D0151459

VIRGIL AND THE MODERNS

THEODORE ZIOLKOWSKI

Virgil and the Moderns

PRINCETON UNIVERSITY PRESS

PRINCETON, N. J.

Copyright © 1993 by Princeton University Press
Published by Princeton University Press, 41 William Street,
Princeton, New Jersey 08540
In the United Kingdom: Princeton University Press,
Chichester, West Sussex

ALL RIGHTS RESERVED

Library of Congress Cataloging-in-Publication Data
Ziolkowski, Theodore.
Virgil and the moderns / Theodore Ziolkowski.
    p.   cm.
Includes bibliographical references and index.
ISBN 0-691-03248-3
1. Virgil—Criticism and interpretation—History.
2. Latin poetry—History and criticism—Theory, etc.
3. Literature, Modern—Roman influences.
4. Modernism (Literature)   5. Rome in literature.
I. Title.
PA6825.Z56 1993
871'.01—dc20   92-41209

This book has been composed in Adobe Garamond
Designed by Jan Lilly

Princeton University Press books are printed on
acid-free paper and meet the guidelines for permanence
and durability of the Committee on Production
Guidelines for Book Longevity of the
Council on Library Resources

Printed in the United States of America

10   9   8   7   6   5   4   3   2   1

"Mis noches están llenas de Virgilio"

Jorge Luis Borges,
"Al idioma alemán"

——— ❧ ————————————————————————

FOR MY GRANDCHILDREN

Saskia, Ada, and Yetta

Alexander and Lara

Theodora

whom Virgil still awaits

CONTENTS

———— ❧ ————————————————————————

CONTENTS

Virgil is too important to be left to the classicists.

By this remark I intend no disrespect for classics scholars. On the contrary: I have the greatest esteem for, and more than a little envy of, those colleagues who have devoted their lives and careers to the study of our Graeco-Roman heritage. I mean, rather, that the rest of us stand to suffer an immeasurable loss if we are content to leave Virgil to the tutelary benevolence of the classical philologists or hidden in the sacred wood of the "canon"—to the extent that a canon can still be said to exist in the cultural world of the present. No doubt every national literature can identify writers best left to the solicitude of specialists—but Virgil is not one of them. For Virgil has permeated modern culture and society in ways that would be unimaginable in the case of most other icons of Western civilization.

In this country today, for instance, with every financial transaction involving a dollar bill we are, quite literally, letting the words of Virgil slip through our fingers because three different quotations from his works are engraved on that instrument that many consider as fundamental to our society as the Constitution. In the eighteenth century the discovery, and in the nineteenth century the westward expansion, of the United States were regularly equated with Aeneas's journey to establish a new Troy in Italy. During the 1930s Virgil's name and works, especially the *Eclogues* and *Georgics*, were invoked by poets and cultural critics as a touchstone in the social and political discussions of the day. The fabric of American history—at least in the understanding of our ancestors—is inextricably interwoven with Virgilian threads.

The situation in the United States mirrors circumstances elsewhere in the Western world although, as we shall see, the lines of cultural continuity vary in their length and breadth from nation to nation. For reasons discussed in Chapter 1, Virgil came to signify the archetype of the man of letters in a time of political and social turmoil. In this capacity, his life and works entered the modern cultural consciousness to such an extent that many major works of the era between the first and second world wars cannot be adequately comprehended without the context of associations provided by the Roman poet. We need Virgil today not simply because his works constitute an indispensable cultural possession: We are impoverished if we do not possess the *Eclogues*, the *Georgics*, and the *Aeneid*. We need him, in addition, because his poems provide the patterns, the images, the values, the very words that inform many central works of American, English, French, German, Italian, and other literatures of the twentieth century.

This pervasive presence has been noted in the case of a few specific writers, e. g., T. S. Eliot, Hermann Broch, Allen Tate, André Gide, and Giuseppe Ungaretti. However, what Donald Davie remarked about T. S. Eliot—that the consideration of Virgilianism in modern poetry has been "mesmerized" by the figure of one individual poet[1]—applies with equal validity in other national literatures. Only a few scholars have tentatively investigated the impact of Virgil on groups of writers. Usually a single dominant figure has been considered largely in isolation from fellow writers in his own country as well as other countries. As a result, the discussions of Eliot do not take into account, say, Vita Sackville-West, much less Hermann Broch and André Gide. For that reason, the students of Robert Frost or Paul Valéry or Salvatore Quasimodo often remain unaware of the overarching generational factors motivating the specific figures with whom they are dealing. I hope to remedy that deficiency with an overview that approaches the question with a comparative perspective.

Recent decades have seen a surge of interest in pastoralism, including its manifestations in twentieth-century literature. Although these studies normally cite Virgil as an exemplary model (along with Theocritus), they swerve off all too easily into "the pastoral" and lose sight of specific texts. As a result, writers are introduced whose works may display elements commonly regarded as pastoral, but who betray no knowledge of Virgil or his *Eclogues*. In addition, generic discussions of "the pastoral" often fail to make the necessary distinctions between the *Eclogues* and the *Georgics*, with the result that fundamental differences—for all their acknowledged indebtedness to Virgil—among, say, the French bucoliasts, the English georgicists, and the American agrarians go unremarked. As a study of "Virgil and the Moderns," rather than "Virgilianism" or "Pastoralism" among the moderns, this book sets out to illustrate some of the underlying affinities among modern writers who admired Virgil as well as to display certain characteristic differences between them.

What began as a purely literary project—an exercise in literary reception and cultural continuity—turned out to have significant political implications. It soon became apparent that the writers and cultural critics who turned to Virgil did so not merely or even primarily for "literary" reasons but because they saw in his works, along with a profound insight into the ambivalence of human nature and its history, a set of values and an image of security that they missed in a world transformed by World War I. At the same time, they recognized in his life a model of dignified survival in the face of social disorder and political turmoil that provided a certain strength for their own lives in troubled times. While the writers drawn to Virgil were affiliated, generally speaking, with the political and cultural conservatives of their age, their responses to the differing circumstances in their countries varied radically—from the fascism of Robert Brasillach in France to the anti-Nazi opposition of Theodor Haecker in Germany, from the agrarianism of Allen Tate and his friends to the inner emigration of the Italian hermeticists, all in the name of the same Roman poet!

Speaking of that name, I have chosen to employ the form "Virgil," which is used by the majority of writers and secondary sources to which I refer (e.g., the *Enciclopedia Virgiliana*). Inevitably this practice produces inconsistencies because I have retained the spelling "Vergil" in those cases where it appears in the original titles and in quotations of the writers with whom I deal. (In translating into English, however, I have in most cases routinely normalized the form.)

As for the other substantive of my title, it will become apparent that I am using the term *moderns* to designate generally the writers and intellectuals active in the decades between the two world wars—and in distinction to both the Victorians who preceded and the postwar generations that followed them. At the same time, many of them also happen to belong to that group of artists whom we recognize as the "classics" of modernism. No work of this sort, of course, can aspire to absolute completeness; it is possible, even likely, that I have missed important examples that have simply eluded my attention. Yet I believe that the writers I have identified are representative of those transitional generations and that the various groupings are valid enough to accommodate other examples that may occur to readers.

All translations, unless otherwise noted, are my own. I have felt free to work with translations in cases where it is the substance, rather than the language itself, that matters. But in those many cases in which it seemed to me important to point out the recurrence of Virgil's words in a modern text, I have quoted liberally in Latin as well as in the appropriate modern languages. In most cases the writers with whom we are dealing here were capable Latinists and knew their Virgil in the original. It goes without saying that neither Virgil nor the modern Virgilians used "gender-neutral" language, and I have not presumed in my translations or paraphrases of their works to accommodate their style to contemporary preferences.

I first became aware of the potential dimensions of this topic in 1978 when I was preparing a paper on "Broch's Image of Vergil and Its Context" for a symposium on Broch held at Yale University in 1979 (*Modern Austrian Literature* 72 [1980]: 1–30). A preliminary sketch of the central themes appeared under the title "Vergil und die Moderne: Politisierte Bukolik" in *Poetik und Geschichte: Victor Zmegac zum 60. Geburtstag*, ed. Dieter Borchmeyer (Tübingen: Niemeyer, 1989), 136–49. In the fall of 1992, I had the opportunity to present much of the material as a series of lectures, in German, to a knowledgeable and responsive audience at the University of Munich. Although I have been reading Virgil and modern Virgilians for many years, the bulk of the writing was accomplished in the summers of 1990 and 1991 and during those evenings and weekends that I was able to reclaim from a full-time position as dean of the Graduate School at Princeton University— when, with Borges, I was often able to say that "my nights were full of Virgil."

It would have been difficult to write this book without the unusual resources and resourceful staff of Princeton University's Firestone Library and, in particular, the Junius S. Morgan Collection of Vergil. I am also indebted to Yale University's Beinecke Rare Book and Manuscript Library and to Christa Sammons, the curator of its Collection of German Literature, who helped me on several occasions. Fachoberlehrer Bruno Seitz of Teesdorf, Austria, generously provided information from the archives of the Hermann Broch-Museum.

Again, Robert E. Brown stewarded my work through the editorial process from submission to publication. Thanks to his good offices, I benefited from the knowledgeable readings of two fine scholars, Virgil Nemoianu and Susan Ford Wiltshire, both of whom provided magnanimous encouragement as well as incisive suggestions that I took to heart. Marta Steele brought to the manuscript the high quality of editing that authors at Princeton University Press are privileged to expect.

Finally, I am grateful to Jan M. Ziolkowski for reassuring me on a few points of translation from post-Classical Latin texts. (I am of course alone responsible for any errors.) My wife Yetta, who usually senses where I am heading before I know it myself, presented me with the bust of Virgil, who has been the *genius loci* of my study as I wrote this book and who now graces the dust jacket of the volume.

Theodore Ziolkowski
Princeton, New Jersey
die natali P. Virgilii Maronis MCMXCII

ACKNOWLEDGMENTS

───── ❧ ─────────────────────────────────────

   The author wishes to thank the following publishers and persons for permission to quote excerpts from various works of poetry:
   Basil Blackwell Ltd., for *The Singing Farmer: A Translation of Vergil's 'Georgics'* by L.A.S. Jermyn, published 1947 by Basil Blackwell Ltd.
   Jonathan Cape Ltd., and the Estate of Robert Frost, for British rights to *The Poetry of Robert Frost*, edited by Edward Connery Lathem (for copyright dates, see Henry Holt and Company).
   Curtis Brown and John Farquharson, for lines from *The Land*, copyright Vita Sackville-West 1927, reproduced by permission of Curtis Brown, London, on behalf of the author's estate.
   Devin-Adair, Publishers, Inc., Old Greenwich, Connecticut 06870. Permission granted to reprint "Virgil" and "Sub Ilice," from *Collected Poems of Oliver St. John Gogarty*. Copyright 1954 by Devin-Adair. All rights reserved.
   Faber and Faber Ltd., for "Memorial for the City" and "Secondary Epic" from *Collected Shorter Poems, 1927–1957* by W. H. Auden, copyright © 1966 by W. H. Auden, published by Faber and Faber Ltd.; for British rights to T. S. Eliot, *Collected Poems 1909–1962*; for *The Waste Land: A Facsimile and Transcript of the Original Drafts including the Annotations of Ezra Pound*, edited by Valerie Eliot, copyright © 1971 by Valerie Eliot; for British rights to Robert Lowell, *Selected Poems 1938– 1964*; and for "An Eclogue for Christmas" and "Eclogue by a Five-Barred Gate" from *The Collected Poems of Louis MacNeice*, edited by E. R. Dodds.
   Ruth Fainlight, for "Aeneas' Meeting with the Sibyl" in *Sibyls and Other Poems*. Copyright 1980 by Ruth Fainlight.
   Farrar, Straus & Giroux, for excerpts from "Aeneas at New York," "Aeneas at Washington," and "The Mediterranean" from *Collected Poems 1919–1976* by Allen Tate. Copyright © 1977 by Allen Tate. Reprinted by permission of Farrar, Straus & Giroux, Inc.
   Editions Gallimard, for *Les Bucoliques* in Paul Valéry, *Oeuvres I*. Copyright 1957 by Librairie Gallimard.
   Harcourt Brace Jovanovich, Inc., for excerpts from "The Waste Land" in *Collected Poems 1909–1962* by T. S. Eliot, copyright 1936 by Harcourt Brace Jovanovich, Inc., copyright © 1964, 1963 by T. S. Eliot, reprinted by permission of the publisher; for excerpts from "East Coker," and "The Dry Salvages" in *Four Quartets*, copyright 1943 by

T. S. Eliot and renewed 1971 by Esme Valerie Eliot, reprinted by permission of Harcourt Brace Jovanovich, Inc.; for excerpts from "Falling Asleep over the Aeneid," in *The Mills of the Kavanaughs*, copyright 1948 and renewed 1976 by Robert Lowell, reprinted by permission of Harcourt Brace Jovanovich, Inc.

D. C. Heath and Company, for "Virgil, 1930" by J. M. Beatty, Jr., and "Virgil's First Eclogue Remembered" by John H. Finley, in *Master Virgil: An Anthology of Poems in English on Vergil and Vergilian Themes*. Copyright 1930 by D. C. Heath and Co.

The Hogarth Press, and the Estate of the author, for "Arms and the Boy," in *The Poems of Wilfred Owen*, edited by Jon Stallworthy. Copyright © 1963 and 1983 by the Executors of Harold Owen's Estate.

Henry Holt and Company, Inc., for "Build Soil" from *The Poetry of Robert Frost*, edited by Edward Connery Lathem. Copyright 1936 by Robert Frost. Copyright © 1964 by Lesley Frost Ballantine. Copyright © 1969 by Holt, Rinehart, and Winston. Reprinted by permission of Henry Holt and Company, Inc.

Houghton Mifflin Company, for "Invocation to the Social Muse" in *Collected Poems 1917–1982*, by Archibald MacLeish. Copyright © 1985 by The Estate of Archibald MacLeish. Reprinted by permission of Houghton Mifflin Company. All rights reserved.

Macmillan Publishing Company, for "Experience in the West" by John Peale Bishop, reprinted with permission of Charles Scribner's Sons, an imprint of Macmillan Publishing Company, from *The Collected Poems of John Peale Bishop*, edited by Allen Tate. Copyright 1933, 1941, 1948 Charles Scribner's Sons. Copyrights renewed.

University of Minnesota Press, for "Lines Written for Allen Tate on His Sixtieth Anniversary," in *Poems 1922–1961*, by Donald Davidson. Copyright 1966 by Donald Davidson.

Arnoldo Mondadori Editore, for "Ecloga" in *Poesie I: Ossi di Seppia* by Eugenio Montale, copyright 1948 by Arnoldo Mondadori Editore; and for "La terra promessa" in *Vita d'un uomo. Tutte le poesie*, by Giuseppe Ungaretti, copyright 1974 by Arnoldo Mondadori Editore.

New Directions Publishing Corporation, for *The Cantos of Ezra Pound*, copyright 1934, 1937, 1940, 1948, © 1956, 1959, 1970 by Ezra Pound.

The Peters Fraser & Dunlop Group Ltd. for world rights to lines from *The Georgics of Virgil*. Copyright 1940 by Cecil Day Lewis.

Sterling Lord Literistic, Inc., for U.S. rights to lines from *The Georgics of Virgil*. Copyright 1940 by Cecil Day Lewis.

Suhrkamp Verlag, for "Bucolica" from *Gesammelte Werke in fünf Bänden* by Rudolf Alexander Schröder. Copyright 1952 by Suhrkamp Verlag.

ACKNOWLEDGMENTS

Viking Penguin, for "The Dawn," from *A Son of Earth* by William Ellery Leonard. Copyright 1928 by The Viking Press, Inc., renewed © 1955 by Charlotte C. Leonard. Used by permission of Viking Penguin, a division of Penguin Books USA Inc.

VIRGIL AND THE MODERNS

CHAPTER ONE

Introduction

Flectere si nequeo Superos, Acheronta movebo.
(Aeneid 7.312)

The twentieth century opens under the auspices of Virgil. With the sonorous hexameter that Sigmund Freud inscribed as an epigraph on the title page of *The Interpretation of Dreams* (*Die Traumdeutung*, 1900), the father of psychoanalysis adumbrated the murky realm of the unconscious that he proposed to explore through the medium of dreams. As he wrote to Wilhelm Fliess while preparing the work for publication, the epigraph—"If I cannot sway the powers above, I shall stir up the underworld"—was meant in psychoanalytical terms to "hint at repression."[1] In the *Aeneid* the words introduce the scene in which Juno, enraged to discover that Aeneas has succeeded, despite all her efforts, in reaching the shores of Italy, summons the baleful Fury Allecto (*luctificam Allecto*) from the infernal shades of the underworld and looses her with her "thousand arts of ill" (*mille nocendi artes*) to disrupt the fragile peace established between the Trojan leader and King Latinus. But the words of the vengeful Juno also anticipate ominously the ideological forces about to be unleashed on the modern world. In her implacable opposition to the progress of history embodied by Aeneas—from the semibarbarous tribal culture of Turnus and his Latin allies to the new Roman society governed by humane laws, *pietas*, and *ordo*— Juno prefigures the reactionary forces of totalitarianism that emerged from the chaos of World War I.[2] (That Freud's invocation of Virgil's words did not go unnoticed by his contemporaries is suggested by the fact that in "The Dreams of Maria Dunin"—part 1 of the symbolist-psychoanalytical novel *The Hag* [*Paluba*, 1903] by the Polish writer Karol Irzykowski—the heroine's father is named Acheronta Movebo.)

Three decades later, with the First World War a vivid memory while a second one loomed on the horizon, Arnold Toynbee found reason to believe that Western men and women had already penetrated that Virgilian underworld that Freud had contemplated from the security of his analyst's chair. The motto to the first volume of *A Study of History*

(1934) is also borrowed from Virgil. But the words *nox ruit, Aenea* (*Aen.* 6.539) are those that the Sibyl, standing with Aeneas at the crossroads of Hades, utters to warn him that night is swiftly approaching and that they must make haste if they hope to find their way safely back to the upper regions before being overtaken by the powers of darkness. It is fair to assume that in the bleak days of the 1930s Toynbee could not be at all sanguine about which road humanity might follow—the lefthand path to *impia Tartara* or the righthand way to Elysium.

This modern appropriation of Virgil, as exemplified by Freud and Toynbee, differs strikingly from the view pervasive throughout the nineteenth century and anticipates the "dark" readings characteristic of recent decades. If we take as exemplary the volume of international tributes published by the Accademia Virgiliana of Mantua to commemorate its celebration in September 1882 of the nineteenth centenary of Virgil's death, the difference in tenor is instantly striking. We should remember, first, that the public mood in late nineteenth-century Italy had little in common with the spirit of Europe around the time of World War I. Following the turmoil of the risorgimento, the United Kingdom of Italy under Victor Emmanuel had been recognized in 1861, and Rome was coopted as its capital as recently as 1872. In 1878 the new kingdom had lost its political and spiritual leaders, King Victor Emmanuel and Pope Pius IX. Under a new king, Humbert, and a new pope, Leo XIII, the country was attempting to assert its political maturity through its first major diplomatic pacts, notably the Triple Alliance of 1882. In this state of euphoria, Italy was obsessed with its political present: The past was not a warning mirror but a glorious history to be resurrected and nurtured. The group who contributed to the Mantuan commemorative volume in six different languages—Italian, Latin, French, Spanish, German, and English—were unified by the hope that Virgil could be restored as a glorious herald of the new kingdom.

The tone is set by the introductory account of the celebration. It is the will of the people, along with royal perseverance ("volere di popolo e costanza di re"), we learn, that have made the star of Italy shine at last.[3] But the rise of the new star did not eclipse the memory of the past; on the contrary, it dissipated the oblivion obscuring the shades of the great forefathers, so that the city of Mantua naturally turned its thoughts to celebrating the next centenary of its greatest citizen. The theme of rescuing Virgil from obscurity is pursued by the French representative, who begins by observing that genius, like princes, requires a guard who watches at the door and heralds who proclaim it to a distraught world (55). It is the responsibility of Mantua to protect Virgil against the insolent assaults of the age and of men, no less than against the shadowy invasions of ignorance ("contre les tentatives insolentes du temps et des hommes, non moins que contre les ténébreux envahissements de l'ignorance"). In a Sapphic ode "A Virgilio," another admirer assures the pitiable shade ("ombra pietosa") returning to his birthplace that time, whose tooth has corroded even the power of Rome and its marbles, has not presumed to touch Virgil, who lives eternally in his poetry (65):

> Il tempo, che del suo dente corrosa
> La potenza ha di Roma ed i suoi marmi,
> La tua, che ferve, di toccar non osa,
> Viva nei carmi.

The author of one of the several Latin *carmina* that adorn the volume urges Virgil to leave his immortal companions and return to Italy and to Mantua, whom he has honored and who now summons him with her maternal voice (79):

> Virgili, io! socios et sedem sperne parumper,
> Huc ades, in terras Italiamque redi:
> . . . .
> Cui tantum meritae tribuisti gratus honoris
> Materno exultim Mantua corde vocat.

> (Virgil, ho! put aside for a while your comrades and your seat. Come hither, return to your country and to Italy: . . . Mantua, on whom you have gratefully bestowed so much deserved honor, elatedly calls you with a maternal heart.)

The dean of the Metropolis of Ferrara concludes his sonnet "Al sommo poeta" (III) with the claim that our age can learn from Virgil's works the three values of ancient Italy: courage, industry, and simple manners.

> Apprenda nostra età dal tuo Volume
> Che fur tre i vanti dell'Italia antica:
> Valore, industria e semplice costume!

Against this background we read with more understanding eyes the ode "To Virgil" that Tennyson, at the request of the people of Mantua, wrote specifically for inclusion in this volume (147–48). Like other readers of his century (e.g., Victor Hugo), Tennyson was not insensitive to Virgil's "sadness / at the doubtful doom of human kind." In general, however, his poem apostrophizes the "Poet of the happy Tityrus / piping underneath his beechen bowers," the *vates* who praises "Universal / Nature moved by Universal Mind." In no phrase, no line,

5

do we sense that Tennyson regards Virgil as a prophet of modernity. It is poetic admiration alone that elicits Tennyson's greeting:

> I salute thee, Mantovano,
>   I that loved thee since my day began,
> Wielder of the stateliest measure
>   ever moulded by the lips of man.

The 1882 commemorations would seem to bear out Robert Graves's thesis that "whenever a golden age of stable government, full churches, and expanding wealth dawns among the Western nations, Virgil always returns to supreme favour."[4] In the twentieth century, however, it was precisely the troubled era *entre deux guerres* that sent scholars, writers, and readers back to the Roman poet who seemed to have anticipated so much of the turmoil of our times. To appreciate how the modern view of Virgil emerged, we need to recall the crisis of history in the early twentieth century, the Roman analogy that came to dominate much historical thinking at that time, and the reassessment prompted by the bimillennial celebrations in 1930 of Virgil's birth.

THE CRISIS OF HISTORY

The early twentieth century was by no means the first age to experience a crisis in its historical consciousness. It could be argued that Virgil's contemporary, the historian Livy, was addressing precisely such a "crisis" in the preface to his own account of Roman history, which begins by questioning the value of his undertaking (*facturusne operae pretium sim*), goes on to contrast the seemingly conventional nature of his own approach with the methodological and rhetorical innovations of the *novi semper scriptores*, and confesses that he is turning to the past in order to liberate himself from contemplation of the steadily worsening ills that have afflicted recent Roman society.[5]

In one sense the modern crisis of history is simply another aspect of the more general crisis of values heralded by Nietzsche and other prophets of modernity. In one of the representative documents of this crisis, *Man in the Modern Age* (*Die geistige Situation der Zeit*, 1931), Karl Jaspers argued that the world that for centuries and millennia had appeared to be our reality was at present collapsing and that the public consciousness had become so keenly aware of this problematic disorder that every newspaper featured a daily crisis.[6] According to Jaspers, and for reasons that he analyzes at length, the modern crisis is accompanied by a hostility to traditional culture and education (*Bildungsfeindlichkeit*, 105) that has interrupted any sense of historical continuity. "The break is the most profound one ever experienced in Western civilization" (106). As a fatal consequence of this loosening of historical contexts, humankind disintegrates into a heap of interchangeable individuals that are nothing more than functions in the social nexus while the individual dissolves into the foreshortened perspectives of his or her immediate present (169). Similarly Rudolf Pannwitz, a member of the circle surrounding the vatic poet Stefan George, observed in his book on the crisis of European culture (*Die Krisis der europäischen Kultur*, 1917) that in an age when the intellectual axis of the earth has shifted "there is nothing more unhistorical than history."[7]

Jaspers and other philosophers regarded the crisis of history as simply one aspect of a general disintegration of values in the modern world. The sense of cultural crisis was especially acute in Germany, which emerged from World War I as the vanquished land. In victorious France, as Ernst Robert Curtius had occasion to observe, most intellectuals—albeit not such leading figures as André Gide or Paul Valéry, whom Curtius took to be exceptions—regarded the defeat of the Germans as a sign of the reestablishment of traditional Western values, of which they considered France the appropriate spiritual center.[8]

Historians, especially but not only in Germany, focusing on their own intellectual domain, tended to take the crisis most seriously. Ernst Troeltsch's monumental survey and analysis of contemporary history (*Der Historismus und seine Probleme*, 1922) begins with a chapter on "The Present Crisis of History." Troeltsch stresses his conviction that the crisis is not a predicament in professional historiography, which in his opinion has never been more vigorous, but rather in the historical consciousness of the general public.[9] "The crisis is to be found, therefore, in the philosophical elements and relations of history, in that which can be called its context and its significance for one's view of the world [*Weltanschauung*], whereby the relationship is wholly reciprocal: a significance of history for our view of the world, and of our view of the world for history" (7).

In the paragraphs that follow, Troeltsch defines the issue as "the problem of so-called historicism" ("das Problem des sogenannten Historismus," 9)—the recognition of the essentially historical character of all human existence that can be traced back to Vico and Herder and whose genesis Friedrich Meinecke was to analyze in his masterwork, *Die Entstehung des Historismus* (1936).[10] Historicism, called by Meinecke "one of the greatest intellectual revolutions that Western thought has experienced" (1), implies generally the historicization of human phenomena that, from the eighteenth century on, paralleled mathematicization in the sciences: the tendency, that is, to understand all political-social life in a historical context and against the background of history, and not simply logically and abstractly from the standpoint of natural law. It was this fundamental historicist attitude regarding all human institutions that appeared to have been shattered by the crisis of history.

There is a certain ironic parodox inherent in Troeltsch's claim. The general crisis of history was generated in part by the conspicuous successes of professional historiography of the nineteenth century, which was so thoroughly indebted to historicism that another critic of the field defined historicism as simply "the historiography of the period around 1900."[11] The recognition of the historicity of all human life and institutions led gradually to a profound skepticism regarding the possibility of any historical certainty or of any meaning in history. If all historical being is relative, then how can we continue to believe in the priority of Christianity and the Western values that had formerly provided the center of meaning in Western civilization? (Indeed, the controversy surrounding historicism in the twenties strikingly anticipated in its issues and arguments the educational debate of the 1980s concerning the priority of Western civilization and its canon.) At the same time, the new techniques of documentary analysis and archival research, which after Ranke produced the monumental compilations of the nineteenth century, led historians increasingly away from writing presentations for a general educated public, as had been the practice from classical antiquity down to the late eighteenth century, and into creating ever more highly specialized monographs instead. As professional historiography grew in sophistication, becoming at the same time and in every country more nationalistic in thrust and factual in substance, it lost the audience that from Sallust to the present had been drawn to history for its philosophical—that is to say, ethical—implications.

Because history first became an academic discipline in Germany and, during the nineteenth century, achieved its greatest distinction there, the crisis of history was felt most acutely in that country.[12] According to Troeltsch's spectrum of cultures, the crisis affected next most keenly the politically and philosophically lively peoples of continental Europe, less so the more placid Anglo-Saxons, and "least of all naturally the Americans, who have only little history and regard Europe as a museum. . . . They have more future than past."[13]

If the growing depersonalization of professional historians prepared the ground for the crisis of history, and if the controversy regarding historicism was itself a symptom of that crisis, it was the experience of such social cataclysms as World War I and the Russian Revolution that led the public to question the ability of professional history, at least as it had defined itself during the pre-war era, to come to grips with and explain historical reality.[14] Because the overwhelming documentation now available in the press as well as archival sources was unsurveyable, the previous tyranny of facts was called into question. Moreover, even the "facts" of war and revolution often turned out by the measure of personal experience to be false or self-contradictory. This new skepticism regarding our understanding of present historical reality was soon transposed to the past. If we are incapable of making sense even of the events of our own immediate experience, how can we hope to come to terms with the past? Consequently the public longed for a synthesizing history that would be capable of explaining current reality and putting it back into larger and more meaningful contexts. This longing was summed up in the title of Theodor Lessing's book, *History as Giving Meaning to the Meaningless* (*Geschichte als Sinngebung des Sinnlosen*, 1916), in which this cultural critic, writing in the tradition of Nietzsche, argued that history, having no objective validity, amounts to a mythic construct imposed on an unknowable reality in order to give it some semblance of meaning.[15]

In response to the public longing to make sense of the chaos into which the world had been plunged by the overwhelming mass of contemporary historical reality, a stream of often spectacularly successful works began to be published, immediately after the war, that belonged to the category that Troeltsch, without contempt or disparagement, called belletristic rather than scholarly (*Literatentum* rather than *Gelehrtentum*, ix) and that sought to explain the present against a background of world history set forth with a pronounced ideological thesis. The first of these was Oswald Spengler's *The Decline of the West* (*Der Untergang des Abendlandes*, vol. 1, 1918), which attempted to make philosophical sense of history by introducing into it a morphological principle appropriated from Goethe's theory of biological metamorphosis. Less important for our context than Spengler's generally pessimistic view of the three cultures into which he divides Western history—Arabian or "magical," classical or "Apollonian," and modern or "Faustian"—is the author's awareness, expressed in the preface to the first edition of volume 1, that his book, "though concerned with a general philosophy of history, constitutes nevertheless in a more profound sense a commentary on the great epoch under the signs of which its principal ideas have taken shape." In other words, Spengler reintroduced into history the large view as well as the subjective element that had been excluded by positivist history of the nineteenth century.

H. G. Wells's *The Outline of History* (published serially in 1918–19; first book publication, 1920), while exemplifying a different kind of attempt to provide, according to the subtitle, "A Plain History of Life and Mankind," also emerged directly from the experience of the war.

There were many reasons to move a writer to attempt a World History in 1918. It was the last, the weariest, most disillusioned year of the first World War. Everywhere there were unwonted privations; everywhere there was mourning. The tale of the dead and mutilated had mounted to many millions. Men felt they had come to a crisis in the world's affairs. They were too weary and heart-sick to consider complicated possibilities. They were not sure whether they were facing a disaster to civilization or the inauguration of a new phase of human association; they saw things with the simplicity of such flat alternatives, and they clung to hope.[16]

Wells realized that men and women searching for meaning in the postwar era found in the history of their schooldays "an uninspiring and partially forgotten list of national kings or presidents" (2).

They tried to read about these matters, and found an endless wilderness of books. They had been taught history, they found, in nationalist blinkers, ignoring every country but their own, and now they were turned out into a blaze. It was extraordinarily difficult for them to determine the relative values of the matters under discussion.

Historians were for the most part "very scholarly men" who went about "in fear rather of small errors than of disconnectedness" (3). To fill the need for connectedness, Wells undertook the "epic immensity" of his *Outline*, opposing to Spengler's profound and Germanic cultural pessimism the optimism of his progressive socialist vision, which provided the mythic meaning for his view of history from the earliest emergence of the genus *Homo* through the major civilizations of the world down to the League of Nations: "We have traced throughout this history the gradual restriction of the idea of property from the first unlimited claim of the strong man to possess everything and the gradual realization of brotherhood as something transcending personal self-seeking" (811). The enormous popularity of the work, which sold millions of copies and was repeatedly revised with the assistance of a cadre of distinguished scholars, suggests the urgency with which the crisis of history was felt by readers between the two world wars.

To take a third example, the studies of Marxian dialectics that Georg Lukács published under the title *History and Class Consciousness* (*Geschichte und Klassenbewußtsein*, 1923), while not a world history after the model of Spengler and Wells, represented an attempt to bring meaning back into history by reverting to the young Marx's conception of historical materialism (and leaping over the concept of dialectical materialism that had been introduced rather confusingly by Engels and Lenin). "It is not the predominance of economic motives in the explanation of history that distinguishes Marxism decisively from bourgeois science, but the standpoint of totality."[17] As Lukács explains elsewhere in the book (357), historical materialism

> was doubtless a scientific method to comprehend the events of the past according to their true essence. But in contrast to the historical methods of the bourgeoisie, it simultaneously enables us to contemplate the present under the aspect of history, that is to say, scientifically, and to see in it not only the superficial phenomena, but also those more profound historical motivating forces by which the events in reality are moved.

Symptomatic again is the fact, which Lukács details at length in his 1967 preface to a new edition, that the essays of the volume arose in specific response to the events surrounding the Russian Revolution in 1917 in an effort to make sense of the new world being brought forth by Communism.

In sum, the postwar crisis of history, prepared by the increasing specialization of professional historians along with their rejection of the philosophy of history, and precipitated by the seemingly inexplicable sociopolitical events of the early twentieth century, produced in the public at large a longing for synthesizing accounts of history that would help them to make sense of the world in which they lived. Spengler's cultural pessimism in a morphological framework, Wells's socialist optimism in a progressive vision, and Lukács's historical materialism are only three representative examples, among the many published in the twenties, of efforts to bring meaning back into history. For instance, Johan Huizinga's conception of the responsibilities of cultural history, first outlined in a speech of 1926 ("De taak der cultuurgeschiedenis"), shared the contemporary dissatisfaction with what Troeltsch called "seminar history" but at the same time worried about the effects of an aestheticizing history written by dilettantes for essentially literary effects.[18] He therefore proposed a morphological understanding and description of the course of civilizations, but one that would restrict itself to cultural process without degenerating, as did Spengler's, into mythology.

Beyond these structural approaches one might recall, in addition, the biographies associated with the group around Stefan George—Friedrich Gundolf's history of Caesar's fame (*Caesar: Geschichte seines Ruhms*, 1924), Ernst Bertram's analysis of the mythification of Nietzsche (*Nietzsche: Versuch einer Mythologie*, 1918), or Ernst Kantorowicz's study of a medieval emperor (*Kaiser Friedrich II*, 1928)—all of which attempted through a kind of phenomenological analysis of being (*Wesensschau*) to determine a static and timeless *Gestalt* of the individual in contrast to the relativizing views of historicism. The Roman analogy and, ultimately, the powerful appeal of Virgil to modern thinkers can be seen as another manifestation of this same urgent attempt to find meaning in history.

THE ROMAN ANALOGY IN MODERN THOUGHT

In his introduction to the first volume of *The Decline of the West* (1918) Spengler, setting out to determine the "morphological" situation of modern Euro-American civilization, finds the closest analogy in ancient Rome.[19] A comparative analysis, he argues, exposes the "simultaneity" of our contemporary world, and especially the highpoint designated by World War I, with the transition from the Hellenistic period to the Roman period. "Romanism [*das Römertum*]—with its rigorous sense of factuality, lacking in geniality, barbaric, disciplined, practical, Protestant, *Prussian*—will always provide us in our search for analogies with the key to the understanding of our own future." Rome, he suggests, is the true *alter ego* of our culture, which between 1800 and 2000 was to attain a similar stage of cosmopolitan imperialism.

Spengler warns that the Roman analogy has hitherto been applied misleadingly by historians, who fall into what he calls a "materialistic" or an "ideological" manner of viewing antiquity. The danger of the materialistic view, represented by most nineteenth-century professional historians, is an "intelligent superficiality" that regards antiquity as nothing but a bundle of social, economic, political, and physiological facts. The ideologists, in contrast, are belated Romantics—Spengler had in mind the brilliant triumvirate of Basel professors: Johann Jacob Bachofen, Jakob Burckhardt, and Friedrich Nietzsche—who see in antiquity little more than a mirror image of their own problematic sensibilities.

The comparison with Rome dominates the thousand pages of Spengler's opus, providing in the final paragraphs of volume 2 (1922) the main clue to the future of Western civilization. When the forms and institutions of democracy have been exhausted, as happened in late republican Rome, meaning is vouchsafed solely by the sheer personal authority that the emperor or his counterpart exerts through his own abilities. If mind and money celebrate their highest victories in the blossoming of civilization, "the age of the Caesars represents in every culture the end of a politics of mind and money."[20] This was the situation in Augustan Rome. "Caesarism I call that form of government which despite all its constitutional formulations is once again wholly formless in its essence."

Although Spengler does not draw out his ultimate analogy, his implication is clear. By the end of the book he has expounded the morphological parallels between republican Rome and modern Europe, and he has depicted the emergence of the strong man, the Caesar, who inevitably steps forth to fill the vacuum when constitutional forms collapse. "The rise of Caesarism," he writes in his final section, "shatters the dictatorship of money and its political weapon, democracy." This analogy, he concludes, shows us in which direction we must proceed, Europeans *entre deux guerres*, "whom destiny has placed into this culture and this moment of its development, in which money celebrates its final victories and its heir, Caesarism, approaches quietly and irresistibly."

If the Roman analogy thrust itself upon Spengler in the course of his somber meditations during World War I, it was no less compelling for Arnold Toynbee, as he composed his monumental *Study of History* in the course of the next two decades. Writing in 1939, only a few weeks before World War II broke out, he tells us that "the contemporary atmosphere in which the present three volumes were produced was painfully appropriate to the themes of 'breakdown' and 'disintegration' which these volumes have for their subjects."[21] During those years, when it often appeared that a catastrophe might shatter his world at any moment, Toynbee "fortified his will," he tells us, by recalling that St. Augustine composed *De Civitate Dei* during the very years when bands of barbarians were beleaguering the walls of Rome. And the detailed analysis of the process of disintegration provides an even closer analogy. The disintegration phase in the history of any civilization, he argues, displays a rhythm marked by the breakdown of the civilization, which is succeeded by a "rally" acccompanied by the founding of its "universal state," which in turn is followed by the breakdown of its *Pax Oecumenica*, a rout that "runs on unchecked until it results in annihilation."[22] As his cardinal example Toynbee adduces the Roman Empire, which was characterized by a *Pax Romana* interrupted by two periods of turmoil (ending, respectively, with the Battle of Actium in 31 B.C. and the fall of the empire in A.D. 378).

When he turns to "Symptoms in Western History," Toynbee finds that our modern Western history conforms in an alarming manner to "the pattern of a disintegrating society's 'Time of Troubles,'" in which the Wars of Religion represent the first interruption of our *Pax Oecumenica* and the nineteenth-century Wars of Nationality the second paroxysm.[23] The table of Universal States that concludes the volume illustrates Toynbee's view that the Danubian Hapsburg Monarchy (1526–1918), representing the Universal State of modern Western society, constitutes a precise analogy to the Roman Empire from Augustus to the fall of Rome.

Of course, not only the grand theoreticians of world history were tempted by the Roman analogy. Friedrich Gundolf began his study of Julius Caesar's fame with the statement: "Today, when the need for a strong man is loudly expressed, when people, weary of the babblers and fault-finders, content themselves with sergeants rather than leaders . . . we would like to remind these jumpers-to-hasty-conclusions of the great man to whom supreme power owes its very name and, for centuries, its idea: *Caesar*."[24] Gundolf was obsessed with Caesar. Two decades earlier he had written his dissertation at the University of Berlin on "Caesar in German Literature" ("Caesar in der deutschen Literatur," 1903), and two years later he was to publish a volume on the reception of Caesar in the nineteenth century (*Caesar im 19. Jahrhundert*, 1926).

But Gundolf's obsession with Caesar and Rome, though better informed, was no more urgent than that of the noncommissioned officer to whom he was no doubt alluding in his belittling remarks on German leadership. Adolf Hitler referred constantly to Roman history. On many occasions he drew parallels between the political turmoil in late Roman antiquity, from which Christianity emerged, and the chaos of the twenties, from which communism threatened to explode all over Europe. In his table conversations during the war, he was fond of deducing theories from Roman military and administrative organization.[25] Accordingly it is no surprise to find in *Mein Kampf* (1925–27) a passage on the value of history for humanistic education and, especially, the study of antiquity for the meaning of the great battle raging in the present. "Roman history, properly comprehended in its broad outlines, is and remains the best teacher not only for today, but indeed for all times."[26]

Hitler's views were often paralleled in the works of contemporary scholars of Roman antiquity, albeit not always in his sense.[27] In an address on "The Spiritual Presence of Antiquity" ("Die geistige Gegenwart der Antike"), delivered in 1929 to commemorate the hundredth anniversary of the Archaeological Institute of the German Reich, the distinguished classicist Werner Jaeger stressed the many commonalities of consciousness, ethics, and politics that bind us more intimately to the Romans than to the Greeks. "The Romans are simply closer to us historically, the bringers of Greek culture for the West and North of Europe."[28] Historians of the 1930s returned obsessively to the period of Augustus, in whose career they implicitly analyzed the phenomenon of dictatorship arising from the chaos of civil war. In perhaps the most distinguished British work on Roman history of that period, *The Roman Revolution* (1939), the author, Ronald Syme, explicitly states in his introduction that "the present inquiry will attempt to discover the resources and devices by which a revolutionary leader arose in civil strife, usurped power for himself and his faction, transformed a faction into a national party, and a torn and distracted land into a nation, with a stable and enduring government."[29] The success of Robert Graves's *I, Claudius* (1934), a historical novel beginning in the reign of Augustus and extending into the early years of the principate, provides a further indication of the popular appeal of the Roman analogy.

While some scholars were concerned with the emergence of a strong leader from political chaos, others were attracted to Rome because of their fascination with the phenomenon of social chaos itself. Three years before Hitler took office, Walther Rehm dedicated a book to the theme of the decline of Rome in Western thought as a chapter, as he put it, in the continuing "European Rome-discourse."[30] To portray the disintegration of the Roman empire, he begins, may be the greatest and most difficult task that the historian can undertake, and the question concerning that disintegration—*Roma fuit*—has been asked over and over again "especially when an age was itself stirred and disquieted by a sense of decadence, when it desired to obtain certainty about the historical and spiritual position it occupies in its life."[31] In sum, the study of the decline of Rome unites historical awareness with existential consciousness—a conjunction that we will encounter repeatedly and, indeed, thematically in the course of the following pages.

It was of course not only in Germany and England that Roman history became a renewed and central concern during the twenties and thirties. As Rehm noted in 1937, the ruins of ancient Rome speak once more in the Roman present, when a new generation consciously recalled their national past "in order to see their own deeds confirmed and their own future consecrated."[32] The Fascists through the school reform initiated in 1923 by the philosopher Giovanni Gentile (*Riforma Gentile*) cleverly introduced their ideology into the course of instruction through compulsory study of Latin as well as Roman history.[33]

It was not only the *fascio littorio*, which Mussolini called the symbol of unity, of power, and of justice, that the Fascists appropriated from ancient Rome. Many of the designations used by the Fascist volunteer militia (*Milizia volontaria per la sicurezza nazionale*) were adapted from the Latin. The common soldier, known in the army as *soldato*, was termed *milite*, while the officers were known as *capomanipolo, centurione, seniore,* and *console*. The *milizia* itself was divided into *legioni, coorti, centurie,* and *manipoli*. Schoolboys, who had to spend many hours each day studying Roman history, were known as "sons of the [ancient Roman] she-wolf" (*figli della lupa*), and their exercises in Latin syntax drew heavily on the comparison of past and present. To illustrate hypothetical clauses: "If we Italians were not worthy heirs of Roman *virtus*, we would not have won the great fame of which Fascist Italy today is proud, and we could not have created the new *imperium.*" The pupils were expected to translate excerpts from Mussolini's speeches into Latin and to respond to Latin questions bearing allusions to current events: "Cur Aethiopes animo benevolo militibus Italicis fuerunt?" ("Why were the Ethiopians well-disposed toward Italian soldiers?")

The history of ancient Rome, in turn, was illustrated by analogy to modern politics. An influential biography of Julius Caesar—U. Silvagni's *Giulio Cesare* (Turin, 1930)—began with the claim, expressed without Marx's ironic caveat about tragedy and farce, that history repeats itself. Caesar's crossing of the Rubicon was repeated first in 1799 when Napoleon took the decisive step of dissolving the directorate to become leader of the government and a second time in 1922 when Mussolini set out on the great march to Rome and seized power. But it was not just the Italians who accepted the analogy of ancient and modern. Edmund G. Gardner concluded the Annual Italian Lecture of the British Academy in 1931 by noting:

> For that "ritmo accelerato della vita italiana"—the epoch-making phrase with which the great Leader of the Fascist Revolution defined the essential characteristic of the new Italy of to-day—is an energetic renewal of Italian life in the spirit of ancient Rome adapted to the new conditions of the modern world. Its motto, its keynote, may well be found in the Virgilian salutation to Italy in the *Georgics*, of which we see it achieving the realization. *Magna parens frugum*! We know how the Fascist regime has set itself to make every sod of Italian earth—even the once desolate Meramma and the most arid regions of Calabria and Sicily—yield its utmost measure of production. *Magna parens virum*! . . . Thus it is with a renewed conviction that we salute Italy to-day in Virgil's words:
>
> Salve, magna parens frugum, Saturnia tellus,
> magna virum.[34]

In 1930 the French cultural journal *Latinité* reprinted a two-page Latin paean by Joannes de Casamichela addressed to *VIRO EXCELLENTISSIMO BENITO MUSSOLINI,* congratulating him on his election in 1922 *ad officium Italicae civitatis moderandae* and dated *Anno I a fascibus restitutis.*[35] The paean is followed by two short poems written eight years later (*Anno VIII*) in Latin distichs *In Benitum Mussolini*

Ducem Nostrum and apostrophizing the Great Leader in extravagant terms reminiscent of Horace's *Carmen Saeculare*:

> Magne Dux, quo nil majus toto orbe revisit
> Qui caelum ac terras, qui maria alta videt
>
> . . . .
>
> Vive Dux, Dux alme diu: tibi supplicat orbis
> Dum Itali tuas laudes et benefacta canunt.

(Great Leader, he who surveys heaven, earth, and the deep seas, beholds nothing in the whole world greater than you. . . . Hail, Leader, long our dear Leader: the world entreats you while the Italians sing your praises and good deeds.)

In the United States, Joseph M. Beatty, Jr., also hailed the rebirth of Italy under the new Caesar.

> Once more, exultant legions proudly stand
> At steep Trentino's borders, and once more
> A Caesar rules supreme from shore to shore
> His loyal race obedient to command;
> In peasant cottages on every hand
> Hearths burn with sloth-consuming patriot fire,
> While high on wings imperial of desire
> The Roman eagle guards his native land.[36]

Beatty's praise of Mussolini and Fascism as the modern counterpart of ancient Rome occurs, symptomatically, in a sonnet entitled "Virgil, 1930." The sestet concludes:

> Virgil, awake from bimillennial sleep!
> Once Roman, now the world's, your poet-voice
> Can sing triumphant harmonies sublime
> In praise of far-flung peace; upwelling, deep,
> A paean that will make the folk rejoice
> In realms yet unrevealed by looming time.

THE BIMILLENNIAL CELEBRATIONS

Ernst Robert Curtius remarked in 1951 that "it would not be very interesting to survey the German contributions to the Virgil celebrations of 1930" because "they amount to as much, or as little, as the manifestations for the Dante celebration of 1921 or the Goethe celebration of 1932."[37] The great Romanist, who had himself provided a notable contribution to the Virgil bimillennial celebrations,[38] was perhaps too close to the events to be able to assess them properly. Apart from their individual value, the contributions display collectively a representative character of considerable significance for the history of literary reception and constitute a specific case of the general Roman analogy that was prevalent at the time. The bimillennial celebrations of Virgil's birth, which had been announced in 1924 by a Latin proclamation of the Società italiana per la diffusione e l'incoraggiamento degli studi classici,[39] assumed international dimensions that appreciably exceeded the relatively limited national celebrations for Dante in 1921 and for Goethe in 1932.

The occasion, as one would expect, produced its most splendid festivities in Italy, where the new Fascist government recognized an opportunity for the first large-scale experiment in politico-cultural propaganda.[40] The grand bimillennial celebrations for Emperor Augustus in 1937 were to be characterized by wholly different, and essentially militaristic, emphases because the war of aggression in Ethiopia had by then taken place. But the year 1930 marked the moment of greatest political stability and consensus for Mussolini's regime, which hoped through the occasion to achieve various propagandistic goals. By focusing on Virgil and emphasizing the patronage of Augustus and Maecenas, the government intended to strengthen the rapport between culture and power in Italy. The nature of Virgil's poetry offered the opportunity to celebrate such Fascist themes as rural agrarianism, an imperialistic teleology, and the ultimate victory of the Occident over the Orient. On April 21 (the legendary date for the founding of Rome: *ab urbe condita*) ceremonial lectures were delivered simultaneously in thirty cities from the poet's birthplace of Andes by way of Rome to his beloved Naples.[41] In addition to the speeches, festivals, and exhibitions, pilgrimage sites were designated in Mantua, Cumae, Pozzuoli, and other places that played a role in Virgil's life and works, to which patriotic students conducted tourist groups coming from all over the world.[42] The highest classes in the Italian *licei* competed in an essay contest on Virgil's agrarian teachings and the rural policies of Fascism ("L'insegnamento agrario di Virgilio e la politica rurale del Fascismo"), a topic specified by the Duce himself.[43] In Mantua a *bosco sacro* was laid out by Mussolini's brother Arnaldo, containing specimens of all the plants and trees mentioned in the poet's works, while near Naples the poet's tomb was restored along with the Sibyl's cave at Cumae.

In general, the Virgil celebrations offered a favorable opportunity to emphasize the parallels between ancient Rome and Mussolini's Italy— beyond the symbolic initials *S.P.Q.R.* (*Senatus Populusque Romanus*), which were affixed to many public buildings, and the so-called Roman salute. The Italian government, as well as the Vatican and San Marino,

printed a series of commemorative postage stamps representing episodes and quotations from Virgil's works intended to stem the tide of
emigration (e.g., a scene from the *Georgics* portraying prosperous farm
life) and to heighten national pride (e.g., a picture of Turnus in battle
gear and displaying prominently the unmistakable physiognomy of
Mussolini).[44]

The more official occasions were accompanied by literary manifestations. The handsome and sumptuously illustrated commemorative volume published by *L'Illustrazione Italiana* under the title *Virgilio* and
edited by Vincenzo Ussani and Luigi Suttina (1930–31) begins symptomatically with chapters on "Virgilio e la terra" and "Virgilio e l'im-
pero." Volumes entitled *Studi Virgiliani* were published both by the
Accademia Virgiliana of Mantua (1930) and the Istituto di Studi Ro-
mani (1931). Other celebratory works also saw modern Italy as moving
in the footsteps of the past, e.g., Oddone Tesini's book *De Virgilio a
Mussolini* (Treviso, 1930) or Francesco Quattrone's Latin *oratio* with
the title *De Virgilio et fascium regimine* (Reggio, 1930). The standard
two-volume bibliographical work of Giuliano Mambelli, *Gli studi virgiliani nel secolo XX* (Florence, 1940), was published in the series *Guide
Bibliographiche dell' Istituto Nationale di cultura fascista* (No. 7). And
the grand project of the *Enciclopedia Virgiliana*, whose five magnificent
volumes finally appeared in the 1980s after years of intense labor, was
conceived during the bimillennial (vol. 1:xi). The bibliographies provide some sense of the frenetic publishing activity—commemorative
volumes, scholarly works, critical editions, and much more—that occurred not only in Italy, but all over the Western world.

In comparison with the cooptation of Virgil as a national
property in Italy, we can observe a process of popularization in the
United States, where ever since the beginning of the republic Virgil had
belonged among the most beloved school-authors, where his epic about
"the pilgrim fathers of the Romans" was regarded as the archetype of
every voyage of discovery, where twenty-two states could boast of a
town named Troy, and where even the dollar bill bore Latin phrases
based on quotations from Virgil (*novus ordo seclorum, annuit coeptis,*
and *e pluribus unum*).[45] The American Classical League organized a
nationwide Virgil celebration, which in addition to exhibitions, text
editions, and translations also stimulated dramatic performances on
Virgilian themes, established a prize of $100 for the best Virgilian
poem, commissioned an anthology of English poems about Virgil, and
had a medallion struck of the poet's bust encircled by the inscription
hinc vsqve ad sidera notvs.[46]

The Bureau of University Travel invited interested admirers to

Virgilian Pilgrimages, Virgilian Cruises, and Aeneid Voyages, on one of which Professor E. K. Rand of Harvard University delivered a series of lectures on "Virgil the Magician."[47] The honor society Phi Beta Kappa arranged for simultaneous lectures on Virgil to take place on October 15, 1930, at 466 schools in 46 states.[48] The pupils of the Germantown Friends School presented an open-air pageant *In honorem P. Vergili Maronis poetae MM jam anno florentis,* which began with a recitation of Horace's *Carmen Saeculare* and concluded with tributes to Virgil by Petrarch, Dante, Chaucer, and other poets of aftertime.[49] At the College of William and Mary, following a lecture on "The *Aeneid* as a National Poem," the visit to the underworld from *Aeneid* 6 was performed in five scenes (after the translation by Dryden) to celebrate the occasion.[50] An Actus Vergilianus in a Jesuit Seminary culminated in the singing of "The Star-Spangled Banner" in Latin.[51] The Authors Club of New York reprinted for distribution to its members "the greatest of essays on Virgil ever written by an American scholar."[52] A one-time professor of Latin at Hunter College, who had given up his position to write poetry on classical themes, published a collection of twelve epistles in blank verse supposed to have been written to Pliny the Younger by two friends on a variety of topics from the life and works of Virgil with many passages translated or paraphrased from Horace, Lucretius, and Martial as well as Virgil's own works.[53]

Exhibitions were mounted at the Library of Congress, the New York Public Library, the Newark Public Library, and elsewhere, while a consortium of associations produced in Carnegie Hall a Virgilian Festival featuring music, dance, pageant, theatrical performances, recitations, and readings.[54] Commemorative lectures were delivered on many campuses, but, thanks to the Italy-America Society of San Francisco, the bay area led the way. At the University of California at Santa Clara, Henry Woods, S. J., produced a 152-line poem celebrating "Mantuan! Roman! Latest of Seers! All Hail!"[55] The poem begins with a hymn to the "Mantuan land" that amounts to a paraphrase of the *Georgics,* it continues with praise of the national poet in lines reminiscent of the *Aeneid* (e.g., "How long a work to found the Roman name"; *Tantae molis erat Romanam condere gentem* [1. 33]), and concludes with a Catholic motif based on the Fourth Eclogue:

> In Pollio's babe he parables the true
> > Saviour of men. He tunes his Roman lyre
> To that of Israel's seer. . . .

Not content with this effort, Woods also produced a 121-line poem in Latin hexameters that amounts to a modified *cento* from Virgil's works, tracing the poet's development from birth to death:

Mantua te genuit; matrem tibi dicere foetam
Frugibus, armentis, apibus, gregibusque juvabat;
Seu tenui Musae Siculae modulatus avena
Aut male despectos miseri pastoris amores,
Alterno aut cantu certantes voce sonora;
Seu plectro Ascraeo, audito non ante Latinis,
Agricolas, quales validi, dum sera moratur
Acris hiems, soleant duram diffindere glebam,
Dicebas; necnon, vitam quod tangit agrestem,
Aut quae cura boum valeat, quidve insit equorum;
Arvo et mendaci tempusque modusque medendi.[56]

(Mantua bore you; it delighted you to sing your mother, fertile
with fruits, cattle, bees, and flocks. Whether, playing on the slender reed of the Sicilian Muse, you sang the pathetic loves of the
poor shepherd or, with sonorous voice, told of [shepherds] com-
peting in alternating song; whether with the lyre of Hesiod, not
previously heard by Latins, you sang of the sturdy farmers who,
while winter tarries late, are wont to cleave the rough clod; and
also what concerns the rural life or what care is needed for cattle;
and what benefits horses; and the time and means of curing the
infertile field.)

(The reader with the *Eclogues* and *Georgics* in mind recognizes almost
every line of this introductory passage.) John Henry Nash, who printed
Woods's Latin poem privately, also published a curious volume for the
celebration that took place at Mills College: an imaginary dialogue between Walter Savage Landor and the Icelandic scholar Willard Fiske on
"the status of Virgil in the scheme of the *Divine Comedy*."[57] (It is the
fiction of the short work that the conversation takes place thirty-six
years after Landor's death while Fiske is in the Villa Gherardesca near
Florence collecting books for the Cornell University Library.)

The celebrations were not limited to North America. In
Mexico Virgil's birth was celebrated by the Academy of Arts and Sciences on October 27, 1930, and two weeks later a commemorative address was delivered in the presence of the President of the Republic. In
the introduction to the volume containing these speeches, *Homenaje de
Mexico al poeta Virgilio en el segundo milenario de su nacimiento* (1931),
which was published at the initiative of President Pascual Ortiz Rubio,
Virgil is hailed as the "gloria de la latinidad" (9)—a motif of Latin pride
that repeatedly crops up in the course of almost six hundred pages of
essays, speeches, translations, and poems. (Approximately half the volume consists of a sequential commentary on the work by Francisco de

P. Herrasti.) It is conspicuous that the various contributors keep referring to the first Eclogue and specifically to the unfortunate social circumstances produced by the land expropriations underlying Virgil's
text ("la tristeza y el abatimiento que se apoderaron de Italia a raíz de la
nueva repartición agraria," 490), and to the gratitude that Virgil expressed for the restoration of his own properties: "Virgilio le da las
gracias a Octaviano por haberle repuesto en sus posesiones mantuanas"
(72). In Mexico, after two decades of revolutionary activity, a conservative government had come back into power and reversed many of the
land reforms. So it can be regarded as a political statement that the
volume closes with an annotated translation of the Bucolics by Tirso
Saénz.

A similar mildly political slant is evident if we turn to the "fiestas
bimilenarias de Virgilio" in Ecuador, where from the end of the nineteenth century increasingly liberal governments had deprived the Catholic church of its influence as well as many of its properties. The ceremonies, described in a volume dedicated to the Archbishop of Quito,[58]
begin with the customary declaration of the worldwide renown of the
"vate latino." The *acto académico* performed in the historic Colegio San
Gabriel de Quito by students and professors of the Seminario de Cotocollao continues with an interpretation of the Eclogues of expropriation ("Las Eglogas de la expoliación") and a study of the "Poeta de la
patria italiana" followed by a recitation of the ninth Eclogue in elegant
Castilian, an alcaic ode by P. Chacón, and a translation of Tennyson's
ode, "To Virgil." Following a speech on "Virgil's Living Poetry" by
Aurelio Espinosa Pólit, the leading representative of humanism in Ecuador, the program was completed with music, notably an orchestra-
tion of Tennyson's ode. The Virgilian enthusiasm in Ecuador did not
end with the bimillennial celebrations. Three years later, in its aftermath, the students of rhetoric at the Colegio de Cotocollao held a
public *acto* on Virgil culminating in the declamation of three sonnets:
an Italian one by Carducci, a French one by the Jesuit Alexis Hanrion,
and a Spanish one by Dr. Manuel María Palacios Bravor—a triptych
that Aurelio Espinosa Pólit took to exemplify "the spiritual assumption
of Virgilian criticism"—an ascent, that is to say, from Carducci's secular appreciation to the religious apotheosis in the words of Palacios.[59]

In France the acknowledgment of the bimillennial was remarkably
sedate, though displaying a poetic as well as a political emphasis. The
Collège de France sponsored two public ceremonies with the goal of
establishing a closer union between the French and Italian intellectual
aristocracy.[60] At the Sorbonne the occasion was celebrated on March 25,
the legendary anniversary of the encounter between Dante and Virgil:
in the great amphitheater of the Sorbonne, where a fresco by Puvis de
Chavannes portrays the Muse of lyric poetry holding the lyre of Or-

pheus, the Orphic passage from Book 4 of the Georgics was recited to the accompaniment of Monteverdi, in a symbolic association of the musician of Mantua with the poet of Mantua.[61] The journal *Latinité* published a special number featuring a piece on "Virgile politique." And in 1931 the scandalous first work of the young fascist Robert Brasillach appeared, a remarkable fictionalized biography that one reviewer characterized as "une sorte d'épopée d'Action française."[62] We shall return in the next chapter to Brasillach, in whose hands Virgil becomes a protofascist preaching political order in an agrarian society. For the most part, however, the reception in France was neither nationalistic in the Italian fashion, nor political in the Hispanic, nor popular in the North American style, but elitist-literary, as we shall see when we look more closely in Chapter 3 at the collective translation of the *Eclogues* undertaken by a group of conservative littérateurs.

Beside the Italo-American folk festivals, the Latin American politico-poetical celebrations, and the French fêtes littéraires, the German ceremonies seem academically sober. The essays in cultural magazines as well as the festive addresses at various universities by distinguished scholars and intellectuals—Rudolf Borchardt in Kiel, Johannes Stroux in Munich, Eduard Fraenkel in Berlin, Wolfgang Schadewaldt in Freiburg, Walter F. Otto in Frankfurt am Main[63]—routinely begin with laments about the German remoteness from Virgil (*Vergilfremdheit*).[64] Ulrich von Wilamowitz-Moellendorff, stating that Virgil is not so important for the rest of the world as for the Italians and the other Romanic peoples and that very few Germans have experienced a lasting effect from his works, concedes that "it ought to be time to shed some light on this contrast but also to do justice to the great artist."[65] The classical philologist Carl Hosius in Würzburg concluded his rectoral address "On Virgil's Two Thousandth Birthday" with the defensive words:

> Germany can also celebrate the bard of Mantua, and even if it does not do so with pilgrimages to the bard's birthplace or grave, as the English intend; if it does not preempt radio and movie theater and postage stamps into the service of its veneration, like the Americans; if it refuses to render homage to the Latin cultural community, which France (always pleased to be political) likes to make of the occasion: still it knows that Virgil also belongs to the elements that cannot be thought out of German culture without producing confusion and injustice.[66]

But the stylistic difference should not distract our attention from certain symptomatic similarities. Two themes above all dominate the speeches: loss and peril, or in other words, the parallel past and present, whereby Virgil is regarded as the father of the Western spirit in a time of crisis. And the appeal to Virgil almost inevitably occurs within a conservative group appalled by the disappearance of order and tradition in the modern world.

Many other countries observed the occasion although, generally speaking, the celebrations were limited to Western Europe and the Western hemisphere.[67] In Poland, for instance, the Roman poet whom Mickiewicz in *Pan Tadeusz* (4.608–17) called "our brother Maro" had long been popular and his bimillennium was celebrated grandly, generating many orations and essays in Latin.[68] (In the Soviet Union, by way of contrast, Virgil was little known and 1930 passed unnoticed.[69]) Even in South Africa the bimillennium was commemorated by a volume recapitulating most of the characteristics previously mentioned. *Vergil in the Experience of South Africa* (Oxford: Blackwell, 1931), by T. J. Haarhoff, professor of classics at the University of Witwatersrand, contains a Latin *praefatio* as well as two dedicatory sonnets in Afrikaans characterizing Virgil as "a peasant's son from Mantua, unfashionable in his disarrayed toga and ill at ease in the city bustle, whose eye penetrates into the very depths of the human soul":

> 'N Boereseun van Mantua se land,
>   Met toga skeef, onmodies, skaam-verloor
>   In stadsgewoel, met oog wat kan deurboor
> Tot in die siel se dieptes; . . .

The book is based on the assumption that the South African *Voortrekker* displays almost precisely the characteristics of the Roman citizen-soldier: *gravitas*, strict morality, wariness of foreigners, and a vague prejudice against art (11). Against this background of analogy, Haarhoff explores "the application of this Vergilian humanism to the circumstances of his time and of South Africa" (60), with particular reference to Virgil's sense of traditional religion (86), his balance between native character and the ideas of an older civilization (104), and even his views on slavery (67). "It is part of the continuity and universality of his spirit, that he should have a meaning for us, too, if only we learn to understand and interpret it aright" (120).

What struck most thoughtful readers of Virgil at the time, then, was the conspicuous parallel between the Augustan past and the European and American (and South African) present. Alice Freda Braunlich wrote in *The South Atlantic Quarterly* of Virgil's appropriateness to serve as a moral leader for the modern world.

Though Virgil was born two thousand years ago, his world was in many respects like ours; for the Augustan Age was characterized, as is our day, by an increasing complexity of business and social relations, by extremes of wealth and poverty, by lavish expenditures, by disillusionment following after a great war, and by changing moral standards.[70]

The scholar-novelist John Erskine explained Virgil's modernity through the similarity of ages: "Now that we realize that the weakness belongs to our civilization also, that our imperialism is only a development of the Roman and carries with it the same or greater cruelties, Vergil lives afresh as our poet."[71]

John William Mackail, the poet-critic who published in 1922 a widely read appreciation of *Virgil and His Meaning to the World of To-Day*, presented in a German periodical the translation of a talk that began with the claim: "The age in which Vergil lived and upon which he made his imprint, greatly resembles ours in many respects. Like ours, the world of that time was a shattered world that had gotten off the rails, a world close to the edge of ethical and economical bankruptcy."[72] In the introduction to his translation of *Les Bucoliques* (Paris, 1946), Henry Charpentier asserts something similar: "Virgile vécut en des temps qui ressemblèrent au nôtre. Les guerres, longues et cruelles, étaient suivies de confiscations et d'exils. Les vainqueurs étaient durs; les poètes doux et craintifs" (83). ("Virgil lived in times that resembled ours. Long, cruel wars were followed by confiscations and exile. The victors were harsh; the poets gentle and apprehensive.")

Wolfgang Schadewaldt characterized the world of Virgil with words that leave no doubt as to their hidden point of reference. "Virgil's work is the child of a troubled and confused time. The state without authority, a shell decrepit with age, passive, vulnerable to the brutal political interests of the party bosses. The society without stability, nervous and greedy, haughty about its traditions and apprehensive about the future."[73] And Friedrich Klingner, leaving little to the imagination as he wrote from the depths of World War II, observed that Virgil lived through

> a boundary situation between the ages, surrounded [*umwittert*] by the horror of the end, of nothingness. The idea of Rome's decline was in the air. All around unspeakable suffering without escape, thousandfold decline. . . . In order properly to understand his gentle games, one must constantly imagine as their background the frightfully devastated life that surrounded him as he composed them: civil war, revolution, fratricide, proscription, misery, brutality, and depravity.[74]

The commonplace was so widespread that Theodor Haecker, in what was probably the most popular Virgil book of the time, exclaimed in annoyance, "Nowadays our age is being compared to antiquity *ad nau-*

seam."[75] But even Haecker regarded Virgil as the "Father of the West," while Curtius designated him as "the spiritual genius of the Occident" (42) and Borchardt called the *Aeneid* "the Old Testament of the entire occidental West."[76]

In sum, then, the reception of Virgil in the decades embracing the worldwide bimillennial celebrations in 1930 can be understood as a specific case of the general Roman analogy that was invoked by many thoughtful people in Europe and the Americas in response to the pervasive crisis of history precipitated by World War I. In the effort to bring meaning into the world of the 1920s and 1930s the Roman poet was invoked, who two thousand years earlier had succeeded in distilling beauty and order from the political and social horror of his own age: civil war, revolution, expropriation, brutal agrarian reform, exile, dictatorship, and imperial aggression. But the response, including the preference for specific works, varied from country to country and from individual to individual, depending upon political, social, and even religious orientation. Virgil's texts, almost like the *sortes Virgilianae* of the Middle Ages, became a mirror in which every reader found what he wished: populism or elitism, fascism or democracy, commitment or escapism. It is against this background, ultimately, that we can properly appreciate the literary image of Virgil among the moderns.

The Ideological Lives

In some sense, no doubt, every biography is ideological. Just as past centuries tailored the lives of heroes *ad usum delphini,* modern American publishers scramble each year to accommodate their history texts to the latest educational fads in California or Texas or New York. Readers can choose among Marxist exposures, Freudian analyses, feminist insights, and a host of other approaches to their favorite biographical subjects. Small wonder that such figures as Julius Caesar, Napoleon, or Goethe have often (in the field of study known to French scholars as *imagologie*) been taken up as mirrors in which the ages see themselves reflected.[1]

Among these specular figures, none affords a steadier image through the ages than Virgil. In 1922 the author of a still important study of Virgilian lives observed that "the figure of the poet may be used as a kind of constant by which to measure the progress of human thought. Every age has tended to fashion a Vergil after its own image, as it were."[2] It is true that the earliest lives of Virgil were written within a century of his death and that, since that time, rarely a generation has passed without shaping its own view of the poet. At the same time, it is probably safe to say that no earlier period in history produced as many biographies of Virgil as did the decades between the two world wars of the twentieth century.

THE ANCIENT VITAE

It is a token of his fame in antiquity that the most extensive and detailed biography that we possess of any Roman writer is a life of Virgil.[3] (As one modern scholar has pointed out, Virgil's life is "much better known than Shakespeare's, but not nearly so well known as Milton's."[4]) This vita was known for many centuries as the *vita Donatiana,* because it was prefixed to a fourth-century commentary on Virgil by Aelius Donatus, the teacher of St. Jerome, who was so famous as a grammarian that the word *Donat* or *donet* came to be used in the later Middle Ages to signify a textbook. In the mid-seventeenth century, however, it was established that the *vita Donatiana* was not an original

composition: It was based upon a lost life of Virgil written early in the
second century by Suetonius for the section *De poetis* in his biographical encyclopedia *De viris illustribus.* The extent of Donatus's borrow-
ing, or of his interpolations, has remained for over three hundred years
a matter of considerable debate among classical philologists. In general,
hardly a line of the roughly two hundred lines of the work now usually
designated as VSD (= *Vita Suetonii [vulgo] Donatiana*) has not been
challenged by one scholar or another.[5]

At the same time, this document contains most of the information
upon which our knowledge of Virgil's life, such as it is, is based—the
framework to which all further speculation must be attached and accommodated. Between his birth on October 15, 70 B.C., at a village near
Mantua and his death in Brundisium on September 21, 19 B.C., the life
is presented in typical Suetonian form. The introduction (about
twenty-five lines[6]) relates the circumstances of Virgil's family, the
dreams and legends surrounding his birth, and his early life: school in
Cremona, then studies in Milan, and his move to "the city." At this
point the chronological sequence is interrupted by some hundred lines
(27–129) in which Virgil is characterized more systematically: his appearance, health, sexual preferences, and sense of privacy (27–42); his
wealth and property (43–47); the deaths of his father and two brothers
(48–51); his studies of medicine, mathematics, and law (52–55). Finally
we hear about Virgil's poetry: his earliest works and his motivations for
writing the *Eclogues,* the *Georgics,* and the *Aeneid* (56–84). This is followed by a longer section (85–129) describing his method and stages of
composition (three years for the *Eclogues,* seven for the *Georgics,* and
eleven for the *Aeneid*) along with some circumstances surrounding his
reading of his works. This brings the author of the vita back to chronology (130–44) and to Virgil's decision, in his fifty-second year, to spend
three years in Greece polishing the epic. Encountering Augustus in
Athens, he is persuaded by the emperor to return with him to Rome;
but afflicted by the heat in Megara, Virgil becomes ill and dies shortly
after the return to Brundisium. His remains are transported to Naples,
where they are buried in a tomb bearing the famous inscription that
sums up his life and works:

> Mantua me genuit, Calabri rapuere, tenet nunc
> Parthenope; cecini pascua rura duces.

> (Mantua bore me, Calabria tore me away, Naples now
> Holds me; I sang meadows, fields, leaders.)

The last quarter of the text attributed to Suetonius relates the terms of
Virgil's will, his wish to have the *Aeneid* burned at his death, and the
editing of his works by his friends Varius and Tucca (145–76). The

conclusion of the vita (177–200) recapitulates criticisms by Virgil's detractors (*obtrectatores*) and a quotation from Virgil generally accepted as genuine: that it is easier to wrest a club away from Hercules than a verse from Homer (*facilius esse Herculi clavam quam Homero versum subripere*).

Late antiquity knew several other briefer lives of Virgil: notably Servius's fifty-line introduction to his standard commentary on the works (late fourth century); the thirty-line biographical sketch prefixed to the commentary by Pseudo-Probus (fifth or sixth century); and a 100-line vita in hexameters attributed to the fifth-century grammarian Focas. But of these *vitae vetustiores*, it was the *vita Donatiana* (or VSD) that constituted the basis for biographical knowledge of Virgil through the Middle Ages and down to modern times.

During late antiquity and the Middle Ages, the life of Virgil was not related for its autonomous biographical interest, as was the biography written by Suetonius, but used for two very specific purposes.[7] First, it was functionalized, and in the process usually streamlined (as in the case of Servius), for use as an introduction (*accessus*) to editions of Virgil's works and commentaries on those works. Accordingly, it was reprinted with various degrees of editing in scores of editions over the centuries and became very widely known. Second, it provided the framework for fanciful expansion as Virgil acquired the reputation of a sage or magician, as Domenico Comparetti demonstrated in his great study *Virgil in the Middle Ages* (*Virgilio nel medio evo*, 1872).[8]

The later lives (*vitae recentiores*) that sprang up during the Renaissance contain no new biographical evidence but simply interpolate apocryphal elements from the medieval romances.[9] The most important of these "expanded lives" is the so-called *Donatus Auctus*, a fifteenth-century vulgate text incorporating various medieval elements—e.g., Virgil's veterinarian skills and his wisdom as a sage—into the *vita Donatiana*.[10] Because the *Donatus Auctus* was repeatedly reprinted in dozens of editions down to the mid-nineteenth century—including the fourth edition of C. G. Heyne's standard edition as revised by G. P. E. Wagner (vol. 1, 1830), which was widely used into the twentieth century—its influence can be felt even in writers of the mid-twentieth century (as we shall have occasion to observe when we consider Hermann Broch).

It was one of the principal challenges of modern philological research to prune away the legendary material in an effort to get back to the basic facts of Virgil's biography—a task that was reasonably well accomplished by the second half of the nineteenth century with the biographical *prolegomena* that Otto Ribbeck prefixed to his edition of the *Opera* (1866) and the account that Nettleship provided in his edition of the *Ancient Lives of Virgil* (1879). Nevertheless, as Werner Suerbaum warns in his study of the vitae, any biography of Virgil should still be written in the interrogative form or with extensive qualifications for every statement.

Suerbaum, of course, is talking about scholarly biographies. Biographies written for a general audience approach their subject with greater latitude. And apart from creative imagination and ideological motivation, those writers have at their disposal a considerable body of material. First, of course, there is the basic chronology of Virgil's life, which has been accepted in outline at least since Donatus, along with its direct quotations from Virgil and its documentary evidence (notably the will and testament). Then there is the potentially rich evidence from Virgil's poetry, which is adduced to suggest his frame of mind (e.g., the constitutional melancholy suggested by such lines as the famous *sunt lacrimae rerum* at *Aen.* 1.462), the landscape he knew as a boy near Mantua, important events in his life (notably the expropriation of his land near Mantua), and indications concerning his circle of friends. In this connection, writers in the twentieth century have attached much weight, as a source of biographical information, to the young Virgil's poetry, known since Scaliger collectively as the *Appendix Vergiliana*, which was virtually ignored by the older vitae. In addition to this internal evidence, we have the testimony of friends (e.g., Horace's account of their journey to Brundisium around 37 B.C. in *Satires* 1.5), the attacks of enemies (the so-called *obtrectatores*), and tales like those recounted by Servius in his commentary and Macrobius in his *Saturnalia*, which quotes passages allegedly from the correspondence between Virgil and Augustus. Resourceful writers have also been able to make use of their knowledge of Roman history during Virgil's lifetime to establish certain probabilities (e.g., that Virgil as a schoolboy in Cremona read accounts of Caesar's wars in Gaul).

Yet it is important to remember that the modern popularizing lives, no less than the ancient and medieval ones, are related either as *accessus* in connection with interpretations of Virgil's works, or in the context of expanded biographies presenting the Roman poet as a sage for the twentieth century.

THE POPULARIZED VIRGIL

It was in this mode that the nineteenth century brought forth, alongside the rigorously scholarly works of Ribbeck, Nettleship, and others, two monumental lives addressed to a general reading public. Sainte-Beuve's exquisite *Etude sur Virgile* (1857) is essentially an appreciation of the *Aeneid*, but it opens with several chapters proclaiming Virgil's enduring status in France and characterizing his personality. Virgil is a poet, Sainte-Beuve begins, who has not ceased to be known and loved in France by everyone. "But why do I say 'in France'? Virgil, since the hour when he appeared, has been the poet of Latinity as a whole."[11] Virgil's eternal appeal lies, for Sainte-Beuve, in his gravity ("ce sérieux"), his quality of noble reflectiveness, and his lofty serenity (49). The book closes with a survey of Virgil's reputation in France from Scaliger to Chateaubriand.

Sainte-Beuve's work, which sought to combine French connoisseurship with the new German philological methods and defended Virgil against his Homeric detractors, had a mixed reception.[12] Presented initially in 1855 as a series of public lectures following his appointment to the chair of Latin poetry at the Collège de France, the work implied an analogy equating Virgil and Augustus with Sainte-Beuve and his government, which precipitated demonstrations by liberal students and Sainte-Beuve's resignation (which was not accepted). But in serial form in the *Moniteur* and in its subsequent publication as a monograph, the *Etude* was received enthusiastically and rapidly entered the canon of European Virgil criticism. Yet his Virgil is not so much a model for the present as "l'enchanteur Virgile" (30). As society has become gentler and culture has spread, Virgil has again found his true climate. More profoundly understood, he is admired in his serenity and artistry, cherished for his piety and compassion, for that "tristesse" that had colored the French view of Virgil ever since Chateaubriand's *Le Génie du Christianisme* (1802)—an image whose influence can also be felt in English literature from Tennyson's Virgil, "majestic in thy sadness at the doubtful doom of human kind," to T. S. Eliot, as we shall see in Chapter 4.

The magisterial volume on Virgil in W. Y. Sellar's *The Roman Poets of the Augustan Age* (1877) was for many decades the standard work in English. The eminently readable book, beginning with substantial chapters on the Augustan Age and Virgil's place in Roman literature, cites Sainte-Beuve (60)[13] to mark the undeviating loyalty of French criticism to the great poet of Latinity and notes a gratifying resurgence of his reputation in England as a reaction against German philology. The third chapter presents a lively and knowledgeable account of the sources and details of the poet's life along with an analysis of his personal characteristics. The remaining three hundred pages deal at length with the three major works to conclude, in sharp contradistinction to subsequent twentieth-century appraisals, that although the Latin poet provides "a bond of union with the genius and culture of Europe in other times" (91) his thought "may not help us to understand the spirit of our own era."

Attitudes toward Virgil changed dramatically around the time of the First World War, as a result of various factors: the Roman analogy that we have already noted, along with the approaching bimillennial celebrations; the new scholarly interest in the *carmina minora* as a possible biographical source; and the popular craving for biography, which was evident in the fictionalizing works of such authors as Emil Ludwig, Stefan Zweig, and André Maurois as well as the phenomenological lives associated with the circle surrounding Stefan George. Between André Bellessort's *Virgile. Son oeuvre et son temps* (1920) and W. F. Jackson Knight's *Roman Vergil* (1944), over a score of often immensely popular lives appeared in German, French, Italian, Spanish, and English. Many of these biographies are written according to formula—often the formula of the series in which they appear—while others amount to reasonably straightforward efforts by scholars to produce reliable and readable appreciations for a public newly awakened to an interest in Virgil. Several of the most interesting ones, finally, display a pronounced ideological slant: Virgil is appropriated for, or accommodated to, the political, religious, or cultural interests of the author. In this chapter we shall examine four of these "ideological" lives. But before doing so, we need to look at several other biographies that served as important points of reference for the "ideological" lives.

André Bellessort's "works and times" begins with an apology to professional Latinists, who will quickly realize, he says, that he is not offering a new interpretation (vii).[14] What we find is not a new scholarly-critical effort but a thoroughly knowledgeable *accessus* by a professor of French and Latin at the Lycée Louis-le-Grand, a skillful translator of the *Aeneid*, and a future member of the Académie Française, who is writing for those who know Virgil only by reputation or as a vague memory from schooldays, in the hope of acquainting them with the historical background and analyzing for them the beauties of his works. This introduction to Virgil, written with all the skill of a popular novelist, poet, travel-writer (to North and South America, the Philippines, and Japan, among other places), and experienced biographer (of Saint Francis Xavier, Balzac, and Voltaire), was widely read and went through ten editions within the first decade.

But Bellessort, who was a reactionary critic of the social and political institutions of France and during the 1930s a contributor to the fascist newspaper *Je suis partout*, had a pronounced intellectual bias. In the first place, this radical Germanophobe intended to take up arms in "the cunning war that the historians, the philosophers, and the philologists of Germany have long waged against us" and, specifically, against the cause of Virgil (330). It was the detested Niebuhr, he wrote, who had set the tone for subsequent German criticism. "The cult of the unconscious, around which the Germanic soul loves to perform its incantations, translated itself into a spiteful contempt of everything that attests in art the patient will and the full consciousness of the artist" (330), a tendency that led the Germans to denigrate Virgil in favor of Homer. Bellessort urges his readers to return to the Roman poet at times when they wish to hear a voice of antiquity that resembles our own (331). Virgil, he argues, is not simply one of the finest geniuses, but "the most noble inspiration of our art, the father of our modern poetry, whose oeuvre reflects, like the shield of Aeneas, all the glory and the humanity of Latin civilization" (viii).

Bellessort informs his readers that he undertook his book just at the time when France was emerging from "the rudest peril" by which it had ever been threatened—France, the true heir of Rome and of everything that Rome and France represented in past and present. Germany had to submit to "a just and shameful capitulation" (ix); once again "the gods of Actium triumphed over the barbarian." During this period it was the verses of Virgil that sounded the joy of victory and of deliverance. Bellessort confesses his immense gratitude toward the poet whose lines spring to our lips in the great crises of life. "Nineteen hundred years ago, he proclaimed to men 'a new order of the centuries.' On the day after the war, I reread with delight this proclaimer of new times" (ix). In Bellessort's portrayal, as level-headed and learned as it is, we sense clearly a nationalistic bias that causes him to reject the subtleties of Teutonic *Wissenschaft* in favor of an immediate apprehension of the poet's modern sensibility, and a veneration for traditional order that he opposes to the anarchic quest for originality that he deplored in the contemporary France of the 1920s. To this extent, Bellessort's *Virgile* exemplifies perfectly the crisis of history and the Roman analogy discussed in the Introduction above.

The widely reviewed *Vergil* (1922) by Tenney Frank, professor of Latin at the Johns Hopkins University—controversial because it generalized so extravagantly from hypotheses—also proclaimed a pronounced thesis. Rejecting Donatus's "meager *Vita*" as "a conglomeration of a few chance facts set into a mass of later conjecture" plus a later "accretion of irresponsible gossip" (v),[15] Frank takes the juvenilia in the *Appendix Vergiliana* to be a reliable record of the poet's daily life, his occupations, and his ambitions: "Best of all they disclose the processes by which the poet during an apprenticeship of ten years developed the mature art of the *Georgics* and the *Aeneid*" (vi). Eschewing both literary history (notably, the question of Virgil's sources) and literary criticism, Frank undertakes a detailed account of the poet's early life based on textual hints in the *Culex*, the *Ciris*, the early epigrams, and the *Eclogues*. (Only the last quarter of his two hundred pages is devoted to the *Georgics* and the *Aeneid*.) In the process he argues against prevailing views to make the case that Virgil was more of an Epicurean than a

Stoic, and he affirms that the landscapes portrayed in the pastoral works are the landscapes of Naples, where Virgil was writing, and not scenes of his childhood around Mantua.

A different kind of thesis is evident in the still eminently readable *Virgil and His Meaning to the World of To-Day* (1922) by John William Mackail. Mackail (1859–1945), a professional writer with socialist leanings who published works on topics as diverse as Shakespeare and William Morris, was in great demand as a lecturer on literary and cultural subjects. The standing of this all-round man of letters who produced a number of editions (e.g., of Russian poetry, Erasmus, and Dante), was attested by his election to a five-year term as Professor of Poetry at Oxford (1907–11). A fervent advocate of the importance of Latin and Greek in modern society, he wrote an often reissued history of Latin literature (1895), brought out an edition of Latin poetry, translated the *Pervigilium Veneris* for the Loeb Classical Library as well as the complete works of Virgil, which were collected in the Modern Library Editions (1934). His *Virgil* (1922) was written for the series *Our Debt to Greece and Rome*, whose editors noted in their preface "the remarkable similarity between our own times and the days of the Roman poet" and Virgil's message "that lives with spirit and power for us at the present moment" (v).[16]

The book amounts to a fine introduction to Virgil—one that is still placed on reading lists for college courses on Roman culture and literature. It opens with a chapter on "The Divine Poet: The Interpreter of Life for All Time," which sets the tone by emphasizing the social significance of Rome and Latin. "Not only is the civilization of Europe and America based on Roman foundations; not only have our machinery of government, our municipal institutions, our jurisprudence and our theology, their roots in Rome; but the language which we use daily as the instrument of thought and the vehicle of expression has been moulded by Latin influence" (5). He discusses "Virgil's Predecessors" and "Virgil's World: Its Meaning for and Its Likeness to Our Own World" (11–21). The work ends with a chapter on "The Virgilian Hexameter," in which Mackail, as a poet, makes clear the huge achievement of Virgil in perfecting for Latin literature such a "foreign metrical structure" as the dactylic hexameter.

Mackail's thrust emerges most clearly in the biographical chapters, where circumstances from Virgil's life are explained for the reader in modern terms. Virgil's father married his employer's daughter and heiress, "like the father of Keats" (29). The schools of Milan that Virgil attended "corresponded broadly to a modern provincial university" (33). The *Eclogues* are the Selected Poems or *Poesie Scelte* of the young poet (36); like Spenser's *Shepherd's Calendar*, they marked a new age of poetry (50), although his reluctance to publish them reminds Mackail of Milton's "reluctant consent to the publication of his *Ludlow Masque*" (49). When Virgil meets Maecenas, the grand patron is serving as "Home Secretary and Minister of Reconstruction (to use modern phraseology)" (37). And the precocious brilliance of Gallus "acted as a stimulus of immense force on Virgil's more slowly maturing and more laboriously working mind (somewhat as Coleridge in early years acted on Wordsworth)" (40).

This systematic interpretation of the ancient life in modern terms prepares the way for Mackail's demonstration of the relevance of ancient times for the understanding of our own present reality. Aeneas's "single lapse into barbarism"—his command to immolate bound prisoners of war over Pallas's funeral pyre—is rationalized by the statement "We ourselves have in recent years seen atrocities as great perpetrated in the daylight by men who called themselves civilized and Christian. So thin is the crust which, now as then, separates mankind from the abyss" (105). Like many of his socialist contemporaries, Mackail (writing *before* the Fascist march on Rome!) believed that "the unified and Roman Italy which was Virgil's primary ideal" had been reborn in his time (140). "Those are yet living who saw the first creation since a thousand years back of an Italian kingdom; our own days have seen its slow unification, its extension to its natural boundaries, the larger hope of its concord or coalescence with the spiritual power which still lives in the name of Rome" (140–41).

But beyond the specific political circumstances of Italy, Virgil is invoked for a more general human purpose. "We stand now, as Virgil stood, among the wreckage of a world; he can give light and guidance to us in the foundation of a new world upon its ruins" (141). It is not, in the last analysis, simply a new appreciation of Virgil and a new insistence on the value of a classical education that Mackail is offering, but a spiritual and moral reclamation of Virgil as a source of strength and inspiration for Western civilization in the chaotic social aftermath of World War I.

Unlike Bellessort, Mackail, and Frank, who could take for granted the uninterrupted cultural traditions of France, England, and the United States, Walter Wili (born 1900), a Privatdozent of classics at the University of Bern, who was known also as a scholar of Plato and Horace—and probably the only biographer of Virgil who became president of a Swiss bank[17]—was seeking with his life to reestablish a line of continuity that had been shattered in German-speaking countries. Wili's *Vergil* (1930)—astonishingly, the first biography of Virgil in German—opens with a quick survey of the poet's image that, continuous in "Romania," was undermined in Germany in the second half of the eighteenth century, when Winckelmann and Voss, along with Herder and Goethe, appropriated Homer as the "naive" poet, in whom nature and art attain absolute harmony (5).[18] As a corollary to this glorification of Greece—what E. M. Butler in the title of her influential book aptly called *The Tyranny of Greece over Germany* (1935)—German thinkers and writers from Herder on, with the notable exception of Schiller, tended to reduce Rome to that imperialistic aspect embodied by Julius Caesar and to regard art as utterly dispensable in the life of the Roman people. This German indifference toward Virgil, which according to Wili reached its nadir around the *fin de siècle*, was turned around in scholarship by the epochmaking work of Richard Heinze, *Vergils epische Technik* (1902); but Heinze's principal finding—that Virgil amounted to more than a simple imitator of Homer—remained essentially a negative fact. Few contemporaries in Germany were still aware, in 1930, of his true significance and standing. Indeed, despite the outstanding editorial accomplishments of German scholars from Heyne to Ribbeck (whose biographical *accessus* and commentaries were written in Latin), there was no life of Virgil available to the interested German reader.

It is this gap that Wili set out to fill, encouraged by the fondness of the age for biography, which had emerged during the 1920s virtually as a new literary genre. "In this book Vergil and his art are presented as simply and basically [*wesentlich*] as possible," we learn from the preface. Inspired evidently by the great biographies being written by members of the circle surrounding Stefan George (and specifically by Gundolf's *Julius Caesar*), Wili argues that, for all its difficulty, intellectual biography ("die geistesgeschichtliche Biographie") is the only adequate way of approaching Roman history and culture. Accepting the criteria underlying the biographies of the George Circle—that they must be exemplary, that they must highlight the Roman basis of modern civilization, and that they must have an educational mission—he states it as the goal of his work "to portray Virgil from the center of his creation and thinking" (122)—a goal thoroughly in keeping with the phenomenological tendencies of the decade. Although his book emphasizes facts rather than any thesis, Wili points out that his collaboration with Rudolf Alexander Schröder, who provided the translations for his volume, is the most telling evidence that his book aspires to be a document of Western culture. (Accordingly the volume features no distracting footnotes or scholarly references and limits itself to three pages of discreet endnotes.) Indeed, it was this collaboration of poet and scholar that excited several early reviewers of the volume.[19]

Working with extensive translations of Virgil's own words—e.g., both the third and fourth *Eclogues* are quoted in full—Wili provides a readable account of the poet's life in four major sections entitled "Form" ("Gestalt," or early life), "Dream" (the *Eclogues*), "Country" (the *Georgics*), and "State" (the *Aeneid*). In general the life provides few surprises: Wili accepts the authenticity of the early pieces of the *Catalepton* but rejects the other *carmina minora*, and he adduces with critical judiciousness the appropriate passages from the vitae and from such contemporaries as Horace. He designates the fourth *Eclogue* as "the most famous poem of Latin literature" (36) and concludes that the mysterious child can be none other than the anticipated heir of Octavian and Scribonia (42). Despite his admiration of the elegance of the *Georgics*, Wili insists, contrary to the traditional view, that they in no way transcend the poetic perfection of the *Eclogues*. And in his discussion of the historical background to the *Eclogues*, he makes the by now conventional point that posterity has come, across the centuries, to regard the figures of that tumultuous age as symbols for world-historical turmoil (40).

Following Heinze, Wili discusses the sophisticated *imitatio* of the *Aeneid*, but insists that the work is primarily a "religious" epic (112) and, to that extent, un-Homeric. The *Aeneid* was the first work of Roman literature that represented the ideals of the people (138) and, in the process, the ideals of Augustan humanism (139). Lucretius may have been a greater thinker, Horace an equal artist, and Ovid more talented inherently; but Virgil transcended them all in the sublimity of his goal (134). To the extent that the *Aeneid* incorporates the Roman ideal of *justitia* and *virtus*, Virgil comes to embody the sense of Roman community (*Gemeinschaft*, 143).

The originality of Wili's book is evident not so much in his portrayal of the life itself or in his literary and historical judgments, but rather in the pattern that he imposes on both: an "inner *bios*" and a "Virgilian *psyche*" (135). The pattern of development that Wili perceives in the *bios* is a pendulation from the stillness of youth to the gay and abandoned life of his young adulthood in Rome; then a sudden renunciation—not as a relapse into solitude but as a serious desire; and during these years of wisdom the experience of great encounters. In Wili's scheme this pattern corresponds to a movement leading from a bucolic period of romantic dreams and myths, by way of a pastoral epoch of agricultural plannings, to a final affirmation of the community embracing the acceptance of cosmic, historical, political, and religious forces (134–35). This *bios* corresponds on the *psychic* level to a tough force of will that stands in sharp contrast to the gentle exterior, a fundamental religious sense of the soil that is close to Roman traditions, and a powerful longing for fulfillment that approaches reality always with a hopeful affirmation (135).

Wili's undertaking seeks in the course of almost one hundred fifty pages both to reestablish the lines of continuity shattered by more than a century of German Graecophilia and to accomplish this by approaching the Roman poet with categories familiar from the phenomenological biographies of the period. In view of his success, it is with an enormous sense of astonishment that we come to the last paragraph, only to learn that Wili regards Virgil's achievements—a perfection lacking intellectual power ("das denkschwache Vollkommensein"), a slavish self-subordination to alien forms, and a new communal discourse ("die neue Gemeinschaftssprache")—as ultimately "un-Greek and un-German" (144–45). Although Wili aspires through a final paradox to claim that these very qualities, in their strangeness, bring Virgil closer to the contemporary observer, it is the surprising implication of his book that Wili himself cannot quite overcome the traditional German prejudices against the Roman poet.

All four of these lives by French, American, English, and German scholars advance a certain thesis. Bellessort advocates a traditional humanism, albeit with a strong nationalistic tinge, against German *Wissenschaft*; Tenney Frank wants to make the case for the authenticity of the *carmina minora* as reliable sources for the poet's life; Mackail reclaims Virgil as a source of moral strength for modern society; and Walter Wili hopes to reestablish the shattered lines of continuity in Germany by approaching the Roman writer with patterns familiar from contemporary phenomenological biographies. All of them, though controversial, were widely cited and played an important role in the discussion about Virgil around the bimillennial celebration. All stressed the relevance of Virgil for the twentieth century. Yet none had the pronounced bias that is evident when we turn to the next set of four works, each of which conspicuously sought to appropriate Virgil for explicitly ideological purposes.

THE PROTOFASCIST VIRGIL

By far the greatest number of modern "lives" was produced, as might be expected from everything said in Chapter 1, in Italy. From introductions written expressly for a general audience (e.g., Giuseppi Lipparini's *Virgilio: l'uomo, l'opera, i tempi* [1925], Giuseppi Fanciulli's *Virgilio: la vita e le opere* [1927], and Alberto Mocchino's *Virgilio* [1931]) to pamphlets produced according to the formula of inexpensive series (Enrico Turolla's *Virgilio* in *Profili* [1927], Lionello Levi's *Virgilio* in *La coltura classica* [1929], and Cesare Verlato's *Virgilio* in *Scrittori ed opere* [1930]), not to mention translations into Italian of the works of Bellessort and Tenney Frank,[20] Italian writers kept the presses busy with works turned out expressly to capitalize on the bimillennial. From this outpouring I want to single out, as perhaps the best and certainly the most representative, Paolo Fabbri's *Virgilio: Poeta sociale e politico* (1929) because its sociopolitical motivation is evident from the title onward and from the explicit dedication, "Agl' ideali della patria rinnovata."

Fabbri was a classicist whose familiarity with Latin Augustan literature had been demonstrated by a study of Roman customs based largely on the works of Horace and Martial (*Da Orazio e da Marziale*, 1924) and who later produced a major edition of Ovid (1940). His scholarly competence in matters Virgilian is evident on every page of his book, which refers with expert ease to the relevant classical sources as well as the international scholarship in English, German, and French.[21] (Fabbri frequently cites Bellessort's *Virgile*, which he characterizes as "libro importantissimo e geniale" [7].) At the same time, the preface makes it clear that Fabbri is writing not for specialists but for "la nuova generazione italica"—that is, for the youth of the secondary and higher schools as well as "cultivated persons whose love of knowledge and art is united with a passion to improve and to aggrandize our *Patria*, which was specifically Virgil's passion" (viii). Perhaps no writer in modern times, Fabbri suggests, has been the subject of such ambivalent responses, such sympathy and antipathy, as Virgil, from whose poems emanates an effluvium that attracts some spirits and repels others. Fabbri views it as his task to resolve this issue of idealism and materialism that divides temperaments along moral and political lines (vii) and to "relocate him [Virgil] in his proper sphere, both material and ideal, both civil and political" (viii).

While protesting on the first page that his book should not be confused with the "romanzi virgiliani" that have flooded the market, Fabbri concedes that he has taken certain liberties with the historical reconstruction, especially in the opening chapter, in order to create a livelier narrative. Fabbri begins his biography with the dramatized account, transmitted by Tacitus and Servius, of the public performance of the sixth *Eclogue* by the actress Volumnia, which first established Virgil's reputation. "On that day the theater of Pompey was more crowded and noisy than usual" (1). The story then circles back to the facts and legends associated with Virgil's birth and quickly establishes the theme of *Latinitas*. After reviewing the scholarly conjectures regarding the poet's ethnicity, Fabbri concludes, "But of whatever blood he may have been—Celtic, Etruscan, or Latin; and we firmly believe it was Latin, just as his name is Latin—Virgil fashioned himself according to the culture, the thought, the patriotism of Rome, and more than any other writer he acquired the right to be called Roman" (7).

Fabbri covers the accepted facts reliably but allows himself a number of conjectures introduced by such phrases as "chi sa": "Who knows how often in the solitude of the fields and the meadows or in the shade of some tree the youth paused to listen to these and other sounds. . . . Who knows how often in the serene nights he fixed his large innocent eyes to admire these lights in the skies" (10). Or "Who can tell the enthusiasm that invaded these spirits" when they learned of Caesar's victories (13). The section dealing with Virgil's schooldays in Cremona is a fiction composed of the sparse facts from Virgil's life plus details culled from Caesar's *De bello Gallico*: "One day, while he was walking to school accompanied as usual by his servant, who was carrying his satchel and waxed tablet, Virgil saw written on the walls of Cremona, 'The barbarians of Helvetia wish to invade our province, but we will not permit it'" (12). Other conjectures are introduced by "forse," as when Virgil leaves Cremona to study rhetoric at Milan: "Perhaps, considering his passion for poetry, someone proposed to introduce him to Valerius Cato, the master of poets and likewise a native of Cisalpina" (16). The following pages, dealing with Virgil's years as a member of "il cenacolo di poeti nuovi" (19), rely heavily for background material on Cicero's account of these "*poetae novi, neoteroi*" and "*cantores Euphorionis*" as well as the fast-moving political events in Rome from 53 to 46 B.C.

In the course of his fictionalizing account, Fabbri takes issue with certain scholarly findings. For instance, he rejects the identity of Virgil with Tityrus in the first *Eclogue* and the implied restoration of his family estate in Mantua (42). He likewise refuses to accept the *Appendix Vergiliana* as a reliable biographical source (42–43), in contrast to Tenney Frank and many other scholars of the twenties. The chapter is rounded off by Virgil's visit in Rome to Cornelius Gallus, where he meets Volumnia (the actress, whose performance opens the chapter) and ends with a highly fictionalized account of Virgil's first encounter with Maecenas. "On that same day Maecenas, who had not only conceived but already initiated the famous circle, had a conversation with Varius and Tucca, and on the following day had Cornelius Gallus summoned to his house: he wanted to know not only the origins but the characteristics of Virgil and, above all, his ideas and his political attitudes" (45).

After chapter 1, the biographical survey gives way to three chapters focused, respectively, on the major works. But the inquiry of Maecenas regarding Virgil's political views provides the focus of everything that follows. The discussion of the *Georgics*, for instance, begins with a portrayal of the contemporary social circumstances in Italy, where the land was cultivated by means of slaves on vast estates, while sheep rearing, in violation of the ancient restrictive laws, tended to remove great territories from agricultural use (89). At the same time, the distribution of land to the veterans, whereby Octavian had hoped to reinvigorate agriculture by augmenting the number of small landholders and thereby breaking in some measure the practice of latifundia, had actually done nothing but increase the confusion.

In response to this situation, Fabbri writes, "Virgil wrote the *Georgics*—for himself, for Maecenas, for the little landowners, for those who desired the improvement and progress of agriculture, for those who loved the life of the countryside, and saw in it an inexhaustible school of sober citizens and of strong soldiers for the homeland" (91). The "moral law of life" ("la legge morale della vita," 94) that emerges from the *Georgics* is summed up by the famous phrase *labor omnia vicit / improbus* (*Geo.* 1.145–46). The message that finally remains in this, his loveliest work, is "the poet's love for the country of Italy, the most beautiful *Patria* that exists in the world" (110).

The discussion of the kingdom of the bees in Book 4 of the *Georgics*, in which Fabbri sees Virgil's declaration of faith in monarchy ("dichiarazione di fede monarchica," 137), provides a transition to the *Aeneid*. Virgil's death is mentioned almost in passing (150) during the discussion of the *Aeneid*, presumably so that the temporal fact of his demise will not detract in any way from Fabbri's conception of the eternal message of this "epopea della Romanità." Fabbri sees in the *Aeneid* a prophetic work that anticipates the most salient aspects of Roman history (151), a work rich in significance and teachings ("ricca veramente di significati e di ammestramenti è la poesia virgiliana," 222–23). It is the moral and social message of the *Aeneid* that good can be attained only by way of suffering and striving ("attraverso il dolore e lo sforzo," 223)—the conjunction that produced the sense of human tragedy and religious devotion that springs from the poet's heart to all humanity. What national affirmation is stronger than the precept bequeathed at *Aeneid* 6.853 to all future Romans:

parcere subiectis et debellare superbos

(to spare the vanquished and to tame the haughty)

To pardon the vanquished is an act of piety and a criterion of Roman politics that has its complement in the responsibility to punish the haughty—that is, "not to permit the existence of competitors capable of threatening the Empire" (224). For Fabbri this precept represents "the ideal of generosity and of valor joined to political wisdom as conceived by Romans of the most beautiful centuries" (224). Fabbri concludes his moving revival with the assertion that Virgil is closer to us at the end of his second millennium than ever before, a fact suggested by the degree to which humanity, and specially Italy, is again turning to him. More even than Dante, he is "the bard of virtue and of all the qualities dear to the renewed *Patria*, the bard of sacrifice and work, of devotion and power, of love and glory" (225). On this ecstatic note Fabbri ends his paean, which epitomizes the enthronement of Virgil as the incorporation of all the virtues of modern Fascist Italy.

By all odds the most curious life produced by the bimillennial celebrations was *Présence de Virgile* (1931) by Robert Brasillach, the brilliant young intellectual whose romantic fascism led him into an unapologetic collaboration with the Nazi occupation, for which he was tried and executed in 1945. At the time he wrote his life of Virgil, however, the twenty-year-old *normalien* was still in the process of shaping his anarchistic views, which were characterized largely by negative valences—anticapitalist, antiliberal, anti-Marxist, and antibourgeois— into a positive political vision. As a result, his effort presents us with a Virgil who is part *bohémien* and part protofascist.

Brasillach (1909–45) was born at Perpignan but spent most of his childhood in Sens, where his mother moved when she remarried following the death of his father, an officer in the colonial infantry.[22] In 1925 the bookish, ambitious, and socially alienated youth arrived in Paris to continue his studies at the Lycée Louis-le-Grand. The precocious lycéen had already published articles in a provincial weekly, *Le Coq Catalan*, and during the next few years he continued to turn out articles, poems, and reviews at a feverish pace for a variety of local and student newspapers and journals, activities that led to his engagement in 1930 by the right-wing *Revue universelle*. Brasillach's most illustrious teacher at Louis-le-Grand was none other than André Bellessort, who introduced his classes to rigorous critical thinking. They learned through Tacitus the relevance of classical texts for the analysis of modern society; and, thanks to the author of the enormously successful life of Virgil, came to appreciate particularly the great Roman poet.

Bellessort's reactionary views represented an important stage in the political development of his impressionable pupils, several of whom— including Brasillach's most immediate circle of friends—later became associated with the fascist newspaper *Je suis partout* and the Action française. In 1928 the brilliant student was accepted at the Ecole normale, where he was able to continue the *vie de bohème* to which he had become accustomed. Indeed, the literary life occupied Brasillach so obsessively that he failed his *agrégation* in 1931 and again in 1932. However, his professional life as an aspiring *homme de lettres* thrived: Working first as a tutor and as an occasional translator (of, among other things, a Renaissance Latin text on alchemy), he gradually began to support himself through his writing, primarily for right-wing journals.

The *normalien* who in 1930 undertook a life of Virgil for his first book did so explicitly in response to the bimillennial.[23] But this twenty-year-old was also a first-rate Latinist, trained by one of the foremost Virgilian scholars in France, to whom the preprint in *Revue universelle* was dedicated. A bookworm inexperienced in life and politics, Brasillach was extremely well read in a variety of fields and filled with nostalgia for the student *bohème* that he saw soon coming to an end. At the same time, his political and social views were rapidly coming together in a kind of romantic fascism inspired by developments in Italy. "In the courtyard at Louis-le-Grand we spoke of [Italian] fascism with affection."[24] For these boys in search of an ideal, *homo fascista* represented the appropriate successor to the Christian knight as a defender of Western values.[25]

The tone of Brasillach's book, which one reviewer called "une sorte d'épopée d'Action française,"[26] is suggested by the circumstance that it was published through the assistance of Henri Massis, a star of the radical Right, a friend of the extremist Maurras, a notorious polemicist against Gide and other literary figures, an important entrepreneur of the right-wing literary establishment, and a ghostwriter for Pétain during the Vichy regime. Brasillach's *Présence de Virgile*, which another critic has called "l'inventaire anticipé des thèmes de son oeuvre à venir"[27] and which constituted his first literary success, marks Brasillach's initiation into the politics of the extreme Right and, ultimately, to fascism.

What was the appeal of Virgil to this young *bohémien* with totalitarian political aspirations? How did he shape the life to suit his goals? What were the sources for this precocious classicist without professional philological training? If we begin with the last question, we are informed by Brasillach's "Note pour le lecteur bienveillant" (240–43)[28] that he was familiar with the classical vitae, with the arguments of Tenney Frank for the validity of the *Appendix Vergiliana*, and of course with the work of his own teacher. He disclaims any intention of writing a work of literary history or criticism "because there is already an excellent one written by André Bellessort" (243). Moreover, although Brasillach is not explicit on this point, there is hardly a factual detail in his book that is not to be found in the splendid edition of Plessis and Lejay (1919),[29] which replaced the *Virgile* of Eugène Benoist (1873) as the standard school text and whose quality Bellessort had acknowledged in the *avant-propos* of his study (ix).

Above all, Brasillach relies on Virgil himself for all those "éléments véritables" that he did not find in the secondary studies: "le soleil, la

mer, l'herbe des prairies" (242). Many descriptive passages amount to
little more than a paraphrase of the Latin text. For instance, he speaks
of the peasant lore that Virgil picked up from the conversations of his
father and the farm workers. "Il savait sous quelle étoile il fallait ouvrir
le sol et marier la vigne grimpante à l'ormeau, la manière de multiplier
le bétail" (8). Readers will recognize this sentence as an adaptation of
the opening lines of the *Georgics*, in which the poet outlines the contents of his work, which will deal with planting, viniculture, and animal
husbandry:

> Quid faciat laetas segetes, quo sidere terram
> Vertere, Maecenas, ulmisque adjungere vites
> Conveniat, quae cura boum, qui cultus habendo
> Sit pecori, . . .

(What makes the crops bountiful, under what constellation,
Maecenas, it is best to turn the soil and to attach vines to the elms,
what care is needed for cattle, what tending for flocks, . . .)

(where the last word is glossed by Plessis and Lejay as "le petit bétail,
opposé à *boum*"). Similarly, when the seventeen-year-old from northern Italy arrives in Rome, he is stupefied by the enormity of the urban
metropolis. "Il croyait d'abord, dans sa simplicité, que Rome ressem-
blerait à Mantoue ou à Crémone, comme une chienne à son chiot"
(12)—a reference to the first *Eclogue*, where Tityrus recalls for his friend
Meliboeus his naive belief that Rome was comparable to their own
town:

> Urbem quam dicunt Romam, Meliboee, putavi
> Stultus ego huic nostrae similem, . . .
> Sic canibus catulos similes, sic matribus haedos
> Noram, sic parvis componere magna solebam.
>
> (I. 20–24)

(The city they call Rome, Meliboeus, I foolishly believed similar
to ours, . . . Just as I knew that pups were similar to dogs, and
kids to their dams, thus I was used to comparing the large to the
small.)

Returning to Mantua following his studies, Virgil finds again the
rural landscape in which the evening smoke furls up from the roofs of
cottages: "ce monde où les fumées lointaines montent naturellement
des toits de métairies" (65)—virtually a translation of the concluding
lines of the first *Eclogue: et iam summa procul villarum culmina fumant*
("and already in the distance the rooftops of the cottages are smoking").

When Virgil looks out from his property, "Devant lui était cette colline dont la pente s'abaisse doucement, et ce fleuve étalé, et le hêtre rompu" (66), a description taken directly from the *Eclogues*:

> Certe equidem audieram, qua se subducere colles
> Incipiunt mollique jugum demittere clivo,
> Usque ad aquam, et veteres, jam fracta cacumina, fagos . . .
>
> (9. 7–9)

> (Indeed I had heard that, where the hills begin to rise and then to depress their ridge in a gentle slope, down to the water and the old beeches with their broken tops . . .)

Citing André Maurois's book on Shelley as his model (240), Brasillach affirms that he has not attributed to Virgil a single phrase or thought that is not based on an ancient text or, at least, a modern conjecture. But if Brasillach remains close to his sources for his details, how does he shape his life? Here the young littérateur adopted a wholly different method.

Despite the authenticity of the details and the atmosphere, Brasillach had no desire to write a conventional historical novel. Rather, he "wanted the reader to begin the book as though it were the story of a young Italian of the year 1930" (242). Accordingly the opening pages contain no dates, no names, and no technical terms of ancient Roman life. Brasillach does not wish so much to say new things about Virgil as to present the familiar life in a wholly new light. It is his ambition to have this life read "comme une vie moderne" (242)—to present Virgil as "un homme du temps *présent*" (243).

When Virgil arrives in Rome, like the young Brasillach arriving in Paris from the provinces, he is attracted by the intellectual avant-garde which, at that time, cultivated orientalism, religious myth, and preciosity of style. During this age of political crisis and civil war, Virgil and his fellow students attended the lectures of the fashionable Greek intellectual Parthenios and cherished the memory of Catullus. When Cicero—"un écrivain célèbre, avocat, essayiste, vulgarisateur" (36)—publishes the work of Lucretius, an unknown poet-philosopher who is said to have committed suicide after having lived his last days in madness, the analogy to Nietzsche and his impact on Brasillach's own generation is implicit. Renouncing this "littérature de cénacle" (39), Virgil spends several years in Naples studying with the philosophers Siro and Philodemus. Later he is introduced to the *vie de bohème* surrounding Horace, who is characterized as though he were a figure from a fashionable novel:

C'était un petit homme myope, rond, court et vif. Il riait, aimait le vin, les belles filles, le goût du pain. Il avait des vulgarités, des plaisanteries faciles. Il se plaisait à l'emphase affectée et truculente. Il était drôle—et un peu plus. (107)

(He was a short myopic man, rotund, abrupt, and lively. He liked to laugh, loved wine, beautiful girls, the taste of bread. He was not averse to trivial conversation, to facile witticisms. He delighted in an affected and truculant pomposity. He was droll—and something more than that.)

Later in his career Virgil's books, which were much in demand, were handled by a shrewd literary agent named Eros, "a Greek who knew his way around in business and whose name lent itself to facile puns about the eternal alliance of love and money" (182).

In addition to the modern terms in which the ancient world is depicted, Brasillach uses analogy to help his readers understand the situation of Virgil and his friends. It was no doubt from his teacher Bellessort (cf. *Virgile*, 152) that Brasillach learned that Virgil first composed his epic in prose, as did Racine his dramas (193). The Racinian analogy, favored by Bellessort as well as Plessis and Lejay, occurs frequently throughout the text: "He said nothing but simple and ordinary things, but he said them in that almost colorless form, reduced to a precise and pristine nakedness that later would be the style of Racine" (126; see also 196 and 235). In another place Virgil's memorial to noble Roman families in the *Aeneid* is compared to the *Almanach de Gotha* (205). In characterizing the *Eclogues*, whose dreams are rooted in visible reality, Brasillach speaks of Alain Fournier, whose *Le grand Meaulnes* was similarly compounded of experienced peasant reality and lost illusions of youth (126). In his attempt to define Virgil's unique role as a national poet, Brasillach adduces two other contemporary examples: "He had in fact the poetic sense of a union with the land and the dead, like Maurice Barrès, and a pagan enthusiasm and pride like Gabriele d'Annunzio" (181). Speaking of Virgil's research trip to Greece, in the course of which he died, Brasillach reminds his readers of André Maurois, who died while visiting sites beloved by Byron (230). Virgil inserts everyday names of places and things into his poetry as does Mistral, using the banal terms familiar to Provençal peasants. (Here, no doubt, Brasillach was influenced by the common bimillennial coupling in France of Virgil and Mistral.) And in a macabre image, Brasillach maintains that Virgil loved the blood-soaked lands of his "cité charnelle" (199) just as Péguy loved the "terre charnelle" that he celebrated in the poem *Eve*.

Ultimately, of course, this technique of modernization—the portrayal of the ancient world as though it were being experienced by a young Italian of 1930 and analogous to the contemporary *vie de bohème*—serves Brasillach's as yet inchoate political objectives. This Virgil, like Brasillach himself in 1930, is a protofascist, a man who senses that power and a strong man are necessary to preserve a country in political disarray and without order. "Pour sauver ce pays et cet ordre, il savait que la force était nécessaire." But he did not fear to appeal to this power; he loved it "as is natural at his age" (61). Brasillach extrapolates from his own physical weakness to assume that Virgil reacted against his sickliness to admire, in contrast to such fearful babblers as Cicero, brutal conquerors who violate laws in order to impose new ones. "Par regret d'être lui-même trop faible de corps, trop rêveur encore d'esprit pour agir, il aimait les grands vainqueurs qui violent toutes les lois jusqu'au moment où ils en donnent aux autres" (61).

First exposed to the romanticism of power in the person of Julius Caesar, "who seized power as one becomes a priest . . . a force that resides in the exercise of power and that transforms men," Virgil "longed for him passionately" (29). In keeping with this romance of power, the poet regarded the young Octavian with a mixture of terror at his cruelty and admiration for his prodigious intelligence, realizing that this man of execrably bloody tendencies curbed his cruelty for political reasons "because now he regarded himself as at one with the Roman people" (147). With fascination the poet listened to the young ruler speak of his projects: to humble the mighty, to create an indispensable middle class of citizens, to reestablish the old traditions and the national religion, to send the peasants back to the deserted countryside.

It is Maecenas who enables Virgil to understand how he can assist Octavian in his political plans and his agrarian projects. "He advised him to apply his love of the country to other subjects than these pleasant pastorals. He showed him how important it was for the nation to create a movement of opinion in favor of the land" (147). Virgil undertakes the *Georgics*, a work combining a manual of agriculture with a ritual of religious ceremonies. Although Virgil grasped the poetic project immediately, "the political and social program was less easily assimilable to poetry" (153). Gradually, however, as he contemplated the great landed estates that had transformed the exploitation of the countryside into a mechanical operation without beauty, Virgil began to dream of free workers, organized by families and under the protection of the prince. "It was this idea of the free trades, grouped under a strong authority, which, better than the artificial opposition between the town and the country, permitted poetry to filter between the lines" (155).

Paradoxically, his memories of his father, the beekeeper, pursuing his mysterious preoccupations "like the priest of a dangerous religion" (161), lead Virgil in the fourth book of the *Georgics* to "ses plus claires idées de la politique et même de l'univers" (161).

From this vision of the political ideal it is a logical step to the outline of a political theory ("ébauche de politique," 198) evident in the *Aeneid*. Although the epic lacks the precision that produces in the *Georgics* a veritable treatise expounding a complete system, it presents in poetic guise a striking lesson in obedience, modesty, and sacrifice in service of the country—"the story of a man who identifies himself, whatever it may cost, with his nation" (198). Observing Octavian, this "économe du sang de son peuple" (197), Virgil saw him organize the provincial freedoms and prepare just social laws. He had long followed Octavian in his design to subjugate the upper classes in order to create the indispensable middle class. Brasillach concludes from this that, with these thoughts, Virgil was addressing the future—the youth of his own country as well as the young people of all centuries, providing them with "un modèle d'héroïsme accepté" (198). Ultimately this Virgil, in his reverence for traditional values, the strong ruler, and submission to law, resembles no one so greatly as Brasillach himself. "He proposed to the politically minded a traditional monarchy, with a long retinue of memories; to the disquieted, a union with the world and submission to laws that rule all living creatures; to all he proposed love, friendship, combat, the family, even if he was himself not precisely acquainted with all these benefits" (227). Unfortunately, Brasillach did not content himself with the patriotism, nationalism, and political conservatism that he sensed in Virgil. The political developments of the next few years along with his own impulse to blood and violence led him to the reactionary values of fascism and, only fifteen years later, to his death.

The Proto-Christian Virgil

It would be difficult to imagine a sharper contrast to Brasillach than Theodor Haecker, who, having barely survived various Nazi interrogations, died in the same year as did the French fascist. Haecker (1879–1945) was in almost every respect the polar opposite of Brasillach.[30] An autodidact who finally passed his *Abitur* at age twenty-five but never completed a university degree, Haecker was an outspoken anti-Nazi who maintained a steady course of courageous oppositional activity until he was prohibited from further public appearances and his books were proscribed. His wartime journals, posthumously published under the title *Journal in the Night* (*Tag- und Nachtbücher*, 1947), constitute one of the finest documents of German resistance thought. A freelance writer and convert to Catholicism, he supported himself by translating Kierkegaard, John Henry Newman, Hilaire Belloc, and Francis Thompson. A gifted essayist and aphorist, he was an enthusiastic polemicist and intransigent critic who turned his considerable energies and satiric pen against what he considered the unprincipled liberalism of the twenties, against industrialism and urbanism, and against the tide of nationalism everywhere in Europe. Thus in 1923 he observed, in a gloss on Mussolini, that "the deification of the state proceeds at the same pace as the beastification of man."[31]

Haecker's interest in Virgil antedated the bimillennial celebrations. In 1923 he published a translation of the *Eclogues* in a luxury edition with twenty woodcuts by Richard Seewald.[32] And during the bimillennial year, he lectured on Virgil in Munich, Zürich, and Vienna. (The book was written as a series of essayistic chapters that lend themselves easily to separate delivery.) In any event, *Vergil. Vater des Abendlands* (*Virgil: Father of the West*, 1931) became his most famous book: It was frequently reprinted; rapidly translated into English (1934), French (1935), Italian (1935), Dutch (1942), and Spanish (1945); widely reviewed; and influential, as we shall see, in the works of T. S. Eliot and Hermann Broch.

The book has all the hallmarks of Haecker's style, including the polemics. He finds occasion for numerous sideswipes as, for instance, against the "modern type-mad ignorance" of Oswald Spengler (84–85).[33] He also mocks the fashion of the Roman analogy, asserting that "nowadays our age is being compared to antiquity *ad nauseam*" (40). He regards the festive tributes to Virgil as largely superficial—"a wretched remnant of the learning and experience that Germans of the Holy Roman Empire of German Nation down to the eighteenth century shared with every good European" (127). And he rejects "the currently all too abrupt constructions of Romanitas and Latinitas and Germanitas—nothing but closed and therefore false systems that exclude any insight into the natural catholicity of the true and the beautiful" (128).

With this final criticism, we approach the positive principles underlying Haecker's work. It is his ambition, as he explains in the preface, to expose "Virgilian Man" not as a particular and limited type of Western man but as Western Man par excellence (20). He aspires to encompass the totality of this Western, Virgilian Man and not to present simply a philological-aesthetic interpretation of Virgil and his work: That would be like the decomposition (*Zersetzung*) produced by other disintegrating minds (21). Although he hopes to proceed objectively and to exclude irrelevancies, Haecker states his intention of ascertaining the "faith" (*Glauben*) that motivates Virgil and his figures (19). It is the absence of faith that precludes both popular biographers like Emil Ludwig and the historians of the George Circle from penetrating to any essential truths about the past (24). The large question that concerns Haecker is, How was it possible for a Christian Rome and the Christian West to emerge from pagan Rome (26)? In other words, How was it possible for this adventist pagan, this *anima Vergiliana* that constituted the loftiest soul of ancient Rome, only a few years before "the fullness of time," to anticipate the Christian mysteries of grace and of freedom?

In his summary of Virgil's life ("Ecce Poeta"), which is based on the traditional vitae, Haecker stresses several characteristic features: Growing up in the provinces far from Rome, which was disintegrating into anarchy, Virgil was able to absorb the puritanical old morals of the republic (29). From Lucretius he learned that the greatness of all art "stands in a direct relation to the value of its philosophy and theology" (33). Despite the philosophical profundity of his work, his poetic language is characterized by the use, in his most powerful as well as his most tender verses, of simple words that every Roman of his day spoke and wrote. In accordance with this "inexorable law of classical art" (36), he achieved the most uncommon verse with the most common words, rising to the *gloria* of the pure word. The brief biographical *accessus* closes with the paradoxical observation that Virgil was fortunate to have died at the peak of his career and the plenitude of the Empire (43).

Haecker's discussion of the *Eclogues* and *Georgics* is tied in each case to a thematic quotation. Under the motto *omnia vincit amor* (*Ecl.* 10.69), he traces the tragic force of love—in contrast to the Lucretian love that motivates all nature—from the *Eclogues*, by way of the *Georgics*, down to Dido. In his discussion of the *Georgics*, "the most classical work that can be imagined" (64), the tag *labor omnia vicit / improbus* (1.145–46) leads Haecker to point out that Virgil's portrayal of the pastoral life has nothing in common with the romantic escapism of, say, Rousseau. Rather, the Roman poet wants to make the point that true culture, in its etymological associations with agri*cultura*, is possible only through hard work (70). The effect of ultimate simplicity can be achieved only through the utmost rigor and effort.

Haecker's treatment of the *Aeneid* is presented in the form of five brief essays. He begins by stressing that Virgil had the greatest subject ever offered to a writer before the Christian era: one in which *mythos* and history could be approached not through fantasy but through reality. But it was Virgil's classical sense of totality that enabled him to deal with his subject in such a manner that "a single verse of the *Aeneid* contains all Rome, a single verse the entire Virgil" (78). His excursus on Aeneas's *pietas* points out that the Roman notion differs from the conventional associations of German *Frömmigkeit* (or, for that matter, English *piety*) by combining internal devotion with the external sense of divine mission that motivates Virgil's hero (ch. 5). It is this sense of mission that distinguishes Aeneas unmistakably from Odysseus (and hence removes Virgil from the mindless charge of plagiarism). Indeed, the *Aeneid* is the only book of antiquity besides the Holy Scripture that contains prophecies pointing beyond the time and circumstances of its own days (ch. 6).

The theological meaning of the *Aeneid* is not to be found, however, in the many deities that play a superficial role, but rather in the mystery of *fatum*. The distinction between the Roman concept, which invokes the notion of utterance, and the German vocable *Schicksal*, which involves Faustian associations of action, leads Haecker to ruminations on the religious quality of Virgil's work (ch. 7). The "sea of tears between man and *fatum*" (115) suggested by "the least translatable phrase of Roman literature" (116), the mysterious *sunt lacrimae rerum* (*Aen.* 1.462), introduces speculations on the term *res*, which Haecker calls the "heartword [*Herzwort*] of the Latin language" (117)—that is, one of those untranslatable expressions that contain the key to the intuitions lying behind every language. It is Virgil's sense of the ineffable sadness of reality that entitles him, according to Haecker, to be regarded as "the greatest and sole tragic writer of Rome" (122). Chapter 10 recapitulates the by now familiar theme of Virgil's standing in Germany, *in partibus infidelium*. Although Haecker does not regard the fourth *Eclogue* as a literal prophesy of the savior, he sees in it a "mythic presentiment of divine salvation history" (136). It is this presentiment in the thoroughly Roman poet, in a humble soul that is *humilis* like the Italian soil itself, that qualifies Virgil as an *anima naturaliter christiana* (140).

In his epilogue Haecker surveys the appeal of the Roman poet to other *animae Vergilianae* through the centuries, from Augustine to Cardinal Newman, as evidence for the claim that Virgil is truly "the Father of the West." In a long essay catalyzed by his book—and that turns into an analysis of political developments in Germany culminating in an attack against the Nazis[34]—Haecker sought to explain this notion more extensively. Just as the Church is independent of time and space, of races and peoples and states, so too the unity of humanity is essentially of the spirit and not of the blood. Particularity emerges in specific historical situations determined by time and place. With his book Haecker was addressing humanity in its historical manifestation as "Western Man," of whom Virgil is the spiritual father. "I can well imagine," Haecker continues, "that, if the Chinese should become Christians, they would find a natural predecessor in whom they would recognize the more or less prepared 'nature,' the adventist of their race and their individual spirit for the super-nature of the God-man—I can well imagine that one of them might write a little book entitled 'Laotse, Father of the Orient' " (437).

We have already encountered Aurelio Espinosa Pólit as a motivating force behind the elaborate "fiestas bimilenarias de Virgilio" that were celebrated in Ecuador (ch. 1). Espinosa (1894–1961) was a leader in the distinguished tradition of Jesuit education that began in Ecuador in the mid-nineteenth century when President Gabriel García Moreno persuaded the Roman Catholic church to send a group of European Jesuit scholars to become teachers in the country's schools. The author of many works on pastoral theology, Espinosa also edited a series of titles important for the history of Ecuador and translated into Spanish not only Sophocles' two Oedipean tragedies but also one of the literary curios cited earlier, *La pastoral virgiliana* by Whicher (Quito, 1937). Most of Espinosa's principal impulses—the pastoral, the pedagogical, and the classical—came together in his powerful presentation of *Virgilio. El poeta y su misión providencial* (1932), which has been authoritatively termed "the most elegant work dedicated to the Latin poet in the Spanish language."[35]

Espinosa's five-hundred-page work is based on a thorough acquaintance both with the Virgilian texts and with the major international scholarship. Sainte-Beuve and Bellessort, Tenney Frank and Mackail, Nettleship and Rand, along with many others, figure in his notes. Above all Espinosa, with true Latin pride, takes issue with the German critical reaction from Niebuhr to Wilamowitz that interrupted the hitherto continuous tradition of admiration for the *universal paternidad* of Virgil in Western letters (4).[36] Indeed, the first half of the book, dedicated to Virgil the Poet, is concerned mainly with the rehabilitation of the Roman poet in the face of the Teutonic attacks. Following a rapid survey of the centuries during which Virgil provided "el modelo universal" (5) for writers in every European country, Espinosa arrives at the "formidable reaction" initiated by such nineteenth-century German scholars of Roman antiquity as Niebuhr, Mommsen, and Teuffel (12). Espinosa attributes this shift to the *social* reaction of a revolutionary age against a monarchical poet and to the *scholarly* reaction of a generation that regarded the Roman writer as artificial in comparison to the originality of the Greeks, and particularly Homer. If the twentieth century is coming to a greater appreciation of the essence of Virgil ("el conocimiento del alma de Virgilio," 22), the reason is that he has again emerged from beneath the shadow of Homer.

Espinosa argues that the conventional parallel of Homer and Virgil is absurd because genius cannot be judged through comparison (ch. 2). Imitation, which is held against Virgil by his German critics, is in fact a universal trait that can be detected in Dante, Shakespeare, and most other major writers (ch. 3). Espinosa adduces Victor Bérard's epoch-making studies, which were appearing in the 1920s, to remind his readers that even Homer had sources that he imitated—Mediterranean maritime logs, Egyptian narratives, and Phoenician epics (ch. 4). Rather than being a criterion for criticism, imitation is a universal law that helps to explain the fecundity of genius (ch. 5). From time to time, Virgil imitated unnecessarily—e.g., in certain epic conventions; in general, however, it is solely the quality of the imitation that should count in evaluation (ch. 6). In this respect Virgil was truly original because his works provided his contemporaries with the sensation of novelty. How? "Virgilio no es un texto. . . . Es un hombre que habla a otros hombres" (136). In contrast to the impersonality of classical Hellenism, where the author sought to conceal himself behind the perfection of his work, in Latin literature—e.g., Catullus or Caesar—each book is the living reflection of a soul (ch. 7).

In his effort to define Virgil's originality, Espinosa reviews the facts of the poet's life, which, sparse though they may be, take on life in his works. It is "la fuerza reveladora de su radiante poesía" (172) that converts the aridity of the historical data into vibrant human reality, in which we recognize a core of sensibility both balanced and exquisite—one that, across the centuries, strikes us as new and, at the same time, wholly our own. In seeking the first impulse for this sensibility, Espinosa points to the occasion when "the strings of his lyre felt their first vibration at the touch of the hand of grief" (173)—the expropriation of his family's lands. Espinosa stresses that this primal experience of grief, *dolor*, was not produced, as in the case of most poets, by the sorrows of love but by the sense of human solidarity. "In this aptitude of compassion and sympathy for all the grief of men, we perceive a first essential difference between him and all his models, particularly the Greeks" (175). because he is incapable of contemplating the miseries of grieving humanity with the impassive serenity ("impasible serenidad," 176) of Homer, Virgil's tears, "like a suspension in his soul," endow his voice with that "pathetic vibration," that "penumbra of melancholy majesty" always evident in his verses (176).

Precisely this "fecundant omnipresence of grief" (179), according to Espinosa, provides another of the most characteristic and original traits of Virgil's poetry: its power of suggestion. A third trait is the sense of gravity and profundity that manifests itself in the *Eclogues* in the shift from descriptive realism into lyricism, in the *Georgics* in their greater moral scope, and in the *Aeneid* in the conception of a grand finality. As a result of these three characteristics, Virgil succeeded in transforming every one of the three genres that he touched (ch. 8).

Virgilianismo can be defined in the last analysis as "feeling" (*sentimiento*)—a feeling that is more profound, more cordial, more ample, more harmonious than that of his models, a sentiment born of a heart made to live its entire life in solitude. It is this factor that explains the survival of Virgil's poetry, for true poetry ("poesía viva"), as the loftiest human expression of beauty contemplated and felt, is "the visible trace of the Creator in the moral and physical world" (211) and hence ultimately religious (ch. 9). But poetry of this sort, far from being mere imitation, is in fact a new creation, for which Virgil had to prepare himself through solitude, study, closeness to nature, and observation (ch. 10).

The chapters on Virgil's poetic art constitute the prelude to the topic that concerns Espinosa in the second part of his book: Virgil's "providential mission." The superior order of Virgil's poetry is evident in at least three facts: the unity of his life focused solely on the composition of his works; the radical difference of these works vis-à-vis other pagan works; and, finally, his unique survival within Christianity and among such Christian writers as Augustine and Thomas Aquinas (ch. 11). If Virgil became a "half-unwitting instrument" ("instrumento semiinconsciente," 279) of his lofty mission, the cause was his fidelity to his vocation: Virgil had to be a poet before he could become a prophet or educator of humanity (280–81). And that fidelity can be attributed, in turn, to the virtues of integrity, purity, and truth that are strikingly evident in his personality (ch. 12).

Confronted with the horrors of moral decadence that characterized his age, Virgil saw it as his responsibility to reawaken the sense of religiosity. To that end, in the *Aeneid*, he linked to the conception of the providential mission of Rome in the world the transcendent notion of religion. To make this point Espinosa cites the opening lines of the *Aeneid* (1. 5–6), which link the founding of the city to the introduction of the gods (*dum conderet urbem / inferretque deos Latio*). Espinosa argues that Virgil's conception of deity, despite the multitude of gods, is essentially monotheistic. His monotheism, in addition, is combined with a clear belief in original sin: *si qua manent sceleris vestigia nostri* (*Ecl.* 4.13) (ch. 13). Accordingly, this "maestro entre las gentiles" quickly became an "apostle of peace"—the herald of a pagan Rome destined by God to pacify the world in anticipation of the coming of Christ (ch. 14). Because the fourth *Eclogue*, long held by fathers of the Church to be a mysterious proclamation of the birth of Christ, cannot be explained by natural reasons, it is necessary to believe in a higher providential inspiration (ch. 15).

For all these reasons, then, Espinosa concludes that Virgil was held for centuries by the Christian fathers to be a "maestro de humanidad" (ch. 16). And still today he can fulfill an essential role as a "pedagogue for Christ" ("pedagogo hacia Cristo"). Indeed, Virgilian poetry can be regarded as the best basis for the refinement of Christian education, in contrast to the many pagan texts that are not susceptible to any Christian accommodation, e.g., the atheistic materialism of Lucretius or the absolute moral indifference of Catullus. But in Virgil there is nothing that is not accessible to a Christian interpretation or to what Espinosa calls "compenetración íntima con el espíritu regenerador del cristianismo" (434). The lesson of modesty (*pudor*) that permeates Virgil's works amounts to a constant protest against pagan corruption as displayed in much ancient literature. Espinosa even cites passages involving the vocable *fortunatus* to suggest that Virgil formulated Christian beatitudes in his works: e.g., *fortunatus et ille deos qui novit agrestes* (*Geo.* 2.493).

In sum, the Virgilian virtues of purity, humility, and charity constitute an excellent preparation for the mysteries of divine *caritas* (ch. 17). Certain passages in Virgil cannot be satisfactorily explained without a Christian criterion: Espinosa cites, for instance, the repentance of the blasphemous Mezentius in the second part of the *Aeneid*. And he reflects how Virgil might have modified the *Aeneid* had he been born a century later. Certainly he would have changed the mythological apparatus; the Fates would have been called Providence, and the various theological inconsistencies and vacillations would have disappeared. Otherwise not much would have been altered, for "Virgil has given us in Aeneas something similar to Christian sanctity" (493). At most he would have added "a sparkle of serene joy to his countenance" and would have transformed his resignation into "amor de su cruz" (ch. 18).

In his epilogue Espinosa observes that the twentieth century has learned to venerate Virgil as he merits—with a love based on scientific appreciation. Having overcome the limitations of Virgil's nineteenth-century detractors, we recognize that Homer and the Greeks were restricted to humankind and the world ("el hombre y la tierra") while Virgil penetrates into the center of souls. If we see his glorious providential mission in his preparation of a moral and social order for the pagans and of a pedagogical and esthetic order for the Christian generations (506), we can appreciate the beneficial influence of his poetry within Christianity and in the education of youth and in the ideas of maturity. Once again we can call out with Dante, "Virgilio, dolcissimo padre!" Espinosa consciously located himself in a tradition that goes back by way of Dante to Emperor Constantine, who opened the Council of Nicaea by reading the fourth "messianic" *Eclogue*, and by so doing sought to regain for the twentieth century the tradition shattered by a German romanticism and Teutonic *Wissenschaft* that felt the need to discredit Virgil in order to praise Homer. In his work, therefore, we see the spiritual conversion of Virgil as another response to the bimillennial celebrations.[37]

Our survey of these representative lives has shown, in sum, how the same limited set of biographical facts and the identical literary corpus produced, under the impetus of bimillennial enthusiasm and the influence of local ideology, several radically different faces of Virgil: in Italy, a Latin nationalist with conservative messages for the present on government and agriculture; in France, a protofascist emerging from the bohemian life of the *rive gauche* of ancient Rome; in Germany, an agrarian *anima naturaliter christiana* destined to become Father of the West in opposition to the rise of Nazism; and in Latin America an apostle of peace among the pagans with the providential mission to serve the generations as a pedagogue for Christ. Although the political readings range from conservative to totalitarian, the religious views from pagan to Christian, and the ethnic stamp from narrowly national to broadly occidental, the response was triggered in every case by the powerful conviction that Virgil in his works offers a message of compelling relevance for the morally chaotic and socially anarchic present *entre deux guerres*—a view that strikes us, in retrospect, as particularly poignant because we know today what followed those hopeful bimillennial appeals to Virgilian *ordo, pietas,* and *humanitas.* In the following chapters we shall have occasion to see how these popularizing and ideological lives reflected, and sometimes directly influenced, the literary manifestations of the bimillennial Virgil.

Virgil on the Continent

THE FRENCH BUCOLIASTS

On the occasion of the bimillennial celebrations, Paul Hazard remarked that "Virgil has been one of the great educators, the greatest one perhaps, of our sensibility."[1] Abundant examples from nineteenth-century literature in France attest the truth of that assertion.[2] Perhaps the predominant example is Victor Hugo (1802–85), who called himself as a schoolboy (in a letter of August 31, 1817) "un élève de Virgile." His earliest literary exercises prove the point, including as they do several extensive passages from Virgil—notably the first and the fourth *Eclogues*. Entering the turmoil of Romanticism with its emphasis on "natural" genius, Hugo developed a more ambivalent attitude toward Virgil. "Avec toute sa poésie," he opined in the famous preface to *Cromwell* (1827), "Virgile n'est que la lune d'Homère." Only ten years later, however, he returned almost obsessively to the Roman poet in the volume *Les Voix intérieures* (1837).[3] The poem "A Virgile" (No. 7) begins with the apostrophe: "O Virgile! ô poète! ô mon maître divin!" and goes on for fifty-two riming alexandrines to invoke many passages specifically of the *Eclogues*, equating the ancient setting to his own Meudon. (E.g., he alludes to *Ecl.* 10 when he says that his beloved "would be my Lycoris if I were your Gallus"; and the last line— "Les satyres dansants qu'imite Alphésibée"—paraphrases *Ecl.* 5.73: *saltantis Satyros imitabitur Alphesiboeus.*) Poem No. 18 ("Dans Virgile parfois, dieu tout près de être un ange, / Le vers porte à sa cime une lueur étrange.") appeals to the proto-Christian Virgil of *Eclogue* 4. Two of the poems borrow their titles from Virgil: "Sunt lacrymae rerum" (No. 2; from *Aen.* 1.462) and "Tentanda via est" (No. 25; from *Geo.* 3.8). Two others invoke Virgil in connection with Dante (Nos. 8 and 27). And many of Hugo's subsequent works bear epigraphs and mottos from Virgil.[4]

Not every French writer, to be sure, shared the general Virgiliophilia. The later nineteenth century brought forth the virulent attack on Virgil in the third chapter of Joris-Karl Huysmans's *A rebours* (1884), where the Roman poet is called "one of the most terrible pedants, one of the most dismal bores that antiquity ever produced." Huysmans, speaking through Des Esseintes, appears to harbor a particular contempt for the

Eclogues, whose "scrubbed and bidizened shepherds unburden themselves, each in his turn, of pots heaped full of sententious and glazed
verses." Even "the tedious twaddle that these marionettes exchange
among themselves" amounts in his opinion to little more than "impu-
dent plagiarisms." But Huysmans represents a conspicious exception in
a period otherwise enthralled by Virgil. And in France it was the *Eclogues* in particular that caught the literary imagination.

Renato Poggioli was the first scholar to stress the importance of the
generic term *églogue* that is specified as the subtitle of Mallarmé's
L'Après-midi d'un faune (1876).[5] Poggioli does not mention Virgil in his
essay, and the Roman poet does not play the same conspicuous role in
Mallarmé's thought and art as in that of Hugo. Yet with its 110 broken
alexandrines Mallarmé's "églogue" is almost precisely the length of
most of Virgil's *Eclogues*, and the situation of the faun recollecting his
pursuit of the two slumbering nymphs amounts to an ironic inversion
of the sixth *Eclogue*, in which two youths and a maiden capture the
drunken Silenus and force him to sing his great mythological song.
(The faun is eventually caught by other nymphs, who entwine his
horns with their tresses, just as the sleeping Silenus is bound by the
wreathes fallen from his own head.) Throughout the faun's monologue—a form common to *Eclogues* 2, 4, 6, and 10—the attentive ear
catches reminiscences of *Eclogue* 1, beginning with the setting (the
faun's *marécage* is surely Tityrus's *palus*) and including such touches as
the murmur of bees and ripe fruit:

> Tu sais, ma passion, que, pourpre et déjà mûre,
> Chaque grenade éclate et d'abeilles murmure.
>
> hinc tibi, quae semper, vicino ab limite saepes
> Hyblaeis apibus florem depasta salicti
> saepe levi somnum suadebit inire susurro.
>
> (1.53–55)

(On this side of the nearby property-line, as always, the willow
hedge whose blossoms are tasted by Hyblaean bees, will often
soothe you to sleep with its gentle murmur.)

And:

> sunt nobis mitia poma,
> castaneae molles.
>
> (1.80–81)

(We have ripe apples, tender chestnuts.)

The period can display other bucolic texts that, although less poetically compelling than Mallarmé's masterpiece, are more evidently Vir-

gilian. Thus, among the more than thirty volumes of Paul Fort's *Ballades françaises* we find two books of "Idylles antiques" (1900), which include several *poèmes en prose* that are specifically indebted to the *Eclogues*.[6] One (No. 6) deals with Silenus in terms not unlike *Eclogue* 6; another (No. 7) brings together Menalcas and Amaryllis, as in *Eclogue* 9; in No. 8 Menalcas praises the decorations on his goblet, as in *Eclogue* 3; and still another, entitled simply "L'Eglogue" (No. 9), is a poetic dialogue in which the goatherd Mélibée mediates between Daphnis and his beloved Thyrsis in a manner evoking several of the *Eclogues*.

To take another example: The eleven "Eglogues" composed by Francis Jammes following his return to Catholicism in 1905 are for the most part remote in any formal sense from Virgil.[7] Only the introductory seven-part "Eglogue de Printemps" displays the rimed alexandrines normally used in French as the equivalent of Latin hexameters and Virgilian echoes: the small farmstead ("métairie") with its stream, where the poet sings his modest song ("mon poème modeste"=Tityrus's *deductum carmen* of *Ecl.* 6.5) on his simple flute ("sa flûte grossière"). Most of the others are brief epiphanies of vaguely rural situations. Yet Jammes is using a form with Virgilian associations to give shape to his Christian sentiments, as he was to do again only a few years later in his more famous *Géorgiques chrétiennes* (1912).[8]

It is no accident that André Gide, in his "In Memoriam" for Mallarmé (1898), observed that *L'Après-midi d'un faune* produces "a poetic emotion quite similar to that which we seek in Virgil."[9] Gide was remarkably sensitive to the works of the Latin poet, to whom he returned obsessively in the course of his long literary career. In an unpublished note on his reading in 1891, Gide observed:

> Finished Vergil's *Eclogues*. Read in Latin, one every morning. Ecstatic surprises at first; a little boredom some time after, because of the monotony of the themes and the fact that they are almost all a bit flaccid. I think the first is the best—and the IVth. I don't like Silenus. The VIIIth is boring. I know by heart the IInd and Xth, which Delacroix brought to my attention.[10]

In a journal entry from November 1894, he added:

> I have gone back to Vergil's *Eclogues*. I thought I knew them by heart; I feel as if I had never read them; the poet's marvelous gift of being always new. All the rest, thoughts and numbers, can be grasped, learned, retained. But the actual harmony of the verses, colors, shapes, music remains something *incomprehensible*. Memory can do nothing with it; it remains outside, and stands before us, and every time we behold it, we experience new stupefaction.

It is symptomatic that the first work published under his own name, the symbolist experiment entitled *Le Traité du Narcisse* (1891), bears a motto from one of his favorite *Eclogues*, *nuper me in littore vidi* ([*sic*]; 2.25); and that one of his last works, the moving *mémoire* of his wife Madeleine (written 1938–39; published 1947), got its title, *Et Nunc Manet in Te*, from a passage in the *Appendix Vergiliana* (*Culex* 269) referring to the punishment suffered by Eurydice for Orpheus's backward glance.

In the fifty intervening years Virgil, and particularly the *Eclogues*, provided a host of names, titles, and epigraphs in Gide's works. The allusion to the poet's dark-skinned lover, *Quid tum si fuscus Amyntas* (*Ecl.* 10.38), appears with fateful symbolism as the motto to book 7 of *Les Nourritures terrestres* (1897), where the writer is on the point of departure from Marseille to what turns out to be his homoerotic adventure with a dark-skinned Arab boy in North Africa. The same passage reappears thirty years later as a comment in Gide's autobiography, *Si le grain ne meurt* (1926). Amyntas, who is cited as the only worthy competitor in singing for Mopsus (*Ecl.* 5.8) and elsewhere as the love object of Menalcas and Damoetas (*Ecl.* 3.66 and 83), supplied the title for another North African travel book (published in 1906), in which Gide revisits the Algeria where, ten years earlier in 1893, he had experienced his first liberation from the sexual constraints of France and the literary atmosphere of Paris. (Gide was rereading the *Eclogues* in 1903 during that sixth trip to North Africa.)

Further examples abound. *Le Voyage d'Urien* (1893) bears as its motto the phrase *Dic, quibus in terris* that is used twice in *Eclogue* 3 (104 and 106) to introduce riddles. Gide's favorite second *Eclogue*, which he knew by heart and which begins with the famous expression of homoerotic passion, *Formosum pastor Corydon ardebat Alexim*, provided the title, *Corydon*, but not much else, for the daring apologia for homosexuality that Gide wrote mainly in 1910 and completed in 1918 (published 1924; Gide's Corydon is a doctor of medicine and author of a book on homosexuality, which he discusses in a series of dialogues with the homosexual narrator.) Mopsus, who engages in a singing contest with Menalcas in *Eclogue* 5, provides the title as well as the motto (*Incipe, Mopse, prior*) for the brief North African travel sketch *Mopsus* (1899),[11] in which Mopsus discovers in a desert oasis a realm outside of time: "Pays clos, tranquille, Arcadie! . . . J'ai trouvé le lieu du repos." Here, listening to the bleating of the flocks, the cooing of the doves, and the songs of the shepherd's pipes, he recalls the last line of the third *Eclogue*:

Claudite jam rivos, pueri; sat prata biberunt.

(Close the sluices, boys; the meadows have drunk their fill.)

The piece concludes with the note that Mopsus writes to his friend Ménalque, urging grieving lovers—notably Gallus from *Eclogue* 10—to join him in his desert climes, where he will guide their steps into oblivion. "Here no nourishment for their pain; a great calm upon their thoughts.—Here life is more voluptuous and more useless, and death is less difficult." That same Ménalque, one of the principal speakers in two of the *Eclogues* (3 and 5), was already familiar to Gide's readers from book 4 of *Les Nourritures terrestres*, where he recounts his autobiography and establishes his identity in Gide's oeuvre as the exemplary figure of the nomadic sensualist. Ménalque reappears importantly in *L'Immoraliste* (1902) as a counterfoil to the hero, Michel.[12]

The single work that exemplifies most dramatically Gide's early obsession with Virgil's *Eclogues* is by any measure the satire *Paludes* (1895). As Gide reported in his afterword to the second edition of *Paludes* (which itself bears a motto echoing the irony of *Ecl.* 8.55, *Sit Tityrus Orpheus*; Gide's Tityre is as unlike Orpheus as is Virgil's), he returned from his first trip to North Africa in 1893 almost wholly transfigured by his experiences there. During a year when he had largely banished books from his life and torn down the barriers between himself and nature, he had succeeded in "harmonizing at last his life and his thoughts."[13] Living among a people with a different religion and a different sense of morality, he came to regard with fresh eyes the fashionable anxieties of his former associates, "the agitation of these men of the North who always believe that beyond the Good it would be possible to obtain a preferable Better." From this new perspective, Gide perceived the ridiculous side of the Parisian literary life that had formerly enchanted him—the Tuesday evenings at Mallarmé's, the gatherings of Parnassians at Heredia's apartment on the rue Balzac, the interminable gossip of the *cénacles*.

In recounting six days from the life of the nameless narrator—the work is in the form of a journal—along with his friends Hubert, Richard, and Angèle, Gide satirizes the tedious circularity of existence among people so totally obsessed with themselves, their ideas, and their precious little activities that they reject all fresh impressions from outside. We hear about their literary evenings, their *soirées musicales*, their talk of Wagner and Mallarmé, their pointless little expeditions. The narrator—Gide protests in his afterword that "I am not the one who says *I* in *Paludes*"—is a man so physically withered that he is incapable of social action or even sexual desire for Angèle, with whom he maintains a strictly Platonic relationship. He refuses to travel—even a trip to Montmorency exhausts him—or to permit any new experience to enter his life. Because he has no talent for verse or drama and "my aesthetic principles are opposed to conceiving a novel" (146),[14] all his energy is drained into the little prose poems that constitute his total literary production. The sterility of this futile existence is emphasized when Hubert, an early avatar of the Ménalque figure, suddenly departs for North Africa, leaving behind the narrator to his precious little literary endeavors. The circularity of this existence is exemplified structurally in the last lines of the narrative by the verbatim repetition of the opening scene, where a friend enters and remarks, "So you're working?" to which the narrator replies, "I'm writing" (91 and 146)—an exchange that drives home the notion that, with the exception of Hubert, this circle of acquaintances live not for life itself, but for their writing.

How does Virgil enter into this closed world of aesthetes? Like Gide's first work, *Les Cahiers d'André Walter* (1891), and like *Les Faux-Monnayeurs* (1925) thirty years later, this satire involves a narrator who is writing a work that is itself included within the text. The work that Gide's nameless narrator is composing, and that he reads section by section to his friends, is a prose poem entitled *Journal de Tityre ou Paludes*. The allusion, as he explains to Hubert on the first page, is to Virgil's first *Eclogue* (47–48), where Meliboeus comments on Tityrus's farm:

Et tibi magna satis quamvis lapis omnia nudus
Limosoque palus obducat pascua junco.

(And [your lands] are sufficiently large for your needs although bare stones and a swamp with slimy rushes covers everything.)

Paludes is not a standard French vocable; it is the Latin plural of the noun *palus, paludis* (="marsh" or "swamp") and merely appears to be a normal French plural.[15] (The amusement that the title produced among Gide's friends was no doubt due in no small measure to the fact that Virgil's *Eclogues* were so familiar to them.[16])

Tityrus surrounded by his swamp—he can even fish from the window of his tower with "a multiplication of lines (symbols)," as Gide puts it—exemplifies the man so content with his own lot, as imperfect as it may be, that he is unwilling to change. "*Paludes* is particularly the story of anyone who does not wish to travel; —in Virgil he is called Tityrus; —*Paludes*, it's the story of a man who, possessing the field of Tityrus, does not force himself to leave it but, on the contrary, is satisfied" (91). The swamp, in turn, is the perfect contrast to the liberating desert of self-discovery that Gide had experienced in North Africa and for which Hubert-Ménalque always departs—the perfect image for what Gide perceived as the stagnation of the symbolist aestheticism of Paris in the 1890s. As the narrator seeks to explain his project to his friends, he points out that Virgil, in the first line of his *Eclogue*, characterizes Tityrus as *recubans*: "*Paludes*, it's the story of the man who's always lying down" (117; "l'homme couché"). As he inscribes the lines of Tityrus's journal—"Between you and me, great flat landscapes attract me,—monotonous moors,—and I would have undertaken long voyages to find lands of pools, but I find such landscapes surrounding me here.—Do not believe that I am sad; I am not even melancholy; I am Tityrus and solitary and I love scenery that is like a book that does not distract me from my thoughts" (103)—the narrator is also characterizing the monotony of the aestheticizing life he leads with his coterie of like-minded friends.

The work ends when six days have passed, when Hubert has left for North Africa, and when the narrator has finished his prose poem *Paludes*. Wondering how he will pass his time now that his friend has gone and his work is finished, he decides to take up "my former topic of POLDERS" (146). When his friend Gaspard enters his apartment at six o'clock, like Hubert at the beginning of the story just a week earlier, and finds him "working," the narrator again responds with the same words: "I'm writing"—but now, as the new week begins with a new friend and a new work, "I'm writing *Polders*" (146). There is an intentional irony in the fact that the narrator has again chosen an exotic foreign word for his title: *Polder* is the Dutch term for marshlands reclaimed by drainage. Whether Gide has in mind primarily again the sense of flat, bleak landscape, as in *paludes*, and hence mindless repetition of the same recurring existence, or whether there is a glimmer of hope in the progression from swamp to land reclamation (as might be suggested by Gide's fascination with Goethe's *Faust*, which ends with Faust's ambition to create a new society on land reclaimed from the sea)—that ambiguity is left open to interpretation.

It is also a matter of interpretation, though the figure does not appear in *Paludes*, to assume that Gide's own sympathies would lie, in the first *Eclogue*, with the Ménalque-like Meliboeus—who, driven from his land, must now set off on journeys to the remote corners of the earth—rather than with the settled Tityrus on his stony, marshy farm. In this case, however, we have evidence for the interpretation because Gide returned, a few years later, to the story of Tityrus in *Le Prométhée mal enchaîné* (1899).[17] In this playful satire, Gide brings back a number of figures from classical mythology and sets them down in modern incarnations—Zeus as a rich banker and Prometheus, denounced and arrested for manufacturing matches without a license—and in unexpected situations stage-managed by a café waiter who likes to perform "actions gratuites" by the manner in which he arranges seatings and conversations among his customers.

One of the tales (told by Prometheus) is "The Story of Tityrus," in which Tityrus, becoming bored with his paludal existence, drains his farmstead and becomes so prosperous that he must hire laborers, establish an economy, enter labor negotiations, become mayor, and pursue other activities until finally "Tityrus was happy, for he felt that his life was useful to others, excessively occupied" (336).[18] Extending his field of activity, Tityrus builds additions to his house, takes an interest in national government, and establishes a lending library with a reference librarian named Angèle, from whom he learns metaphysics, algebra, theology, and music. Gradually, however, Tityrus finds that he is being consumed by his activities and lets himself be persuaded by Angèle to leave his marshlands. Thus they find themselves in Paris on the boulevard that leads from the Madeleine to the Opéra. Taking a seat in a café, they learn from the waiter that the crowd outside has assembled in eager anticipation of Moelibée, who is accustomed to pass that way each evening between five and six o'clock. When Moelibée, who is completely naked and playing his flute, reaches their table, he stops abruptly and is admired by Angèle. "Oh! exclaimed Angèle, leaning against Tityre, how handsome he is! how fit his loins! how adorable his flutes!" (339). Tityrus, a bit peeved, asks where he is going, and Moelibée replies in Latin that he is going to Rome ("*Eo Romam*"). Because Angèle doesn't understand, he elaborates with words from the first *Eclogue* (where they are actually spoken by Tityrus): "*urbem quam dicunt Romam.*" Enchanted by his language and by the thought of seeing Rome, Angèle takes Moelibée's arm and strolls down the boulevard with him until they disappear in the twilight. As the crowd, distracted by the evening newspapers, disperses "like unconfined water," "Tityrus found himself alone and completely surrounded by swamp" (339).

Gide's exploitation of the *Eclogues* for his various purposes—notably for the symbolic exemplification of the two sides of his own character in Tityrus and Meliboeus-Mopsus-Amyntas and notoriously for the justification of homosexuality in the figure of Corydon—was possible largely because Virgil's text was so familiar to his contemporaries that the allusions were instantly accessible. Even the issue of the ethical ambivalence of homoeroticism was delicately raised for the generation in the standard school edition that Gide and his contemporaries used. In his preliminary comments on the second *Eclogue*, Eugène Benoist observes, "Jusqu'à quel point cette anecdote peut-elle nous autoriser à incriminer les moeurs de Virgile, c'est ce qu'il est difficile de déterminer."[19]

This general familiarity with Virgil, and with the *Eclogues* in particular, provided the uninterrupted continuity with the literary generations after World War I.[20] The specific dominance of Gide in this line of continuity is evident in the work of Marguerite Yourcenar. Yourcenar, who studied Latin and Greek intensively for her 1919 *baccalauréat*, was intimately familiar with the classics, which provide the background for some of her best-known works, notably *Mémoires d'Hadrien* (1951).[21] In her oeuvre Virgil plays a resonant, though hardly constitutive role. *Anna, soror*, written in 1925 as part of a larger (abandoned) work, was first published ten years later in a collection of three nouvelles.[22] The story, which recounts the incestuous love of Anna de la Cerna y los Herreros for her brother Miguel in sixteenth-century Naples, has nothing to do with Virgil. But the author counts on the instantly recognizable title, which is taken from the first words of Dido's confession to her sister at the beginning of perhaps the most famous book of the *Aeneid* (4.9), to arouse associations that are then ironically exploded: Dido's apostrophe to Anna when she confesses her powerfully awakened love for Aeneas becomes Miguel's erotic appeal to his own sister. Similarly, the source for *La nouvelle Eurydice* (1931) is Virgil's version in the *Georgics*, but Yourcenar's tale of a love triangle betrays no further classical analogies.

Alexis ou le Traité du Vain Combat (1929) displays more interesting associations. The *récit* consists of a letter written by the narrator to justify his desertion of his virtuous young wife and son to seek more liberated sexual pleasures. The letter turns into the autobiographical account of this scion of impoverished Bohemian nobility, who, raised by the women of his family, discovers his gift for music and soon thereafter undergoes his first homosexual experience. His studies in Vienna lead to further liberation from his Moravian prejudices, but his growing success as a pianist, his marriage to the beautiful Monique, and the birth of their son Daniel do not provide the freedom for which he longs. "Not having known how to live according to common morality, I endeavor at least to be in harmony with my own," he concludes.[23]

Although the narrator's name occurs nowhere in the text, Yourcenar has stated explicitly that the name, "and hence the title of the book, is borrowed from the *Second Eclogue* of Virgil, 'Alexis,' from which, and for the same reasons, Gide took the Corydon of his controversial essay."[24] In that *Eclogue* (2.1), it will be recalled, Alexis is the beautiful youth for whom the shepherd Corydon longs ardently: *Formosum pastor Corydon ardebat Alexim*. Through her indirect allusion to Gide's controversial essay, which had appeared five years earlier, the young author established a connection that would have been quickly apparent to readers of the decade. And just in case the Virgilian allusion should not suffice to establish the continuity, Yourcenar supplied a subtitle, *Traité du Vain Combat*, that echoed the subtitle, *Traité du Vain Désir*, that Gide appended to the second edition (1899) of *La Tentative amoureuse* (1893), the vaguely bucolic account of the misbegotten love of Luc and Rachel.

If Yourcenar's work demonstrates the continuity of the eclogic tradition in France, which was transmitted unbroken from the *fin de siècle* into the 1920s, another group of writers exemplifies dramatically the specific response to the bimillennial celebrations in France. In April of 1930 a group of Parisian hommes de lettres, gathered at the apartment of Henry Charpentier, came up with the project of translating *à dix* Virgil's *Eclogues* and of publishing them on the occasion of the bimillennial.[25] Each of the ten took on the translation of a designated *Eclogue*, and they agreed on a period of three months to complete the assignment. (We should pause long enough to note that the tradition of classical education in France was still continuous enough in 1930 to make it feasible for a group of ten writers to conceive and undertake a plan of this sort. The headings of the individual poems suggest, by the way, that the collaborators used the standard nineteenth-century school edition by Eugène Benoist as their basis, rather than the more recently published edition by Plessis and Lejay, which lacks the headings.)

The project was completed, at least in part, and the collective translation appeared in the September-October issue of the journal *Latinité*, edited by Jacques Reynaud.[26] Evidently not all the original collaborators fulfilled their commitments, for in the collective enterprise Reynaud is himself responsible for two *Eclogues* (1 and 2), and the third is represented in the version by Jacques Delille (1738–1813), the so-called "Virgile français" of the eighteenth century.[27] For the rest, however, we find renditions by such more or less well-known literary figures as Xavier de Magallon (4), Roger de Pampelonne (5), Edouard Marye (6), Henri Ghéon (7), Alexandre Gaspard-Michel (8), Eugène Bestaux (9), and Henry Charpentier (10). The translations range in style from fairly literal renditions in the traditional rhymed alexandrine (1, 3, 4, 6) by way of the more exotic unrhymed alexandrines (5) and regular eight-foot lines (8) to straightforward rhythmic prose (2, 7, 9, 10). (The collaborators make no effort to preserve the elaborate structural pattern of Virgil's book, which links the individual poems through various formal and thematic groupings.)

However, it is not the individual efforts as such that are of interest here, but rather the collective initiative. Charpentier himself, in the afterword to his own translation of the complete *Eclogues* that he published sixteen years later, recaptured the mood of the collaborators.[28]

The flow of the centuries always recommences. Virgil lived in times that resembled ours. Long, cruel wars were followed by confiscations and exile. . . . But despite his day-to-day worries, three essential concerns filled Virgil's life and soul: the contemplation of nature in its mysterious and lovely cyclicity; the extraordinary

Eros that joins and divides all beings; and finally the metaphysical secret, the solution to the problem of destiny that lets itself be glimpsed, ever so feebly, only by the man capable of summoning to his aid science, mythology, and magic—or, if you prefer, observation, analogy, and intuition.

(83)

We recognize the theme of the Roman analogy that was common to the times. And Fernand Mazade's preface to the complete *Bucoliques*, which Xavier de Magallon went on immediately to translate on his own in ten successive days, adds the hope that the *Eclogues*, with their context of civic feeling, Roman grandeur, and respect for law and order, will provide "salubrious reading" for the times (13).

It is symptomatic that the translations appeared in Jacques Reynaud's journal. *Latinité* had been founded only a year earlier with the explicit commitment, according to the legend on the editorial page, "to establish a liaison among all the Latin countries, for world peace, in the memory of common glory, in dignity, power, and honor." This *Revue des pays d'occident* was so conservative in its editorial policy that it printed in its pages such items (mentioned in Ch. 1 above) as the Latin exhortation to Mussolini (*Viro excellentissimo*) along with two poems *in ducem nostrum* in Latin elegiacs (2 [1930]:478–80). In his introduction to the issue for September-October 1930, which was dedicated to "Hommage à Virgile et à Mistral," Reynaud observed that "the year 1930 will have been the year of Latinity." "Menaced by boundless appetites and monstrous egotisms excited throughout the world by a materialist idolatry," every individual feels the need to take stock and to seek other masters. But rather than taking on new masters who will simply impose their will of flesh and blood, Reynaud continues, "it is with spiritual rulers that we contemplate and imagine, in the future, the happiness—or the misfortune—of the race." Dante, in his own day, had chosen Virgil. "We too, in his succession; and with Virgil, Mistral. We, Latins. Their message of power and of reason, of serenity and of beauty, is appropriate for a doleful humanity."

The issue continues, following essays on "Virgile et les Alexandrins" and "La femme et l'amour dans la poésie de Virgile," with a study by Albert Guillaume on "Virgile politique" (105–26), where the nationalist-conservative theme is extended. "It is especially Virgil's intention to create a national work that stirs and interests us" (105). "Man loves power, and he obeys it in order to share in it" (106). Guillaume goes on to say, however, that patriotism exists in precise proportion to love of the family and that it is necessary to restore family virtues if one wishes to restore the patriotic virtues. It is these ideas that sparkle in all the poems of the Mantuan. "The intelligent veneration of a past better known and the restoration of the national language constitute the worthy prelude to the renaissance of the country" (126).

Clearly things have changed in the short years since Gide and Yourcenar. Far from representing the theme of personal development toward sexual liberation, Virgil is here being coopted by the editors and writers of *Latinité* in the service of moral and patriotic renewal with a strongly nationalist emphasis (within the framework of Latinity). To be sure, the individual contributors may have been moved by elements that were more purely poetic. Thus Mazade asserts in his preface that "the Virgil of the *Eclogues* has a delicate, calm, studious soul; he is a contemplative man, impressionable, affectionate" (7). Yet he acknowledges the common theme of Latin unification in the face of political threat: Xavier de Magallon's translation "arrives at a timely moment for these Virgilian and Mistralian fêtes of Latin fraternity above a stormy sky" (13).[29] And Charpentier, while stressing that he sought in his translation "to demonstrate that Virgil is first and foremost a poet" (84), nevertheless emphasizes the tumultuous times in which Virgil lived—times that resembled the period of the bimillennial (83).

Both Xavier de Magallon and Charpentier, as we have noted, were stimulated by the collective enterprise to translate the *Eclogues* in their entirety. And at least five other French writers also published translations of the *Eclogues* during these same years.[30] However, the most significant rendition of the poems that emerged from this period in France was unquestionably *Les Bucoliques* that Paul Valéry completed, as one of his final literary efforts, from 1942 to 1944.[31] Valéry's translation was undertaken, at the urging of its president, Dr. A. Roudinesco, for the bibliophile society *Scripta et Picta*, which wanted to publish a dual-language luxury edition of the *Eclogues* with illustrations by the lithographer Jacques Villon. Valéry initially turned down the commission on the grounds that he was not a Latinist, that he had not looked at Virgil since his schooldays, and that a "grammairien" would be able to provide a more suitable translation.[32] Even though Roudinesco assured him that the society wanted not a translation but a "transposition" with verses like those of Valéry's masterpiece, *La Jeune Parque*, the poet still had his doubts. He could not provide rhymed alexandrines, and it would be extremely difficult to render a line-by-line translation because Latin is a far more economical language than French. But he promised to think it over and, two days later, agreed to make an attempt. "I have reread the *Eclogues*, and they're a bit puerile. Moreover, these shepherd-poets seem to me to practice rather strange love affairs." But he assured Roudinesco that rhymes would be unnecessary and that the lines would "sing" even without them. A month later the first *Eclogue* was finished to Roudinesco's enormous delight: "It was as though Virgil were speaking in French verse." Within a year all ten were done.

Valéry's *Les Bucoliques*, taken simply as a translation, constitutes a remarkable achievement. It could be argued, to be sure, that the alexandrines with their pronounced caesura have a certain lapidary quality not characteristic of Virgil's more fluid hexameters. Consider the first five lines of the first *Eclogue*:

> Tityre, tu patulae recubans sub tegmine fagi
> Silvestrem tenui musam meditaris avena;
> Nos patriae finis et dulcia linquimus arva;
> Nos patriam fugimus; tu, Tityre, lentus in umbra
> Formosam resonare doces Amaryllida silvas.

(Tityrus, lying beneath the spreading beech you sing the woodland muse on slender reed: we are leaving our country's borders and its sweet fields; we [must] flee our country: You, Tityrus, relaxed in the shade, teach the woods to resound [the praises of] lovely Amaryllis.)

> O Tityre, tandis qu'à l'aise sous le hêtre,
> Tu cherches sur ta flûte un petit air champêtre,
> Nous, nous abandonnons le doux terroir natal,
> Nous fuyons la patrie, et toi, tranquille à l'ombre,
> Tu fais chanter au bois le nom d'Amaryllis.

The French alexandrines lack the shifting caesurae and the flowing enjambements that characterize Virgil's sonorities. Yet the precision of Valéry's translation, accomplished with no violence to the French, is astonishing. Indeed, in the entire first *Eclogue* Valéry omits only three phrases from Virgil's highly concentrated verse in order to maintain the line-by-line correspondence:

> Sic *canibus catulos* similis, sic matribus haedos
> Noram.
>
> (1.22–23)

Je voyais les chevreaux ressembler à leurs mères.

"Pascite, ut ante, boves, pueri; *submittite tauros.*"   (1.45)

"Garçons, comme jadis, paissez votre bétail."

Hinc *alta sub rupe* canet frondator ad auras.   (1.56)

Le chant de l'émondeur s'élèvera dans l'air.

The last two lines constitute a marvel of concentration:

> Et jam summa procul villarum culmina fumant,
> Majoresque cadunt altis de montibus umbrae.

> Vois: au lointain déjà les toits des fermes fument
> Et les ombres des monts grandissent jusqu'à nous.

Never satisfied, Valéry continued to propose revisions even as the printer produced the proofs. For the conclusion, for instance, he contemplated (and then rejected) the following variant:

> Vois: des fermes là-bas les hauts faîtes qui fument
> Et les ombres des monts s'étendent jusqu'à nous.[33]

In this case, it would seem, he was striving for the greater precision of "au lointain" (for *procul*), the inclusion of the temporal notion "déjà" (*jam*), the simplicity and directness of "les toits des fermes" (as opposed to the inversion "des fermes . . . les hauts faîtes"), and the metaphoric power of "grandissent" to capture the sense of *Majoresque cadunt . . . umbrae*. The close comparison of Valéry's rendition with Virgil's text, especially in light of the variants, affords an excellent exercise in poetic analysis.

Valéry tells us that he used his old "Virgile de classe" (1: 209), which must have been Eugène Benoist's *Oeuvres de Virgile*. Although Valéry protests that "the notes which manifest all the erudition of a professor" are useful to no one but the author and that students take care not to consult them, it is evident from his translation that he was not so scrupulous in ignoring them. Benoist annotates *Eclogue* 4.61 (*Matri longa decem tulerunt fastidia menses*) as follows: "*Fastidia*. C'est ce mot qui semble déterminer le sens du vers précédent: Pour consoler ta mère des longs ennuis de dix mois, pendant lesquels elle t'a porté dan son sein."[34] Valéry translates with precisely the same emphasis and freedom: "(Qui, durant six longs mois, t'a porté dans son sein)." Or with reference to *Eclogue* 7.26 (*invidia rumpantur ut ilia Codro*), Benoist remarks: "Phrase proverbiale: qu'il meure, qu'il crève de jalousie." And Valéry renders it accordingly: ". . . et que Codrus crève de jalousie." The careful collator can find many other cases where the poet accepted the assistance of the scholar.

However, it is in Valéry's introduction, "Variations sur les *Bucoliques*," rather than the translation itself, that we see how his enterprise recapitulates the modern French appreciations of the *Eclogues*, from pure poetry to political statement. As we know from Roudinesco's preface, Valéry at first resisted the notion of writing an introduction. "My translation is going to set the grammarians and the philologists against me, and now you want to set me at odds with the historians" (1:1692). Yet several months later (on August 20, 1944), he produced an introduction that Roudinesco regards with not too much exaggeration as "le testament poétique de Valéry."

Valéry begins by characterizing the density of Latin, which requires fewer words than French does and which, moreover, enjoys a syntactical liberty impossible in French. Considering the enormity of the challenge—to provide a faithful line-by-line translation despite the difference in the two languages—he was initially tempted to refuse. His little bit of schoolboy Latin, after some fifty-five years, was nothing but the memory of a memory, and in the course of three or four centuries many lettered and erudite men had translated the poems. We should not be distracted too much by Valéry's ritual lament of incompetence. In fact, although there is no reason to doubt Valéry's claim that Latin was not his favorite subject at school, he did acquire enough skill to write letters in Latin to his friends in the 1890s and to participate intelligently in conversations with Gide and others about Virgil and Latin literature.[35]

Beyond his protestations regarding Latin, moreover, as the native of a seaport surrounded by no fields but only sand and salt water, Valéry continues: "I confess that bucolic themes do not excessively excite my spirit. Pastoral life is alien to me and seems boring. The agricultural industry requires precisely all those virtues that I do not possess. The sight of furrows saddens me,—including that that my own pen traces" (1:208). However, abandoning himself, as was his wont, to "these agents of destiny that one calls the 'Others,'" Valéry reopened his school text of Virgil and set out to translate the *Eclogues* line by line, one alexandrine for every hexameter. He did not even dream of rhyming the alexandrines, "for it would assuredly have constrained me to take liberties with the text, whereas I hardly permitted myself any omissions of detail" (210).

The question of language leads Valéry to reflections on its cultural dimensions. Protesting once more that he belongs to those Latinists least sure of themselves, "this slight and mediocre acquaintance with the language of Rome that has remained with me is infinitely precious to me" (212). For Latin is not only the father of French: "It is also its preceptor in matters of the grand style" (213), and the assimilation of the writings of Cicero, Livy, and Tacitus constituted the essential condition in the first half of the seventeenth century for the formation of abstract prose, "which is the most extraordinary and most enduring thing, in the order of Letters, that France has produced" (213).

As he became increasingly absorbed by his translation, Valéry was seized by the familiar sensation of a poet at work and reexperienced the "orientation of sensibility" underlying the poems. Disclaiming any scholarly erudition concerning biography or interpretation, Valéry nevertheless ponders discreetly the Gidean question as to whether the poet himself practiced the kind of love that he attributed to his shepherds (215). Emphasizing that the *Eclogues* are a poetry of youth, he confesses that Virgil's poems drew him for several instants from his advanced age and took him back to the time of his first verse. Valéry presents these highly personal observations, he continues, to explain that he ultimately surprised himself through an almost unseemly, yet inevitable attitude of familiarity vis-à-vis a work of his own profession. Penetrated by such sentiments, he was unable to refrain from applying to the Latin text the same kind of attention that he brought to French verse (217). "In sum, my illusory identification suddenly dispelled the schoolroom atmosphere, the tedium, the memory of lost hours and of rigid schedules that weigh upon these unhappy shepherds, upon their flocks and the various kinds of love, and which the sight of my 'classic book' restored to me" (218).

With this new sense of identity, Valéry approached Virgil's poems in an effort to comprehend them intuitively, from the standpoint of the youth who composed them in the year 40 B.C., before peasants, still living in a mystic unity with nature, became farmers. Virgil was, to be sure, a small landowner, "petit propriétaire" (219), but quite different from the modern equivalent, who is constantly obsessed with the economic results of his labors. This "Virgile à double vue" (220), who shared the hopes and fears of the Italic countryman and, at the same time, was developing higher and more literary ambitions, suddenly became a victim of the disorders of civil war and its brutal consequences.

> In sum: a poet whose desire and craft are developing; a man of the countryside, but a man menaced by expropriation, ruined by the extortions of the victorious soldateska, reduced to appealing to the powers of the day and asuring himself of protectors—this is the triple condition of the author of the *Eclogues*. Virgil's entire poetic career will amount to the most graceful expansion of the Latin language and its musical and plastic resources in a field of political forces.
>
> (220)

This line of reasoning, which has led from a purely poetic consideration of Virgil's language and craft by way of identification with the poet and his personal problematics to the raw political circumstances of the age, brings Valéry to a concluding meditation on the relation of the poet with power, which culminates in an astonishing justification of political collaboration. Valéry begins by acknowledging that the problem admits a multitude of solutions, depending on individual conditions and general circumstances—economic and moral solutions, in short. Regimes can be seductive through their external triumphs, the genius of their leaders, and their liberality. In other cases, reactions of opposition are excited by public affairs, which cause the spirited individual to revolt or to withdraw into his own work. Valéry concedes with ruthless honesty that every individual who is distinguished by his talents tends to locate himself in a certain aristocracy, not to identify with the masses, and to observe that democracy is incapable of supporting a poet. Virgil, he concludes, had no tolerance for disorder and extortion. Plundered, deprived of his means of existence by political expediency, threatened by the loss of his freedom to be and to become himself, "how could one expect that he would not welcome the favors of the tyrant and that he would not extol the one who assures him of tranquil days and thereby restores to him his raison d'être?" (221–22) Virgil, therefore, did not vacillate between the independence of the citizen and that of the poet. Indeed, he may not even have been aware that he was sacrificing anything by becoming the praise-singer of Caesar. Writing in 1944, Valéry permits himself only the most tangential application of these daring thoughts to present circumstances. "One imagines all the phrases that could be written pro or contra this attitude, accordingly as one judges from a modern standpoint or takes into account the reality of feelings and circumstances" (22).

Valéry concludes his remarkable apologia by noting that the insoluble problem of conscience becomes particularly interesting if it is translated into an issue of values. If submission to despotism and acceptance of its benefits, which degenerates into expressions of gratitude or even praise, is the condition for the production of works of the first rank, then how is one to decide? what is one to do? what is one to think? This line of reasoning exposes infinities that Valéry in his last sentence declines to enter. Yet Valéry's remarkable testament, moving from the most personal to the most political, touches upon every dimension of the *Eclogues* that fascinated French writers of the twentieth century, from Gide's musings on homosexuality to the nationalistic ruminations of the *Latinité* circle and Valéry's own profound meditations on the moral implications of colloboration, withdrawal into a self-enclosed universe of pure poetry, or courageous resistance.

In conclusion we should note that Valéry, during the very months he was translating the *Eclogues*, produced his own gloss on the opening lines of the first *Eclogue*. When he read his "Dialogue of the Tree" before the annual joint session of the Cinq Académies on October 25, 1943, the poet explained that "une certaine circonstance" or "un hasard" had recently brought him back to Virgil's *Eclogues* and that "this return to school days inspired me to write, like a school exercise, this fantasy in the form of a pastoral dialogue."[36] In Valéry's version it is not the fugitive Meliboeus but the philosopher-poet Lucretius who encounters Tityrus reclining at ease beneath the beech tree, holding his fragile reed. The situation is patently based on the first five lines of Virgil's *Eclogue*, and the prose gives way frequently to the alexandrines that Valéry was using concurrently in his translation of the *Bucoliques*. Thus in response to Lucrèce's initial greeting (3), Tityre responds: "Je vis. J'attends. Ma flûte est prête entre mes doigts." And at the end (25) Tityre comments to the increasingly voluble Lucrèce: "Mais tu deviens toi-même un arbre de paroles." But there the similarity ends. Lucretius, who gradually becomes the dominant figure, transforms the meaning of the Virgilian vocable *meditaris*, which in *Ecl.* 1.2 means little more than "to practice" or "to play":

Silvestrem tenui musam meditaris avena.

(You rehearse the sylvan muse on slender reed.)

In the second half of the dialogue, *meditaris* becomes a key word: By the end it is no longer Tityrus who is "meditating" and teaching the forest to sing, but the tree itself. Tityre, as Lucrèce informs him, has been concerned exclusively with the externality of the tree, projecting his own imaginings onto it. Lucrèce, in contrast, urges him to contemplate the spiritual essence of the tree and to become aware of the powerful meditation ("cette méditation puissante" [23]) taking place within it. Tityre, astonished to hear that a tree can meditate, replies in a perfect alexandrine: "Peut-être de ce mot le sens m'est-il obscur?" But Lucrèce assures him that "if anyone on earth does meditate, it is the Plant, so active and yet so coherent in its design."

To conclude this remarkable efflorescence of the *Eclogues* in early twentieth-century France, we should note the introductory essay that Jean Giono wrote for an anthology of "immortal pages" from Virgil commissioned by the publisher Corrêa in 1942.[37] Although Giono, unlike most of his French contemporaries, had no Latin, it was not wholly irrational of the publisher to select him for this commission. Giono, who was born in 1895 in the Provençal town of Manosque and had himself tended sheep as a boy, was almost prototypically a Mediterranean pastoralist. He had begun his career with an imaginative account of Ulysses' adventures in Mediterranean seaports before the return to Ithaca (*La Naissance de l'Odyssée*, 1930) and gone on to make his reputation with a so-called "Pan Trilogy" of novels glorifying lives of simple people who still are capable of enjoying an uncomplicated relationship with the Mediterranean landscape of sea, sun, and mountains. Through extensive reading, moreover, he had succeeded in acquainting himself with Virgil as thoroughly as is possible in translation.

The introduction that he submitted under the title "Virgile" must have stunned the publisher—not simply for its length (over one hundred pages in the first edition) but mainly for its contents.[38] The piece begins with a life of Virgil based on the *vita Donatiana* as retold by Saint-Denis in his edition of the *Eclogues*.[39] Giono follows Saint-Denis quite closely, appropriating specific phrases from time to time, and he also refers for details to notes in the school edition of Plessis and Lejay.[40] But he feels free to expand at length when he is describing Virgil's youth among the peasants along the Mincio—passages based evidently upon Giono's own boyhood experiences.

Following the account of Virgil's life, which concludes with Saint-Denis's rendition of the famous epitaph "Mantoue m'a donné le jour; la Calabre m'a ravi; aujourd'hui Parthénope me possède. J'ai chanté les pâturages, les champs et les héros" (1025), we are astonished to find that the introduction continues with a long semiautobiographical fiction dealing with the author's own life and his encounter with Virgil. Giono had already made use of the genre of semiautobiography in his novel *Jean le Bleu* (1932), which dealt in fictionalized form with his youth in Manosque. Moreover, Saint-Denis's "Vie de Virgile" begins (v) with the statement that "les vies romancées" are not an invention of our epoch, pointing out that Virgil's biography had been embellished with legendary elements already in antiquity. By personal literary preference, then, as well as scholarly authority, Giono felt justified in using this unusual form for his essay on Virgil. Introducing a number of purely fictional as well as lightly fictionalized characters, Giono relates three episodes from his life: his escapades with a group of schoolfriends in 1907 when he was twelve years old; his decision, motivated by the illness of his father, to leave school and go to work as a delivery boy for a bank in the fall of 1911; and, in 1943, a gathering of four friends from his schooldays, who spend an evening talking about the state of the modern world.

How does Virgil fit into all this? In 1907 it is only the atmosphere of Provence in his boyhood that strikes Giono, looking back some thirty-five years later, as Virgilian. "The tone of the last phrases that I have just written might be that of Virgil's shepherds while speaking of their past life in the Elysian Fields," he observes at one point (1035). The first encounter with Virgil does not come until 1911. "The school in Manosque did not teach Latin," Giono begins (erroneously). "So it was the poet that I came to know, and at the very moment when I needed a poet" (1041). To educate himself after he left school, Giono saved his paltry salary and ordered books in the Classiques Garnier from Paris. On December 20, 1911, the mailman delivered his Virgil. In the long passage that follows, Giono tells us how, for several days, he simply savored the book itself—its typography, its weight, its yellow cover, its sheer physicality. Finally, on Christmas Eve, when the bank employees had a free afternoon, Giono walked up into the neighboring hills with his Virgil and, opening it to the *Eclogues*, encountered the "pure race" of Virgil's world, those shepherds who "were conscious of this immense order that modern man no longer comprehends and that he therefore calls disorder" (1058).

This Virgilian theme becomes the leitmotif when the friends gather in 1943 and lament the decline of civilization. "Our civilization has been analyzed to death" ("Notre civilisation meurt d'analyse," 1037), one of them observes. Another follows up with the by now familiar refrain: "The twentieth century began in 1914. . . . one is hardly able to designate as civilization the manner in which men lived from 1914 to 1943." At the end of the essay Jules Verne, in his unrestrained admiration for technology, is cited as the embodiment of all the ills of a misbegotten modern world. In a quick transition, Giono recalls an expedition in which he had gone out on the water with a friend and looked down through a piece of glass at the ocean world below. "Thus," he concludes, "like the glass at the bottom of a raft floating on the sea before warring shores, Virgil permits us to make out beneath us the flotsam of a great shipwreck and the palaces of Atlantis" (1068). Again, then, Virgil fulfills his traditional role as the window through which we can look back from our troubled times and see a world of *pietas* and *ordo*—an image of stability in a time of turmoil.

Giono later explained to his publisher that it had been his intention to compose "a *Virgil* subjective to the point at which he speaks only of me and at which the reader sees Virgil only by way of my veins and arteries, as one might perceive a bird in the branches of the beech tree" (3:1563)—a statement that sums up the view of most of the French bucoliasts.

THE GERMAN MILLENNIALISTS

In France the Virgilian tradition survived so continuously that writers in the first decades of the twentieth century could feel free to allude casually to the *Eclogues* in the conviction that their implications would be immediately understood. To many lettered French people around 1930, nothing seemed more natural than to celebrate the bimillennial with translations of those treasured works. They exemplified Curtius's observation, in *European Literature and the Latin Middle Ages* (1948), that "from the first century of the Empire down to the Age of Goethe all Latin culture began with the reading of the first *Eclogue*. It is not saying too much to claim that anyone who does not have this little poem in his head lacks one key to the literary tradition of Europe."[41] In Germany the situation looks quite different.[42]

Until the middle of the eighteenth century, Virgil enjoyed the same esteem in Germany as elsewhere in Europe. The literary reformer Gottsched said that Virgil imitated Homer so intelligently that he excelled him in many areas—a fact that Gottsched does not find astonishing because Virgil belonged to a much finer and more refined age.[43] Even the Swiss critic Breitinger, inclined though he was to favor natural genius, conceded: "Homer was the greatest genius, Virgil the best artist. In the one we admire the master, in the other the work."[44] Yet despite this respect for Virgil's art, no major German writer can be said to be a Virgilian in the same sense as Milton or Racine.

In the second half of the century, owing to the phenomenon that E. M. Butler aptly labeled "the tyranny of Greece over Germany," even the modest educational role that Virgil fulfilled was reduced. The discovery of Greek culture—indeed, the veritable addiction to everything Greek—caused a general rejection of Rome in favor of Hellas. In his philosophy of history Herder does not trouble to conceal his disdain when he turns from the Greeks, Etruscans, and other "gentler" peoples to the haughty, bloodthirsty Romans. Dismayed that Germans, who have so little in common with the Roman mind and spirit, must study Latin as the tool for education, Herder is condescending toward Roman "poesie," which he regards as an exotic flower that managed to blossom beautifully in Latium but was unable to bring forth any native germinations.[45]

Applied more specifically to Virgil, the unfavorable comparisons of Greek and Roman produced such evaluations as Lessing's in the eighteenth chapter of *Laokoon*, which contrasts Homer's description of Achilles' shield with Virgil's portrayal of Aeneas's shield. The latter, Lessing argues, is so cold and tedious that it required all the poetic decoration that Virgil could muster to make it tolerable.[46] In Virgil's works, he continues, "the witty courtier" ("der witzige Hofmann"), with his glittering manners and obsequious allusions, is everywhere evident, but not the great genius who, trusting the inherent vigor of his work, disdains external means of rendering his material interesting. Goethe, for all his love of Rome, has astonishingly little interest in Virgil. In the standard compilation of Goethe's utterances on classical antiquity, almost a hundred pages are devoted to Homer during the period 1766 to 1831; yet from the same sixty-five years fewer than ten pages on Virgil can be gleaned, and of those remarks most are condescending.[47]

Schiller was virtually the only major writer drawn to Virgil, largely because he felt temperamentally attuned to the Virgilian pathos.[48] Indeed, Virgil was the only poet of classical antiquity with whose works he was reasonably familiar in the original. Predictably, when Schiller decided to render Virgil into German ottava rima, he chose Books 2 and 4 of the *Aeneid* for his text. Schiller was not the only poet of that melodramatic age attracted by the Dido episode, which led a life of its own, divorced from the other books of the *Aeneid*, in eighteenth-century drama and opera.[49] However, the history of the Dido theme in German literature amounts to a depressing catalogue of third-rate works. The deplorable record is relieved only by occasional unintentional humor, as when Frau von Stein after her break with Goethe seized upon the legend of the forsaken Carthaginian queen as a suitable vehicle through which she could render in dramatic form her bitterness at her faithless admirer.[50]

Most writers of the age shared Goethe's disdain for Virgil. Friedrich Schlegel argued in his Vienna lectures of 1812 that Lucretius and Ovid are superior as poets to Virgil, who surpasses them only in the degree of his national consciousness.[51] August Wilhelm Schlegel concluded in his Berlin lectures of 1802–3 that even the positive achievements of the *Aeneid* cannot be credited to Virgil, who is no more than "a talented mosaic-craftsman" skillfully assembling borrowings from other poets.[52] Caroline Schlegel epitomized the Romantic attitude toward Virgil when she first encountered his work in Voss's translation. "I could never have imagined that it was so bad."[53] As far as Caroline is concerned, Virgil is closer to the popular melodramatist Kotzebue than to Homer.

Under the circumstances it is hardly surprising that Virgil was more frequently travestied than translated. The most popular of the parodies was published from 1784 to 1788 by a Viennese ex-Jesuit named Alois Blumauer, who transposed Virgil's epic into an attack against the Church.[54] Playing with the translation of *pius* as "fromm," Blumauer converts the father of heathen Rome into the founder of the Vatican who, when he descends into the underworld, encounters such figures as Saint Plato and Saint Lessing. Dido is caricatured as a coquettish queen who lies on her couch reading *Werther* until she can summon up the courage to hang herself on a hair ribbon left behind by the faithless Aeneas.

Small wonder, in view of the critical and popular contempt, that Virgil was unable to maintain any position in the German literary hierarchy of the nineteenth century. He was not ignored by scholars, to be sure: Thanks to the magnificent achievement of Christian Gottlob Heyne's edition and commentary, which provided the basis for all subsequent texts, Virgil continued to be studied by generations of German classicists, who were primarily intent upon demonstrating the extent of his alleged plagiarisms. But he was read without love. The historian Niebuhr remarked that Virgil provides the remarkable example of a writer who missed his calling: Although his early poems prove that he had the makings of a lyric poet like Catullus, the *Aeneid* is nothing but a potpourri of erudition from which only the antiquarian can profit.[55] The classicist Wilamowitz conceded his respect for Virgil's industry and artistic judgment, but he regretted that the poet of the *Georgics*, giving way to Maecenas's importuning, had turned out a national epic destined to remain no more than an aesthetic construct (*Kunstfigur*).[56] And the author of the standard German history of Roman literature speaks disparagingly of the blind enthusiasm that inspired the Virgil cult in Romance lands. He approves of the more profound understanding prevalent among the Germanic peoples, who downgrade Virgil in their appreciation of Homer.[57]

As a result of such developments, Friedrich Klingner was justified in speaking of a century and a half of alienation and misunderstanding that conditioned the German image of Virgil—a lack of appreciation that had reached its nadir around the turn of the twentieth century.[58] In 1926 Ernst Robert Curtius sadly affirmed the depressing truth of a skeptical commentary in the *Frankfurter Zeitung* that asked, "Who reads Virgil today?" ("Wer liest heute Vergil?").[59]

Against this cultural background, a translation of the *Eclogues* was not an act of collective affirmation, as it was in France, but virtually a provocation. Given the radical break in the Virgilian tradition, Germany was unable to compete with the more than half-dozen translations that France produced with such seeming ease, much less the remarkable enterprise of the *Latinité* collaborators. But two of the three German translations that did appear in the 1920s—the first in some seventy years[60]—amounted to major statements by conspicuous literary figures. Although they share with the French translators the sense that the turmoil of the times reflects the sociopolitical situation portrayed by Virgil in the first and the ninth *Eclogues*, that insight produces in the two groups a wholly different response. The French commentators tended in general to respond to the political turmoil by moving into the personal realm—the exotic adventures of Gide's Ménalque or the homosexual license of his Corydon, the aestheticism of the *Latinité* authors, the absolute poetry of Valéry, or the pastoralism of Giono. The German translators and publicists emphasized the broader millennial conception underlying the fourth *Eclogue*—both in its political and in its religious implications.

Rudolf Alexander Schröder (1878–1962), a prolific poet and essayist associated with writers known as the Conservative Revolution and the Christian Renewal, is generally acknowledged to be the most important German translator since August Wilhelm Schlegel. In addition to the complete works of Homer, Virgil, and Horace, he also provided the German public with renditions of works by Corneille, Racine, Molière, Shakespeare, Guido Gezelle, T. S. Eliot, and other modern poets. In 1910 Schröder established himself as the most promising German translator of the period with a splendid rendition of the *Odyssey*, which was published by the recently established Insel Verlag in a handsome bibliophile edition with titles and initials by Eric Gill and woodcuts by Aristide Maillol. The printing of the luxury edition of 425 copies was supervised by Count Harry Kessler, to whom, as its initiator and sponsor, Schröder dedicated the first popular edition of his translation. It was therefore natural that Kessler invited Schröder to provide the translation for a bibliophile edition of the *Eclogues* that he planned to publish at his Cranach Press in Weimar, featuring Maillol's woodcuts and using handmade paper with special typography to "emulate the unity of text and illustrations which we see in Carolingian manuscripts and in the illustrated incunabula."[61] (For the French and English editions of the work Kessler used prose translations by the poet Marc Lafargue and the typographer J. H. Mason.)

Maillol set to work immediately, and the gradually emerging design of the edition is evident in the various *Probedrucke*, or "made-up volumes" of sample proof sheets, that were printed from 1910 on the handpresses of the Cranach Press with woodcuts and a Latin text edited by Thomas Achelis.[62] Schröder completed his translation in 1913,[63] and in 1914 the final printing was already under way when the outbreak of World War I interrupted the plans. The volume, which constituted the most expensive and elegant of the various bibliophile enterprises with which Schröder was involved, was finally printed in 1926[64]—by now two years after his translation of the *Georgica* had already appeared in a bibliophile edition in Schröder's own Bremer Presse (1924).

In France the standard equivalent for the Latin hexameter was the (rhymed or unrhymed) alexandrine. In English verse, despite various ambitious experiments since the sixteenth century and such occasional successes as Longfellow's "Evangeline," the hexameter has rarely provided a comfortable vehicle for poetic expression. In Germany, in contrast, the classical hexameter was developed to a point of high expressiveness and fluidity in several great works of German classicism—notably Goethe's epics *Reineke Fuchs* (1794), *Hermann und Dorothea*

(1798), and *Achilleis* (written 1799; publ. 1808); Schiller's philosophical poems in elegiac distichs (e.g., "Der Spaziergang" of 1795); and the complete Homer published by Johann Heinrich Voss in 1793. And the meter was kept supple by various poets writing throughout the nineteenth century. Accordingly Schröder had at his disposal Virgil's own poetic meter—a meter, moreover, in which he had obtained great skill through his translation of the *Odyssey*. All his craft is evident in his rendition of the *Eclogues*, which maintains considerable rhythmic elasticity while remaining remarkably close to the original. The opening lines of the first *Eclogue*, which achieve the rhythmic variation and flow that mark the original, are typical.

> Tityrus, unter dem Dach der schattigen Buche gelagert,
> Pfeifst du, dir selber zur Lust, auf geschnittenem Halme dein
>   Waldlied;
> Wir aber wandern, wir fliehn der Heimat holde Gebreite,
> Fliehen das Heimatland. Du, Tityrus, lässig im Grünen,
> Lehrest den horchenden Wald Amaryllidis Namen erwidern.[65]

While Schröder appended no introduction or notes to the bibliophile editions (as he did to later reprintings), we know from his various comments where his own emphasis lay in his comprehension of Virgil's poems. Like the contemporary admirers of the *Eclogues* in France, Schröder began with the situation of the first poem, which displayed parallels to Europe in the 1920s. In an essay of 1930, he points out that the first *Eclogue* celebrates Octavian, "who in the turmoils of proscription protected the Mantuan Virgil from the loss of his paternal estate."[66] Schröder moves on quickly to stress that all the principal themes of the mature Virgil are resonant already in the *Eclogues*—namely "the world-famous fourth with its 'Christian' prophesy" and "the 'Roman' center of thought and sensibility" hidden behind the "Sicilian masquerade" (163). Schröder has made it clear that he does not accept the simplistic notion that the fourth *Eclogue* was "a visionary depiction" referring to unspecified events in the future.[67]

But his emphasis on the fourth *Eclogue* reveals the preoccupation of this highly devout German poet with the religious aspect of Virgil's character. In 1931 he devoted an essay to a refutation of "the widespread contemptuous view of Roman piety."[68] Behind the crude animism and sometimes scurrilous observances lies "a total concept of world-moving and world-enriching profundity, namely, that a sacrum worthy of reverence is inherent even in the most unholy manifestation of the phenomenal world" (169). Virgil deserves our attention because "he succeeded, on the basis of the unique Italic form of piety, in bestowing on Hellenistic-Roman syncretism a transcendence of unparalleled radiance and penetration ["Verklärung und Durchdrungenheit"]" (170–71). He achieved what no one in antiquity before him had managed, "the appropriation of the spiritual heritage of the mature Greek secular and religious wisdom into poetic existence" (171). It was this epoch-making act that explains the reputation for *vaticinatio* for which the Middle Ages ranked Virgil along with the Sibyls and Prophets. "Only in this sphere of religious transfiguration" was it conceivable that the encounter between Virgil and the other great syncretist, Dante, could take place.

Schröder's translation enjoyed an enormous *succès d'estime*. Widely regarded as the "official" German translator of Virgil, he was invited to speak and write on numerous occasions during the bimillennial celebrations. He provided translations for the quotations in Walter Wili's 1930 biography of Virgil, and it is again symptomatic that Wili, whose central theme is Virgil's praise of the Golden Age, cites the fourth *Eclogue* (as well as the third) in full—in sharp distinction to the French preference for the second. As we noted earlier (Ch. 2), Wili defends the *Eclogues* against detractors who regard the *Georgics* more highly, and, although he points to the significance of the first *Eclogue* as a symbol for world-historical turmoil, he designates the fourth as "the most famous poem of Latin literature."

This privileged position, which coincides with Schröder's view of the poem, stems from Wili's belief, as expressed in his own bimillennial essay, that "the final goal of the Virgilian longing for fulfillment was the *aetas aurea*, the Golden Age. It had been discovered by the poet quite early and definitively in the fifth and fourth *Eclogues* and remained from that point on the absolute in his life as in his art. The poet thus aligned himself with the sublime seekers after the Golden Age."[69] Wili goes on to explain, however, that he does not wish to restrict Virgil to the conception of the Augustan epoch as a Golden Age. Rather, the anti-Greek, chthonic powers of Roman culture, "growing and strengthened by Virgil's creativity, nourished the most effective form of the myth of world domination: the Christian one. Christianity is therefore in the most profound historical sense Roman" (753).

This "Rome idea" in its religious and supratemporal dimensions, shared by Wili and Schröder, was the basis for the appreciation of their joint undertaking. In a review of the two works, Max Rychner makes this clear.[70] Noting first that the "Rome idea" has found eager defenders among Catholic writers, he stresses that it should not be limited to Catholic politics.

Walter Wili's book, *Vergil* (to recommend which these lines were written), is the work of a young enthusiast who knows our age and its literature, as well as the needs that it has aroused and others that it does not even suspect. He shows what Virgil can be for us if we approach him with a readiness for supratemporal values, whose appeal to us corresponds to our longing for them.

(728–29)

Observing that the quotations in Wili's book were translated by Schröder, he asserts:

In Rudolf Alexander Schröder the feeling for Virgil's grandeur and style is the liveliest among German poets since Schiller. This great master of language, whose German Homer will remain a lasting monument, has also translated the *Bucolica* and *Georgica*. I don't know what classic poetic translations since Schlegel's Shakespeare German literature could set beside Schröder's. . . . It is now up to us not to lose this newly won Virgil all over again."

(729)

Rychner's enthusiasm for the joint accomplishment was echoed in the Catholic cultural journal *Hochland*.[71]

Not everyone shared the general admiration for Schröder's translations. The first edition of Theodor Haecker's *Vergil. Vater des Abendlands* (1931; see Ch. 2) included a two-page diatribe against Schröder, citing him as "one of the most typical examples for the unintelligent misunderstanding by German 'leaders of the spirit'" ("Führer des Geistes") because he seeks to render mystery by using uncommon words artificially rather than common words artfully (37). Haecker singles out a line from the *Aeneid*, not the *Eclogues*, in order to scoff at Schröder's rendition; but he heaps his scorn on the entire translation, its advocates, and even its publisher! Schröder, he says, invents German words so monstrous that "only an anthropomorphic hippopotamus" could find them utterable (38).

But impotent privy councillors and virulent lecturers in classical philology and georgics [here he has in mind Wili, at the time a Privatdozent for classics at the University of Zürich] scuttle about in an anti-Roman manner on their arrogant knees before the uncommon translator's art of Herr Rudolf Alexander Schröder, to which in turn the Bremer Presse takes pains to give bibliophile expression in an Antiqua that stands in the same relationship to antiquity as does heresy to the dogma of the Church.

(38)

Leaving aside the polemical animus that characterizes all of Haecker's writings and the special hostility that the Catholic convert here brings to the author of popular Protestant hymns, how do we explain the unusual degree of virulence? It is no doubt motivated in no small measure by a sense of literary competition. In 1923, three years before the postponed publication of Schröder's translation finally appeared, Haecker had brought out his own translation of the *Eclogues* in a limited bibliophile edition of 720 copies with woodcuts by his friend Richard Seewald (1889–1976).[72]

Haecker's antagonism toward Schröder and Wili is particularly ironic in view of the fact that he shares their evaluation of the *Eclogues*, and notably the eschatology of the fourth, "messianic" *Eclogue*. The first *Eclogue* that Haecker translated was the fourth, which appeared in 1920 in the cultural journal *Der Brenner* with a dedication to Richard Seewald, who was already planning his illustrated edition.[73] In an essay entitled "Truth and Life" (1930), Haecker wrote a passage that he subsequently quoted in his book on Virgil:

> Virgil was not a prophet like Isaiah; he did not prophesy the birth of the savior like the angels and the patriarchs and the prophets. How could he have done so since he was neither an angel nor a patriarch nor a prophet? But he gave shape to a mythic subject that had a relation to the eternal truth of the angels and patriarchs and prophets at a moment that not he but providence itself determined—providence that in turn singled out specifically him in the advent mood of heathen antiquity for this task of shaping because he was in an eminent sense before Christ an anima naturaliter christiana.[74]

It is true enough that Haecker's translation tends to be more immediate and more idiomatic than Schröder's. Let us consider as an example the first lines from his own translation that Haecker cites in his chapter on the *Eclogues*:

> Tityrus hinc aberat. ipsae te, Tityre, pinus,
> ipsi te fontes, ipsa haec arbusta vocabant.
>
> (Ecl. 1: 38–39)

(Tityrus was gone. The very pines, Tityrus, the very fountains, the very groves were calling you.)

Schröder:

> Tityrus fehlte der Flur, dich, Tityrus riefen die Fichten,
> Riefen die Quellen zurück, dich rief das Rebengeländ hier.

Haecker:

> Fort war Tityrus. Aber die Pinien, o Tityrus, riefen,
> Selbst die Quellen, selbst diese Reben hier riefen nach
>   dir nur.

Haecker's rendition of the first phrase is certainly more idiomatic than Schröder's rather precious "Tityrus fehlte der Flur"; and his repetition of the intensifier *selbst*, in contrast to Schröder's repetition of the verb *rief(en)*, is closer to Virgil's rapid line. Haecker believed that the *Eclogues* contain "Virgil's sensually loveliest and most perfect verses" from a purely literary standpoint—albeit not the most profound or sublime ones (60). It is this poetic quality to which he seeks to do justice with his translation.

Otherwise Haecker is fully aware of the "tragic tone from history and politics, the reminiscence of the civil wars and their consequences" in the *Eclogues* (58–59), and he also acknowledges the centrality of Eros, which attracted Gide. But the centrality of the fourth *Eclogue* in his understanding of Virgil is evidenced by Haecker's discussion of that poem not in the chapter on "Shepherds," in which he talks of love in the *Eclogues*, but in the concluding chapter entitled simply *Anima naturaliter christiana*.

The third German translation of the period stands apart from the controversy surrounding Schröder and Haecker. In 1929 the Berlin classicist Adolf Trendelenburg, who had previously produced the first twentieth-century rendition of the *Aeneid* (1928), completed his edition of Virgil with a translation of the *Eclogues* and *Georgics*, which he dedicated to the Royal Virgilian Academy of Mantua in honor of the bimillennial celebrations of October 15, 1930.[75] Trendelenburg, who was in his eighties when he undertook his translations, explicitly ignores the battle of the translators taking place in the literary forum, stating in his preface that Virgil's pastoral poems "hitherto have been little known to broader circles" (vi) and that readers with little Latin will now be able to decide for themselves whether Virgil is a mere imitator of Homer or has independent artistic significance of his own. The translations, in dactylic hexameters, lack the energy of Haecker and the elegance of Schröder, as can be judged from Trendelenburg's version of *Eclogue* 1:38–39.

Tityrus war ja fern! Selbst Pinien, Tityrus, riefen
Laut nach dir, der murmelnde Quell, nach dir die Gebüsche.

(Note the unnecessary expansion of *fontes* to "der murmelnde Quell" and the repetition of "nach dir.") In addition, the translator has added epigraphs to each poem that suggest a certain Rococo cuteness: "Ungleiches Los" ("Unequal Destiny," 1), "Trost bei verlorener Liebesmüh" ("Consolation for Love's Labor Lost," 2), "Unentschiedener Wettstreit" ("Undecided Contest," 3), and so forth. The virtue of his translation that Trendelenburg singles out for emphasis is that he has had the benefit of consultation with various professors of geology, botany, and veterinary medicine for the natural-historical details of his work. In fact, his translations amount to little more than cribs with which the reader can decipher Virgil's original.

However, the generational similarity to the other German translations is evident in the notes, which devote four full pages (32–35) to the fourth *Eclogue*. Trendelenburg begins by warning that access to this much discussed poem has been made more difficult by the extensive scholarship with which it has been burdened. He advises the reader to approach the poem with simple directness. Sketching the historical background, he turns to the unusual visionary form that Virgil gives to his poem, "in which he sees as become reality what he wishes in his heart" (34). Referring to the most recent scholarship, Trendelenburg assumes that the child whose birth heralds the return of the Golden Age is meant to be Octavian's son. But even if the birth of a daughter rather than a son precluded the fulfillment of the prophecy, a new era began with the consulate of his friend Pollio, to whom the poem is dedicated. For within ten years, Octavian secures the borders of the empire, closes the temple of Janus, and prepares the way for the Golden Age of Roman literature.

All three German translations, we see, differ conspicuously in emphasis from those of the French. Even though all the translators, on both sides of the Rhine, begin with the assumption of the Roman analogy in the first *Eclogue*, the French were moved by that insight to seek a kind of personal salvation in adventure, homoerotic love, or pure poetry, while the Germans all give a privileged position to the fourth *Eclogue* with its promise of a new Golden Age for society—cultural, religious, or merely literary. How can we account for this pronounced difference in emphasis?

It should be stressed, first, that the emphasis was shared by most of the German commentators at the time of the bimillennial celebrations. Curtius tells us that his interest in Virgil was stimulated shortly after the turn of the century by a chance encounter with a magical phrase *mille meae Siculis errant in montibus agnae*, from the second *Eclogue* (line 21) beloved of the French.[76] But by 1930 he shares the German millennialist sentiment. "Virgil's most secret yearning is the Golden Age and its materialization in pastoral circumstances."[77] Curtius associates Virgil's soteriological hopes, his expectation of a *restitutio in integrum* and specifically the prophesy of the fourth *Eclogue*, with a cyclical theory of history according to which things will get worse—*ruere in peius* (*Geo.* 1.200)—before they get better again. Curtius acknowledges Virgil's poetic beauty and cites as examples various passages from the *Eclogues*. But if he can be regarded as "the spiritual genius of the occident" (42), the reason is that the "Oriental prophesies extending into the fourth *Eclogue*" reveal a portentous radiance from worlds of the beyond, "a sibylline piety" that appears to look forward with impatience toward the revelation.

Similarly Wolfgang Schadewaldt, in the address he held in 1931 for the Virgil celebration, singles out the first and fourth *Eclogues*, in which his bucolic poetry is fulfilled.[78] The first poem reveals the dialectics of two destinies with their gratitude and despair and the opposition of a lost and a redeemed world. But the fourth *Eclogue* expands to embrace the expanded space of the cosmos and the distance of infinite time. Schadewaldt takes cognizance of scholarly efforts to remove the messianic prophesy from all political reality and to explain it on the basis of religious sources. But Schadewaldt insists that it was not a private religious impulse that motivated Virgil to the prophesy of the Cumaean Sibyl:

> The poem is a great politico-religious symbol: its experiential basis Virgil's own present, comprehended with sympathetic feeling; its spiritual content religious hope and political conviction; its coloring bucolic, and Oriental nothing but the literary motif that the poet appropriated along with the subject from the prevailing mythological-religious koine.

Accordingly the fourth *Eclogue* rounds off the circle of the bucolic poems, which began with the private destiny of loss and restoration of property, events that first focused Virgil's gaze on the political reality surrounding him.

This typically German view of the *Eclogues* is repeated wherever we look. Eduard Fraenkel concludes his thoughts on the occasion of a German Virgil celebration with the wish for the future that "a new German understanding of Virgil might begin first of all with the *Georgics* and perhaps also with the fourth, the ninth and the loveliest, the first *Eclogue*."[79] Friedrich Fuchs claims that the fourth *Eclogue*, with its reminiscences of Isaiah's prophecy concerning the messianic child, amounts to "a key to the whole of the Virgilian opus."[80] And the sentiment grows poignantly in strength as external circumstances worsen. Thus, Alexander Schenk von Stauffenberg, in a talk on "Virgil and the Augustan State" that he delivered in 1941, argues that any prophesy of such a general and binding character as that of the fourth *Eclogue* should be applied only to a general situation. If the Middle Ages recognized in it a situation of Christian salvation, the modern age has the right to see in it the prophesy of the Augustan realm of peace, as did antiquity (186). But Stauffenberg goes on unmistakably to draw the lesson for his own times. "Here in the fourth *Eclogue* the *vates* Virgil became the voice for the confused longings of his terribly afflicted time, to whose expectation of salvation he gave expression" (187). And it is impossible to read Bruno Snell's classic essay "Arcadia: The Discovery of a Spiritual Landscape" (first published in 1945) without sensing that the great classicist sought his own inner emigration during the last years of World War II in the vision of harmony expressed in the *Eclogues*. Snell recounts the three spiritual characteristics that appear here for the first time: a poetic-visionary quality, an encompassing love, and a sentimental suffering. These indicators

> point far into the future, and it is not contingent alone on the prophesy of the fourth *Eclogue* that Virgil was regarded by the Middle Ages as a forerunner of Christianity. His Arcadia is not only a midway-land between myth and reality, but also a midway-land between the ages, a here in the beyond, a land of the soul that is longing for its distant home.[81]

What historical factors can be adduced to account for this remarkable turn to the fourth *Eclogue* in Germany in the years around 1930? In part, no doubt, the phenomenon is due to the impact of Eduard Norden's enormously influential book, *Die Geburt des Kindes: Geschichte einer religiösen Idee* ("The Birth of the Child: History of a Religious Idea," 1924). As Norden noted in his preface to the second printing, the book had already justified its existence by stimulating scholarship: Virtually a small library had grown up around the problem of the fourth *Eclogue* since its publication seven years earlier.[82] By way of example, both Curtius and Schadewaldt in the previously mentioned essays referred to Norden's theory that Virgil had in mind no historically real child but rather incorporated in his poem a variety of soteriological notions current in the decades preceding the birth of Christ: Egyptian myths, Greek gnosis, Hebrew prophecies, and Gospel narrative.

Yet I believe that another important fact must be taken into account. At least by 1918, when the first volume of Spengler's *The Decline of the West* appeared and immediately made its impression on the mind of thoughtful Germans in the postwar era, the ancient notion of a Golden Age, a "Third Kingdom" toward which humanity aspires, again became current and popular. "The ancient mind with its oracles and auguries only wishes to *know* the future; the Western mind wishes to *create* it. The *Third Reich is the Germanic Ideal*, an eternal tomorrow to which all great men from Joachim of Fiore to Nietzsche and Ibsen have attached their lives—arrows of longing to the other shore, as Zarathustra puts it."[83] In 1923 the phrase was appropriated by Arthur Moeller van den Bruck as the title for the enormously popular and influential book, *Das dritte Reich*, in which he outlined a program for the "conservative revolution" through which Germany, "the land of the middle," would create a new political destiny beyond and unconstrained by the goals of existing political parties.[84] Moeller died by his own hand in 1925, before he could see the perverted realization of his vision in the mad views of Adolf Hitler. But the phrase, as well as the notion of a future Third Kingdom in which the tribulations of the present would be resolved, had captured the German imagination.

In many minds the incantatory phrase has been debased through its abuse by the Nazis and such intellectual opportunists as Professor Julius Petersen, a distinguished literary scholar who became an academic rationalizer for the Nazis and in 1934 published a book entitled *The Longing for the Third Reich in German Legend and Poetry*, in which he sought to demonstrate that the venerable ancient myth of the Golden Age progressed through six historical stages until it reached its fulfillment in a seventh stage manifesting the National Socialist conception of a people's realm (*Volksreich*).[85] (In Petersen's scheme Virgil and the fourth *Eclogue* stand at the beginning of the second stage, the theocratic conception of a chiliastic kingdom of God [11].)

Yet we must not allow the perversions of the Nazis to obscure the significance of the vision of a Third Kingdom for many writers and intellectuals of the 1920s and 1930s. Stefan George used a variant of the phrase as the title for the volume in which he collected his poems of the preceding twenty years, *Das Neue Reich* (1928). And until 1933 Hermann Hesse used the expression "Drittes Reich," in full consciousness of its ancient historical associations, to designate his chiliastic vision of the spiritual rebirth of humanity.[86] It is this urgent sense of the need for spiritual renewal—of the individual as well as humanity as a whole—born from the political turmoil of the 1920s and the intellectual despair in Germany that prepared the way for a renewed interest in the ancient vision of the Golden Age or Third Kingdom. Through the skillful rhetorical inversions of the Nazis, the phrase appealed to the basest instincts of many Germans. But on another level altogether, I would like to suggest, it was this venerable conception that made German thinkers and poets especially responsive to Virgil's fourth *Eclogue* with its ecstatic prophesy of an ultimate age sung by the Cumaean Sibyl, of a new order of the centuries, of justice and the reign of Saturn, and of a new humanity.

> Ultima Cumaei venit jam carminis aetas;
> Magnus ab integro saeclorum nascitur ordo.
> Jam redit et Virgo, redeunt Saturnia regna;
> Jam nova progenies caelo demittitur alto.

(At last the final age of the Cumaean song has arrived; the great order of the centuries is born anew. Already the Virgin returns, the reign of Saturn returns, already a new generation descends from high heaven.)

The Italian Hermeticists

In his bimillennial lecture on "Virgil's Survival in the Romance Literatures," a German observer stated the thesis that "Virgil has remained truly alive only in the Romance countries."[87] As the exemplary embodiment of Latin culture and an inexhaustible source that constantly refreshes poets, "Virgil is the most powerful and most frequently invoked symbol of the unity of the Romance lands." And among the cultures that constitute "Romania," none displays a more continuous tradition of Virgiliana than Italy does.[88] The European poet most closely identified with Virgil—indeed, unthinkable without him—is Dante, who invoked his Roman predecessor as "lo mio maestro e 'l mio autore" at the start of his journey through the Inferno (*Inf.* 1.85). Whether the long silence from which Virgil faintly emerges—"chi per lungo silenzio parea fioco" (*Inf.* 1.63)—is to be read as the false image of Virgil as a magician during the Middle Ages or as Dante's own neglect of him during his wandering from the path of virtue,[89] Virgil's appearance as Dante's guide in *The Divine Comedy* marks the spectacular beginning of his progression through the minds and works of such Renaissance admirers as Petrarch, Sannazaro, Ariosto, and Tasso. And he continued to be acknowledged as a master and guide through the Baroque and the eighteenth century down to such nineteenth-century classicists as Ugo Foscolo, Giosuè Carducci, and Giovanni Pascoli (whose *Myricae* of 1891, for instance, are directly modeled on the *Eclogues*). Despite a certain slackening of interest during the nineteenth century, Vladimir Zabughin was speaking for many of his fellow Virgilians when he expressed the hope in 1923 that "Virgil should now again become what he was for the Renaissance: the palladium of Romanità, of the idea of the civilizing power of Rome, which is preserved by the free peoples of the Occident and denied to the descendants of Alaric and Totila."[90]

It did not work out quite that way. We have noted, to be sure, the well-nigh feverish celebrations of the bimillennium in Italy, which revolved around the efforts of the Fascists to coopt Virgil for their own purposes—celebrations that encompassed landscape gardening as well as architecture and postage stamps, laudatory orations and group tours as well as scholarly editions. The nationalistic bimillennium also produced such literary efforts as Ricciardi Maria Bosi's "heroic poem" *Sulle grandi orme* ("In the Footsteps of the Great," 1932), consisting of fifty-six sonnets that establish analogies between ancient and modern *maiestas*, between the Trojan fugitives and the soldiers returning from World War I, between the Harpies and the diplomats of Versailles, and between Aeneas's arrival in Italy and Mussolini's *marcia su Roma* in 1922.

Apart from Fascist propagandists, however, most serious Italian writers of the 1920s and 1930s resorted either to actual or to inner emigration. Thus Silone went to Switzerland, a safe haven where he was able to write novels that dealt overtly with social and political problems in Italy under the Fascists. Those who remained in Italy were restricted ideologically in their choice of theme. As a result, many tended to turn inward and, under the influence of the *poésie pure* of French symbolism, to cultivate a terse, complex poetry known as *Ermetismo*.

The poets identified with Hermeticism essentially define the best Italian poetry of the period: Eugenio Montale (1896–1981), Salvatore Quasimodo (1901–68), and Giuseppe Ungaretti (1888–1970). To the extent that the Hermeticists were determined by the literary tradition from which they emerged, Virgil figured large in their imagination. For them, however, the turn to Virgil represented an escape from a present reality to which they were opposed: Both Montale and Quasimodo were actively anti-Fascist, and Ungaretti, following an initial infatuation with what he regarded as the humanistic aspect of Fascism, spent the years from 1936 to 1942 in Brazil (after which, to be sure, he returned to a chair at the University of Rome—albeit a position with no political commitment). Characteristically, the experience of the war years eventually led all of them—Ungaretti perhaps least of all—out of the absolute poetry of Hermeticism to a position that Quasimodo was to define as *poesia sociale*. Yet within the conspicuously small poetic output of all three writers, Virgil stands out as a prominent image.[91]

In a thoughtful essay on "Virgil in Modern Italian Poetry," Herbert Frenzel has identified three traditional themes that characterize the image and use of Virgil among the Hermetic poets: his role, at least since Dante, as the guide in the underworld; his image as a poet with a well-nigh magical force of language; and his patriotic function as the singer of *laudes Italiae*[92]—in sum, what might be called the social, the aesthetic, and the national aspects. We must be cautious in our assessment of yet another function that is at play here, the so-called Orphic role. It is hazardous to identify the Orphic theme with Virgil specifically because it is treated not only in the fourth *Georgic* but also by Horace and Ovid. More importantly, the "Orphic atmosphere" that pervaded the Continent, and especially France and Germany, in the nineteenth and early twentieth centuries made the theme of Orpheus and the underworld accessible to many writers who had no appreciation of its classical sources.[93]

In some cases, in short, writers no doubt turned to Virgil because of their interest in orphism: They were not brought to orphism by their interest in Virgil. But the first three themes are clearly constitutive in the relevant writers. The guide to the underworld offers images for the writer's descent into the unconscious or the past as well as for the act of social communication. The "magical" Virgil provides a code for the secret or "hermetic" language cultivated by this group of writers. And the *laudes Italiae* supply a model for the landscape poetry that offered a safe topic for poets in a politically ambivalent time.

The last quality is evident in Montale's first volume *Bones of the Cuttlefish* (*Ossi di seppia*, 1925), which contrasts the eternal austerity of the Ligurian coastal landscape with the artificiality of the Riviera in the 1920s and portrays the sea as an image of purity against which to measure modern humanity's inner despair. The Virgilian echo is conspicuously evident in the poem "Egloga," which describes a hot summer day in a Ligurian olive grove.[94] Certain elements of the description point to passages in the tenth *Idyll* of Theocritus.[95] More relevant for our context, however, is the fact that the poem begins with a scene distinctly reminiscent of Virgil's first *Eclogue*, where Tityrus is reclining at leisure beneath the speading beech. Here the trees beneath which the poet recalls sitting are olive trees, but the other motifs of the bucolic *locus amoenus* are present:

> Perdersi nel bigio ondoso
> dei miei ulivi era buono
> nel tempo andato—loquaci
> di riottanti uccelli
> e di cantanti rivi.[96]

(To lose myself in the waving gray of my olive trees was good in times past—talkative with quarrelsome birds and with singing brooks.)

He recalls how the silver olive leaves lying on the ground felt to his feet and how his thoughts wandered in the still air. But where the tensions arise in Virgil's *Eclogue* in the persons of Tityrus and Meliboeus, here they arise from the contrast of past and present. Today the calm is disturbed by the noise of a train, the sound of a gunshot in the distance, an airplane roaring through the sky. The poet longs for the rebirth of the idyllic moment: "Tosto potrà rinascere l'idillio." But the abrupt and disconnected images, although conveying a vivid impression of the landscape, suggest no return of bucolic peace: the Saturnalian heat ("questi saturnali del caldo"), the fleeting apparition of a woman who turns out not to be a Bacchante. The modern poet's wanderings are fruitless ("nostri vagabondari infruttuosi"), his walk among the briar bushes (Montale uses the Virgilian vocable *vepri*) is disconsolate (*turbati*). Although the poem—in title, in scene, in image—is clearly calculated to remind us of the first *Eclogue*, a reversal of roles emphasizes the dark side of Virgil's poem. Tityrus and Meliboeus are not separate people but different aspects of the poet, who can only remember—and hope for the return of—the vanished idyll of Tityrus. In the linguistic energy and visionary intensity of this early hermetic poem, the allusion to Virgil is the principal key to the poet's longing for an escape from the despair of a chaotic present into the serenity and certainties of a better world.

The most "Orphic" of modern Italian poets is no doubt Quasimodo, who specifically invoked Virgil's Orpheus in his poem "Dialogo" (1949). But Quasimodo's turn to the figure of Orpheus resulted from a conscious decision following the Second World War to reject the emotional seclusion and *poésie pure* of Hermeticism in his effort to work toward a rehumanization of mankind through the renewal of dialogue and communication[97]—a goal that he stated in various essays, and most eloquently perhaps in his 1959 Nobel Prize acceptance speech, "The Poet and the Politician." Before and during the war, however, his motivation was quite different. A kind of Virgilian *laus Italiae* is a conspicuous component of Quasimodo's major collection, *And Suddenly It's Late* (*Ed è subito sera*, 1942), which replaces Montale's Liguria with the seaside of his native Sicily. But the principal document of Quasimodo's Virgilianism is another work that appeared that same year, his translation of selections from the *Georgics, Il fiore delle Georgiche* (Milano, 1942).[98]

During the final three decades of his life Quasimodo, having given up his career as a civil engineer, published close to thirty volumes of translations from the Greek, Latin, English, Spanish, and French and became known as one of the great Italian translators. The translation from Virgil was one of the earliest, preceded only by an anthology of lyrics from the Greek (*Lirici Greci*, 1940). And his turn to the *Georgics*, which he calls Virgil's most difficult work, "disdained and forgotten" ("disprezzata e dimenticata"), was patently motivated by the poet's wish to reveal "the power of his [Virgil's] writing" and the countryman's desire to seek solace in the soil from the dictator's ravages—what Quasimodo, quoting the concluding lines of Virgil's poem, calls "the sweet condescension of a man of the soil in comparison with the authority of Caesar."[99] Quasimodo's selection features eight passages of varying length, including some of the most famous setpieces of the *Georgics*: from the description of the seasons (1.244–423) by way of the praise of Italy (2.136–74), praise of rural life (2.475–540), and praise of love (3.219–85) to the tale of Orpheus (4.317–558). But of interest here is the "Translator's Note," in which Quasimodo discusses the metrical devices through which he sought to render Virgil's cadences and, above all, his reasons for undertaking the translation.

An encounter with Virgil, especially with the *mansuetus* ["gentle"]
Virgil of the *Georgics*, might suggest today a desire to "leave" time
or to force it into a Never-Never-Land dear to poetic usage. But
Virgil, with his continual invention of nature, interrogates himself
but does not address questions to others, does not impose occasions upon his song. In his voice we may recognize ourselves as
ancients through that "sentiment of solitude," which is the reflection of human distress, of absolute grief. . . . This resignation to
solitude, in contrast to Lucretian sorrow, brings Virgil closer to us
than any other Latin poets of classical antiquity. . . . Any justification of my work ought to be of a poetic nature, the only kind that
legitimizes the reading of a text always present through the centuries of an achieved European civilization.

(531–32)

In short, the same ambivalent longing for escape that we observed in
Montale's "Egloga" first brought Quasimodo to Virgil—not an evasion
of human anxiety, but rather a retreat from the turmoil of the present
that obscures through its exigencies the eternal verities of European
civilization accessible in Virgil's words. Although Quasimodo included
the famous passage about Orpheus among his selections, it was in his
later social phase that Orpheus as the poet of discourse and dialogue
became important to him. In his Hermetic period, he was concerned
with the magic of Virgil's language, with the praise of Italy, and with
the reassurance in a time of distress of the permanence of human values.

If Montale's sense of landscape brought him to the *Eclogues* and
Quasimodo's Orphism along with his love of ancient Italy—not to
mention the *labor improbus* that produced the steady stream of translations—brought him to the *Georgics*, Ungaretti turned with a kind of
inevitability to the *Aeneid*. Born in Alexandria to an Italian construc-
tion worker, educated in France at the Sorbonne, and later spending
many years outside Italy, Ungaretti came to identify himself with
Aeneas, whom he defined as "beauty, youth, ingenuousness ever in
search of a Promised Land."[100] Because Ungaretti did not enjoy the
rigorous classical education that would have been the norm in Italian
lycées or gymnasiums,[101] he did not have this tradition routinely offered to him but had actively to repossess it, which resulted in the
advantage that his view of Italy's timeless past, including Virgil, was
free of the "complacent provincialism" that otherwise characterized the
nationalistic age.[102]

Ungaretti's nonclassical schooling also explains why he came to Virgil in a manner different from that of Montale and Quasimodo. In fact,
the few references to Virgil in writings prior to 1932 are limited to brief

secondary mentions in connection with other writers (notably Dante and Leopardi). Then in late 1931, as a correspondent for the Torino *Gazzetta del Popolo,* he made a series of trips (including his first return to Egypt after some twenty years) that took him to a number of sites around Naples that are closely identified with Virgil and the *Aeneid:* notably Cumae, where Aeneas visited the Sibyl and undertook his journey to the underworld, and Capo Palinuro, the landmark where Palinurus is supposed to be buried. The following year (1932) he published a number of articles in the newspaper recounting his experiences at those places as well as the ruins of such ancient cities as Herculaneum, Pompeii, and Paestum.[103]

It is from that year and that trip that we can date Ungaretti's growing obsession with Virgil and notably the *Aeneid.* (Unlike Montale and Quasimodo, Ungaretti shows almost no interest at all in the *Eclogues* or *Georgics.*) A statement that he made (in French) a quarter-century later sums up his mature view:

> The *Aeneid* proposed to glorify Rome's predestination to world domination: it is not this that still attracts us to the poem but the universally human aspects that one discovers in it: love, death, the immutably powerful truth of the shifting allures of nature's spectacles, the aging of all things—of human beings as well as civilization—the tragic destiny of man and the incomparable beauty of the human adventure.[104]

At the same time, the statement helps us to understand why he began soon thereafter (in 1935) to compose his most Virgilian poem, *La terra promessa,* which was not published until 1950. And, finally, it helps us to understand a remark in the notes that he subsequently wrote to explain his obscure poem, where he observed that "the *Aeneid* is always present in *La terra promessa,* along with the places that belong to it."[105] For it is not so much the *Aeneid* in any textual detail that underlies *La terra promessa,* but rather a selective and highly personal recollection of the poem, along with a physical sense of place.[106]

Ungaretti's poem, as originally conceived, was to begin "at the point where, Aeneas having reached the Promised Land, the recollection of past experience awakens in his memory to attest how his present experience, and all that may follow, will end, until, at the end of time, it is given to men to know the true Promised Land."[107] As published, however, the poem consists of three parts: a central section of nineteen short poems entitled "Choruses Descriptive of Dido's States of Mind" ("Cori descrittivi di stati d'animo di Didone"), a forty-one line introductory "Canzone" describing the poet's state of mind, and a concluding "Recitativo" of Palinurus in the rigorous form of the sestina.[108] All of the

poems are written in the terse, highly concentrated, imagistic, and obscure language characteristic of extreme Hermetic poetry. Yet through
his use of such medieval Romance forms as the canzone and the sestina
as the vehicle for classical material, Ungaretti seems to be striving for
what has been called a "Mediterranean" synthesis.[109]

The initial "Canzone," one of Ungaretti's most thoroughly analyzed
poems,[110] portrays the epiphany in which the poet, from the underworld of despair to which he has descended to drink forgetfulness from
the waters of Lethe, first glimpses the primal image, "la prima imma-
gine" of beauty—an image that seems to exclude us and that is ever
fleeting, but that reveals to the poet the shores of the promised land
that he is determined to pursue. Although the poet finds himself in a
situation that could almost be called Aenean, such an identification
would be too specific; for he also feels himself to be Odysseus, as the
allusions to the fleeing walls of Ithaca and the unraveling web suggest.
At this point, despite the Virgilian experiences of 1931, the poet is still
primarily the nomad, the wanderer, the seeker.[111]

It is only with the long central section that we are clearly in the
Aeneid, for Dido, as Ungaretti puts it in his preface, "came to represent
the experience of one who, in late autumn, is on the point of passing
beyond it; the hour in which living is about to become solitary; the
hour of one from whom, awesome and dreadful, the final frisson of
youth is about to depart."[112] Dido's "choruses" begin with reminiscences about her youth "in the distance of years when disquietude did
not yet lacerate" (i):

> In lontananza d'anni
> Quando non laceravano gli affanni.

But quickly recalling (iii) that she is now "a thing in ruins and abandoned" ("cosa in rovina e abbandonata"), she portrays a soul ravished
by desire and not yet weaned (*divezzati*) of youthful longing (v). As she
rehearses in her memory her lover's features (viii), she wonders what
good these images are for her, forgotten as she is (ix):

> Le immagini a che prò
> Per me dimenticata?

As her thoughts turn (x) to the pyre through which she intends, that
evening, to "make beautiful her fall" ("il mio declino abbellirò, sta-
sera"), she recalls the arrival of the Trojan fleet (xii), her bewilderment
at Aeneas's radiance, and her unrequited love (xiv). Attributing her
wrongs to fate, she spends her nights in sleepwalking (xvi) while her
days are dominated by images of barren fields, destroyed cities, and
heron-filled swamps—and of the reeking fame that remains her last

claim to the past (xviii). Her final "chorus" (xix) is the ultimate resignation: Renouncing even her pride, she lays it among the horrors, among the desolated errors:

> Deposto hai la superbia negli orrori,
> Nei desolati errori.

These nineteen "choruses" succeed brilliantly in illuminating through quick flashes the sequences of mood of a disillusioned individual, of a disenchanted civilization. At the same time, only the title gives us the slightest indication that these "states of mind" are Dido's rather than, say, Phaedra's or any other in a sequence of rejected women known to literary history. Ungaretti has not set out so much to portray Dido, who by the way is a figure close to his own North African origins; rather, he is portraying a state of mind, a condition of society, for which he appropriates a few vivid images from Books 1 and 4 of the *Aeneid* (e.g., the image of fire, which recurs most frequently[113]). As his explanatory notes make clear, these choruses represent "the last glimmers of youth of a person, and also of a civilization since civilizations also are born, grow, decline, and die."[114] This Spenglerian pessimism, in turn, accounts for the images of autumn that pervade the entire work.[115]

It is the irony of *La terra promessa* that neither of the figures actually portrayed in the poem ever reaches the goal: Dido of course remains behind to die in Carthage, and Palinurus falls overboard on the trip from Sicily to Italy.[116] (To be precise: Virgil's Palinurus does not die at sea; he reaches the shore of Italy, where he is immediately slain by the natives.) Again it is only the title that specifies Palinurus as the speaker of the "recitativo." But the sequence of rhyme-words that are skillfully varied in the strophes of the sestina—*furia* ("fury"), *sonno* ("sleep"), *onde* ("wave"), *pace* ("peace"), *emblema* ("emblem"), and *mortale* ("mortal")—belongs to the realm of experience of the pilot who, overcome by sleep despite the fury of the storm and the waves crashing on the treacherous cliffs of the Sirens, succumbs to his mortal weakness and falls overboard to watery depths where he finds no peace from what Ungaretti calls his "hopeless loyalty" ("disperata fedeltà"[117]).

Palinurus's vain pursuit of the promised land and the ideal embodied by Aeneas is suggested in the sequence of the strophes by changes in the qualifiers attached to the word *emblema*: "feigned" (*finto*), "lonely" (*deserto*), "of despair" (*di disperanza*); he is the "vanquished pilot of a scattered emblem" ("Piloto vinto d'un disperso emblema"). In the concluding envoy, he finally succeeds in reaching land; but it is only as stone (a reference, of course, to the geographical Capo Palinuro) that he has managed to become an "emblem of peace" ("emblema della pace"). (Ungaretti borrows his image from two different accounts of the incident. In *Aeneid* 5 the sea is calm and Palinurus is presumed drowned; but when Aeneas meets Palinurus in the underworld, the pilot mentions the stormy seas and Aeneas promises that a funeral mound will be raised on a place that will bear his name.)

In the bleak pessimism of *La terra promessa*, then, Ungaretti portrays in Palinurus and Dido the defeated man of action and the defeated woman of passion; it is only in the poet, the contemplative man, that he leaves open any room for hope.[118] However, through his very absence Aeneas is a constant presence in the poem: as the foil against which Dido's despair and Palinurus's failure can be measured and as the "emblem" of the promised land. Although the victorious Aeneas will later emerge only in a few fragmentary "choruses" published a decade later (in the volume *Il taccuino del vecchio*, 1961), it is not unreasonable to suggest that Ungaretti's old age is "largely dominated by a single mythological figure with whom he appears virtually to identify himself"—Aeneas.[119] As he put it in an essay published in French, "l'esprit de Virgile n'est pas mort":

> the spirit of Virgil is not dead . . . it lives, in this very moment while we are speaking of it, in our spirit; and if it is true that he has modified and impregnated our entire culture, he remains constantly alive and present within us.[120]

It was only after the war, after the despair and defeat of Dido and Palinurus, that this image of the mature, existential man could develop. Even in *La terra promessa*, however, it is only by reference to Virgil, and by such "experienced geography" as North Africa and Capo Palinuro, that we are able to make our way through the otherwise impenetrable language of Ungaretti's hermetic images.

All three poets of *Ermetismo*, then, return to Virgil in their effort to reclaim a threatened cultural heritage in a time of political and social turmoil: Montale through the *Eclogues*, Quasimodo through the *Georgics*, and Ungaretti through the *Aeneid*. At the same time, for all of them the turn to Virgil marks a distinct retreat from present reality into the *terra promessa* of Virgilian landscapes and Virgil's past.

Virgil in Britain

In 1962, in response to T. S. Eliot's essay on "Virgil and the Christian World" (1951), Robert Graves launched a vigorous counterattack against what he perceived as Eliot's "task of restoring the Virgil cult, long driven underground by ribald pessimists . . . to the high altar of the English-speaking world."[1] The intensity of Graves's animus is exposed by the fact that, despite his demonstrated familiarity with the classics, he makes several egregious errors in his text, attributing a well-known passage from the first book of the *Aeneid* to the sixth (13) and confusing the fourth *Georgic* with the third (22). Otherwise, however, his contemptuous view of Virgil is based on a thorough acquaintance with the texts. The *Eclogues* are "drawing-room pastorals" portraying a "*salon* life [that] anticipates the French eighteenth century" (20–21). The *Georgics* constitute a "monotonous entertainment" by a "patronizing city-man" who puts a good face on Augustus's moves to undermine traditional Italian agriculture (24–25). In the *Aeneid* Virgil's "chief delight was to mourn beautiful boys cut off in the flower of their youth" while his Aeneas, "a cad to the last," responds to Dido's passionate pleas "with the cold and formal rhetoric of an attorney" (27–28). Taking issue with Virgil's admirers from Propertius and Augustine by way of Dante and Dryden to Tennyson, Graves maintains that "few poets have brought such discredit as Virgil on their sacred calling" (35). In fact, Graves argues, it was Virgil's negative qualities—pliability, subservience, narrowness, denial of imaginative freedom, lack of originality— that "first commended him to government circles, and have kept him in favour ever since" (14).

Although Graves's indictment of Virgil as a government toady was not written until the early 1960s, his essay reflects attitudes that he held half a century earlier. Recalling questions of logic and style that he raised as a schoolboy about the *Aeneid*, he points out that "my adult eye was offended by numerous other examples of poetic bad manners" (30). Mainly, however, he attacks the doctrine of imperialism implicit throughout the *Aeneid*, as in the famous words in which Jupiter assures Venus that the Trojans are destined to establish an empire without geographical or historical bounds and to impose their own law and order on all the peoples of the world:

> His ego nec metas rerum, nec tempora pono:
> Imperium sine fine dedi.
>
> (*Aen.* 1.278–79)

"This heady doctrine, to which as a young Romano-British imperialist I too was asked to subscribe a few years later, Mr. Eliot still cherishes" (14).

It is true that, during and immediately after World War I, many young British soldiers who had been schooled on the *Aeneid* were led by their experience of battlefield reality to reject the Virgilian ideal of *imperium romanum* and its implicit acceptance of war. In his poem "Arms and the Boy" (1918), Wilfred Owen anticipates the disenchantment of the youth who, having learned to intone *arma virumque cano* mindlessly, is then exposed to the brutal reality of modern warfare:

> Let the boy try along this bayonet-blade
> How cold steel is, and keen with hunger of blood:
> Blue with all malice, like a madman's flash;
> And thinly drawn with famishing for flesh.[2]

But Owen's fury is not directed against Virgil personally: his equally ardent antiwar poem, "Dulce Et Decorum Est" (1917), takes as its title and subtext the familiar lines from Horace (*Odes* 3.2.13) proclaiming how sweet and fitting it is to die for one's country, which he calls "The old Lie: Dulce et decorum est / Pro patria mori" (55).

Although the centrality of Virgil as a force in British education and culture may have been "challenged" by the horror of World War I, it goes too far to suggest that he was "rejected."[3] In the first place, the challenge applies almost wholly to the political message of the *Aeneid* and not to Virgil's other works. And in the second place, even in the case of the epic we see an ironic relativization rather than the savage rejection of Graves. Ezra Pound relates an anecdote that he heard from Yeats:

> A plain sailor man took a notion to study Latin, and his teacher tried him with Virgil; after many lessons he asked him something about the hero.
>   Said the sailor: "What hero?"
>   Said the teacher: "What hero, why, Aeneas, the hero."
>   Said the sailor: "Ach, a hero, him a hero? Bigob, I t'ought he waz a priest."[4]

However, even the otherwise non-Virgilian Yeats resorted to the *Aeneid* (2.255) for the title of his volume *Per amica silentia lunae* (1915), the lovely phrase describing the moonlit silence through which the Greek fleet closed in stealthily for its final attack on Troy.

It is more accurate perhaps to speak of a new ambivalence toward Virgil that replaced, after the Great War, the previous unquestioning acceptance of what was regarded as his imperialistic message. In this sense, the new attitude toward Virgil is simply another manifestation of that general sense of irony that Paul Fussell attributes to the generational loss of innocence in the trenches of World War I.[5] For it is not at all the case that Virgil disappeared from the curriculum. In his 1945 presidential address to the Classical Association on "A Classical Education," Maurice Bowra pointed out that the number of classical students at British universities from 1919 to 1939 remained virtually constant.[6] J. W. Mackail stated that his bimillennial edition of the *Aeneid* (dedicated to *Principi Poetarum Natali MM*) was designed not for professional scholars and students but "for readers and lovers of great poetry" even though it featured only the Latin text with no translation or vocabulary.[7] Noel Annan has emphasized that the education of the British clerisy of his generation, from which so many writers (and their readers) emerged, continued to have the same basis in Greek and Latin as it did before the war, and reminds us that the classical curriculum could number among its achievements not simply cultural snobbery but also the training of cryptographers "who deciphered enemy traffic with all the skill of Housman in emending a corrupt text."[8] Indeed, Maurice Bowra in his 1945 address maintains that "the strength of the classical education in England and its peculiar qualities are due to this close association with fine literature and especially with poetry" (60). Accordingly, writers continue throughout the 1920s and 1930s, as did Owen, to count on the recognition of the familiar Virgilian texts. This is immediately apparent if we look at the fate of the *Eclogues* in England.

THE *ECLOGUES* PARODIED

It is almost predictable that Oliver St. John Gogarty, the author of bawdy songs that amused his friend James Joyce, would be instinctively attracted to the *Eclogues* and their praise of *amor*. His poem to "Virgil" is based almost wholly on images borrowed from the *Eclogues*:

From Mantua's meadows to Imperial Rome
Came Virgil, with the wood-light in his eyes,

Browned by the suns that round his hillside home
Burned on the chestnuts and the ilices.
And these he left, and left the fallows where
The slow streams freshened many a bank of thyme,
To found a city in the Roman air,
And build the epic turrets in a rhyme.
But were the woodland deities forgot,
Pan, Sylvan, and the sister nymphs for whom
He poured his melody the fields along?
They gave him for his faith a happy lot:
The waving of the meadows in his song
And the spontaneous laurel at his tomb.[9]

Another poem in the same volume, with the bucolic title "Sub Ilice,"[10] recalls earthily his encounter in Italy with "a tall fair student girl from Dresden," to whom, by way of seduction, he points out the famous sights: "'This is Virgil's / Confiscated farmstead which his friend in Rome restored'"; or

"'Is this Virgil's birthplace?' Scholars are uncertain—
You cannot be a scholar if a thing is too well known—
There's the Idylls' ilex: if we use it for a curtain,
You can sit on half my raincoat and my half will be a throne."

The vision concludes with a punning play on the third *Eclogue*, where Damoetas challenges Menalcas with his wax-jointed pipe (*fistula cera /iuncta*) to a singing contest: *Vis ergo inter nos, quid possit uterque, vicissim / experiamur.* ("Well, would you like for us to see, turn about, what each can do?") Gogarty's challenge to a girl he names Phyllis (from the same eclogue) leaves little to the imagination:

"Virgil was Menalcas: let me call you Phyllis.
Now look up the Idyll where they tried what each could do:
There! 'Vis ergo inter nos', and 'turn about's', 'vicissim';
My pipe though not wax-jointed yet can play a tune or two."

Louis MacNeice, an Oxford-educated classics don, opens his volume of *Collected Poems 1925–1948* with four "eclogues" written in the mid-1930s and modeled on the amoebaean poems in Virgil's collection. "An Eclogue for Christmas"—at 142 lines roughly twice the length of most of Virgil's *Eclogues*—is the dialogue between an urban aesthete ("A.") and a countryman ("B."), who are equally disenchanted with the state of the world.

A. I meet you in an evil time.
B.   The evil bells

Put out of our heads, I think, the thought of everything
    else.
A. The jaded calendar revolves,
    Its nuts need oil, carbon chokes the valves,
    The excess sugar of a diabetic culture
    Rotting the nerve of life and literature.[11]

But MacNeice's countryman refuses to offer any hope of rural consolations:

B. Analogue of me, you are wrong to turn to me,
    My country will not yield you any sanctuary,
    There is no pinpoint in any of the ordnance maps
    To save you when your towns and town-bred thoughts
        collapse.
    It is better to die *in situ* as I shall,
    One place is as bad as another.

The following "Eclogue by a Five-Barred Gate" is a conversation between Death and two Shepherds, whose "sheep" are their poems. In true Virgilian fashion, Death offers them a competition:

D. Look, I will set you a prize like any of your favourites,
    Like any Tityrus or tired Damon;
    Sing me, each in turn, what dream you had last night
    And if either's dream rings true, to him I will open my gate.

                                          (25)

Death finds that both their dreams deserve a prize. But he cautions them to "take another look at my land before you choose it." The two shepherds observe that the realm of Death looks cold and its sheep do not breed or couple. Yet, being human, they decide to try the unknown land in exchange for their familiar territories, and Death remains at the gate:

D. So; they are gone; life in my land . . .
    There is no life as there is no land.
    They are gone and I am alone
    With a gate the façade of a mirage.

                                          (26)

MacNeice's somber eclogues radically invert the Virgilian form to accommodate a bleak vision of the contemporary world. Like his French counterparts, he appreciates the political potential of the genre; but unlike the German millennialists he displays no interest in the "Messianic" eclogue.

But Gogarty and MacNeice were exceptions. Paul Fussell has suggested that the second *Eclogue*—a poem that "every young officer from a public school had read" and that "recommended itself especially by virtue of usually being skipped by teachers making assignments in Virgil"[12]—must have been recalled in the poppied fields of Flanders by the "pseudo-homosexuals" of the British army. But that "complex and poignant experience," if it in fact occurred, does not seem to be supported by textual evidence. In general, and in contrast to the situation in France and Germany, it was not so much the *Eclogues* that seized popular attention in Britain as the *Georgics*.

THE MODERN GEORGICISTS

Virginia Woolf does not tell us, in *To the Lighthouse* (1927), which work it is that occupies Mr. Carmichael, "who liked to lie awake a little reading Virgil."[13] But the position of the emphasized reference—we are reminded a few pages later, when Mr. Carmichael blows out his candle, that he is still "reading Virgil" (192)—suggests that it is in all likelihood the *Georgics* that keeps him awake. The passage opens the brief middle section of the novel, "Time Passes," which covers the period between the first part, which takes place one day in the summer of 1914, and the conclusion ten years later. The passage of time is described in terms of nature's eternal recurrence, with its seasons and constellations, and the inevitability of human toil distinctly reminiscent of the bleak message of the *Georgics* (1.145–46):

> Labor omnia vicit
> improbus et duris urgens in rebus egestas.

(Harsh toil conquered all things, and need that oppresses in adverse circumstances.)

As Mr. Carmichael blows out his candle, the narrative continues:

> But what after all is one night? A short space, especially when the darkness dims so soon, and so soon a bird sings, a cock crows, or a faint green quickens, like a turning leaf, in the hollow of the wave. Night, however, succeeds to night. The winter holds a pack of them in store and deals them equally, evenly, with indefatigable fingers. They lengthen; they darken. Some of them hold aloft clear planets, plates of brightness. The autumn trees, ravaged as they are, take on the flash of tattered flags kindling in the gloom of cool cathedral caves where gold letters on marble pages describe death in battle and how bones bleach and burn far away in Indian sands. The autumn trees gleam in the yellow moonlight, in the light of

harvest moons, the light which mellows the energy of labour, and smooths the stubble, and brings the wave lapping blue to the shore.

It seemed now as if, touched by human penitence and all its toil, divine goodness had parted the curtain and displayed behind it, single, distinct, the hare erect; the wave falling; the boat rocking, which, did we deserve them should be ours always. But alas, divine goodness, twitching the cord, draws the curtain; it does not please him; he covers his treasures in a drench of hail, and so breaks them, so confuses them that it seems impossible that their calm should ever return or that we should ever compose from their fragments a perfect whole or read in the littered pieces the clear words of truth. For our penitence deserves a glimpse only; our toil respite only.

(192–93)

The text contains other hints. Mr. Carmichael is named Augustus, after the emperor who is repeatedly lauded in the *Georgics*—at the beginning, at the conclusion, and at several points in between. Although Mr. Carmichael is un-Virgilian in appearance—an umkempt old man whose beard is stained yellow with opium—he becomes a famous poet, and his work is described in terms characteristic of Virgil's poetry. Lily Briscoe, though she has never read a line of his work, "thought that she knew how it went though, slowly and sonorously. It was seasoned and mellow. It was about the desert and the camel. It was about the palm tree and the sunset. It was extremely impersonal; it said something about death; it said very little about love" (289–90). And on the last page, when Mr. Carmichael and Lily watch as Mr. Ramsey and his son James finally reach the lighthouse, he extends his arms in a vatic gesture.

He stood there as if he were spreading his hands over all the weakness and suffering of mankind; she thought he was surveying, tolerantly and compassionately, their final destiny. Now he has crowned the occasion, she thought, when his hand slowly fell, as if she had seen him let fall from his great height a wreath of violets and asphodels which, fluttering slowly, lay at length upon the earth.

(309)

If Mr. Carmichael is meant to be a Virgilian figure, then we may regard it as a final irony in Woolf's masterpiece, and a comment on the social changes between pre-war and postwar England, that the book he is holding on this occasion, as he stands "looking like an old pagan god, shaggy, with weeds in his hair," is no longer the Virgilian text specified twice before but "only a French novel" (309).

If the Virgil analogy, and specifically the allusion to the *Georgics*, requires further substantiation, we should remind ourselves that during the very years when Woolf was writing *To the Lighthouse* her intimate friend Vita Sackville-West was completing *The Land* (1926), which has been called "perhaps the best of English georgics"[14] and "probably the most Vergilian of all recent poems."[15] Immediately capturing a popularity that lasted for decades, *The Land* went though fourteen printings in its first year, was awarded the Hawthornden Prize in 1927, and by 1971 had sold 100,000 copies in Britain.[16] When she conceived and started writing this characterisically Virgilian poem, Sackville-West had allegedly "never read one line of the *Georgics*, either in Latin which I was never taught or in any translation."[17] But the literary parallels to her project were evident to others. As early as 1921, when she first thought of writing a major poem in praise of English country life, her husband, Harold Nicolson, noted that "Vita has an idea of writing sort of English Georgics."[18] In 1925 a friend to whom she showed selections presented her with Lord Burghclere's translation as well as the Loeb edition of the *Georgics*, "and I was appalled to see that my poem must appear to be a fake or an imitation."[19] In the event, she decided to capitalize on the similarity by acknowledging frankly the analogy and building on it. As published in 1926, the poem bears a Latin motto from the *Georgics* (3.289–90) expressing cautiously, in the words of the Loeb translation with which Sackville-West was familiar, "how hard it is to win with words a triumph herein, and thus to crown with glory a lowly theme":

> Nec sum animi dubius, verbis ea vincere magnum
> quam sit et angustis hunc addere rebus honorem.

Though divided like Virgil's work into four books, the seasonal organization of *The Land*, moving from winter to autumn, is different from the topical arrangement proclaimed in the opening lines of the *Georgics*, which begins with the crops, their sequence, and meteorological signs; moves on to the nurture of trees and viniculture; treats the care of animals both large and small; and concludes with a treatise on beekeeping that culminates in the myth of Aristaeus. Sackville-West's theme, "the mild continuous epic of the soil," is defined at the outset in terms that stress its universal aspects, the identity of the farmer's life and labor in England or abroad, in the present or in antiquity:

> I sing the cycle of my country's year,
> I sing the tillage, and the reaping sing,
> Classic monotony, that modes and wars

Leave undisturbed, unbettered, for their best
Was born immediate, of expediency.
The sickle sought no art; the axe, the share
Draped no superfluous beauty round their steel;
The scythe desired no music for her stroke,
Her stroke sufficed in music, as her blade
Laid low the swathes; the scythesmen swept, nor cared
What crop had ripened, whether oats in Greece
Or oats in Kent; the shepherd on the ridge
Like his Boeotian forebear kept his flocks,
And still their outlines on our tenderer sky
Simple and classic rear their grave design
As once at Thebes, as once in Lombardy.

(3)

The author emphasizes the common humanity of farmers in all times and all places:

Shepherds and stars are quiet with the hills.
There is a bond between the men who go
From youth about the business of the earth, . . .

(6)

Like Virgil, she is keenly aware of the toil that dominates the farmer's life:

But I, like him, who strive
Closely with earth, and know her grudging mind,
Will sing no songs of bounty, for I see
Only the battle between man and earth,
The sweat, the weariness, the care, the balk;
See earth the slave and tyrant, mutinous,
Turning upon her tyrant and her slave,
Yielding reluctantly her fruits, to none
But most peremptory wooers.

(7)

She begins by describing the landscape of the Weald of Kent, "the country that shall claim my theme" (11), and goes on to characterize the two principal figures in that landscape, the yeoman and the shepherd. Stressing that "There's no beginning to the farmer's year,/ Only recurrent patterns on a scroll / Unwinding" (30), the author surveys the rituals of spring: sowing, rotation, care of orchards and young stock, the responsibilities of the bee-master, and the flowers that decorate the landscape "in wood and dell" as well as "in lane and wood." Summer brings the time to shear and wash the sheep, to harvest and hay, and to combat the weeds. It also employs such craftsmen as basket-makers, osier-weavers, bricklayers, and dowsers. "All craftsmen share a knowledge. They have held / Reality down fluttering to a bench" and their "Tools have their own integrity" (81). Autumn, finally, is the time for ploughing, threshing, hedging, ditching, tending to orchards, and making cider.

Although the sempiternal routine of the farmer generates many astonishing parallels between *The Land* and the *Georgics*, it is only in the later pages that specific references to Virgil enter the text.

> Homer and Hesiod and Virgil knew
> The ploughshare in its reasonable shape,
> Classical from the moment it was new,
> Sprung ready-armed, ordained without escape,
> And never bettered though man's cunning grew,
> And barbarous countries joined the classic reach.
>
> (89)

The poem concludes with a visionary passage linking the ritual of harvest in Kent with that celebrated by Virgil in the *Georgics*:

> Yet I recall
> Another harvest, not beneath this sky
> So Saxon-fair, so washed by dews and rain;
> Another harvest, where the gods still rouse,
> And stretch, and waken with the evenfall.
> Down from the hill the slow white oxen crawl,
> Dragging the purple waggon heaped with must,
> Raising on sundered hoofs small puffs of dust,
> With scarlet tassels on their milky brows,
> Gentle as evening moths.
> . . . .
> Here the long sense of classic measure cures
> The spirit weary of its difficult pain;
> Here the old Bacchic piety endures,
> Here the sweet legends of the world remain.
> Homeric waggons lumbering the road;
> Virgilian litanies among the bine;
> Pastoral sloth of flocks beneath the pine;
> The swineherd watching, propped upon his goad.
> Under the chestnut trees the rootling swine,
> Who could so stand, and see this evening fall,
> This calm of husbandry, this redolent tilth,

This terracing of hills, this vintage wealth,
Without the pagan sanity of blood
Mounting his veins in young and tempered health?

(105-6)

Who, in short, could observe this scene and not "know himself for Rome's inheritor"? This association triggers the concluding invocation of Virgil, "O Mantuan! that sang the bees and vines,/ The tillage and the flocks" (107). Even though she came late to Virgil, Sackville-West recognized in his *Georgics* a shared sense of the humanity and dignity in the farmer's struggle with the soil and the common desire to bear testimony to that eternal struggle, "as a man who knows"

That Nature, tender enemy, harsh friend,
Takes from him soon the little that she gave,
Yet for his span will labour to defend
His courage, that his soul be not a slave,
Whether on waxen tablet or on loam,
Whether with stylus or with share and heft
The record of his passage he engrave,
And still, in toil, takes heart to love the rose.

Then thought I, Virgil! how from Mantua reft,
Shy as a peasant in the courts of Rome,
Thou took'st the waxen tablets in thy hand,
And out of anger cut calm tales of home.

The initially unwitting Virgilian form of *The Land* along with the success of the work reminds us of the continuing popularity in England of generally "georgic" poetry—that is, poetry that does not simply praise beautiful landscapes of indolence but that emphasizes the necessity and dignity of work, Virgilian *labor*. Anthony Low has shown that the georgic spirit, which he defines as an ideological revolution attacking the prevailing aristocratic ideal, began to be reflected in English poetry in the course of the sixteenth century—roughly from the second installment of Spenser's *The Faerie Queene* (1596) down to Milton's *Paradise Regained* (1671).[20] But it was not until 1697, with Dryden's tone-setting translation of the *Georgics*, which the poet in his dedication called "the best Poem of the best Poet," written when Virgil was "in the full strength and vigour of his age,"[21] that Virgil's poem moved into the center of the English poetic consciousness. The impact of Dryden's translation was enhanced by Addison's introductory essay (written in 1693), in which the young critic called it "the most complete, elaborate, and finished piece of all antiquity."[22] Dryden, understanding that Virgil's *Georgics* could not be reduced to the formula of mere didactic poetry, insisted on the need to distinguish between georgic and pastoral poetry. Although Theocritus and Homer were unmatched in pastoral and epic, Virgil excelled all models in "the middle style" of the georgic, which he defined as "plain and direct instruction" on matters moral, philosophical, or practical (12–13).

Dryden's translation, coupled with Addison's critical appreciation, inspired a wave of generally "georgic" poetry in eighteenth-century England, which culminated in Thomson's *The Seasons* (1726–30).[23] It was through *The Seasons*, into which in the course of successive revisions Thomson incorporated more and more Virgilian borrowings,[24] that the *Georgics* affected not only European literature generally but also the painting, landscape gardening, and music of the eighteenth century. The structure, finally, of a descriptive landscape poem divided by season into four parts and displaying less a didactic than a philosophical thrust, is evident as late as Sackville-West's *The Land*. Thus, the georgic mode maintained itself in England down to the twentieth century, showing up, for instance, in such popular works as Edmund Blunden's *The Shepherd and Other Poems of Peace and War* (1922). Blunden, who was later to translate the Latin poems of Milton and Marvell into English, had won prizes for Greek and Latin at Christ's Hospital and a classics scholarship to Oxford just at the moment when his career was interrupted by the war and service on the front. Despite its pastoral title, *The Shepherd* contains no bucolic idylls but, rather, poems that deal with the seasons and agricultural rhythms of the Kentish countryside measured against the turmoil of war in the background. But for all its georgic impulse the collection, which like *The Land* was awarded the Hawthornden Prize, displays no allusions to Virgil or to the *Georgics*.

It was this tradition of georgic poetry to which Cecil Day Lewis (1904–72) was referring in the foreword to his translation of *The Georgics.*

> The fascination of the Georgics for many generations of Englishmen is not difficult to explain. A century of urban civilization has not yet materially modified the instinct of a people once devoted to agriculture and stockbreeding, to the chase, to landscape gardening, to a practical love of Nature. No poem yet written has touched these subjects with more expert knowledge or more tenderness than the Georgics. In our love of domestic animals, in the millions of suburban and cottage gardens, we may see the depth and tenacity of our roots in earth to-day.[25]

Day Lewis, as he reports amusingly in his autobiography, was early made aware of Sackville-West's poem. As a young schoolmaster at Summer Fields (in North Oxford) in 1927–28, he writes:

I noticed a very small boy reading a book of poetry. I leant over his shoulder to see its title. He was reading *The Land.*

"Is that a good book? Do you like it?" I asked.

"Of course it's a good book," he politely replied. "My mother wrote it."[26]

It was years after this encounter with the young Nigel Nicolson, and for more complicated reasons, that Day Lewis undertook what turned out to be one of the great translations of the *Georgics*. His characterization of Virgil in the "Dedicatory Stanzas" to Stephen Spender suggests that a certain sense of spiritual identity may have bound the quiet clergyman's son from Ireland with the Roman poet:

> Virgil—a tall man, dark and countrified
> In looks, they say: retiring: no rhetorician:
> Of humble birth: a Celt, whose first ambition
> Was to be a philosopher: Dante's guide.
> But chiefly dear for his gift to understand
> Earth's intricate, ordered heart, and for a vision
> That saw beyond an imperial day the hand
> Of man no longer armed against his fellow
> But all for vine and cattle, fruit and fallow,
> Subduing with love's positive force the land.[27]

Day Lewis has indicated that it was a thoroughly Virgilian sense of "*pietas*—a habit of respect for gods, ancestors, parents, country, institutions, and a sense of involvement with them"[28]—that prompted him to fulfill his obligation to his past by writing his autobiography. It is a reasonable assumption that the same *pietas* also underlay the lifelong preoccupation with Virgil that led, following his rendition of the *Georgics* (1940) to translations of the *Aeneid* (1952) and the *Eclogues* (1963). (The mysteries that Day Lewis began publishing in the 1930s under the pseudonym of Nicholas Blake feature an Oxford-educated classicist, Nigel Strangeways, whose theory of detection is based on Latin syntax[29] and who frequently cites Latin tags, among which Virgil figures conspicuously.)

Day Lewis's *Georgics* is not so much a translation as a recreation in modern colloquial English of Virgil's text—a fact readily apparent if we compare his rendition of the opening lines with those of an almost contemporary English version, whose author sought "to reproduce the original meter as nearly as the structural differences between the two languages will permit."[30]

> What giveth us glad crops, what star makes timely the
> ploughman's

> Labour, or his that mates, Maecenas, vine to the elmtree;
> How cattle ask tendance; how a sheepfold rightly is order'd;
> How to manage bee-thrift needs long-tried mastery—hence I
> Mean to ordain my song.

Leaving aside the metrical awkwardnesses (e.g., the non-idiomatic emphasis in line 1 on *us*, in line 3 on the second syllable of *tendance*, and in line 4 on the second word in the compound *bee-thrift*), the hexameter also requires, in order to fill out the English line, the kind of lengthening suggested by *giveth* or the expansion of the second phrase: *quo sidere terram / vertere* in such a manner that the person (ploughman) is emphasized rather than the task (turning the soil). The effect is finally stilted, lacking the earthy immediacy of Virgil's Latin.

Day Lewis, in contrast, uses a six-beat line based on the Latin hexameter but consistent with contemporary speech rhythms.

> What makes the cornfields happy, under what constellation
> It's best to turn the soil, my friend, and train the vine
> On the elm; the care of cattle, the management of flocks,
> The knowledge you need for keeping frugal bees:—all this
> I'll now begin to relate.
>
> (15)

The result is a smooth-flowing, natural line that permits an ingeniously literal translation of Virgil's words within roughly the same space of lines. Day Lewis also uses a basically Anglo-Saxon vocabulary that has an effect analogous to that of Virgil's Latin, which clearly betrays its rural origins in vocabulary and agricultural metaphors.[31]

> Vero novo, gelidus canis cum montibus umor
> liquitur et Zephyro putris se glaeba resolvit,
> depresso incipiat iam tum mihi taurus aratro
> ingemere, et sulco attritus splendescere vomer.
> illa seges demum votis respondet avari
> agricolae, bis quae solem, bis frigora sensit;
> illius immensae ruperunt horrea messes.
>
> (1.43–49)

> Early spring, when a cold moisture sweats from the hoar-head
> Hills and the brittle clods are loosening under a west wind,
> Is the time for the bull to grunt as he pulls the plough deep-
>   driven
> And the ploughshare to take a shine, scoured clean in the
>   furrow.
> That crop, which twice has felt the sun's heat and the frost
>   twice,

Will answer at last the prayers of the never-satisfied
Farmer, and burst his barns with an overflowing harvest.

(16)

Because Day Lewis is writing "chiefly for readers who have no Latin
and because classical allusions have ceased to be commonplaces for even
the highly educated" (8), he seeks to make the various allusions self-
explanatory in the text itself. Accordingly, Ceres becomes "the corn-
goddess," Pales the "goddess of sheepfolds," Jupiter the "Father" or
"Father of agriculture" (19), and Virgil's *fata* (1.199) are rationalized into
"a law of nature" (21). Even Virgil's patron Maecenas, who encouraged
him to undertake the *Georgics* and who is mentioned by name at the
beginning of each book, becomes simply "my friend" (as in the first
passage cited above). And in Book 4 the kings (*reges*) that rule the hives
and enable Virgil to establish a precise analogy between the organization of the bees and human governments are modernized with entomo-
logical precision into "queens."

But other factors are at work here besides the innovations of a brilliant and resourceful translator, who read classics at Oxford under the
tutelage of Maurice Bowra. Like many of his friends during the early
1930s—Auden, MacNeice, Spender, and others—Day Lewis was a
lapsed Christian and disenchanted liberal who, out of a sense of religious longing and romantic humanism, was drawn toward communism.[32] A member of the Communist party of Great Britain from 1935
to 1938, he left it finally not out of any hostility to the ideals of the
movement but because he "had to choose between political work and
my writing."[33] In 1938 Day Lewis moved with his wife to a cottage on
the Devon-Dorset border, where "at last, in the village life I seemed to
share that genial and positive sense of community which I had so long
desired."[34] It was here, while running the local Home Guard, that he
was asked by his wife's brother, a master at Winchester, to provide a
verse translation of a short passage from the fourth *Georgic* which had
been designated for an examination. "The passage excited me—particularly the line about bees holding little stones to ballast them when they
flew in a gusty wind."[35] Deciding that he would like to translate the
whole of the *Georgics*, he set to work, "my imagination quickened
and enriched by all that I had come to love here—the places and the
people—and by a sense that this work might be a valediction to
them."

It was this experience that acquainted Day Lewis with Virgilian
pietas.

As I worked on into the summer of 1940, I felt more and more
the kind of patriotism which I imagine was Virgil's—the natural
piety, the heightened sense of the genius of place, the passion to

praise and protect one's roots, or to put down roots somewhere while there is still time, which it takes a seismic event such as a war to reveal to most of us rootless moderns. More and more I was buoyed up by a feeling that England was speaking to me through Virgil, and that the Virgil of the *Georgics* was speaking to me through the English farmers and labourers with whom I consorted. Again, just as I had never been consciously a patriot, so I had never had much respect for, much sense of obligation to, the past. The inner disturbances created by the war threw up my own past before my eyes, giving it new value. . . . A heightened sense of the past—both my own and that which, through the European tradition of Virgil, I share with many—was added to the enhanced awareness of place, of England, and especially that South-West of England which, because I had been at school there twenty years before, was associated with the *Georgics* I had first read there.[36]

Day Lewis's socialist idealism is evident in the foreword to his translation, where he expresses the hope that "this war, together with the spread of electrical power, will result in a decentralization of industry and the establishment of a new rural-urban civilization working through smaller social units" (7). And the "Dedicatory Stanzas" to Stephen Spender repeat the conviction motivating all modern Virgilians, that "Different from his our age and myths, our toil / The same" (10). As motto, Day Lewis placed at the head of his book the powerful Latin lines at *Georgics* 1.505–11:

> . . . tot bella per orbem,
> Tam multae scelerum facies, non ullus aratro
> Dignus honor, squalent abductis arva colonis,
> Et curvae rigidum falces conflantur in ensem.
> Hinc movet Euphrates, illinc Germania bellum;
> Vicinae ruptis inter se legibus urbes
> Arma ferunt; saevit toto Mars impius orbe.

which he subsequently translates:

> there's so much war in the world,
> Evil has so many faces, the plough so little
> Honour, the labourers are taken, the fields untended,
> And the curving sickle is beaten into the sword that yields not.
> There the East is in arms, here Germany marches:
> Neighbour cities, breaking their treaties, attack each other:
> The wicked War-god runs amok through all the world.
>
> (31)

The translator did not need to spell out for his readers, classically educated or not, the relevance of Virgil's lines to the present of an England where conscription had emptied the farms and industry had been converted to military purposes, all in response to aggression of the Germans, who were once again on the march.[37]

> Soon enough each is called into the quarrel.
> Till then, taking a leaf from Virgil's laurel,
> I sang in time of war the arts of peace.
>
> (10)

We have already observed with what sympathetic virtuosity Day Lewis accommodated Virgil's hexameters and the farm-based Latin vocabulary to the rhythms and language of twentieth-century England. We also noted that the accessibility of his version was achieved through a certain modernization of ancient concepts of deity and fate and even apiary lore. However, Day Lewis modified the tone of Virgil's poem in other ways.

We know today, thanks to recent studies by several classicists, that Virgil's *Georgics* have a dark side that was generally ignored by most of the work's earlier admirers—that, in short, he was not portraying a utopia but the sober reality of Roman farm life along with the political reality of Roman social history. Gary B. Miles has traced the history of two parallel developments that produced an ambivalence toward and, indeed, contradictory visions of rustic life in Virgil's work. Although the countryside exemplified Rome's agrarian past as the source of traditional Roman values, it also represented the lure of escape and refuge from the responsibilities of public life in Virgil's present.[38] David O. Ross, Jr., has recently gone even further by exposing what he calls the "lies" that inform several of Virgil's most famous set pieces (e.g., the natural impossibilities in the *Laudes Italiae* or the clichés in the Praise of Rustic Life) and by making clear the rhetorical pattern according to which virtually every *laudatio* is counterbalanced by a qualifying and relativizing *vituperatio*.[39]

If we scrutinize Day Lewis's translation in the light of these interpretations, we see that he almost consistently, and probably unwittingly, softens the tone in a number of crucial passages. We have already quoted the line from the "Dedicatory Stanzas" which refers to Virgil's vision of man "subduing with love's positive force the land" (10). Now it is possible to speak of the presence of love in the *Eclogues*, where it is claimed that *omnia vincit Amor* (10.69) and where the figures in several poems are preoccupied with various (usually frustrated) love affairs. But love can hardly be called a positive force in the *Georgics*. At most we think of the destructive power of sexual passion in Book 3:

Omne adeo genus in terris hominumque ferarumque,
et genus aequoreum, pecudes pictaeque volucres,
in furias ignemque ruunt: amor omnibus idem.

(242–44)

All manner of life on earth—men, fauna of land and sea,
Cattle and coloured birds—
Run to this fiery madness: love is alike for all.

(62)

Although in his translation Day Lewis renders the passage with appropriate savagery, his introductory poem prepares the reader for a much gentler spirit. We note a similar toning down in his treatment of the lines *labor omnia vicit / improbus* (1.145–46), which conclude the passage (one of Ross's "lies") in which we learn that Jupiter himself put an end to the Golden Age, when the earth brought forth its fruits without human effort (*ipsaque tellus / omnia liberius nullo poscente ferebat*). Instead *pater ipse* determined that the way of the farmer should not be an easy one and that dire need should require humankind, through ingenuity, to invent the skills of agriculture. In this context *labor improbus* is "ruinous toil" that represents a threat to human existence.[40] Day Lewis turns the harsh commentary into a reassuring aphorism:

Yes, unremitting labour
And harsh necessity's hand will master anything.

(19)

To cite a final example, classical scholars have noted the frequent use of military images in Virgil's agricultural terminology.[41] In one passage the farmer hurls his seed (*iacto semine*) like a javelin, rushes into hand-to-hand combat (*comminus*) with his fields, routs (*ruit*) the hostile mounds of sand, and then in martial procession leads (*inducit*) streams of water to his plants:

quid dicam, iacto qui semine comminus arva
insequitur cumulosque ruit male pinguis harenae,
deinde satis fluvium inducit rivosque sequentis.

(1.104–6)

This entire military subtext is played down and lost in Day Lewis's translation:

No need to commend him who, after the sowing, closely
Follows it up by breaking the clammy loam of the field,
Then lets in runnels of water to irrigate the seed-land.

(18)

This tendency to soften the tone of Virgil's text does nothing to vitiate the quality and value of Day Lewis's otherwise splendid translation. But it directs our attention to a crucial aspect of the appeal of the *Georgics* in England. Virgil composed his poem over a seven-year period (37–30 B.C.) concluding a bloody age of civil strife, mob violence at home, and war abroad; and evidence of this turmoil is apparent throughout his text—not just in the violence of nature and the military images of agriculture. We have already cited the conclusion to Book 1 (*tot bella per orbem*), which Day Lewis chose for his motto. Elsewhere Virgil tells us that the very sun hid its head in an eclipse to lament the assassination of Julius Caesar (*ille etiam exstincto miseratus Caesare Romam, / cum caput obscura nitidum ferrugine texit,* 1.466–67). And the work as a whole ends with the reminder that, while Virgil was composing his poem on the cultivation of crops, cattle, and trees, the future Augustus was storming across Asia, bringing Roman law to the conquered peoples and paving his way to Olympus:

> Haec super arvorum cultu pecorumque canebam
> et super arboribus, Caesar dum magnus ad altum
> fulminat Euphraten bello victorque volentis
> per populos dat iura viamque adfectat Olympo.
>
> (4.559–63)

During this time, it is true, Virgil was in Naples, devoting himself in leisure to unheroic poetic pursuits (*illo Vergilium me tempore dulcis alebat / Parthenope studiis florentem ignobilis oti,* 4.563–64). At the same time, the poet was acutely aware of the fact that he had experienced a period of violence and war, and this awareness made itself felt in the poems he was writing. The *Georgics,* in sum, did not constitute an escape from contemporary violence; it amounted to a reflection of that violence in terms of the struggle of farmers with the land, of the agricultural beasts driven by sexual lust, of the bees vying for power in their kingdom.

For the English georgicists, in contrast, their preoccupation with the *Georgics* was one step removed from the reality of the present: For them the rural life represented by the *Georgics* was not, as it was for Virgil, an ambivalent reflection of the harshness of political reality but a refuge from it into a text remote from the present in time, place, and language. This is starkly evident in the translation that L. A. S. Jermyn published in 1947 under the title *The Singing Farmer.*[42] There is nothing particularly notable about Jermyn's blank verse: Apart from the remarkable degree of care in the rendition of agricultural terminology and procedures, the translation is quite traditional and even slightly antiquarian in tone:

What makes the cornfields glad, beneath what star
To plough the soil, Maecenas, or to wed
Vine to her elm, the herdsman's care, the right
Treatment of flocks, the practice long which makes
The perfect keeper of the thrifty bees—
Hence springs my song. Ye constellations bright
That lead the rolling year athwart the sky:
. . . .
Your benisons I sing.

(3)

That VERGIL I, who pastoral ditties made,
And, bold in youth, sang thee, my Tityrus,
Recumbent in thy spreading beechen bower.

(92)

What distinguishes Jermyn's translation, rather, are the circumstances under which it was undertaken and completed: during the author's internment by the Japanese in Singapore between March 1942 and July 1945.[43] With nothing but a secondhand copy of the *Eclogues* and *Georgics* in T. E. Page's edition, Jermyn began and completed his translation of the first book in Changi Gaol before the end of 1942. (The very decision to translate the *Georgics* rather than the *Eclogues* is in itself a characteristically English choice.) Though he had no dictionary available, "I had taken a class of enthusiastic Chinese lads through it six years previously, reading to them, at the end of each lesson, J. W. Mackail's beautiful prose rendering" (v). With the aid of "an indifferent Latin dictionary" that appeared in Changi, Jermyn turned next to "the delightful bees" and managed to complete Book 4 shortly after his arrival in Sime Road Camp, to which he was transferred in May 1944. Here, while he was working on the second book, the prisoners were gratified by the sight of the first big British bombing raid on Singapore: "The flames shot up from petrol-dumps, 'rushing skyward pitchy clouds of smoke', like the fire in Vergil's vineyard" (vi; the allusion is to *Geo.* 2.308–9). The translation of the third book was finished in July 1945, a month before Jermyn's release. "By that time there was such a spirit of confidence throughout the camp that I was able positively to enjoy Vergil's description of the cattle-plagues, even though they reminded us so keenly of our own" (vi).

Again it is evident that yet another English georgicist was turning to Virgil's text as a refuge from the horrors of the present. "Despite the squalor, progressive starvation and other ills, upon which it would be depressing to enlarge, there were many things in our camp-life which seemed to harmonize with the work of translating *The Georgics*" (vi).

The same kind of weevil identified by Virgil appeared in the prisoners' rice rations; the frogs in Sime Road Camp "voiced their ancient moan" like those described by Virgil; one internee, "an enthusiastic bee-keeper," set up several hives in Changi Gaol; and Jermyn is confident that "Vergil would have loved our birds" (vii), which he describes for a full paragraph. The prisoners benefited from the *labor improbus* of their vegetable gardeners, who cultivated their corn by the seed selection recommended by Virgil. And they were cheered, at early parades, by the rise of a Virgilian dawn just as they enjoyed "the glories of the night, those *clarissima mundi lumina*" (viii). It emerges quite clearly from Jermyn's account that the act of translation contributed to the preservation of his own equanimity.

> My method, generally, was to worry out in prose the last ounce of meaning in a particular passage, then to learn the Latin by heart and let the rhythm suggest a rendering. Often the rendering I wanted came to me in the middle of the night, when, as lights were forbidden, I would endeavour to memorize it, and write it down the next morning.
>
> (ix)

After the war Jermyn submitted his translation to Basil Blackwell, who published it on the enthusiastic recommendation of none other than Jackson Knight, who referred Jermyn to several works that enabled him to benefit from the latest Virgilian scholarship.

THE CASE OF T. S. ELIOT

It is against this British background that we can best appreciate T. S. Eliot's attitude toward Virgil.[44] For reasons that will become obvious in the following chapter, Eliot shared few of the values that motivated contemporary American admirers of the Roman poet. Moreover, to the extent that he regarded Aeneas as "an exile"[45] or "the original Displaced Person,"[46] Eliot as an expatriate in England identified personally with his destiny in a manner alien to writers in the United States. At the same time, his attitude did not undergo the same relativization that characterized many of his English colleagues, who had experienced the Great War more directly. As Frank Kermode has observed, Eliot remained in a special sense "an imperialist," stating only a few years after World War I, "I am all for empires."[47] Yet his views—notably regarding the *Georgics*—are very close to those of his British contemporaries.

For all his diffidence when addressing the Virgil Society, "a gathering of people, all of whom may be better scholars than I,"[48] Eliot had a sound classical education. He began Latin and Greek at age twelve at the Smith Academy in St. Louis, where he won a gold medal for achievement in Latin. As a schoolboy, he has remarked, "It was my lot to be introduced to the *Iliad* and to the *Aeneid* in the same year. . . . I found myself at ease with Virgil as I was not at ease with Homer."[49] He observes elsewhere that "at school, I enjoyed very much reciting Homer or Virgil."[50] At Harvard he continued Latin, taking a course in Petronius and Apuleius as well as a course in Latin poetry with E. K. Rand. Yet, for a critic who was to declare that Virgil is "at the centre of European civilization, in a position which no other poet can share or usurp," and, as such, the poet by whom the very concept of "classic" must be defined,[51] Eliot the poet displays surprisingly little direct influence by Virgil. Even the critics who try hardest to make the case for a "Virgilian" Eliot are able to demonstrate his presence in at most a few lines in some half-dozen poems.

At the same time, Eliot's acquaintance with Virgil's works appears to be quite circumscribed. With the exception of a passing reference to the fourth *Eclogue* in his 1951 radio talk on "Virgil and the Christian World" (1951),[52] in which he discusses not the poem itself but the Christian "Messianic" reading of the poem, which legitimized Virgil as "suitable reading for Christians," Eliot displays no familiarity with the *Eclogues* either in his essays or in his poetry. The *Georgics* occupy a position of central importance in Eliot's understanding of Virgil; but that understanding is based, as we shall see, almost entirely on a second-hand acquaintance with the poem, which he knew mainly in translation. As for the *Aeneid*, it is not possible to demonstrate on the basis of his statements that he knew much more than he remembered from his school days: the first six books and especially two episodes, the Dido affair and the visit to the underworld.

Eliot's two major statements on Virgil—"What is a Classic?" (1944) and "Virgil and the Christian World" (1951)—contain astonishingly few textual details (in comparison, say, with his essays on Seneca or Dante or the English poets). Indeed, the earlier essay, which sets out mainly to define the nature of the literary classic, deals with the example of Virgil in only one-third of its pages and includes not a single quotation. The later piece contains only two brief quotations—the one that evoked Graves's wrath (*Aen.* 1.278–79) plus a similar three-line prophecy from Book 6 (851–53: *tu regere imperio populos, Romane, memento . . .*)—and three phrases: one from *Aeneid* 6 (*sed me iussa deum*), one from the fourth *Eclogue* (*cara deum suboles*), and one incorrectly cited from the tenth *Eclogue* (*amor vincit omnia* instead of *omnia vincit amor*).[53] The allusions in any case do not permit us to conclude that Eliot reread Virgil's works in the original Latin. At most, he looked up an occasional quotation and refreshed his memory extensively from translations.

In general, three stages are evident in Eliot's preoccupation with Virgil. Prior to 1930 the references, restricted exclusively to the early books of the *Aeneid*, are highly allusive, conveying images rather than ideas and suggesting the vivid recollection of favorite scenes rather than any ideological communion. The most explicit reference occurs in "La Figlia che Piange" (1916),[54] which bears as its epigraph the words that Aeneas addresses to his mother Venus when she appears to him disguised as a huntress: *O quam te memorem virgo . . .* (*Aen.* 1.327). In this brief vision of a girl who turns aways from a departing lover "with a fugitive resentment," critics, alerted by the Virgilian epigraph, have with some reason detected reminiscences of the characteristic gesture with which Dido turns away from Aeneas when he announces his departure from Carthage (*talia dicentem iamdudum versa tuetur,* "turning away, she gazed for some time at him as he spoke," *Aen.* 4.362) and again, as she bitterly ignores him when they meet in the underworld (*illa solo fixos oculos aversa tenebat,* "turned away, she kept her eyes fixed on the ground," *Aen.* 6.469).[55] Yet this fleeting allusion, which Eliot could hardly have expected most readers to catch, supplies little more than a crutch for the poet. "The Virgilian echoes do not elucidate a situation or action. . . . The emotions that come from Virgil's poem float freely in Eliot's."[56] Other critics—much less persuasively, in my opinion—detect Virgilian echoes in "Dans le Restaurant" (1917), where a shabby old waiter describes a childhood sexual experience in which, as a seven year old, he took refuge from a cloudburst under the dripping willows and budding brambles with an even younger girl, whom he tickled to make her laugh. "J'éprouvais un instant de puissance et de délire." But it requires a considerable leap of faith to get from this epiphany to the famous scene in the fourth book of the *Aeneid* where Dido and Aeneas take refuge from a sudden hailstorm in a cave and consummate what Dido (though not Aeneas) regards as their marriage.[57]

With *The Waste Land* (1922) we reach firmer ground. Eliot himself, in his notoriously playful notes, provided Virgil as the source for the unusual vocable *laquearia*, which in "A Game of Chess" occurs in the description of the fortune-teller's apartment, where fragrances ascended into the air and "Flung their smoke into the laquearia, / Stirring the pattern on the coffered ceiling." Eliot's note cites lines describing Dido's palace—*dependent lychni laquearibus aureis / incensi, et noctem flammis funalia vincunt* (*Aen.* 1.726–27; "lighted lamps hang down from the golden panelled ceiling, and torches vanquish the night with their flames"). We also know from early drafts of the poem that at one point

Eliot wrote three lines, not finally included, referring specifically to the interview between Aeneas and Venus that provided the epigraph for "La Figlia che Piange":

> To Aeneas, in an unfamiliar place,
> Appeared his mother, with an altered face,
> He knew the goddess by her smooth celestial pace.[58]

(The last line is a paraphrase of *Aeneid* 1:405, *et vera incessu patuit dea.*) Alerted by such details, Hugh Kenner goes on to speculate that

> Mme. Sosostris' cards may remind us of the riddling leaves of the Sibyl of Cumae in the sixth book of the *Aeneid*, whose injunction to Aeneas, when he wanted to visit the Underworld, required him not only to locate the golden bough but to perform for a drowned companion the rite of the burial of the dead. As we brood on the first part of the poem in their first form, points of contact with the *Aeneid* multiply: Carthage and the Punic Wars Dido prophesied, the drowned sailor, the Sibyl and her enigmas, the horn and ivory gates [later canceled], even such a detail as the word "laquearia" (*Aen.* I:726), which hints that the woman in the chair, rendered in the dead luxurious diction of Huysmans or the Mallarmé of *Héro-diade*, is a kind of Dido, to interfere with the traveller's proper destiny.[59]

During the very months when he was making his final revisions of *The Waste Land*, Eliot was also thinking profoundly about Joyce's *Ulysses* and its "parallel use of the Odyssey," to which Eliot in his essay on "*Ulysses*, Order, and Myth" (1923)[60] attributed the importance of a scientific discovery:

> In using the myth, in manipulating a continuous parallel between contemporaneity and antiquity, Mr. Joyce is pursuing a method which others must pursue after him. . . . It is simply a way of controlling, of ordering, of giving a shape and a significance to the immense panorama of futility and anarchy which is contemporary history.

So Kenner can claim a fairly high degree of plausibility when he suggests that Eliot "may well have had in mind at one time a kind of modern *Aeneid*, the hero crossing seas to pursue his destiny, detained by one woman and prophesied to by another, and encountering visions of the past and the future, all culminated in a city both founded and yet to be found, unreal and oppressively real, . . ." Indeed, Kenner proposes that the *Aeneid*, and notably its sixth book, provides a much more plausible "controlling scheme" for the first four parts of the poem than does Jessie L. Weston's *From Ritual to Romance* and Sir James Frazer's *The Golden Bough*, to both of which Eliot proclaims a profound debt in his notes. Yet for all its appeal, Kenner's scheme remains a conjecture based on tentative textual evidence. All that we can know for sure is that here again the *Aeneid*, and specifically the Dido episode, furnishes isolated images for a poem that explicitly takes as its matter "A heap of broken images" (l.22) from the entire Western (and Eastern!) cultural tradition. On what grounds can we claim that Virgil deserves a more central position than does Weston or Frazer or indeed Ovid, Dante, Baudelaire, and other poets cited more frequently in the notes than Virgil is?

This is certainly the case in "The Hollow Men" (1925), where we have absolutely no evidence apart from Eliot's apparent fondness for the sixth book of the *Aeneid* to believe that "the tumid river" where the Hollow Men in part IV "grope together / And avoid speech" is reminiscent of Virgil's Styx.[61] In contrast, "the ivory gates" in part VI of "Ash-Wednesday" (1930), between which "the blind eye creates / The empty forms," are no doubt an allusion to the gates through which Aeneas emerged from the underworld:

Sunt geminae Somni portae; quarum altera fertur
cornea, qua veris facilis datus exitus umbris,
altera candenti perfecta nitens elephanto,
sed falsa ad caelum mittunt insomnia.

(Aen. 6.893–96)

(There are two gates of Sleep; one is said to be of horn, through which an easy exit is granted to true shades; the other sparkles all over with shining ivory, but [through it] the spirits send false dreams into the light.)

The phrase is an apt one for a passage dealing with the illusions of life—"the dreamcrossed twilight between birth and dying." At the same time, it is difficult to see that Virgil has contributed much more than a familiar image.

If up to this point Eliot's poetry displays little more than occasional images demonstrating his fondness for Books 1, 4, and 6 of the *Aeneid*—or, more specifically, for a few isolated scenes from those books—based mainly on recollections of schoolboy reading, the situation changes appreciably after 1930. It may seem surprising at first glance that Eliot's *Criterion*, unlike many other literary and cultural journals of the day, failed to acknowledge the bimillennial celebrations of 1930 by even so much as a note in one of the regular reports from other countries or reviews of foreign journals. But a letter Eliot wrote to Stephen Spender in 1932 may contain the simplest explanation. "What I chiefly dislike about Goethe is the fact that he is having a centenary. I always dislike everybody at the centenary moment."[62] If we can take Eliot at his word, then how much greater the dislike at a bimillennial than at a centenary moment!

However that may be, the evidence suggests that Eliot did take note of the celebrations because in the years after 1930 he begins to refer to Virgil in his essays and in his "Commentaries" for *Criterion*. In his "Commentary" for January 1933, written from the United States, where Eliot believed that "communistic theories appear to have more vogue among men of letters than they have yet reached in England," his review of two works of Marxist literary criticism leads to the conclusion that the Christian critic is capable of appreciating good writing even in a Marxist.

> But the Marxian is compelled to scorn delights . . . and live laborious days in deciding what art ought to be. For this knowledge of literature he is obliged to apply himself, not to the furtive and facile pleasures of Homer and Virgil—the former a person of doubtful identity and citizenship, the latter a sychophantic [*sic*] supporter of a middle-class imperialist dynasty, but rather to the social criticism of Hemingway and Dos Passos.[63]

(We note the recurrence of the term *imperialist*, which still has for Eliot the positive associations that he confessed in 1924.) His 1935 essay on "Religion and Literature" contains the first reference to a bimillennial appreciation that came to play a central role in Eliot's view of the Roman poet: Theodor Haecker's *Virgil, Father of the West*, which Eliot cites as "an example of literary criticism given greater significance by theological interests."[64] His essay on "In Memoriam" (1936) characterizes Tennyson in terms that throw light on his understanding of Virgil. "Tennyson is not only a minor Virgil, he is also with Virgil as Dante saw him, a Virgil among the Shades, the saddest of all English poets, among the Great in Limbo, the most instinctive rebel against the society in which he was the most perfect conformist."[65] These three references make it clear that Virgil now has come to represent considerably more for Eliot than a source of images: His reading about the Roman poet has confirmed Eliot in his conviction that Virgil has political and religious views sympathetic to his own and, moreover, that his social conformity was not the toadyism of which Robert Graves was to accuse him, but in fact an ironic type of rebellion.

What links Eliot most conspicuously to his British contemporaries is the new appreciation of the *Georgics*, which assumed an increasingly central role in his view of Virgil during the 1930s—an importance not anticipated by Edmund Wilson when, in his essay on Eliot, he wrote, "To modern readers, the subjects of the 'Georgics'—bee-keeping, stock-raising, and so forth—seem unsuitable and sometimes annoying in verse."[66] To be sure, Eliot's most explicit statement occurs in the radio talk of 1951 on "Virgil and the Christian World"; but it will become apparent that the talk represents a summation of views developed during the 1930s.

In "Virgil and the Christian World," Eliot sets out to define the "chief characteristics of Virgil which make him sympathetic to the Christian mind" (125), and he proposes to do so by tracing the significance of a few key words—notably *labor, pietas,* and *fatum*—according to the method that he admired in Haecker's *Virgil, Father of the West.* Eliot begins his investigation with the *Georgics,* which he calls "essential to an understanding of Virgil's philosophy" (125). Eliot dismisses the technical agricultural aspects of the work, for which most people "have neither the command of Latin necessary to read them with pleasure, nor any desire to remind ourselves of schooltime agonies." Instead, he recommends to his readers the translation of Day Lewis. (Otherwise, throughout the essay, he quotes translations from the Loeb Classical Library.) Why, Eliot inquires, did Virgil devote his "time, toil and genius" to such a work? He sensibly dismisses any crude didactic conception of the *Georgics* and also the possibility that Virgil was presuming to teach Roman farmers their business or to provide a manual for prospective landowners or even to furnish a historical record of contemporary agricultural techniques. "It is more likely that he hoped to remind absentee landowners, careless of their responsibilities and drawn by love of pleasure or love of politics to the metropolis, of the fundamental duty to cherish the land."

At this point we approach the reason for Eliot's focus on the *Georgics.* "Whatever his conscious motive, it seems clear to me that Virgil desired to affirm the dignity of agricultural labour, and the importance of good cultivation of the soil for the well-being of the state both materially and spiritually" (125). From the early 1930s on, Eliot's "Commentaries" in the *Criterion* returned obsessively to the notion of rural values, which he regarded rather simplistically as the panacea for contemporary social ills. In 1931, for instance, in a review of books by Harold Laski and Lord Lymington, Eliot concluded that neither liberalism nor conservatism offered a doctrine that constituted a worthy adversary for Communism—largely because they ignore the religious foundations of political philosophy.[67] The difficulty, as Eliot analyzes it, is that they present the problem "as primarily an economic or even a military one" (72), whereas Eliot would prefer to see it put in another way.

The essential point is that agriculture ought to be saved and re-vived because agriculture is the foundation for the Good Life in any society; it is in fact the normal life. What matters is not that we should grow the bulk of our own wheat, even if that were possible, in pursuit of the chimera of independence; but that the land of the country should be used and dwelt upon by a stable community engaged in its cultivation.

If only the wages are adequate, "agricultural life is capable of being the best life for the majority of any people." Eliot's peroration culminates in the lofty claim that "only in a primarily agricultural society, in which people have local attachments to their small domains and small com-munities, and remain, generation after generation, in the same place, is genuine patriotism possible."

Similar thoughts are repeated throughout the 1930s. In a piece pub-lished in 1938, just a few months before his journal ceased to appear, Eliot observed that "the two most serious long-distance problems we have, apart from the ultimate religious problem, are the problem of Education and the problem of the Land—meaning by the latter the problem, not merely of how to grow enough food, but of how to obtain a proper balance between country and town life."[68] Unlike such georgi-cists as Sackville-West and Day Lewis, Eliot entertains no thoughts himself of moving to the country in order to participate in this roman-tically glorified communal existence. "I should myself find it as difficult to live in the country as to give up smoking—more difficult, for my urban habits are of much longer standing than the habit of smoking: they are, indeed, pre-natal." Rather patronizingly, he does not wish to see genuine country life ruined by the importation of such urban dis-tractions as the wireless, which can "tempt country folk to stay up too late when they ought to go to bed in order to get up early." Neverthe-less, he clings to his theoretical view that "the real and spontaneous country life—not *legislated* country life—is the right life for the great majority in any nation."

The ideas on social reform that Eliot developed during the 1930s come close to what, a decade later in "Virgil and the Christian World," Eliot was to call "the *spirit* of the *Georgics*" (125): "the attitude toward the soil, and the labour of the soil, which is there expressed, is some-thing that we ought to find particularly intelligible now, when urban agglomeration, the flight from the land, the pillage of the earth and the squandering of natural resources are beginning to attract attention" (126). Whereas the Greeks taught us to appreciate the dignity of leisure and the life of contemplation, "Virgil perceived that agriculture is fun-damental to civilization, and he affirmed the dignity of manual labour"

(126). Noting that the Christian monastic orders conjoined the contemplative life and the life of manual labour, Eliot speculates that "the insight of Virgil was recognized by monks who read his works in their religious houses" (126)—a speculation not confirmed by studies of the reception of Virgil in the Middle Ages.[69] But Eliot is correct in his general assumption that Virgil's "devotion to Rome was founded on the devotion to the land, to the particular region, to the particular village, and to the family in the village" (126)—even though his understanding of Virgil's ruralism lacks the darker aspects that we now perceive there.

We have already noted that Eliot was wholly an urban creature whose experience of the country was almost entirely literary. It has been pointed out that his idealization of rural life as the prescription for social salvation was influenced by Charles Maurras, whose analysis was based upon the situation in France, where a true peasantry still existed.[70] Similarly, his recognition of Virgil as a precursor of rural redemption was probably prompted by others. The allusion in "Virgil and the Christian World" to "schooltime agonies" suggests that he may have been exposed to the *Georgics* at some point in his education. It has been suggested that the title of his first collection of essays, *The Sacred Wood* (1920), as well as the allusion to the "silence from the sacred wood" in the early "Ode" from *Ara Vos Prec* (1919) is based on the passage immediately following the lines about *labor improbus*.[71]

> prima Ceres ferro mortalis vertere terram
> instituit, cum iam glandes atque arbuta sacrae
> deficerent silvae et victum Dodona negaret.
>
> (1.147–49)

(Ceres first taught mortals to turn the soil with iron when the acorns and berries of the sacred wood ran short and Dodona denied them food.)

(But in that case must we turn to the eighth *Eclogue* to explain "The accents of the now retired / Profession of the calamus" that immediately follows those lines or the subsequent "Children singing in the orchard"? At a certain point, surely, one must concede a certain originality of imagination to the poet.) Others have pointed out that a line in the second part of "Coriolan" (1931; "Difficulties of a Statesman")— "And the frogs (O Mantuan) croak in the marshes"—is an explicit reference to Virgil and the "frogs singing their ancient lament in the mire" (*Geo.* 1.378: *et veterem in limo ranae cecinere querelam*).[72] In general, however, it is more likely that Eliot's attention was drawn to the *Georgics* and their relevance to his emerging ruralism not by any first-hand acquaintance with them but by his reading of Theodor Haecker's *Virgil, Father of the West*,[73] to which he had already drawn attention in 1935 and whose author he called in 1946 "that great critic and good European."[74] To be sure, Haecker's chapter on what he calls "Farmers" is much briefer and less detailed than the one on the *Eclogues* ("Shepherds"), which he had himself translated. But he makes essentially the points that Eliot appropriates in "Virgil and the Christian World." It is Haecker's (incorrect) notion that the medieval monks cultivated their fields according to Virgil's prescriptions; he stresses, as Eliot does, the contribution of *labor improbus*, without noting the ambivalence of toil that has been revealed by recent classicists; and above all, he identifies as the unique greatness of Virgil's work its recognition that the true meaning of toil—"one of mankind's greatest problems, and today, when that meaning has been lost, one of the most vexed and perplexed"—is to be found with the farmer, in agricultural life.[75]

By 1940, in short, all the elements were present that were required for Eliot's appreciation of the *Georgics*: the emergence of his agricultural theory of society based on Maurras; the belief, based on Haecker, that Virgil supported his views regarding the rural basis of a healthy society; and the publication of Day Lewis's translation, which made readily accessible the text of Virgil's linguistically most difficult poem. Accordingly, we can agree with considerable confidence when critics point to passages in Eliot's *Four Quartets* that are reminiscent of the *Georgics*.[76] A Virgilian agrarianism is evident especially in "East Coker" (written 1940), which opens with a vision in which the poet watches peasants from the English past joined in "daunsinge":

> Mirth of those long since under earth
> Nourishing the corn. Keeping time,
> Keeping the rhythm in their dancing
> As in their living in the living seasons
> The time of the seasons and the constellations
> The time of milking and the time of harvest
> The time of the coupling of man and woman
> And that of beasts.

Although such passages reflect the spirit and also the images of the *Georgics* and are consistent with the modern georgicism currently common in Sackville-West and Day Lewis, it requires a considerable stretch of the imagination to be persuaded that Eliot needed a Virgilian source for such specific images as "the ragged rock in the restless waters" ("The Dry Salvages" II) or a phrase in the lines ("The Dry Salvages" I):

It tosses up our losses, the torn seine,
The shattered lobsterpot, the broken oar
And the gear of foreign dead men.[77]

For if "the broken oar" is supposed to be inspired by Virgil's *fractos remos* (5.209), then must we turn, say, to Melville for "the shattered lobsterpot" or to Joseph Conrad for "the gear of foreign dead men"? At times there is the danger that Eliot's epigraphs, notes, and other references have stimulated his critics to feats of excessive ingenuity.

If the first stage of Eliot's Virgilianism, as we have seen, consisted principally of a few fragmented images from early books of the *Aeneid* that he shored against his ruins, the second focused mainly on agrarian notions that were developed during the thirties and summed up retrospectively in "Virgil and the Christian World" (1951). To understand the third stage—Eliot's view of Virgil as the exemplary classic, which emerges most sharply in "What is a Classic" (1944)—we must pause to examine the context within which the lecture was written, for it constitutes not so much an utterly original view as, rather, a summation of views current in the early 1940s.

ANNUS MIRABILIS VIRGILIANUS

If the 1930s marked the decade of the *Georgics*, the 1940s witnessed a return to the *Aeneid*, signaled symbolically by the establishment of the Virgil Society.[78] The Virgil Society was the brainchild of Father Bruno Scott James, a convert to Catholicism who cultivated a particular enthusiasm for Virgil. Although the secretary of the Classical Association, whom Father Bruno approached late in 1942, had doubts about the feasibility of the project, he decided to ask for the opinion of Jackson Knight, a classics don at the University College of the South West at Exeter. Knight, respected among British classicists as a Virgil scholar, was at that time correcting the proofs of his book *Roman Vergil*, which he had written rather hastily in the pre-war urgency of the summer of 1939 and the winter of 1939–40.[79] Knight was enthusiastic about the plan because it appeared to him that it might thereby be possible "to link Virgil to the growing problems of the modern world." As Knight expressed his view of the potential scope and membership of the society, "the subject of Virgil is . . . large, co-extensive even with the whole human plight and adventure: for Virgil, and perhaps Virgil alone, is just such a poet—reaching everywhere." Accordingly they announced the proposed society in *The Times Educational Supplement* (January 9, 1943) and arranged a founding dinner on January 12, 1943, to which a few potential sponsors were invited, including T. S. Eliot and Vita Sackville-West.

Knight put Eliot's name on the list no doubt because Eliot had recommended *Roman Vergil* to Faber and Faber, where it was to be published in 1944. Vita Sackville-West was presumably included because Knight, as he proclaimed in the preface to the second edition of *Roman Vergil* (1944), regarded *The Land* as "probably the most Vergilian of all recent poems." Though Eliot was unable to attend the dinner at Brown's Hotel, the society was duly formed in the course of 1943, and Knight was invited to serve as its first president. Knight accepted, but only on condition that Eliot be asked to hold the office first—assuming that Eliot, in view of his public standing as the leading man of letters in England, would be a tactically shrewder choice for the position of founding president. (In his biography Wilson Knight mentions his brother's subsequent disappointment at the circumstance that the presidency did not in fact devolve to him until 1949.) Eliot agreed and in 1944 delivered his presidential address under the title "What is a Classic?" The same *annus mirabilis Virgilianus*, therefore, witnessed in England the establishment of the Virgil Society, the publication of what may be regarded as the major scholarly book on Virgil in the first half of the twentieth century, and a significant affirmation of Virgil by perhaps the leading literary figure of the day.

The scope of *Roman Vergil* is immense, covering the ancient world before Virgil, his life and work, the poetic traditions of antiquity, the historical background and context of his works, his language and style, the manuscript tradition of his poetry, and his subsequent influence. As one contemporary reviewer put it, "Mr. Knight's purpose is to give a comprehensive survey of the whole Virgilian landscape, beginning with Hammurabi in Mesopotamia in 2500 B.C. and ending with Dr. Gogarty to-day—all in 348 admirably-phrased and arranged pages."[80] Noting that "the 'collapse of civilization' was the predominant obsession in Vergil's day," Knight stresses the hopefulness that characterizes Virgil's view of humanity.[81] He concludes, with due warnings about overplaying the analogies, that "comparisons should be increasingly valuable, especially as our own times really reflect more and more the tendencies of antiquity" (316). To make his point, Knight refers repeatedly to such modern poets as Pound, Yeats, Kipling, Robinson Jeffers, W. H. Auden, and Christopher Isherwood; and he approaches Virgil with critical methods adapted from J. Livingston Lowes' study of Coleridge in *The Road to Xanadu*. Above all, he presents Virgil in such a manner that he sometimes sounds like a pre-Christian T. S. Eliot in thought and style.

It is almost predictable that a book approaching Virgil with the insights of Frazer and Jung, with the sensibilities of Eliot and Auden, and with such a bold scope, would not appeal to British scholars of the discipline that had remained least affected by modernism. As a result, Maurice Bowra, who had supported Knight's earlier (and unsuccessful) application for a doctorate (and who, himself lacking the requisite editorial temperament, was chagrined that he had not been appointed to the Regius Chair of Greek at Oxford), advised him not to submit *Roman Vergil* as the basis for a second attempt: "The standards of a D.Litt. are purely academic and bear no relation to the cultural value of a work."[82] But the considerable popular success of Knight's book, which went into a second edition almost immediately and was published by Penguin in a revised and expanded edition in 1966, suggests the readiness of the British public for a new appreciation of Virgil.

To these significant events must be added two other works from the same period. The publication of C. S. Lewis's *A Preface to Paradise Lost* (1942) and Maurice Bowra's *From Virgil to Milton* (1945; completed in 1944), addressed as they were to a general audience of non-classicists, contributed appreciably to the renewed public interest in Virgil among a new generation of readers inasmuch as both works placed Virgil not at the derivatory end of an ancient epic tradition beginning with Homer but at the beginning of a new one extending from late classical antiquity down to *Paradise Lost*. Lewis, distinguishing between what he called the "primary epic" of Homer and the "secondary epic" of Virgil, redressed the balance that since the Romantics had tipped the scales in favor of Homer.

> The truth is that Primary Epic neither had, nor could have, a great subject in the later sense. That kind of greatness arises only when some event can be held to effect a profound and more or less permanent change in the history of the world, as the founding of Rome did, or still more, the fall of man. Before any event can have that significance, history must have some degree of pattern, some design. The mere endless up and down, the constant aimless alternations of glory and misery, which make up the terrible phenomenon called a Heroic Age, admit no such design. No one event is really very much more important than another.[83]

Bowra, picking up the argument (which he rephrases in terms of "oral" and "literary" epic), begins with the assumption that literary epic "flourishes not in the heyday of a nation or of a cause but in its last days or in its aftermath."[84] Accordingly, the poet steps back and attempts with analytical detachment as well as a certain melancholy to sum up the meaning of the historical process. Because Virgil is a "poet of transition," his glorification of the Roman spirit is "tempered by a sense of weariness and futility" (29). Writing during the Second World War, Bowra recognizes that Virgil "sees war from the standpoint of a suffering civilian as a chaos of horror and muddle" (41). He is the poet of war as experienced by the average person. His hero is not the man of single-handed glory but the leader with administrative ability whose goal is social rather than personal (13). In total congruence with the ironic view that emerged from the experiences of the Great War (in which he had served), Bowra presents the *Aeneid* as an epic in which "the old conception of a fight to the finish has been replaced by something nearer to life and in its way more painful and more appalling" (42).

The common denominator implicitly underlying all these statements is the modern view of Virgil as a poet whose vision is dark enough to accommodate the chaos of World War II. As Lewis puts it, "With Virgil European poetry grows up" (37).

If we approach Eliot's "What is a Classic?" in this context, we can see that it exemplifies this widely shared British belief. Most of the address, to be sure, is concerned with the definition of "the Classic" generally. Beginning with the assumption that "a classic can only occur when a civilization is mature" (55),[85] he defines that maturity more precisely as maturity of mind, maturity of manner, maturity of language, and perfection of the common style. He singles out the *Divine Comedy* as the exemplary classic in a modern European language but states his opinion that "we have no classic age, and no classic poet, in English" (59) because the Elizabethan period was not wholly mature and during the age of Milton the language was still in the process of formation.

He then goes on to rehearse the specified characteristics with reference to Virgil. Maturity of mind, in the first place, requires the consciousness of history. In absolute consistency with Lewis, and perhaps under the direct influence of *A Preface to Paradise Lost*, Eliot asserts, "This is a consciousness which the Romans had, and which the Greeks, however much more highly we may estimate their achievement . . . could not possess" (61). Virgil, with his constant adaptation of the traditions of Greek literature along with his understanding of what Eliot calls the historical "relatedness" of the Greek and Trojan cultures, contributed greatly to the development of that consciousness of history. Moving from maturity of mind to maturity of manners, Eliot turns for his example to Aeneas's encounter with the shade of Dido in what we know to be his favorite book of the *Aeneid*, Book 6: "not only one of the most poignant, but one of the most civilized passages in poetry" (62). Eliot appreciates especially the moral subtlety of the scene because "Dido's behaviour appears almost as a projection of Aeneas' own conscience." What matters to Eliot is not that Dido offers Aeneas "perhaps the most telling snub in all poetry" but that "Aeneas does not forgive himself." It is this instance of civilized manners, according to Eliot, that "proceeds to testify to civilized consciousness and conscience." As for the third point—and here Eliot is echoing not only his own thoughts in "Tradition and the Individual Talent" but also Knight's application of those thoughts to Virgil in his chapter "Tradition and Poetry"—the maturity of Virgil's style "would not have been possible without a literature behind him, and without his having a very intimate knowledge of this literature" (63).

Toward the end of his essay, Eliot adds "comprehensiveness" to his list of characteristics of the classic. Although Goethe appears to Eliot to be limited by his age, his language, and his culture, Virgil's universality is evident in the "sense of destiny" that comes to consciousness in the *Aeneid* (68). Aeneas is not a happy or successful man but a "man in fate," exiled for a higher purpose: "He is the symbol of Rome, and, as Aeneas is to Rome, so is ancient Rome to Europe." For this reason "Virgil acquires the centrality of the unique classic; he is at the centre of European civilization, in a position which no other poet can share or usurp" (68). And because Europe, even "in its progressive mutilation and disfigurement," remains for Eliot "the organism out of which any greater world harmony must develop" (69), it is our need to cling to Virgil, "our classic, the classic of all Europe" (70).

Eliot's essay is a fascinating and important summary of views he had been refining for a quarter of a century—at least since "Tradition and the Individual Talent" (1919). However, the passages specifically dealing with Virgil can claim no high degree of originality, indebted as they are to Haecker's *Virgil, Father of the West* for thoughts on Virgil's universality, to Lewis's *A Preface to Paradise Lost* for Virgil's maturity of mind as manifest in his sense of history, and to Knight's *Roman Vergil* for his understanding of Virgil's maturity of language. Even his appreciation of Virgil's maturity of manners is anticipated by Sainte-Beuve, whom Eliot mentions in the opening sentences of his essay and who stated that we can learn from Virgil "une leçon de goût, d'harmonie, de beauté humaine soutenue et moderée."[86] Indeed, the most persuasive argument in support of Gareth Reeves's thesis that Eliot's two essays should not be permitted to cast a retrospective light on his earlier poetry is not the simple chronological fact that they were written later[87] but the critical fact that they are so utterly derivative in content. In the final analysis, however, it was Eliot who was making the pronouncements, a circumstance that assured a degree of attention to which more scholarly works—even those by Lewis, Knight, and Bowra, which attained considerable popular success—might not aspire. Eliot was summing up the views of a generation toward Virgil, and it is no accident that in the wartime of 1944 the Virgil he emphasizes is no longer the author of the *Georgics* but the poet of the *Aeneid*, the same work that Lewis, Bowra, and others were rediscovering. It was this rediscovered *Aeneid* that left its imprint on several writers of the generation.

THE *AENEID* IRONIZED

Cyril Connolly, "the most overeducated boy that Eton produced in this century,"[88] whose literary education was further supervised by Maurice Bowra at Oxford, lived with Virgil throughout his entire literary lifetime. His first publication (1927), a review of a new edition of Laurence Sterne's works, concludes with a reference to Palinurus, the Trojan pilot who—to propitiate Neptune—loses his life on the final leg of Aeneas's voyage from Sicily to Italy. That early review was reprinted in a collection of Connolly's essays which bore an epigraph from the third *Eclogue*: *claudite iam rivos, pueri; sat prata biberunt* ("close the sluices, boys; the meadows have had enough to drink").[89] Shortly following its publication, Connolly wrote an extensive and knowledgeable appreciation of *Roman Vergil* for *The Observer* (April 2, 1944), in which he praised not only Knight's meticulous philology but, in particular, his use of the anthropological methods of Frazer and the mythic insights of Jung.

Years later, Connolly wrote an amusing account of buying a pocket Virgil as a gift for Ezra Pound's eighty-fourth birthday. Seeking an omen for the occasion, he suggested that they attempt a *sors Virgiliana* and, opening the volume at random, put his finger on the concluding lines of the *Georgics*.[90] Under Pound's baleful gaze, Connolly translated the passage in which Virgil tells of dallying in Naples and plying the arts in leisure while Caesar was thundering across the world in war and imposing his laws onto the nations. Connolly presumably was unaware of Pound's distaste for Virgil, and the fatal passage—assuming the anecdote is true—added injury to the insult. But from Connolly's point of view, the selection of that particular gift is simply another indication of the esteem in which he held Virgil from beginning to end. This esteem emerges most vividly in the work that Noel Annan calls Connolly's masterpiece and "the tombstone of the Oxford Wits," *The Unquiet Grave* (1944).[91]

At first glance Connolly's prose poem, which was published anonymously in 1944, contains little to justify the elaborate Virgilian nexus. The work bears the subtitle "A Word Cycle by Palinurus" (that same Palinurus who put in a brief appearance in Connolly's earliest book review), and the title page displays the penultimate line of *Aeneid* 5, which Aeneas addresses to his lost friend: *o nimium coelo et pelago confise sereno* ("o, too trustful of the serenity of sky and sea").[92] The prefatory material continues with three epigraphs beginning with a passage from Lemprière's *Classical Dictionary* identifying Palinurus as Aeneas's pilot who

> fell into the sea in his sleep, was three days exposed to the tempests and waves of the sea and at last came safe to the seashore near Velia, where the cruel inhabitants of the place murdered him to obtain his clothes: his body was left unburied on the seashore.

It goes on to cite a few lines from Servius's commentary on *Aeneid* 6.378, to the effect that the Lucanians (the Italic tribe assumed to have murdered Palinurus), suffering from an epidemic, were told by the Oracle, "The shade of Palinurus must be appeased!" Accordingly they dedicated a cenotaph and a sacred grove to him not far from Velia. As its third epigraph, the first edition contained a passage from Ovid's *Fasti*, which was replaced in the revised edition by a passage from Dryden's translation of the *Aeneid*, describing the cliffs of the Sirens,

> A shelfy Coast,
> Long infamous for Ships, and Sailors lost;
> And white with Bones . . .
>
> (Aen. 5.864–65)

where Aeneas first realized that his pilot had fallen overboard. Finally, the first two sections bear headings referring to Palinurus: *Ecce Gubernator* (Behold the Pilot) and *Te Palinure Petens* ("Seeking you, Palinurus"). And the epilogue, to which we shall return, amounts to a psychiatric analysis of Palinurus entitled "Who Was Palinurus?"

The body of the work (some ninety-five pages in the first edition) amounts to a commonplace book featuring often extensive quotations interspersed with Connolly's own aphorisms and descriptive passages. As Connolly explained in his introduction to the revised edition (xi),

> *The Unquiet Grave* is inevitably a war-book. Although the author tried to extricate himself from the war and to escape from his time and place into the bright empyrean of European thought, he could not long remain above the clouds. He was an editor living in Bedford Square who kept a journal in three little note-books provided by his wise printer between the autumn of 1942 and the autumn of 1943. As a man, he was suffering from a private grief,— a separation for which he felt to blame; as an editor, he was struggling against propaganda (the genial guidance of thought by the state which undermines the love of truth and beauty); as a Lon-

doner, he was affected by the dirt and weariness, the gradual draining away under war conditions of light and colour from the former capital of the world and, lastly, as a European, he was acutely aware of being cut off from France.

Accordingly he set out, through generous quotation, to demonstrate the affinity between French and British thought and, moreover, to "proclaim his faith in the unity and continuity of Western culture in its moment of crisis" (xii) as displayed in the works of those he calls "the Sacred Twelve"—Horace, Virgil, Villon, Montaigne, La Fontaine, La Rochefoucauld, La Bruyère, Baudelaire, Pope, Leopardi, Rimbaud, and Byron—which contain "the maximum of emotion compatible with a classical sense of form" (3). In one sense, then, the book constitutes an anthology of Western culture since the Greeks: in sum, "sanctions rather than originality" (xii).

At the same time, the book is an intensely personal document, and it is here that the figure of Palinurus emerges as the prototype. In his effort to write "at the same level of intention" as do the Sacred Twelve, he announces his plan to share with us

> the doubts and reflections of a year, a word-cycle in three or four rhythms; art, love, nature and religion: an experiment in self-dismantling, a search for the obstruction which is blocking the flow from the well and whereby the name of Palinurus is becoming an archetype of frustration.
>
> (3)

In the first section, "*Ecce Gubernator*," Palinurus (the author's code name) exposes himself to us through his views on various subjects. In the opening sentences, for instance, we learn of his frustration as a writer. Although it is clear "that the true function of a writer is to produce a masterpiece and that no other task is of any consequence" (1), he is ironically prevented by his very literary occupations—in journalism, broadcasting, propaganda, film-writing—from attaining that goal. Similarly, in subsections on "Love and Anxiety" and "Women," he reveals the human failures that have contributed to his anxiety. The two key figures who emerge as archetypes for his state of *Angst*, which leads through thoughts of narcotics to suicide, are Pascal and Leopardi, who dominate "because when they died they were the same age as Palinurus (thirty-nine)" (xiv).

The second section, "*Te Palinure Petens*," beginning with the evocation of four of Connolly's friends who have recently committed suicide, moves very quickly to subsections entitled "Wisdom of Sainte-Beuve" and "Wisdom of Chamfort," two writers who dispel the pessimism of the first section with their resignation and courage. The last section, "La clé des chants," finds "Enemies of Angst" (95) in reminiscences of the streets of Paris and Mediterranean harbor scenes, which are presented in alternating passages under the general auspices of Flaubert and Baudelaire. By the end of the year, on the festival of Lemuria designed to propitiate the wandering evil spirits of the dead, he is finally able to register "departure of my tormentors. Philosophic calm, soaring Hope, manic exaltation, mysterious freedom from Angst. Dare I suppose that a cure has been accomplished, the bones of Palinurus buried and his ghost laid?" (102–3) Having achieved a state of "bio-psychic equilibrium," Palinurus is able to look beyond himself.

> When the present slaughter terminates humanity can survive only through a return to the idea of happiness as the highest good, happiness which lies not in Power or in the exercise of the Will, but in the flowering of the spirit, and which in an unwarped society should coincide with consciousness.
>
> (123–24)

At the end of his year of introspection, the war continues, still disfiguring the landscapes of his memory, but Palinurus through that very act of memory has found the shrine that will bring him peace:

> There, in the harsh sunshine, among the sea-holly and the midday plant, eringo and mesembrianthemum, where the tide prints its colophon of burnt drift-wood and the last susurrus of the wave expires on the sand,—naked under his watery sign shall he come to rest; a man too trustful in the calm of sky and sea.
>
> O nimium coelo et pelago confise sereno
> Nudus in ignota, Palinure, jacebis harena.
>
> (125)

The epilogue, an ironically parodistic "psychiatrist's confidential report" on Palinurus, makes it clear that we have been witnessing an act of spiritual healing through which the shade of Palinurus—"the core of melancholy and guilt that works destruction on us from within" (xiii)—is finally laid to rest. The "report" amounts to a recapitulation and analysis of the myth of Palinurus, with extensive quotations in Dryden's translation of the major passages dealing with the pilot. It begins with the diagnosis "Strongly marked palinuroid tendencies" (126) and a prognosis of "Grave." The "clinical picture" reminds us that the story of Palinurus is found in the third, fifth, and sixth books of the *Aeneid*. However, the fact that in the third book everything is seen through Aeneas's eyes "may be a cause of subjective bias, where the references in that book are concerned." Nothing is known of Palinurus's background, nor is there evidence of any inherited psychopathic tendency. "The first mention of Palinurus exhibits him in a confusion-state and suggests that, although usually a well-adjusted and efficient member of society, the pilot was experiencing a temporary "black-out" (126). Following the description of Palinurus's disappearance (*Aen.* 5.833–71), the psychiatrist continues his report:

> The account is full of difficulties. "Te Palinure petens, tibi somnia tristia portans insonti"—"Looking for *you*, Palinurus, bringing you sad visions, guiltless though you are." But was Palinurus guiltless? If, as we suggest, he was tired of the fruitless voyage, horrified by the callousness of Aeneas, by the disasters which he seemed to attract by his rowdy games, by the ultimate burning of some of the ships by the angry women,—that act unforgivable in the eyes of a man of the seas,—then was his disappearance as accidental as Aeneas supposed?
>
> (132)

Referring to Jackson Knight's earlier book, *Cumaean Gates*, the psychiatrist reminds us that Palinurus's removal of the stern of the ship was "a Virgilian echo of the Babylonian Epic of Gilgamish" (133) and then goes on to describe Aeneas's encounter with Palinurus's shade in the underworld.

> Those are all the known facts about Palinurus. Whether he deliberately tried to abandon Aeneas, whether he was the innocent victim of divine vengeance or a melancholy and resentful character who felt his special nautical gift was soon to become unwanted cannot be deduced from the evidence. His bluff sailor's manner may belie his real state of mind.
>
> (137)

According to the psychiatrist, the alternative we accept comes down to "the claims of reason versus those of revealed religion" (137). But as a myth, Palinurus "clearly stands for a certain will-to-failure or repugnance-to-success, a desire to give up at the last moment, an urge towards loneliness, isolation and obscurity." At the same time, he feels remorse and bitterness at failure. "Palinurus, in fact, though he despises the emptiness of achievement, the applause of the multitude and the rewards of fame, comes in his long exile to hate himself for this contempt and so he jumps childishly at the chance to be perpetuated as an obscure cape" (138).

Connolly's brilliant tour de force is a thoroughly ironic modernization of the *Aeneid*. More, certainly, than in any of Eliot's works, Virgil

is the guiding and shaping force behind *The Unquiet Grave*. Every page
provides evidence of Connolly's classical education and his easy familiarity with the text as well as his assumption of an audience attuned to
Virgil. But Connolly goes well beyond any merely structuring use of
the *Aeneid*. In the first place, his selection of Palinurus—the sea pilot
who falls off his ship!—as an archetype, rather than Aeneas himself,
shows an ironic inversion: We are no longer dealing with the hero of an
imperial epic but with an ambivalent, *Angst*-ridden modern who fails
professionally and thereby endangers his companions. In the second
place, this figure from classical epic is liberated from his original context
of myth and religion, that is to say, from the care of priests and oracles,
and handed over to the scrutiny of that most modern of figures, the
psychiatrist. In his review of *Roman Vergil*, as we noted, Connolly
praised Knight's appropriation of Frazer and Jung. Although he indicates no awareness of the Virgilian epigraph to *The Interpretation of
Dreams*, his own analysis of the Palinurus figure is quite consistent with
Freud's implications. Palinurus, after all, is condemned to that very
underworld that Juno, in her imprecation, threatens to arouse. Connolly, in the last line of his book, suggests that Palinurus's very name,
with its etymologically sexual implications, "opens up possibilities of a
deep analysis on Freudian lines, should time permit—and funds be
available" (138).

It is perhaps worth mentioning that *The Unquiet Grave*, although it
enjoyed considerable critical esteem in England and the United States,
failed to please Evelyn Waugh. In addition to the pose of anonymity
and general hodgepodge of the book, as he pointed out in a caustic
review in *The Tablet* (November 1945), he disliked the use of the Palinurus theme, whereby the author sought to impose a form on what
Waugh considered a shapeless whole. However, the parody of Connolly's work evident in Waugh's war trilogy, published under the collective title *Sword of Honour* (1965), contains no allusion to Virgil. It is
possible to see a burlesque of *The Unquiet Grave* in the Latinizing headings of the first part, *Men at Arms* (1952): "Apthorpe Gloriosus,"
"Apthorpe Furibundus," "Apthorpe Immolatus," and "Apthorpe Placa-
tus." The "*pensées*" that Corporal-Major Ludovic composes in the second novel, *Officers and Gentlemen* (1955), were taken by readers to be a
stylistic mock of Connolly's aphorisms. And Everard Spruce, the man
of letters in volume 3, *Unconditional Surrender* (1961), who publishes
Ludovic's *Pensées* anonymously in his journal *Survival*, was recognized
by Connolly and other members of English literary circles as a carica-
ture of Connolly and his journal *Horizon*. But the larger context linking *The Unquiet Grave* to an English Virgilian tradition is wholly absent in Waugh's trilogy.

We can observe an ironic view of the *Aeneid* similar to Connolly's in the work of another Oxford Wit, W. H. Auden. In his poem "Memorial for the City,"[93] Auden stated his sense that modern man following two world wars is living in a post-epic—that is to say, a "Post-Vergilian"—age.

> Even now, in this night
> Among the ruins of the Post-Vergilian City
> Where our past is a chaos of graves and the barbed-wire
>   stretches ahead,
> Into our future till it is lost to sight,
> Our grief is not Greek: As we bury our dead
> We know without knowing there is reason for what we bear.

Auden's view of Virgil is expressed most clearly in his poem "Secondary Epic," which takes its title from the chapter on Virgil in C. S. Lewis's *A Preface to Paradise Lost.* (The poem first appeared in *Homage to Clio* [1960], but the context—and specifically the allusion to Lewis's book—locates it in the world of the 1940s.) Lewis, it will be recalled, distinguishes primary from secondary epic principally on the basis of the meaning vouchsafed the latter by its awareness of history. As examples of Virgil's enlargement of his epic subject, he cites the forward-looking instances of Jupiter's prophecy in Book 1 (the hymn to *imperium* anathematized by Robert Graves), Anchises' vision in Book 6, and the prophetic scenes on Aeneas's shield described in Book 8. It is precisely these scenes that call forth Auden's objections:

> No, Virgil, no:
> Not even the first of the Romans can learn
> His Roman history in the future tense,
> Not even to serve your political turn;
> Hindsight as foresight makes no sense.[94]

How is it, Auden asks, that Virgil's "shield-making god" is unable to foresee the future beyond 31 B.C.? "Wouldn't Aeneas have asked:— 'What next?'" Virgil's device permits us to imagine a continuation to the eighth book added centuries later by a "down-at-heels refugee rhetorician" for the edification

> Of some blond princeling whom loot had inclined
> To believe that Providence had assigned
> To blonds the task of improving mankind.

(Auden's analogy clearly links the siege of Rome by Alaric and the Visigoths in 408–10 A.D. to the siege of Europe by the Germans in the Second World War.) The next twelve italicized lines, representing such an interpolation, demonstrate Auden's ironic mastery of Virgil's epic style.

The last strophe, beginning again with the negative apostrophe ("No, Virgil, no:"), turns to the vision unfolded for Aeneas in the underworld with the critical judgment, "Your Anchises isn't convincing at all." This time Auden reasons that "A shade so long-sighted" as to foresee the wall to be built around Rome by Romulus and the Golden Age to be established by Augustus would also surely note, with ironic enjoyment, "The names predestined for the Catholic boy / Whom Arian Odovacer will depose." For the last Roman emperor deposed by this first barbarian king of Italy (476–93) was the child-ruler Romulus Augustulus. Auden's poem, like Connolly's book (and unlike Eliot's works), displays a detailed acquaintance with the relevant passages of the *Aeneid*. But in this case, the irony is produced not by psychiatric analysis of a Virgilian figure but by the discrediting of any interpretation of history that seeks to justify present reality through past events: In the process Auden implicitly criticizes both the rewriting of history for political purposes and the suppression of evidence that would qualify the (ironic) course of history. Although written later than *The Unquiet Grave*, Auden's poem is an equally exemplary document of his generation's view of Virgil—not the savage contempt of Robert Graves but an admiration qualified by irony.

Anthony Burgess (born 1917), ten years younger than Auden and a graduate of Manchester University, no longer qualifies for inclusion in what Noel Annan defined as "Our Age." But that very difference in generation and background helps to account for the escalation from irony to full-scale parody of the *Aeneid* that we find in Burgess's first novel. *A Vision of Battlements*, although not published until 1965, was written in 1949, still within the period culminating in Eliot's "Virgil and the Christian World" (1951). The novel is set in Gibraltar, where Burgess spent the second half of his war service (1940–46), and constitutes the writer's effort to come to grips with the artificial life surrounding the Rock that he experienced there.[95] It is therefore a war novel or, more precisely, like the *Aeneid* itself, both a war novel and a postwar novel.

Burgess gives no indication that he is aware of the Virgilian traditions discussed earlier in this chapter. Indeed, his use of an epic framework, "diminished and made comic" (8), was suggested primarily by the example of Joyce's *Ulysses*, which is cited in the epigraph, and not by Connolly or Eliot or Knight. However, having decided on "a tyro's method of giving his story a backbone," Burgess used the *Aeneid* with a vengeance. "The names and personalities and events have more to do with Virgil's *Aeneid* than with remembered actuality." His composer-hero, Richard Ennis (who appears in other works by Burgess), is nominally close to Aeneas; in his lectures for the A.V.C.C. (Army Vocational and Cultural Corps, to which he ironically refers as the "Arma Virumque Cano Corps" [13]) he outlines a utopian society in postwar England. His best friend is another A.V.C.C. sergeant named Agate (Virgil's *fidus Achates*). The parallels are so profuse, and the substance so satirically straightforward, that the novel does not require an elaborate analysis.[96]

The prologue takes place aboard a troop ship bound for Gibraltar, where the piano-playing Ennis is the accompanist for a singer, a big blonde Wren (that is, a member of the Women's Royal Naval Service) named June, who (like Juno invoking the fury of the seas against Aeneas) initially takes a strong dislike to him. Her song, "Ocean, be calm! Storm-winds, do not affright! / For we have got this concert on tonight" (15), precedes a huge North Atlantic storm that terminates the rehearsal and leaves Ennis to think about his embarkation leave and the departure from his wife in a bombed-out London: "The sinister lights of distant burning illuminated her face ghastily, but there was no fear there. Death did not seem all that terrible, their love seemed a Troy that a ten-thousand-year siege could not shatter" (17). Although his wife Laurel does not die in the burning city like Creusa, Ennis "pushed his wife farther back, beyond history, to myth. It was the best thing to do; it would ensure a kind of fidelity" (21). (Ironically, following the emotional back-and-forth described in several letters, his wife decides by the end of the novel to leave Ennis.)

After a year in Gibraltar, Ennis has an affair with a dark-haired Spanish widow named Concepción, to whom he gives music lessons; he also tells the story of his past to her, as does Aeneas to Dido in Book 2 of the *Aeneid* after his arrival at Dido's palace. Ennis's father, we learn, was a piano-player married to a singer named "The Blonde Venus"; during a bomb raid, the father was injured by a falling beam, and Ennis—like his namesake—"took him to safety, dragging his bulk painfully by the armpits" (56). He tells her, further, about a visit to fortune-tellers in Alexandria, who disclosed to him something he did not fully understand—"something about I'd only really know what I wanted when I got so hungry that I'd have to eat the table" (57)—an allusion to the dire prophecy of the Harpy Celaeno in Book 3. The first time they sleep together is during a rainstorm (58) like the cloudburst in Book 4 that drives Aeneas and Dido into the cave. Eventually, however, Concepción marries Barasi (an anagram of Iarbas, Dido's principal suitor).

Ennis is constantly thwarted in his efforts by Major Muir, who plays the role of the opposing deity. At one point Ennis's friend Julian Agate executes "a series of small panels dealing with the loves of Zeus. The god was depicted as descending on Leda, Danae, Europa. The face of Muir crowned the body of the swan, the huge frame of the bull, and glinted through the shower of gold" (128). Although the women in Julian's drawings were intended to represent art, science, and technology—all thwarted by the plebeian Muir—his role as a ladies' man also puts him in a position on one occasion to cuckold Ennis with his wife Laurel back in England. The games of Book 5 are represented by footraces down the anteroom of the Engineers' Mess to get at pints of free gin-and-beer along with fistfights (75). In a drunken stupor, Ennis tries to board a boat to sail across to Spain, where he wants to see Concepción one more time, but he falls into the filthy water and experiences a vision inspired by images from Aeneas's crossing of the Acheron in Book 6 (l. 314): "The helpful faces crowded above, hands held out for him, *tendebant manus*. . . . He mounted the steps, his heavy boots squelching, spitting out oil, his clothes clinging like an unclean familiar. The boat set off to the *ulteriorem ripam* and he was left alone" (79). At the end of Chapter 6, Ennis is "finished with the old life, finished with the dead. He was going to reform" (82).

Although the prologue and the first six chapters of the novel correspond roughly to the first five and a half books of the *Aeneid* (the actual visit to the underworld is postponed to a later point), the second part stretches out into sixteen further chapters. Ennis, learning that he has been betrayed by his wife, meets a beautiful Wren named Lavinia Grantham. In the course of several chapters, he competes for her affection with a "barrel-chested slim-hipped giant" (161), Regimental Sergeant-Major Instructor Turner. Reenacting the contest between Aeneas and Turnus for the hand of Lavinia, Ennis eventually meets Turner at the top of the Rock for a seemingly poorly matched battle; but when Ennis sidesteps Turner's mighty blow, the sergeant-major stumbles over the side and kills himself in the fall.

As a result of this and other scandals, Ennis's commanding officer, who has disliked him from the start, forces him into an early discharge. At this point, in the postponed reprise of Book 6 of the *Aeneid*, his friend Agate proposes that they make one last trip across the border into Spain "to consult the Sybil" ([*sic*]; 211), a schoolmistress named Mrs. Carraway, who lives in "a damp old cavern of a house" and tells fortunes by Tarot cards. As in a mad mixture of the sixth book of the *Aeneid* and part 2 of *The Waste Land*, the wind rises and "draughts indeed knifed them from innumerable crannies, from under the doors, from the badly fitting windows" (213). Mrs. Carroway sees birth and death and a poorly managed love affair. "It's one of the worst I've ever seen" (214). On Ennis's last day in Gibralter, he and Julian make a final trip to Spain to test the validity of Mrs. Carroway's readings, and it turns into a drunken descent into the underworld. First they meet Captain Mendoza (a conflation of Palinurus and the Stygian boatman), a disenchanted Military Policeman responsible for transporting drunks and corpses back to their base by ship, who deserted from the U. S. Army by pretending to fall overboard and drown. Encountering Mr. Barasi, Ennis learns that Concepción has died in childbirth. After several hours of wandering in the underworld, Julian and Ennis realize that they have only three minutes to get to the frontier. Rushing back, Julian reflects that "the descent . . . is so easy. But to return involves overmuch labour. It isn't worth it" (235)—an obvious paraphrase of the Sibyl's words to Aeneas: *facilis descensus Averno . . . sed revocare gradum superasque evadere ad auras, / hoc opus, hic labor est* (*Aen.* 6.126–29).

The next day Ennis boards the ship for home. From a letter he learns that Laurel has left him for an American, but he consoles himself in the embraces of the big blonde Wren from the prologue, who has hardly changed since their first encounter years earlier. Afterward Ennis stands alone at the stern, "looking along the ship's wake at the dwindling past. It shook impotent fists, trying to assert an old power, but it knew that it was becoming too small to be anything but ridiculous or lovable" (240).

In his 1965 introduction, Burgess points out that "readers may see in [Ennis] an anticipation of a particular type of contemporary hero, or anti-hero" (9).[97] Though he made his public appearance later than the antiheroes of the 1950s, in point of creation he actually comes before them. "It's as well to remember that the Welfare State rebels were anticipated by the Army rebels, especially those who, stuck and frustrated, waited in vain for the siege of rocky and invincible Troy" (9). In fact, the novel amounts to considerably more than a parody of the *Aeneid.* Ennis is presented as a decent man (*pius Aeneas?*) with the ambition to be a serious composer and, during his service in the army, with the hope of doing a decent job of providing education and culture for the British troops stationed at Gibraltar. But, as antihero, he is thwarted at every step: by the military establishment in the person of Major Muir; by the cultural establishment in the institution of the BBC, which rejects the *Passacaglia* on which he labors throughout his stay in Gibraltar; by local Spanish society in the persons of Concepción's family; and by the troops in the persons of Turner and his bully boys. Yet he perseveres and, on the last page, jots down on the letter announcing Laurel's desertion the theme of a new composition that he plans to undertake when he gets home to postwar England.

In this late postfiguration of the *Aeneid,* in other words, the genre has been totally inverted into what might be called tertiary epic: going beyond the simple heroics of primary epic and the self-conscious historicism of secondary epic, tertiary epic uses the vehicle of the war novel to deny the validity of the heroic and of history altogether. Ennis refuses to acknowledge the order of the military and the burden of the past. He returns to England as a new man—with no father, no wife, no job—to engage with the new postwar reality. Yet the extent to which Burgess clings to the characters and incidents of the *Aeneid* to give form and structure to his antiheroic novel indicates the degree to which Virgil, as a shaping force, still had hold of the British literary imagination in the years immediately following the Second World War.[98]

Virgil in the New World

For most of the four centuries of our history, Virgil has provided dominating images for the American consciousness. In a compelling study, Leo Marx showed that "the pastoral ideal has been used to define the meaning of America ever since the age of discovery."[1] As Marx continues, "The ruling motive of the good shepherd, the leading figure of the classic, Virgilian mode, was to withdraw from the great world and begin a new life in a fresh, green landscape. And now here was a virgin continent!" The bucolic appeal of withdrawal from society into an idealized landscape, which can be detected in TV westerns and advertising copy as well as in our literary classics—has since the middle of the nineteenth century undergone a symptomatic modification as the rural myth has been threatened by history in the form of advancing technology: the machine in the garden of Marx's title. Although he makes no effort to demonstrate or even to suggest specific literary influence, Marx concludes that this encounter of the idyllic with reality is anticipated most fully in Virgil's first *Eclogue*—that indeed this governing theme of American literature is essentially "a modern variant of the design of Virgil's poem" (24).

Others have discovered a similar model for the American experience in the *Aeneid*. Susan Ford Wiltshire has argued that, because "the defining direction of America has always been westward, in terms of both original colonization and internal expansion," it is hardly surprising that "the figure of Aeneas as explorer and colonizer has been conspicuous almost from the beginning."[2] As evidence she cites the prominent occurrence of Aeneas as an analogue in seventeenth-century English accounts of journeys to the New World, as for instance William Strachey's "True Reportory" of an expedition to Virginia in 1609: "At length, after much and weary search (with their barge coasting still before, as Vergil writeth Aeneas did, arriving in the region of Italy called Latium, upon the banks of the River Tiber) . . . they had sight of an extended plain."[3] Strachey adds that the plain embraced half an acre, "or so much as Queen Dido might buy of King Iarbas, which she compassed about with the thongs cut out of one bull hide and therein built her castle of Byrsa" (79).

As Wiltshire reminds us, Howard Mumford Jones had already shown that "the Aeneas image forms the organizing conception behind *The Proceedings of the English Colonie in Virginia*" (Oxford, 1612). In this narrative Captain John Smith is portrayed as an epic hero who "transplants to unknown shores a divinely guided people and is opposed by Powhatan, like Turnus, a hero of equal eminence. Each is surrounded by lesser heroes and weaker men, each nation appeals to its own deities, each side utters appropriate orations."[4]

It is consistent with this background that Virgil occupied a place of honor in the minds of our Founding Fathers. We have already noted (Ch. 1) that the three mottoes of the Great Seal of the Republic were adopted in 1782 from Virgil's poems. When George Washington retired from military service, he ordered for his mantelpiece a bronze sculpture of Aeneas carrying his father from a burning Troy,[5] and the six bronze busts that John Quincy Adams displayed in his study at Quincy, as his "Household Gods," featured one of Virgil.[6] At the time, of course, Virgil's work was still well known to the educated in the original. In the summer of 1783, John Quincy Adams copied out the Latin text of the *Eclogues* and translated all ten into rhymed couplets; that winter he copied and made a prose translation of the entire *Georgics*.[7] Philip Freneau's poems contain numerous echoes, epigraphs, and references from the *Eclogues*, *Georgics*, and *Aeneid*,[8] and quotations from all three major Virgilian works can be found in Thoreau's writings from 1837 to 1857.[9]

In addition many Latin compositions of the age show clear signs of Virgil's influence: e.g., Edmund Don Griffin's "Columbus" (1818), a 104-line poem in epic hexameters, which uses Virgilian vocabulary, phrases, and even lines to establish the analogy between the voyages of Columbus and Aeneas.[10] For instance, an apparition emerges from the waves to threaten Columbus, just as Virgil's Palinurus is warned:

> Ipse gubernabat navem clavumque regebat,
> quando ecce ante oculos ingens, informis imago,
> teque, Columbe, petens, summa sese extulit unda.
>
> (18–20)

(He himself was steering the ship and guiding the rudder when, lo, before his eyes a vast, shapeless image rose from the wave, seeking you, Columbus.)

But Columbus avoids the fate of the unfortunate Palinurus by telling the spirit:

> Me mea fata vocant, fatisque mihi data tellus.
>
> (29)

(My destiny summons me, and a land has been given to me by destiny.)

Around the middle of the nineteenth century, the image of Virgil began to fade from the American consciousness along with classical learning altogether. As Daniel Webster declared in 1847, speaking at the inauguration of the Northern Railroad and dismissing the pastoral revulsion at the intrusion of technology, "New Hampshire, it is true, is no classic ground. She has no Virgil and no Eclogues."[11] By the end of the century, the classical curriculum had been abandoned at many of the nation's leading colleges and universities.

At the same time, although explicit knowledge may have dwindled, the Virgilian patterns often remained in the American consciousness. In his epilogue Leo Marx observes that Nick Carraway in F. Scott Fitzgerald's *The Great Gatsby*, an unsophisticated Westerner confronted with the vulgar East Coast society, displays a pronounced "propensity to Virgilian fantasies" (361). Summing up, he concludes that "the outcome of *Walden*, *Moby-Dick*, and *Huckleberry Finn* is repeated in the typical modern version of the fable; in the end the American hero is either dead or totally alienated from society, alone and powerless, like the evicted shepherd of Virgil's eclogue" (364). Similarly, although not many twentieth-century American writers may share John Quincy Adams's view that the *Georgics* is "the most perfect composition, that ever issued from the mind of man,"[12] Virgil's faith in the values of rural life is closely reflected in the principles of the Southern Agrarians.[13] Before taking up that major group, however, we need to consider several important examples of the Virgilian tradition.

An exemplary figure for this traditional American view of Virgil may be recognized in Willa Cather (1873–1947). Solidly grounded in classics first by tutors in Red Cloud, then at the Lincoln Latin School, and later at the University of Nebraska, Cather drew extensively on Greek and Latin literature from her early journalism down to her late stories. To be sure, her allusions more frequently hint at analogies and do not establish consistent patterns of reference. Yet it is more than a bon mot when one critic observes that the "implied reader" in Cather's works "is clearly someone who shares her own background in the classics."[14] Although the allusions in her early tales and newspaper pieces sometimes seem mainly decorative and intended to impress the reader with the young writer's learning, they gradually take on deeper significance in her major prose fiction.

In *A Lost Lady* (1923), for instance, it is implied that the romances of Ovid's *Heroides*—"the most glowing love stories ever told"—with which the young Niel Herbert is obsessed, prepare him emotionally to understand later the love affairs of the beautiful Marian Forrester. In *The Professor's House* (1925), Godfrey St. Cloud and his friend Tom Outland read Lucretius together on rainy days. But the true *genius loci et libri* is Virgil: It is the *Aeneid* that initially brings them together when the young man persuades the middle-aged historian of his readiness for college by reciting the first fifty lines of *Aeneid* 2. It turns out that Outland read the entire *Aeneid* on the Blue Mesa of New Mexico and that Virgil's words helped him to an attitude of "filial piety" toward the inhabitants of the ancient city whose cliff dwellings he reverently explored.

Not surprisingly, the novel about the colonization of late-seventeenth-century Quebec that Cather wrote during the bimillennial year, *Shadows on the Rock* (1931), contains several Virgilian motifs. Some of these are purely cosmetic, as when a capricious young bishop is described as being "as changeable and fickle as a woman"[15] (with no explicit reference to the famous tag at *Aen.* 4.569–70, *varium et mutabile semper femina*). Another figure's emotions are explained through a Virgilian allusion: "He was one of the unfortunate of this world. You remember, when Queen Dido offers Aeneas hospitality, she says: *Having known misery, I have learned to pity the miserable.* Our poor wood-carrier is like Queen Dido" (163; *Aen.* 1.630, *non ignara mali miseris succurrere disco*). And elsewhere Euclide Auclair, the philosopher-apothecary, feels a moment of intense exile from France: "Not without reason, he told himself bitterly as he looked up at those stars, had the Latin poets insisted that thrice and four times blessed were those to whom it befell to die in the land of their fathers" (263; *Aen.* 1.94–96, *O terque quaterque beati, / quis ante ora patrum Troiae sub moenibus altis / contigit oppetere!*). Such passages make it clear that Cather is addressing a community of readers still well-versed in Virgil; and this assumption on her part enables her on two occasions to introduce allusions that bear a weightier thematic meaning in this novel, which revolves around the westering theme and the culture-bearing function of the French in Canada. At one point the author explains:

> The Ursulines and the Hospitalières, indeed, were scarcely exiles. When they came across the Atlantic, they brought their family with them, their kindred, their closest friends. In whatever little wooden vessel they had laboured across the sea, they carried all; they brought to Canada the Holy Family, the saints and martyrs, the glorious company of the Apostles, the heavenly host.
>
> (97)

Following such a description, so powerfully evocative of Aeneas and his followers, it is not surprising to encounter (again with no identification of the source at *Aen.* 1.6) the words: "*Inferretque deos Latio.* When an adventurer carries his gods with him into a remote and savage country, the colony he founds will, from the beginning, have graces, traditions, riches of the mind and spirit" (98). Such allusions to the *Aeneid,* both explicit and implicit, and the analogy between the Trojan settlement in Latium and the French colonization of Quebec, help us to understand yet another passage. A woodsman tells Auclair that he had met a mutual friend, Father Hector St.-Cyr, at a remote mission in the Canadian wilderness. Once when he woke up during the night, he thought that he heard Father Hector praying:

> I lay still and listened for a long while, but I didn't once hear an Ave Maria, and not the name of a saint could I make out. At last I turned over and told Father Hector that was certainly a long prayer he was saying. He laughed. "That's not a prayer, Antoine," he says; "that's a Latin poem, a very long one, that I learned at school. If I am uncomfortable, it diverts my mind, and I remember my old school and my comrades."
>
> (143)

For this priest in the forests of the Northeast, the *Aeneid* appears to play the same role as it did earlier for Tom Outland in the Southwestern deserts: It provides a key to insights into the mentality of ancient and, from their standpoint, more primitive peoples, whether they be the Latin tribes, the Canadian Nipissing Indians, or the cliff dwellers of New Mexico.

Yet in all these works, the Virgilian allusions, however pervasive, remain incidental. The single novel by Cather in which Virgil clearly informs the whole, providing a pattern rather than random associations, is the one usually regarded as her masterpiece, *My Antonia* (1918). Alerted by the epigraph, *Optima dies . . . prima fugit* (whose source at *Geo.* 3.66–67 is not identified at this point), the attentive reader gradually comes to realize that Cather's novel constitutes her own elegiac *laudes Americae* and a Virgilian appeal for the preservation of agrarian values in the face of the encroaching industrialization that was everywhere evident in the United States. The saga of Antonia Shimerda, the daughter of a Bohemian immigrant family in Nebraska, is recounted in retrospect by her boyhood friend, Jim Burden, who has grown up to become the legal counsel for a great Western railway—and unhappily married to a cold, handsome woman who exemplifies a society grown effete through wealth and detachment from its native roots.

Jim Burden shares many autobiographical characteristics with Willa Cather. Born like her in Virginia's Blue Ridge Mountains, he moves at age ten to his grandparents' farm outside Black Hawk (=Red Cloud), Nebraska, where his boyhood revolves around his friendship with Antonia (=Cather's girlhood friend Annie Pavelka). In preparation for college, Jim studies Latin that is not included in his high school course and, during his last summer at home, begins Virgil on his own. "Morning after morning I used to pace up and down my sunny little room, looking off at the distant river bluffs and the roll of the blond pastures between, scanning the 'Aeneid' aloud and committing long passages to memory" (231).[16] When he reaches Lincoln, where his room is decorated with a map of ancient Rome and a photograph of the theater at Pompeii, Jim comes under the influence of Gaston Cleric, "a brilliant and inspiring young scholar" (257) who has come West for reasons of health and to become head of the Latin Department of the University. From Cleric, Jim learns about Latin and English poetry, about Italy, about Statius and Dante and their veneration of Virgil. But the text that is explicitly cited is the *Georgics*, to which Jim is introduced in the spring of his sophomore year.

> I propped my book open and stared listlessly at the page of the "Georgics" where to-morrow's lesson began. It opened with the melancholy reflection that, in the lives of mortals, the best days are the first to flee. "*Optima dies . . . prima fugit.*" I turned back to the beginning of the third book, which we had read in class that morning. "*Primus ego in patriam mecum . . . deducam Musas*": "for I shall be the first, if I live, to bring the Muse into my country." Cleric had explained to us that "patria" here meant, not a nation or even a province, but the little rural neighbourhood on the Mincio where the poet was born. This was not a boast, but a hope, at once bold and devoutly humble, that he might bring the Muse (but come lately to Italy from her cloudy Grecian mountains), not to the capital, the *palatia Romana*, but to his own little "country"; to his father's fields, "sloping down to the river and to the old beech trees with broken tops."
>
> (263–64)

Although Jim admires Cleric, he has no ambition to become, like him, a scholar. "I could never lose myself for long among impersonal things. Mental excitement was apt to send me with a rush back to my own naked land and the figures scattered upon it" (262). Every new form and idea to which Cleric introduces him reminds him of the places and people of his own "infinitesimal past." Yet it is through Virgil that he comes to understand and appreciate the figures and the landscapes of his own Nebraskan boyhood. Following a visit from Lena, a friend now working as a dressmaker in Lincoln, he thinks about

the other girls from Black Hawk: the Danish laundry girls and the three
Bohemian Marys.

> It came over me, as it had never done before, the relation between
> girls like those and the poetry of Virgil. If there were no girls like
> them in the world, there would be no poetry. I understood that
> clearly, for the first time. This revelation seemed to me inestima-
> bly precious. I clung to it as if it might suddenly vanish.
>
> (270)

Aside from the fact that Virgil's poetry is hardly renowned for its
portrayal of young girls, it is clear that Cather wants us to understand
Virgil's works, and especially the *Georgics*, as the lens through which
Burden organizes the material of his own experience into recognizable
patterns when, years later, he writes the account of his boyhood with
Antonia. Although his narrative has five books rather than four, it has
a clearly georgic rhythm with a pronounced seasonal movement. Many
of the chapters open with references that seem to tie humankind to the
seasons and landscapes. "While the autumn color was growing pale on
the grass and cornfields, things went badly with our friends the Russians" (50). "When spring came, after that hard winter, one could not
get enough of the nimble air. Every morning I wakened with a fresh
consciousness that winter was over" (119). "July came on with that
breathless, brilliant heat which makes the plains of Kansas and Nebraska the best corn country in the world. It seemed as if we could hear
the corn growing in the night" (137). "Winter lies too long in country
towns; hangs on until it is stale and shabby, old and sullen. On the farm
the weather was the great fact, and men's affairs went on underneath it,
as the streams creep under the ice" (180). Before going off to Harvard
Law School, Jim returns home for a vacation and sees the countryside
with new eyes. "The windy springs and the blazing summers, one after
another, had enriched and mellowed that flat tableland; all the human
effort that had gone into it was coming back in long, sweeping lines of
fertility" (306). "I felt the old pull of the earth, the solemn magic that
comes out of those fields at nightfall" (322).

Although Jim's trips across the continent—from his first journey at
age ten to his later travels for the railroad—acquaint him with the
glories of its landscape and especially "the great midland plain of North
America" (3), it is Nebraska in particular that earns his *laudes*. Indeed,
as Burden wonders "whether that particular rocky strip of New England coast about which he had so often told me was Cleric's *patria*"
(265), it becomes clear that Nebraska is the *patria* that Burden hopes to
immortalize through his own account. And the figure who embodies
the spirit of that landscape is Antonia. Most of the characters of the

novel leave Black Hawk and roam the world—Europe, Alaska, the Caribbean—where for the most part they are childless and unhappy: Jim Burden in his miserable marriage in New York; Lena Lingard as a prosperous single businesswoman in San Fransciso; or Tiny Soderball, who returns from the Klondike to San Francisco, wealthy, thin, and hard-faced, interested in nothing but making money (301).

Antonia, in contrast, emerges as the *magna mater* of the Great Plains. Jim holds her in his memory in a succession of pictures, "fixed there like the old woodcuts of one's first primer. . . . She lent herself to immemorial human attitudes which we recognize by instinct as universal and true" (353). While the friends of her youth—Jim, Lena, Tiny, and all the others—have grown sophisticated and prosperous, Antonia alone has remained in the landscape to which she came as a young immigrant girl. Her life has been unremittingly hard, but it has distilled her character into an object of beauty. "She was a battered woman now, not a lovely girl; but she still had that something which fires the imagination, could still stop one's breath for a moment by a look or gesture that somehow revealed the meaning in common things" (353). Antonia loves the trees she has planted on the plains "as if they were people" (340), and she watches over her children, who burst out of the fruit cellar as from a tellurian womb, like "a veritable explosion of life out of the dark cave into the sunlight" (339). While the others live lives of quiet urban despair, Antonia confesses: "I'd always be miserable in a city. I'd die of lonesomeness. I like to be where I know every stack and tree, and where all the ground is friendly" (320).

Antonia's satisfaction and tranquillity was not easily won. As her husband later tells Jim, " 'It was a pretty hard job, breaking up this place and making the first crops grow' " (365). But as in the *Georgics* (1.145–46), *labor omnia vicit / improbus et duris urgens in rebus egestas*. It is this Virgilian Antonia who fills Jim's memory like a Jungian anima.

> "Do you know, Antonia, since I've been away, I think of you more often than of anyone else in this part of the world. I'd have like to have you for a sweetheart, or a wife, or my mother or my sister— anything that a woman can be to a man. The idea of you is a part of my mind; you influence my likes and dislikes, all my tastes, hundreds of times when I don't realize it. You really are a part of me."
>
> (321)

For Cather, in sum, Antonia represents the agrarian values that she imposed romantically on the Nebraskan landscape of her youth and whose loss she began to lament in the years following World War I when modernization, with the ills accompanying its benefits, swept across America. And Virgil is the poet whose works epitomize the values of that idealized, traditional America.

I know of no better recent example for our national internalization of the *Aeneid* than the autobiography of Penn State football coach Joe Paterno, who devotes an entire chapter to the impact on his character of the Virgil to whom he was introduced by his high school Latin teacher at Brooklyn Prep.[17]

So Virgil, and his hero Aeneas, the founder of Rome, entered my life. More than entered it. The adventures of Aeneas seeped into far corners of my mind, into my feelings about what is true and honorable and important. They helped shape everything I have since become. I don't think anybody can get a handle on what makes me tick as a person, and certainly can't get at the roots of how I coach football, without understanding what I learned from the deep relationship I formed with Virgil during those afternoons and later in my life.

(42)

What attracted Paterno to Virgil's hero is the fact that "Aeneas is not a grandstanding superstar" (45); he is "the ultimate team man" (46). In light of such examples, it is hardly surprising that a foreign observer should have concluded that "it would be possible to write a history of the American spirit with reference to Aeneas, whose archetype has generated a sort of national mythologeme."[18]

What matters in all of these American examples, from the seventeenth century to the present, is that in every case Virgil has been appropriated and accommodated to the American experience. In the European examples that we have considered thus far—in England, France, Italy, and Germany—Virgil's poems were recognized as a consoling analogy or welcomed as an escape from the exigencies of the modern world. But the American writers have almost inevitably seized Virgil's works and taken them as justifying patterns for our national experience—from the exploratory and colonizing pattern of the *Aeneid* to the intrusion of technology into the new Saturnian Hesperia and to the agrarian reforms proposed as the appropriate response. It is this proprietary attitude toward the Roman poet, justifying free play with his forms, that characterizes the American response to Virgil in the twentieth century. It is also not true that all the lines of classical learning were broken in the latter half of the nineteenth century. We shall see that most of the modern Virgilians used the poet's forms consciously and from a detailed acquaintance with the Latin originals. Finally, as a result of what can be called "contamination"[19] of forms, we shall see that it is often more appropriate in the United States to speak generally of "Virgilianism" rather than specifically of bucolicism or georgicism.

THE POLITICAL ECLOGUE

Leo Marx's thesis regarding the importance of the first *Eclogue* seems to be confirmed by such evidence as Elizabeth Nitchie's 1930 "Anthology of Poems in English on Vergil and Vergilian Themes,"[20] because the two poems cited as examples of the *Eclogues* are both based specifically on the first *Eclogue*. "The Dawn"[21] by William Ellery Leonard (1876–1944)—a poet and translator who also made poetic adaptations of various ancient myths and legends—amounts to little more than a recollection, in capable elegiac distichs, of the writer's first encounter, during his Wisconsin boyhood, with Virgil's *Eclogues* in an illustrated edition bought for him by his father.

> There in the homestead at Hilton I sat by the window with
>> Vergil:
>> Under the morning star, words like woods to explore.

The poem takes us through the first five lines of the first *Eclogue* as the boy deciphers them in the light of his own experience;

> *Tityre, tu patulae.* . . . O eery quest in the silence!
>> Magic of dawn on the earth, magic of dawn in the boy!
> Thrilling from letter to letter and every word an enchant-
> ment. . . .
>> *Silvestrem tenui* . . . even ere meaning was known!
> Eager, how eager my fingers divided the glossary's pages,
>> Finding me key after key, golden though printed in black!

There he communed with the spirits of the dead,

> Back by the Mantuan uplands, Mincius stream, and Cremona
>> (Far, how far from the mill, down by the Quarry and Cave).

The phrases seem magical evocations: *Tegmine fagi—*

> Out of that tree, as I fancy, have budded all blossoms and crea-
> tures,
>> Flowed all rivers I know, whispered all winds I have heard.

Similarly *Tityre, lentus in umbra* suggests "Man's mystical union with Nature," while *Dulcia linquimus arva* defines "the love of the acres we've planted." *Formosam Amaryllida* echoed by the forests, finally, summons up "Bessie with ribbon and braid, oriole out in the elm." Although Leonard's poem breaks no ground poetically, it does remind us of the Latin tradition that remained intact into the twentieth century and the experience of a Middle Western American boy that made parts of the first *Eclogue* intuitively accessible to him.

With "Virgil's First Eclogue Remembered,"[22] we are dealing with a much more interesting adaptation. The poem was read in February 1917 at a meeting of the Upper Hudson Phi Beta Kappa Association at Albany by its author, John H. Finley (1863–1940), who at the time was president of the University of the State of New York as well as state commissioner of education. Turning the ancient eclogue into an exhortation for the United States to enter the war against Germany, it begins with a recapitulation of the scene from the "First Century, B.C." in which Tityrus, "reclining 'neath his beech-tree's ample shade," speaks

> To Meliboeus, homeless made by war,
> (A Mantuan who had met a Belgian's fate
> In those pre-Christian days of pagan *pax*).

The poem continues with Finley's free paraphrase of Tityrus's pledge in rhymed couplets:

> Ante leves ergo pascentur in aethere cervi,
> et freta destituent nudos in litore piscis,
> ante pererratis amborum finibus exsul
> aut Ararim Parthus bibet aut Germania Tigrim,
> quam nostro illius labatur pectore voltus.
>
> (1.59–63)

> "*The stags shall pasture buoyant in the sky,*
> *The seas in tree-tops leave their fish to die,*
> *Of Arar shall the distant Parthian drink,*
> *Athirst the German kneel on Tigris' brink,*
> *Ere I'll forget thy face or lightly hold*
> *Thy name, O guardian of my field and fold.*"

The poem then moves to "August, 1916," when once again

> The German presses toward the ancient stream
> (That once as "Hiddekel" from Eden flowed
> But now as "Tigris" dreams of Nineveh)
> And hopes with helmet in his hand to drink
> Beneath the Bagdad sun near Babylon.

While the latter-day Meliboeus, who represents all victims of German aggression, is again driven from his home, Tityrus "in this New World undreamed in Virgil's day" still sings the same old song of thanks in a contemporary version:

> "*The Parthian's sons shall drink*
> *Of Arar's fount; and on the Tigris' brink*
> *Shall kneel the tawny Hohenzollern hosts*
> *To quench their thirst—keeping their long-time boasts;*
> *The Zeppelins shall graze in our own skies*
> *And hostile U-boats in our harbors rise,*
> *Ere I'll forget thy face, who blessest me*
> *With safe and bountiful neutrality.*"

To be sure, this Americanized Tityrus grieves for Meliboeus's cause and provides him with food and medical supplies because

> *My eggs and curds bring prices fabulous*
> *I can afford to be so bounteous.*

By "December, 1916," the poet asks if Americans can "still sing / Our self-contented songs" while not daring to do that which makes our freedom worthwhile. Shall we show no pity and

> Shall Belgian, Serb, Armenian and Pole
> Be left by savagery to famine's dole?

In a bold ellipsis, he suggests by the concluding rhyme the exhortation to battle ("fight") that remains as yet unexpressed:

> Come, let us in protesting word unite
> And say that word with all our heart and might!

By "February, 1917," the poet offers Tityrus another "New World song" to sing beneath his beech-wood tree:

> "*Land of undaunted youth,*
> *Land of the last-born truth,*
>   *For thee one dares to fight;*
> *I will not vaunt nor brag,*
> *But I will guard thy flag,*
>   *Flying for human right.*"

The poem concludes with yet another rephrasing of Virgil's own lines:

> "*The stags shall buoyant pasture in the sky,*
> *The seas in tree-tops leave their fish to die,*
> *Ere I'll forget this flag or, selfish, hold*
> *From earth's stark need, myself, my field, my fold.*"

In an astonishing development, then, Finley, while moving from a reasonably precise recapitulation of Virgil's opening lines to the conclusion of the poem, manages to transform the eclogue into a rousing patriotic hymn in praise of the U.S. flag and of American involvement in World War I. Yet in its very chauvinism the poem reveals its author's recognition of the fundamentally political nature of the eclogue as Virgil reshaped it from Theocritus.

The poems by Leonard and Finley provide a fitting introduction to the poet who was to prove, *pace* Daniel Webster, that New Hampshire could indeed boast both a Virgil and Eclogues. Like Leonard, Robert Frost encountered Virgil in a profound youthful experience; like Finley, he was to appropriate the first *Eclogue* as the pattern for his major poetic statement on public policy. Frost became acquainted with Virgil's works early in life and referred to them with some frequency throughout his life. It was in 1892, during his brief term at Dartmouth, "that something in the *Georgics* of Vergil showed him the way, confirmed him in his poetic purposes."[23] Following his transfer to Harvard, he studied the *Eclogues* with pleasure.[24] Sixty years later he was still quoting Virgil. In a letter of 1950 he wrote: "Wise old Vergil says in one of his Georgics 'Praise large farms, stick to small ones.' Twenty acres are just about enough." (Frost is referring to the passage, *laudato ingentia rura, / exiguum colito* [*Geo.* 2.412–13].) And in the course of a walk, he quoted in Latin the familiar tag (*Aen.* 1.203), *forsan et haec olim meminisse juvabit.*[25]

Critics were not slow to note the Virgilian tone in his early poems.[26] When Frost's second volume, *North of Boston*, was published in England in 1914, Ezra Pound, without developing the thought, entitled his enthusiastic review in *Poetry* (December 1914) "Modern Georgics."[27] Another reviewer, Edward Thomas in the London *Daily News*, characterized the poems as "New England eclogues."[28] Ten years later an anonymous critic began an appraisal, not imperceptively:

> Robert Frost is what the bucolic Virgil might have been, had Virgil, shorn of his Latinity and born of Scotch-New England parentage, spent most of his life where thermometers remain near and often below zero for three months of each year. If Mr. Frost had lived in classical Italy or Greece, he would probably have tended sheep.[29]

The analogy was not fortuitous. Frost himself noted in a copy of his selected poems, with reference to three early poems (from 1905) included in *North of Boston*, "Virgil's Eclogues may have had something to do with them"; and in connection with "Mending Wall" and others, "First heard the voice from a printed page in a Virgilian Eclogue and *Hamlet*."[30] Indeed, Frost initially considered calling the volume *New England Eclogues* but decided against it because not all the poems fit the pattern as he knew it from Virgil's *Eclogues*.[31] As Frost put it in the draft of a preface he wrote for an enlarged edition of the collection, "North of Boston . . . was not written as a book nor towards a book. It was written as scattered poems in a form suggested by the eclogues of Virgil. . . . It gathered itself together in retrospect and found a name for itself in the real estate advertising of the Boston Globe."[32] Frost perceived accurately that some of those early poems "are a little nearer one act plays than eclogues" (vi). At the same time, though the conversational form of others—"The Mountain," "The Black Cottage," "Blueberries"—is reminiscent of Virgil's dialogic eclogues, the characters, the language, and the topics are much closer to the *Georgics*. For the farm folk in these poems speak an everyday idiom that is the American equivalent of Sackville-West's idiom from the Weald of Kent, and not the vaguely poetic language of Virgil's shepherds. And the subjects they discuss are not the loves of Corydon or Gallus, the politically produced tragedies of Meliboeus or Moeris, or the myth of Silenus. Instead, they talk about such matters as picking apples or gathering blueberries, mowing hay and mending wall—the agricultural chores that Virgil describes in the *Georgics*.

As in the *Georgics*, the various chores are not described essentially for their didactic value—even John Quincy Adams recognized that Virgil's poems "will not be of much . . . use to our practical farmers"[33]—but for the moral message that they suggest. "Mending Wall" is not an instruction manual; it is the confrontation of two moral or even political positions—"Something there is that doesn't love a wall" and "Good fences make good neighbors"—that emerge as the two neighbors go about their annual repairs. "The Code" takes hay gathering as an occasion to teach "the town-bred farmer" an important lesson in country manners. In sum, these early poems represent not so much a clear example of "eclogues" or "georgics" as what we have called a "contamination" of the two genres.[34] As W. H. Auden shrewdly observed, Frost in his pastoral eclogues "has taken a sophisticated pleasure in using what is, by tradition, the most aristocratic and idyllic of all literary forms to depict democratic realities."[35] Yet the Virgilian tone is apparent right down to specific verses. The first line of "The Mountain," "The mountain held the town as in a shadow," is not so much a translation as a paraphrase of the two magical closing lines of the first *Eclogue*:

> Et iam summa procul villarum culmina fumant
> maioresque cadunt altis de montibus umbrae.

> (And already smoke is rising from the housetops in the distance, and longer shadows fall from the lofty mountains.)

159

It was almost twenty years after *North of Boston* before Frost wrote his most explicitly Virgilian poem, "Build Soil: A Political Pastoral," which is based formally on the first *Eclogue*, down to the names Tityrus and Meliboeus for the two speakers. The poem, which Frost first read at Columbia University on May 31, 1932, shortly before the national party conventions were to take place, was frankly motivated by his fears of Roosevelt's platform and specifically its farm policy.[36] In the atmosphere of the early 1930s, he worried about a move toward socialism that would disenfranchise private property owners and he feared a movement away from republican democracy toward a totalitarianistic welfare state. The position that Frost developed constituted a kind of Emersonian self-reliance and classical laissez-faire conservatism that was specifically opposed to the kinds of collective action regarded as urgently necessary by many thinkers in the 1930s—especially in its socialist and Marxist variants. Frost's seemingly callous insensitivity toward human suffering produced by the depression that struck some readers as implicit in this attitude would not, incidentally, have been inconsistent with the views of the Virgil who wrote in a famous passage that his happy farmer is neither aggrieved by pity for the poor nor envious of the rich: *neque ille / aut doluit miserans inopem aut invidit habenti* (*Geo.* 2.498–99).

Frost's 292-line amoebaean eclogue begins when Meliboeus, a former potato farmer, encounters Tityrus on an idyllic campus where they had met years before.[37] Meliboeus, forced to give up his farm, has now bought a patch of land on a mountain, "all woods and pasture only fit for sheep." Tityrus, on the other hand, still occupies his farm, where he lives by writing poems. Meliboeus proposes that Tityrus should put his literary abilities at the service of social goals:

> Why don't you use your talents as a writer
> To advertise our farms to city buyers,
> Or else write something to improve food prices.
> Get in a poem toward the next election.
>
> (22–25)

A long dialogue takes place between the laissez-faire conservative Tityrus (=Frost) and Meliboeus, the dispossessed landowner with socialist tendencies. Tityrus concedes the temptation of political activism:

> Oh, Meliboeus, I have half a mind
> To take a writing hand in politics.
> Before now poetry has taken notice

Of wars, and what are wars but politics
Transformed from chronic to acute and bloody?

(26–30)

But in response to Meliboeus's opinion that the times seem "revolutionary bad," Tityrus delicately calibrates the degree:

The question is whether they've reached a depth
Of desperation that would warrant poetry's
Leaving love's alternations, joy and grief,
The weather's alternations, summer and winter,
Our age-long theme, for the uncertainty
Of judging who is a contemporary liar—.

(33–38)

Rather than naming specific names, he prefers "to sing safely in the realm / Of types, composite and imagined people" (48–49). He keeps his eye on Congress, assured that the newspapers are exaggerating the urgency of the situation. As for socialism,

We have it now. For socialism is
An element in any government.
There's no such thing as socialism pure—
Except as an abstraction of the mind.

(68–71)

When Meliboeus suggests that society should be much more extensively socialized for the common good, Tityrus speculates ironically about the results of socializing ingenuity and ambition. Then he states his own economic theory, saying that if he were dictator,

I'd let things take their course
And then I'd claim the credit for the outcome.

(128–29)

When Meliboeus wonders about the value of commerce, which after all has ruined him and forced him to sell his potato farm, Tityrus affirms that "To market 'tis our destiny to go" (172). Then he moves toward the mystical agrarian theology that constitutes the heart of his doctrine:

But much as in the end we bring for sale there,
There is still more we never bring or should bring;
More that should be kept back—the soil for instance.

Tityrus has two basic convictions. On the one hand, he is opposed to the city-dwellers who, in the 1930s, were buying country properties out of a misguided rural romanticism. (Here Frost may well have had in mind T. S. Eliot, who was voicing his own agrarian views in *Criterion*.)

> Let those possess the land, and only those,
> Who love it with a love so strong and stupid
> That they may be abused and taken advantage of
> And made fun of by business, law, and art.
>
> (187–90)

Conceding to Meliboeus that he is preaching "a line of conduct" rather than agricultural policy, Tityrus summarizes, "Let none assume to till the land but farmers" (209). The farmer should aspire to total independence:

> Plant, breed, produce,
> But what you raise or grow, why, feed it out,
> Eat it or plow it under where it stands,
> To build the soil.
>
> (214–17)

The second implication of "building soil" is metaphorical: It refers to the human spirit and the development of the individual.

> I will go to my run-out social mind
> And be as unsocial with it as I can.
> The thought I have, and my first impulse is
> To take to market—I will turn it under.
> The thought from that thought—I will turn it under.
> And so on to the limit of my nature.
>
> (237–42)

Thus Tityrus invites Meliboeus to take charge of his intellectual as well as his economic destiny.

> You see the beauty of my proposal is
> It needn't wait on general revolution.
> I bid you to a one-man revolution—
> The only revolution that is coming.
>
> (264–67)

Modern society forces the individual to renounce his individuality in collectivism. Tityrus enjoins Meliboeus to avoid dehumanizing groups:

> Don't join too many gangs. Join few if any.
> Join the United States and join the family—
> But not much in between unless a college.
>
> (280–83)

The shepherd, confused by this hymn to nation and family in place of any political party-program, promises to keep Tityrus's proposal in mind while cutting posts or mending fence on his farm. The political eclogue ends with the assertion that true consciousness arises when people withdraw from the pressures and claims of society:

> We're too unseparate. And going home
> From company means coming to our senses.

In sum, precisely as in the first *Eclogue*, we are dealing in Frost's "political pastoral" with social turmoil, dispossessed shepherds, and political aspirations in a poetic dialogue that confronts the realistic fugitive Meliboeus with a somewhat complacent Tityrus, who defends the autonomy of the individual and, accordingly, of a *poésie pure*. Although the message of Frost's poem reminds us more of the Epicurean self-sufficiency of Lucretius than the community ethos of the *Georgics*, it can hardly be an accident that, only two years after the bimillennial celebrations, Frost chose to make his major political statement in this explicitly Virgilian form. This decision reflects his appreciation that Virgil's *Eclogues*, as the first poems in Latin to deal with contemporary political events, supplied a basic paradigm for much subsequent political poetry.

Frost's poem was not published until 1936, when it appeared in his volume *A Further Range*, which, though it received the Pulitzer Prize, was generally attacked by the left-wing press.[38] It may, moreover, have been the inspiration, and target, for Allen Tate's rather limp "Eclogue of the Liberal and the Poet" (1938), in which the Southern Agrarian attacked the abstractions of the intellectual left and right alike—those, that is, who ignore the specific reality of the here and now for the image of suffering humanity or the memories of a European past. At the end of their dialogue, the Liberal and Poet join in a concluding unison:

> We must now decide about place.
> We decide that place is the big weeping face
> And the other abstract lace of the race.[39]

However, because it appeared four years after the fact, Frost's poem played no role in the further debate that took place in connection with the 1932 campaigns.

VIRGIL WITH A SOUTHERN ACCENT

Just two weeks before the elections, Archibald MacLeish published in *The New Republic* (26 October 1932) his "Invocation to the Social Muse," in which he vigorously opposed any sort of poetic partisanship—a position hardly surprising from the author of the poetological position paper "Ars poetica" (1926), which ends with the well-known line: "A poem should not mean / But be." Apostrophizing his muse variously as "Señora," "Madame," "Fräulein," "Lady," "Tovarishch," and "Barinya," the poet points out that modern society is a complex phenomenon embracing

> Progress and science and tractors and revolutions and
> Marx and the war more antiseptic and murderous
> And music in every home: there is also Hoover.

Does the lady suggest we should write it out in The Word?[40]

The poet reminds his muse that poets are "whores," that is,

> persons of
> Known vocation following troops: they must sleep with
> Stragglers from either prince and of both views.

The rules prohibit taking sides or participating in maneuvers. Those who infringe enjoy momentary fame and are soon forgotten:

> There is nothing worse for our trade than to be in style.
>
> He that goes naked goes further at last than another.
> Wrap the bard in a flag or a school and they'll jimmy his
> Door down and be thick in his bed—for a month.

The poet should retain only his own nakedness, the things of love and of death. "Is it just to demand of us also to bear arms?"

MacLeish's purist manifesto, which is even more extreme than Frost's declaration of personal independence, infuriated many readers, and in the course of the following weeks—too late, to be sure, to have any influence on the results of the elections—a number of replies were published, among which one is particularly noteworthy. On December 14, 1932, MacLeish's friend and ideological opponent Allen Tate published his reply to MacLeish's poem in the letters column of *The New Republic*: a poem entitled "Aeneas at New York."

In the fourth line of his poem, Tate quotes the concluding rhetorical question that MacLeish had implicitly answered in the negative: "Is it just to demand of us also to bear arms?" But Tate says that his own knowledge of history and war prompts him to precisely the opposite response. In support he cites the scene from the beginning of Book 2 of the *Aeneid* where the priest Laocoön warns the Trojans against accepting within their walls the great wooden horse filled with Greek troops while the deceitful Greek soldier Sinon, allegedly a deserter, successfully persuades them that the Greeks have sailed back home.

> It is just: what manner of man was he
> Sinon who swore at Neptune's priest, swearing
> When the hard spear betrayed the horse's belly?[41]
>
> (70)

The analogy is not absolutely consistent. By arguing that "we are priests ... we are not whores," Tate implicitly ranges MacLeish and others who take the purist position and deny a political role to poets along with Sinon.

> I think Sir that you honoring our trade
> (And nothing is lost save its honor)
> And wishing us our own integrity and calm
> Fall, if I may say it with respect, in error.

He reminds MacLeish that poets, like Sophocles, have from the beginning supported causes they considered just:

> You will remember the name of the poet fighting,
> The young man at Salamis. Was he a whore?
> The poet is he who fights on the passionate
> Side and whoever loses he wins. . . .

Tate attributes to poets "the infallible instinct for the right battle / On the passionate side." The poet does not fight with the arms produced by Mister J. P. Morgan (whom MacLeish had cited disparagingly) but, returning again to his starting point in the *Aeneid*,

> With one's own arms when necessity detects
> The fir-built horse inside the gates of Troy.
>
> (71)

The poet is not concerned with the political machinations with which wars begin and end: "We have nothing to do with Aulis nor intrigues / At Mycenae." Then, in a bold leap from antiquity to the present, Tate presents his own view that it is the poet's responsibility, as it is the priest Laocoön's, to speak up always for the traditional values of the community:

> Have you Penates have you altars, have
> You your great-great-grandfather's breeches?

The poet no longer aspires to fight on the battlefield with the outmoded arms of his forefathers:

Do not I do not attempt to wear the greaves
The moths are fed; our shanks too thin. Have you
His flintlock or had he none have you bought
A new Browning?

What matters is memory, "the ownership / Of the appropriate gun," for this intellectual and spiritual possession provides a strength unknown to such ideologies as communism and "brings / Victory that is not hinted at in 'Das Kapital.'" This is the true war for which the poet must perfect his craft—not the pure poetry of MacLeish but the poetry of tradition and value.[42] Paradoxically, during World War II MacLeish reversed his position and issued a summons for explicitly patriotic poetry—a change for which Tate again took him to task in his "Ode to Our Young Pro-consuls of the Air" (1943).

The Virgilian theme came easily to Tate, who was later to say that "a kind of religious humanism is the moral and spiritual condition which is favorable to poetry"[43] and who identified the two great sources of his own thought and poetry, religion and classical antiquity, by adding as epigraphs to his *Collected Poems* lines in Latin from the Psalms (68.18 of the Vulgate) and from the *Aeneid* (1.462): *Sunt lacrimae rerum et mentem mortalia tangunt.* Tate had taken Latin in high school and he continued that study in college. At that time Vanderbilt still not only required Latin and Greek for admission but expected students to take further courses in both. But under the aegis of their teacher, former Rhodes scholar John Crowe Ransom, who had read "Greats" at Oxford, the classics constituted far more than an academic subject among the aspiring young writers in Nashville in the early 1920s. At a reunion of the Vanderbilt Fugitives half a century later, when the old friends stressed the importance of the classics in their literary development, Tate cited T. S. Eliot on the Southern education in classics. "'You may not have had a very large curriculum in the Southern colleges, but it was sound, because you had the Latin, Greek, and mathematics'" in contrast to the elective system at Harvard. "I think he probably exaggerated the thoroughness of Southern education," Tate continued, "but its very conservatism accounts for some of the things that happened to this group."[44] In fact, when he graduated in 1923, Tate hoped to go on to graduate school in classics—a plan that fell through for want of support.[45] In any case, his early poems from the Fugitive years contain a number of classical allusions,[46] and Tate remained enough of a Latinist to translate the *Pervigilium Veneris* two decades later (1942–43).

However, we hear nothing specifically about Virgil until 1930, when Tate was asked by *The New Republic* to write a piece to commemorate the bimillennial celebrations. Tate's essay[47] begins with a well-informed biographical sketch that draws parallels to the life of John Milton, who also wrote at a time of social disorder and moved from minor forms to the epic. At the same time, Tate manages to make Virgil sound like one of the Fugitives at Vanderbilt, coming as he did from an agricultural background in the provinces, where he enjoyed a good education and the "best intellectual culture of his time." Anticipating Eliot's essays, Tate stresses that the Western mind was shaped essentially by Roman culture, and "at the center of this mind, down to the middle of the eighteenth century, stood Vergil." He singles out for particular notice the first *Eclogue*, whose "joyful melancholy" signaled "the depth of the poet's gratitude" to Octavian for restoring his property. "The poet immediately prophesied the good times to come, in that mysterious fourth Eclogue that fanciful Christians have interpreted as foretelling the Savior." Tate, who along with a group of friends had just published the Southern Agrarian manifesto *I'll Take My Stand* (1930), notes that Virgil "belongs to that stage of civilization which lived by agriculture," but it is for other reasons that the *Georgics* are "perhaps the most perfect poems stylistically in all literature." For Virgil is "the founder of European poetic style," which emerges from his classical purity of vision combined with that "perspicuity" that enabled him to evolve the image most appropriate to every occasion.

Despite the sense of personal identification with a poet whom he regarded virtually as a fellow Fugitive and Agrarian, Tate's essay of 1930 remains fairly representative of most bimillennial comment, focusing as it does on the first and fourth *Eclogues* and accepting almost ritually the perfection of the *Georgics*. It is paradoxical, in fact, that the *Georgics* were to play such a peripheral role for Tate and his fellow Agrarians because Virgil's poem embodied so fully their own ideals. Two more years passed before the *Aeneid* became an urgent factor in Tate's thinking, in "Aeneas at New York" and two other poems written that same year. The circumstances that led to the composition of his poem "The Mediterranean," which was written in 1932 at Cassis, a fishing village between Toulon and Marseilles, have entered the lore of American literary history. As recounted by Ford Madox Ford in a book dedicated to Caroline Gordon and Allen Tate, "who came to Provence and there wrote to 'That Sweet Land' the Poem called 'The Mediterranean,'"[48] Ford invited Tate and a dozen other friends to join him, "on the feast of the Assumption in Provence" (August 15), on a expedition to a cove two or three miles down the coast for the rehearsal of a pastorale that Ford had composed. The *calanque* was a deep fjord edged by blood-red cliffs leading to a beach that could be approached only in boats. The occasion was celebrated by "a Homeric banquet" of bouillabaisse on the beach at which "sixty-one bottles of wine were consumed by sixteen adults" while "twelve cocks stewed in wine with innumerable savoury herbs." It occurred to Ford that the Trojans might have feasted

> in just such a way, off just such viands—for we ate nothing there that the pious Aeneas could not have eaten, cooked in just the way his cooks prepared his viands. And if we did not eat our platters we certainly ate great manchets of bread that had been soaked in that sauce of the bouillabaisse or had lain under the twelve *coqs au vin* in their cauldrons.

The allusion came easily to Ford's mind: In the huge survey of world literature that he was currently engaged in composing, Ford justified the disproportionate space devoted to Virgil by stating flatly: "There is no author, after Virgil, who merits so much attention, not for the divine character of his imagination and the majesty of his mighty line, but for the fact of his standing at so singular a crossway in the history of imaginative writing."[49] As Tate took up the story years later:

> About twilight we pulled ourselves together and got back into our boats and within half an hour we were again in Cassis. As we walked toward the hotel Ford said to me, "In some such place as that calanque the refugees from Troy must have stopped for the famous dinner described in the *Aeneid*, during which the harpies flew over the dinner and defiled it, prophesying that when the Trojans ate so heartily and drank so deeply they would devour the vessels and they would settle in that land forever."[50]

The next day in Toulon, Tate tells us, he bought a secondhand copy of the *Aeneid* and read the relevant passages. "Within a week I had begun the poem."

"The Mediterranean," generally recognized as one of Tate's finest poems, has been much interpreted.[51] The Virgilian allusions begin with the epigraph, which is taken from Venus's speech of reproach to Jupiter for permitting Aeneas and his followers to be tormented so long: *Quem das finem, rex magne, laborum* (*Aen.* 1.241). Tate substitutes *dolorum* for *laborum*, a switch that has elicited a good deal of comment. Tate himself, shortly before his death, dismissed the change as a typographical error.[52] Whether it is toil or woe for which an end is being requested, the motto in any case alerts the reader to the parallels that are developed systematically throughout the thirty-six-line poem (nine strophes of iambic pentameter with alternating rhyme). The other allusion involves the prophecy to which Tate refers in his poem. According to Virgil, the Harpy Celaeno, *infelix vates*, warns the hapless Trojans that they will not surround their promised city with walls until dire hunger and punishment for the wrongs they have inflicted on the Harpies compel them to gnaw with their teeth the very tables on which they eat. (The word *mensa* normally means "table" or a detachable tabletop— hence "platter" or "vessel"; but it can also designate a flat loaf on which offerings are placed.)

> Sed non ante datam cingetis moenibus urbem,
> quam vos dira fames nostraeque iniuria caedis
> ambesas subigat malis absumere mensas.
>
> (*Aen.* 3.255–57)

Later, when the Trojans have landed at the mouth of the Tiber and, having consumed their fare, turn their hunger upon the broad loaves serving as plates for the food, Aeneas's son Iulus jokingly remarks that they have consumed their tables:

> "heus! etiam mensas consumimus," inquit Iulus,
> nec plura adludens.
>
> (*Aen.* 7.116–17)

Thereupon Aeneas, recalling Celaeno's prophecy, rejoices that the terms have now been fulfilled. Tate makes this incident into the governing image of his poem, mentioning it no less than three times (66):

> And we made feast and in our secret need
> Devoured the very plates Aeneas bore.

> Eat dish and bowl to take that sweet land in!

> What prophecy of eaten plates could landless
> Wanderers fulfil by the ancient sea?

Given these explicit quotations and references, it is hardly surprising that critics have looked for further evidence of the *Aeneid* in Tate's poem. It is accepted lore that the first two lines of the poem

> Where we went in the boat was a long bay
> A slingshot wide, walled in by towering stone

incorporate specific images from Virgil: the phrases *in secessu longo* (*Aen.* 1.159) and *vastae rupes* (*Aen.* 1.162) that describe the harbor on the Libyan coast where Aeneas and his men take shelter before their en- counter with Dido.[53] But the sheltered harbor in Libya, whose descrip- tion is a topos of Mediterranean topography based on the *Odyssey* as well as Hellenistic voyagers' catalogues,[54] is quite distinct from the flat mouth of the Tiber, where the Aeneadae "eat their tables." And, ac- cording to the description by Ford Madox Ford, the *calanque* on the Provençal coast was sufficiently dramatic to have suggested the images in itself—especially when specified by the typically American qualification "a slingshot wide." (The waters of Virgil's Libyan harbor, in contrast, specifically spread *late*, "broadly" [1.163].) If a Virgilian source for the passage must be identified, it would seem more plausible to specify Aeneas's account of his adventure with the Harpies on the shores of the Strophades (*Aen.* 3.209–57), where all the requisite elements occur: the phrase *in secessu longo* (3.229), tables (*mensae*), gulls, and a place of prophecy.

Whether the long bay with its walls of towering stone is Virgilian or not, the motto has prepared us for the juxtaposition of ancient and modern and for the timeless realm of classical myth, marked off by high walls, that the poet enters from the realm of modern temporality:

> Peaked margin of antiquity's delay,
> And we went there out of time's monotone.

The poem displays a symmetrical organization into three groups of three strophes. The first three depict the trip down the long bay in the black hull of the small ship before which the seaweed parts, admitting the party to "the murmuring shore," where

> we made feast and in our secret need
> Devoured the very plates Aeneas bore.

The next cluster of strophes juxtaposes past and present in a manner that permits the poet to experience the eternal whose realm he has entered. He first imagines how Aeneas landed and feasted:

> Where derelict you see through the low twilight
> The green coast that you, thunder-tossed, would win,
> Drop sail, and hastening to drink all night
> Eat dish and bowl to take that sweet land in!

The next strophe returns to the present where the modern party is "affecting our day of piracy." But what meaning does the ancient prophecy of eaten plates—that is, as a symbol of the new land discovered—have for these "landless wanderers" of the twentieth century acting out their fantasy by the ancient sea? The experience permits them ever so briefly to "taste the famous age / Eternal here yet hidden from our eyes"—that is, the idyllic moment of Dionysian satisfaction enjoyed by the Trojan adventurers centuries before the Roman empire founded by their landing degenerated into imperialism (or, according to a different interpretation, after Troy was overcome in the war for power):

When lust of power undid its stuffless rage;
They, in a wineskin, bore earth's paradise.

In the final triad Tate imagines how "our live forefathers" felt when they lay down "by the breathing side / Of Ocean" in the days when "the Known Sea" still required a month to cross. Having mastered the hemispheres of the Old World, they look for new countries to conquer and lands in which to "locate our blood."

Now, from the Gates of Hercules we flood

Westward, westward till the barbarous brine
Whelms us to the tired land where tasseling corn,
Fat beans, grapes sweeter than muscadine
Rot on the vine: in that land were we born.

By the daring shift in the last half-line, Tate manages to link "that sweet land" that Aeneas and his men first saw as they came from the East, to the land of lush crops and sweet grapes that was discovered two millennia later in the constant westering movement of humankind.

"The Mediterranean" is important not so much because it was influenced by Virgil but rather because it provided Tate with the occasion to recognize in Virgil a set of values closely approximating his own, as they had been developing through the Fugitive and into the Agrarian period. Virgil's works enabled him to objectify his own experience. It was this discovery of the *Aeneid* as "an analogue for the condition of our culture"[55] and the Virgilian world as "an ideal against which Tate measures the present" and "an image of the potential if unrealized nobility inherent in modern man"[56] at which the poet arrived in 1932 when the meditations of his bimillennial essay were provided with a basis in reality through the evidently moving experience on the beach near Cassis. For the first time, in other words, Tate consciously sensed rather than intellectually knew the ancient roots of his own American culture. The same analogue provides the theme for "Aeneas at Washington," a poem written a short time later. But this time the roles are reversed: It is no longer the modern American traveling to the Mediterranean and imagining himself in Aeneas's position; instead, the Virgilian hero, having undertaken the second phase of his westward course anticipated in the earlier poem, is now in the modern Hesperian world, looking back upon his own past.

The first four lines of the poem amount to a free translation of the passage in which Aeneas recounts to Dido the highpoint of the slaughter at Troy when the Greek warriors cut down the king of the Trojans before the altar at which he was sacrificing:

>   vidi ipse furentem
> caede Neoptolemum geminosque in limine Atridas,
> vidi Hecubam centumque nurus Priamumque per aras
> sanguine foedantem quos ipse sacraverat ignis.
>   (*Aen.* 2.499–502)

> I myself saw furious with blood
> Neoptolemus, at his side the black Atridae,
> Hecuba and the hundred daughters, Priam
> Cut down, his filth drenching the holy fires.

(68)

Aeneas has no reason to be ashamed of his behavior: Indeed, he behaved like a gallant Southern cavalier:

> In that extremity I bore me well,
> A true gentleman, valorous in arms,
> Disinterested and honourable.

But flight was the only response to a time "when civilization / Run by the few fell to the many"—a description that might fit the fall of the South in the Civil War even more closely than the fall of Troy. Taking his father upon his back (in the gesture eternalized in numerous paintings and bronzes like the one on George Washington's mantelpiece), Aeneas saved nothing but his memory of that lost past: "Saving little— a mind imperishable / If time is, a love of past things tenuous / As the hesitation of receding love" (doubtless an allusion to the receding shade of his murdered wife Creusa). And "To the reduction of uncitied littorals"—heavy Latinisms for the conquest of unpopulated shores—he brought only the "vigor of prophecy" anticipated in "The Mediterranean."

In a daring conflation of images from burning Troy and the American South, Aeneas recalls "the thirsty dove / In the glowing fields of Troy, hemp ripening / And tawny corn, the thickening Blue Grass / All lying rich forever in the green sun." The imperial ambitions that he once nurtured have passed: "the towers that men / Contrive I too contrived long, long ago." Now, standing in the rain in the New World, "far from home at nightfall / By the Potomac," he gazes at the great Dome of the Capitol. But he no longer recognizes "The city my blood had built"—an allusion to the land in which Tate/Aeneas in "The Mediterranean" had sought "to locate our blood." The screech-owl that "whistled his new delight / Consecutively dark" has evoked various interpretations; but it may well be simply that owl of Minerva that, according to Hegel, flies only at dusk. The poem concludes with what is probably an allusion to Schliemann's excavations of Hissarlik in

1872–74, which established the existence of nine superposed settlements at the site of Troy:

> Stuck in the wet mire
> Four thousand leagues from the ninth buried city
> I thought of Troy, what we had built her for.[57]

It appears to be the melancholy conclusion of Aeneas/Tate, with the philosophical insight that comes at the end of an era, that Western civilization—which began at Troy, then moved to Rome, and from there to the New World—is inevitably doomed to degenerate into brutality. The only recourse for Trojan warrior and Southern gentleman alike is to maintain a posture both "disinterested and honourable"—that is, a position of honor unsullied by thought of personal gain.

Tate emphasized the specifically Southern identification with Aeneas and his followers when, in his obituary for William Faulkner, he spoke of the centrality for Southern writers of the "Greco-Trojan myth (Northerners as the upstart Greeks, Southerners as the older, more civilized Trojans)."[58] The chief features of this position, as Louise Cowan astutely observed, are the Virgilian qualities of "*fatum*, a sense of mission; *pietas*, duty toward family, country, and the land; *memoria* and the preservation of the sacred; self-discipline; belief in a divine order expressing itself obscurely in history."[59] To this we should add the powerful sense of history that the Southerners shared with Virgil (and that was not shared by Homer and the Greeks): Just as Virgil could anticipate in the fall of Troy the founding of Rome, Tate could see in the fall of Rome the founding of the American Republic and, beyond that, in the fall of the Confederacy some hope for the preservation of its values. All these values, to round the circle, are implicit in Tate's objection to MacLeish's position in his poem "Aeneas at New York."

These values based on the *Aeneid*, hardly unique to Tate, are shared generally by the Southern Agrarians. In his polemical essay "Why the Modern South Has a Great Literature" (1950), Donald Davidson begins by asking us to consider "for a thematic text" the famous passage from the *Georgics* (2.490–502) in which Virgil praises first the intellectually happy man (*felix, qui potuit rerum cognoscere causas*) and then the blessed man who appreciates the boons of country life (*fortunatus et ille, deos qui novit agrestis*).[60] Davidson, the least reconstructed of the Agrarian brethren, reminds us that

> Vergil, like us lived at a time when republican institutions had been undermined by those who were responsible for upholding them. Skepticism and materialism were destroying religion. A

New Deal, headed by a dictator on the make, was pretending to
restore the republic but was actually subverting it.

(159)

He goes on to offer his own revealingly timely paraphrase of Virgil's
text:

But blessed, too (if not happy), is the man who knows that the
God of his fathers is still manifest in the fields, woods, and rivers.
That man does not have to cater to the urban masses of New York
and Detroit. He does not need to beg favors from Roosevelt or
Truman. He has nothing to do with the jealous and traitorous
schemes that split our parties in fratricidal strife. He doesn't spend
his time worrying over where the Russians will strike next, or
about Washington politcs, or over whether the French or British
cabinet will again have to resign.

(160)

Following a lengthy discussion of the passage, in which he insists
that the knowledge of the "happy man" is not scientific knowledge but
philosophical understanding, Davidson goes on to make the point that
the second kind of knowledge—"knowledge that possesses the heart
rather than a knowledge achieved merely by the head" (171)—is the
knowledge that enables the "blessed man" to integrate the various
forms of social experience: economic, aesthetic, philosophical, religious. This quintessentially Virgilian knowledge, in sum, is "the dominant characteristic of Southern society" and the basis for its literature.
Like fifth-century Greece and late-republican Rome, the South from
1920 to 1950 was a traditional society "invaded by changes that threw
[it] slightly out of balance without at first achieving cultural destruction. The invasion seems always to force certain individuals into an
examination of their total inheritance that perhaps they would not otherwise have undertaken" (173)—like Virgil and like the Agrarian brethren themselves.

It is this "shared cultural commitment" that underlies Davidson's
"Lines Written for Allen Tate on His Sixtieth Anniversary."[61] The
poem memorializes evenings at Benfolly, Tate's home on the Cumberland River near Fort Donelson (Dover, Tennessee), where his friends—
Andrew Lytle, John Crowe Ransom, Robert Penn Warren, Frank
Owsley, among others—gathered, summoned by "the creed of memory." On one such occasion, the friends had been discussing the inevitable Southern topic of the Civil War, imagining they could hear the
cannon-fire resounding from the 1862 siege of Fort Donelson:

The sound of guns from beleaguered Donelson
Up-river flowed again to Benfolly's hearth.
Year to familiar year we had heard it run
World-round and back, till Lytle cried out: "Earth
Is good, but better is land, and best
A land still fought-for, even in retreat;
For how else can Aeneas find his rest
And the child hearken and dream at his grandsire's feet?"[62]

Tate responds with an ironic twist, pointing out that the fall of Troy (and, by implication, the fall of Fort Donelson to Union forces) is not a defeat: Indeed, the victor loses himself in the assumption that he has overcome time and history while the "deliberate exiles"—both Aeneas and the Southerner—look forward to a new greening of their culture.

You said: "Not Troy is falling now. Time falls
And the victor locks himself in his victory
Deeming by that conceit he cancels walls
To step with Descartes and Comte beyond history.
But that kildee's cry is more than phylon or image
For us, deliberate exiles, whose dry rod
Blossoms athwart the Long Street's servile rage
And tells what pilgrimage greens the Tennessee sod."

In this assumption of a shared heritage and history, the poet is confident that young Southerners can turn to Tate's poetry to learn the meaning of the past and the meaning of the city that, like Aeneas, they are destined to build:

Exultant with your verses to unlearn
The bondage of their dead time's sophistry;
They know, by Mississippi, Thames, or Seine,
What city we build, what land we dream to save,
What art and wisdom are the part of men
And are your music, gallant and grave.

(The association of Tate and the *Aeneid* appears to have become a commonplace among the poet's friends. For Tate's seventy-fifth birthday his biographer, Radcliffe Squires, wrote "The First Day out from Troy," in which Aeneas envisions the founding of a new city of light "at whose walls barbarians mass / To break the gates.")[63]

For Tate and his fellow Southerners, then, the *Aeneid* represented, in the classical education that they all shared, a profound analogy for their own history and values: the general American westering, the experience of defeat, the preservation of traditional values, the sense of the land. It should be noted in this connection that the Southerners, like Virgil himself in the *Georgics* and elsewhere, never come to grips with the issue of slavery, the institution upon which both cultures—that of Augustan Rome as well as the pre-Civil War South—were based. Indeed, the word *servus* does not even occur in Virgil, while *servitium* is used only four times in the three major works.[64]

The Virgilian analogue was not limited to the Fugitive-Agrarian brethren. John Peale Bishop (1892–1944) was not one of the group; indeed, he sided with MacLeish in the controversy surrounding "Invocation to the Social Muse," arguing that the writer should never desert literature for polemics.[65] But as a friend and fellow Southerner, he shared their belief in "the virtues of an agrarian civilization," as he explained in his essay on "The South and Tradition" (1933).[66] He expressed that affinity in his poems, which Tate edited following his early death.[67] Bishop exploits the Aeneas analogy with great precision in his splendid poetic cycle "Experience in the West" (1936). The first poem, "The Burning Wheel," begins with the image of Aeneas fleeing the burning Troy and bearing on his shoulders Anchises, who has been driven mad by his recollection of his contact with the divine—his love affair, as a young shepherd on Mount Ida, with Aphrodite—that had produced Aeneas.

> They followed the course of heaven as before
> Trojan in smoky armor westward fled
> Disastrous walls and on his shoulders bore
> A dotard recollection had made mad,
>
> Depraved by years, Anchises: on the strong
> Tall bronze upborne, small sack of impotence;
> Yet still he wore the look of one who young
> Had closed with Love in cloudy radiance.[68]

(78)

The following strophes make it clear that the "They" of line 1 are the discovers of America, whose meeting with the natives is likened implicitly to Aeneas's encounter with the Latin inhabitants of the Tiber.

> So the discoverers when they wading came
> From shallow ships and climbed the wooded shores:
> They saw the west, a sky of falling flame,
> And by the streams savage ambassadors.

At first, as they advanced along the "rivers of new gold" where "the wild grapes ripened" and "the bright snake danger coiled," the new Trojans retained their memories of the past:

> They, too, the stalwart conquerors of space,
> Each on his shoulders wore a wise delirium
> Of memory and age: ghostly embrace
> Of fathers slanted toward a western tomb.

But it is Bishop's somber conclusion that, after two centuries, these memories became progressively less substantial and were finally discarded by the heedless sons:

> A hundred and a hundred years they stayed
> Aloft, until they were as light as autumn
> Shells of locusts. Where then were they laid?
> And in what wilderness oblivion?

The following poems make clear Bishop's melancholy belief that America, in the course of developing the new land, forgot history and the values of the past. Thus, the explorers in "Green Centuries" have no thought of the past "When every day dawned Now":

> The long man strode apart
> In green no soul was found,
> In that green savage clime
> Such ignorance of time.
>
> (79)

In "Loss in the West," the man in the coonskin cap has already "had his day" (80). He now merely pursues out of instinct—

> What? Wheel of the sun
> In heaven? The west wind? Or only a will
> To his own destruction?
>
> (81)

In "O Pioneers!" man comes to realize that "The way is lost to fortune." Having lost his father's footsteps, he has gone mad in the delirium of gold and other "daft schemes."

> A continent they had
> To ravage, and raving romped from sea to sea.
>
> (81)

Although he shared what we have come to recognize as the Virgilian virtues of the Southern tradition, Bishop differed from many of his

177

friends in accepting the accusation of having "shown it as already in decline before the Civil War."[69] This ambivalence links him to a much younger member of the group.

The background of Robert Lowell (1917–77) would hardly seem to qualify him for inclusion in the group under discussion. Yet in many ways, this scion of old New England families was closely linked to the Southern Agrarians. As an undergraduate, in the spring of 1937, he had visited Tate at Benfolly, where he "crashed the civilization of the South" and, camping in a tent in the Tates' yard, came into early contact with the Southerners.[70] Encouraged to major in classics by Tate's friend Ford Madox Ford, whom he assisted in the compilation of his volume *The March of Literature* (1938), Lowell found that "all the English classics, and some of the Greeks and Latins were at Tate's elbow." His desire to study with Tate's own mentor, John Crowe Ransom, led him—to the chagrin of his family—to transfer from Harvard to Kenyon College, where Ransom had moved from Vanderbilt in 1937. Since his early poems were written directly under the aegis of these men, it is hardly surprising to find among them one that incorporates the Virgilian analogy. "Falling Asleep over the Aeneid," which first appeared in Lowell's third volume of poetry, *The Mills of the Kavanaughs* (1951), has subsequently won a place as one of his finest poems.

The epigraph sets the scene: "An old man in Concord forgets to go to morning service. He falls asleep, while reading Vergil, and dreams that he is Aeneas at the funeral of Pallas, an Italian prince."[71] Textual hints provide further details: It is a Sunday morning in springtime, sometime around 1945, and the old man now in his eighties, descendant of an uncle who led a batallion of "colored volunteers" in the Civil War, sits in his library overlooking the lake in Concord, reading Virgil as he has done since boyhood.

> The sun is blue and scarlet on my page,
> And *yuck-a, yuck-a, yuck-a, yuck-a,* rage
> The yellowhammers mating.

At this moment he dozes off, and the next sixty-five lines (of the eighty-six line poem) amount to a dreamlike recreation of the passage from the *Aeneid* (11.30–99) he has just been reading. The passage is one of the two scenes in which notoriously Aeneas, forgetting his humanity, gives way to rage and fury at the death of Pallas, the son of his Latin ally Evander, at the hands of Turnus. One such scene takes place at the very end of the epic, when Aeneas, having overcome Turnus and deliberating mercy, catches sight of Pallas's belt, which Turnus is wearing, and buries his sword in his enemy's breast. The other scene takes place immediately following Pallas's death when Aeneas, preparing to send

Pallas's body back to his father, binds the Italic captives with their hands behind their backs and offers their blood in sacrifice to the Shades:

> vinxerat et post terga manus, quos mitteret umbris
> inferias, caeso parsurus sanquine flammas.
>
> (11.81–82)

This is the point at which the old man's day-dream begins, and he assumes the role of Aeneas himself, watching as

> Yellow fire
> Blankets the captives dancing on their pyre,
> And the scorched lictor screams and drops his rod.
> Trojans are singing to their drunken God,
> Ares.

Although the poem eschews all editorial comment, Lowell has chosen with great precision the passage that enables him, the conscientious objector in World War II (and the later antiwar protester during the 1960s), to examine his own ambivalent attitude toward war. Explicitly and implicitly the poem refers to at least five great wars: Aeneas's war against the Italic tribes, the second Punic War, the American Revolutionary War, the Civil War, and World War II.[72] Yet the designated passage from the *Aeneid* presents war in its full horror, embracing as it does both the death of the innocent young and the brutal slaughter of prisoners.

The first lines constitute a phantasmagoria as the old man, between waking and dreaming, confounds the yellowhammers outside his window with the augur (the "bird-priest" who observes and interprets the behavior of birds) who had foretold the young hero's death.

> And I stand up and heil the thousand men,
> Who carry Pallas to the bird-priest.

As he watches the procession, Aeneas's sword, with which Phoenician Dido had killed herself, transforms itself into a bird and utters a Punic (that is, a Phoenician) word.

> I hold
> The sword that Dido used. It tries to speak,
> A bird with Dido's sworded breast. Its beak
> Clangs and ejaculates the Punic word
> I hear the bird-priest chirping like a bird.

Pallas's wounded corpse, into which the old man/Aeneas is suddenly transformed, groans and utters a few words:

I groan a little. "Who am I, and why?"
It asks, a boy's face, though its arrow-eye
Is working from its socket.

Levi Robert Lind has demonstrated in close detail that the next thirty lines of Lowell's poem, which depict the funeral preparations, amount to "both a re-creation and in part a translation" of Virgil's text.[73] Lowell describes how Pallas's male servants, "his harlots," decorate the bier and place on it the handsome youth with his "face of snow." Then Aeneas covers the body with garments that Dido had woven of purple and gold, and the procession is ready. The unfortunate Acoetes (Evander's armor-bearer), consumed by age, is brought in:

> ducitur infelix aevo confectus Acoetes.
>
> (II.85)

Afterward the war-steed Aethon, its insignia removed, follows weeping and wets his face with huge teardrops:

> post bellator equus positis insignibus Aethon
> it lacrimans guttisque umectat grandibus ora.
>
> (II.89–90)

Others carry Pallas's spear and helmet; Turnus, the victor, has taken everything else:

> hastam alii galeamque ferunt; nam cetera Turnus
> victor habet.
>
> (II. 91–92)

Lowell assembles these lines and images as follows:

> Now his car's
> Plumage is ready, and my marshals fetch
> His squire, Acoetes, white with age, to hitch
> Aethon, the hero's charger, and its ears
> Prick, and it steps and steps, and stately tears
> Lather its teeth; and then the harlots bring
> The hero's charms and baton—but the King,
> Vain-glorious Turnus, carried off the rest.

Pallas speaks once more to acknowledge the *fatum* that determined his destiny—"I was myself, but Ares thought it best / The way it happened." Then Aeneas, in a vision, foresees how "my descendants climb / The knees of Father time" to build an empire that will eventually extend beyond the Alps and into remote Africa. As the dream concludes, Aeneas raises his arm in a final salute: "Brother, eternal health.

Farewell / Forever"—an almost literal translation of his words in the *Aeneid* (11.97–98): *salve aeternum mihi, maxime Palla, / aeternumque vale.*

The old man, awakened from his dream by the bells signaling the end of church services, recalls another occasion eighty years earlier when, as a boy not yet eight, he was interrupted in his reading and summoned to church by his mother's great aunt: "Boy, it's late. / Vergil must keep the Sabbath." That memory, in turn, reminds him of the hero in his own family history, Uncle Charles, the young Civil War leader. The "colored volunteers" parading through Concord for his funeral and the English maid who "fold[s] his colors on him" postfigure, of course, the "thousand men" who accompany Pallas's bier and the "harlots" who prepare his body; the Episcopal bishop Phillips Brooks and General Grant, who appeared at his funeral, afford a close analogy to the "bird-priest" and Aeneas himself. At this point the old man, holding onto his uncle's sword for balance, just as Aeneas once "h[e]ld the sword that Dido used," stands up out of the Virgilian past into his own present time, where again the ambivalent interplay of poetry and politics is evident, "for the bust / Of young Augustus weighs on Vergil's shelf." But the times themselves have changed: For now, rather than the sound of the live yellowhammers, "the dust / On the stuffed birds [on top of the bookshelves holding Virgil and Augustus] is breathless." And the bust of Augustus "scowls into my glasses at itself."

The young Lowell has appropriated from his Southern mentors the Virgilian analogy for the Civil War. For Tate, as we saw, the Trojans in their defeat by the upstart Greeks were eventually seen to prefigure the aristocratic South and its culture. Although Lowell's family background gives him a different perspective, he is also able through his choice of scene from the *Aeneid* to use Virgil's text as an analogue for the tragedy of war. Yet his shifting admiration for Pallas as well as Aeneas, for Uncle Charles as well as General Grant, lends to his poem a fascinating ambivalence that sets it apart from the less problematic cooptation of the Southern Virgilians.

AENEAS AMERICANUS

The fact that so few of the Fugitive-Agrarian writers served in World War I (only John Crowe Ransom and Donald Davidson), and that those who did came home safely, caused the American writers to differ markedly from their British counterparts in their perspective on epic generally and on Virgil in particular. The *Aeneid* was not disqualified in its traditional American function as the typological pattern for the national western expansion. And this function was not limited to poetry alone. American literature does not display a novel dominated structurally, like Anthony Burgess's parody, by the *Aeneid*. The Southern dialect classic by Harry Stillwell Edwards, *Eneas Africanus* (1920), might more appropriately be entitled "Odysseus Americanus" because the hero's journey takes him not to a new world in the West but back home to the restored family.[74] The central figure of this picaresque tale, recounted in a series of newspaper reports and personal letters, is an elderly black servant who, before the advancing Union troops, is dispatched to transport the Tommey family silver from a stock farm in northwestern Georgia to the family plantation on the other side of the state, near Louisville in Jefferson County. Because Eneas has never before traveled that road by horse and wagon and because the place-names with which he is familiar—Washington, Jefferson, Macon, Sparta, Thomasville, and others—occur in almost every Southern state, his erratic wanderings take him in the course of some eight years through North Florida, Alabama, Mississippi, Tennessee, North Carolina, and South Carolina as well as various adventures involving a new wife and race horses. (We would probably be forcing the analogy to see in those incidents any parallels to the Dido episode or the games in Book 5 of the *Aeneid*.) In 1872, finally, he arrives at Tommeysville with the intact silver just in time to present the family "Bride's Cup" to Major Tommey's daughter, whose wedding is taking place. But the title of the story and its assumption of a shared literary understanding highlight the centrality in the South of the Virgilian analogy, which still plays an essential role in other works.

This analogy is evident in one of the classics of American historical fiction, Elizabeth Madox Roberts's *The Great Meadow* (1930). Narrated from the standpoint of Diony Hall, a descendant of tidewater gentry who grows up in Albemarle Country, Virginia, the novel depicts the exploration and settlement of Kentucky—the Indian name Ken-tak-ee designates the "meadowlands" of the title—in the years from 1774 to 1781. Throughout the story there are references to the epochmaking events taking place in Boston, New York, and Philadelphia as the news of the Revolution filters through to the remote outposts on the western frontier. The story, like Tate's poem "The Mediterranean," falls into three parts. The first three chapters portray Diony's girlhood on the family plantation in western Virginia and her growing attachment to the young hunter Berk Jarvis and culminate in their marriage in 1777. The next three chapters depict the ordeal of the young couple's journey along the Wilderness Road and through the Cumberland Gap into Caintuck, where they settle near Harrod's Fort. While Diony is pregnant with their first child, she is rescued from an attack of two Indians by Berk's mother, Elvira, who is killed and scalped by the warriors and whose fierce resistance causes her to enter Shawnee legend as "the fighting squaw." Following the completion of his house on Deer Creek and the birth of their son, Berk goes off to avenge his mother and to retrieve her scalp.

In the final cluster of three chapters, Diony waits disconsolately for more than a year and then reluctantly decides to get married again: to her old friend Evin Muir, who had made the journey from Virginia with her and Berk. She has a second child with her new husband before, in 1781, Berk returns from his mission and from months of captivity among the Indians. The novel ends as Diony decides in accordance with the common law of the frontier to go back to Berk; it is implied that Muir will console himself by fighting the British in "another year of mischief" following the battle at Yorktown.

Now the plot in itself, for all the richness in historical fact and local color praised by the novel's admirers, would hardly suggest any Virgilian associations. But Roberts (1881–1941), who attended the University of Chicago in her thirties (1917–21) for a belated formal education, was not unaware of the national Virgilian traditions—an awareness that may have been enhanced by the publicity anticipating the bimillennial celebrations as she was completing her novel. (There is no evidence, only plausibility, to support this conjecture.) In any case, the factors that lent to this historical novel the epic dimensions that account for Roberts's stature among writers of the 1930s are conspicuously Virgilian.[75] The Virgilian context is prepared by a narrative style epic in its level. In the opening pages, for instance, when the Hall family is listening to stories of Dan'l Boon and the new land beyond the mountains,

> The talk sank and flowed about strong men who made brave journeys into the country beyond the barrier, or it lifted and sparkled with the rise of Nathan's hand that set forth a more bold hunter or a more daring exploit with one sharp gesture. The bright yellow smallclothes of the tidewater stranger were a mere ornament in the scene. "Such a country would breed up a race of heroes, men built and knitted together to endure . . . " and another voice, "A new race for the earth."[76]

Diony's name is also a factor that links her, on the one hand, to classical antiquity and, on the other, to the role that she is to play in the new land:

> Diony knew what name she bore, knew that Dione was a great goddess, taking rank with Rhea, and that she was the mother of Venus by Jupiter, in the lore of Homer, an older report than that

of the legendary birth through the foam of the sea. She knew that Dione was one of the Titan sisters, the Titans being earth-men, children of Uranus and Terra. She had a scattered account of this as it came from between her father's ragged teeth as he bit at his quid and spat into the ashes, an elegant blending of tobacco and lore and the scattered dust of burnt wood, the man who limped about before the hearth arising superior to his decay. She could scarcely piece the truths together to make them yield a thread of a story, but she held all in a chaotic sense of grandeur, being grateful for a name of such dignity.

(14–15)

There are passages reminiscent of the *Georgics* in the opening chapters, which recount the different tasks of the farmer in the changing seasons. Before their marriage, Berk brings an old frontiersman to Five Oaks to tell stories about the meadowlands of Ken-tak-ee:

"A fearful country. Every rood a place where a battle has been. The land there is thick with broken battle-axes and under the ground run the bones of many men. A dark country. No red-man lives there."

(51)

These words clearly recall the famous passage in which Virgil anticipates the day when the farmer, toiling at the earth with his curved plough, will find javelins eaten by rusty mould or, with his heavy harrows, will strike empty helmets and marvel at the huge bones in the graves that he uncovers:

scilicet et tempus veniet, cum finibus illis
agricola incurvo terram molitus aratro
exesa inveniet scabra robigine pila,
aut gravibus rastris galeas pulsabit inanis,
grandiaque effossis mirabitur ossa sepulcris.

(*Geo.* 1.493–97)

The parallels with the *Georgics*, although utterly plausible, are still conjectural. The analogy with the *Aeneid*, however, is made explicit by Diony's father, who links her setting off into the wilderness with the voyage of Aeneas. In the weeks before her marriage and departure, her parents try to prepare her spiritually and intellectually as well as practically for the life that awaits her in a strange land. Her mother teaches her to dye and weave her yarn into sturdy travel garments.

Her father's voice:

Arma virumque cano, Trojae qui primus ab oris
Italiam, fato profugus, Lavinaque [*sic*] venit
Litora, multum ille et terris jactatus et alto
Vi superum . . .

His voice breaking from the Latin chant would concede known meanings to all that he had sung, as "I sing of arms and the hero who, fate driven, first came from the shores of Troy to Italy and the Lavinian coast, he, *vi superum*, by the power of the gods, much tossed about, *multum jactatus*, much tossed about on land and sea . . . "

(120–21)

They are both tossed about by the powers of the gods in the course of their journey, but it is Berk who explicitly fulfills the role of the vengeful Aeneas (as in Lowell's poem) by setting out to recapture his mother's scalp, which the Shawnee warrior named Blackfox carries at his belt, "being proud of it because it was marked curiously with one bright gray lock" (205). Like Aeneas obsessed by the shade of Palinurus or the death of Pallas, whose belt was worn in victory by Turnus, Berk justifies his departure to Diony:

"I'll go as I say and no word can hold me. Could I lay me down at night to sleep whilst I know one of those red devils carries my own mother's hair on his belt for a wonder to show?"

(239)

It is Diony who fulfills the Virgilian role as the bringer of order and law and the keeper of the Augustan *pietas* toward God and Country that is as essential to the civilization of the new lands as is the actual physical conquest.[77] While her father quotes the *Aeneid* to her, Diony's mother teaches her the responsibility of *pietas*: "'Hit's not so much matter what the men-folks do that day iffen the women in the home-place hold the Sabbath up for reverence, and seems like hit's the women has got insight and is natured to hold fast to the old customs'" (121). In the course of their journey, the settlers stop at Inglis Ferry to hunt and rest, and Diony talks to an old man who strikes her as "Thomas Hall cut farther away, a new philosophy coming out of his mouth and out of his hand" (144). As he carves a powder horn for her husband, the old paternal surrogate tells him, not unlike Anchises in the underworld: "Berk Jarvis, there's power in your horn. Indian law has not got enough power in it. It's time the law and the women went there" (147). Diony is first troubled by the old man's words.

But presently the evenness of their own going, Berk to the fore, Muir, herself, and Jack, moving in the design already known to her by the way of the plodding horses, restored a design of evenness and order to her mind, and their going became of the order of law, as if they carried the pattern of law in their passage. (153)

Following the attack by the two Indians, in her realization that her mother-in-law sacrificed herself for her and her unborn child—that is, for the future—Diony begins to have daydreams. "She would prolong her reverie until it fell into a clearly defined desire" (207). In her visions, which parallel the prophetic passages in the *Aeneid,* she sees "a new world, the beginning before the beginning. . . . Sitting thus she would see a vision of fields turned up by the plow" (207). These are succeeded by visions of sheep, of stone walls and rail fences setting bounds to the land, of neighbors, of markets, of bridges over streams, of cattle and beehives, of letters and communications back to her family in Virginia, of knowledge and wisdom and beauty—in short, of civilization. But during her first years in the wilderness, Diony is unable to find this Virgilian order anywhere but in her dreams.

Two incidents in particular become thematic for her. When first she meets Daniel Boone, he tells her that he has sometimes felt bewildered in the forests, but "I never felt lost the whole enduren time" (186). This remark becomes a shibboleth for Diony. "'I'm not the Boone kind,' she said. 'I never was. . . . I'd be more at home somewheres else . . . I don't know where'" (187). Second, while Berk is a captive of the Indians, they once threaten to cook and eat him, but he impresses them by his stubborn resistance:

> "You will not put me in your kettle, you brown son-of-the-devil. I belong," I said, "to the Long Knives. Iffen you never heard it said what kind they are, you better go find out. You put me in your kettle and you'll not eat one bit of my strength. You'll eat ne'er a thing but my weak part and you'll breed weakness in your bones."
>
> (331)

By the end of the novel Diony has learned to understand the order of Boone and the strength of Berk as constituting along with her own *pietas* a kind of *novus ordo saeclorum.*

> For a little while she felt that the end of an age had come to the world, a new order dawning out of the chaos that had beat through the house during the early part of the night. Her thought strove to put all in order before she lay down to sleep. She felt the power of reason over the wild life of the earth. Berk had divided the thinking part of a man from the part the Ojibways would have

put into their kettle and into their mouths. . . . Boone moved securely among the chaotic things of the woods and the rivers. . . . The whole mighty frame of the world stood about her then, all the furniture of the earth and the sky, she a minute point, conscious, soothing the hunger of a child. Boone, she contrived, was a messenger to the chaotic part, a herald, an envoy there, to prepare it for civil men.

(337–38)

By the end of the novel, in sum, Diony Hall has become the Titan sister Dione, child of Uranus and Terra, who is destined to bring order to the chaos of the new world—or, in Virgilian terms, to fulfill the *Georgics* in a land conquered by the American Aeneas.

It is hardly surprising that the *Aeneid* analogy is also to be found in *The Fathers* (1938), the only novel by Elizabeth Madox Roberts's fellow Kentuckian, Allen Tate. The story, which takes place immediately before and during the first months of the Civil War, exposes the conflict of two ages as reflected in the lives of two Southern families, the Buchans and the Poseys. The Buchans represent the world of honor and dignity of the Old South—but a world exposed through its very location (in Fairfax County, Virginia) to the threat of the new forces emerging in the North. "Men of honor and dignity! They did a great deal of injustice but they always knew where they stood because they thought more of their code than they did of themselves."[78] Major Buchan's cousin once remarks that the major "is still living before he was born—in 1789. He thinks the government is a group of high-minded gentlemen who are trying to yield everything to one another" (124)—and, in his blindness, contributes to the ruin of the republic. Mrs. Buchan believes that "the State of Virginia (by which she meant her friends and kin) was . . . the direct legatee of the civilization of Greece and Rome" (184). As a boy, appropriately, Lacy Buchan construes Ovid and other Latin classics with his father. Yet all their civilization and classical learning has not taught these people the lesson of history that is implicit in the *Aeneid*: "[P]eople living in formal societies, lacking the historical imagination, can imagine for themselves only a timeless existence: they themselves never had any origin anywhere and they can have no end, but will go on forever" (183). They read of Troy but they do not apply the analogy to themselves. Or more precisely: They apply to themselves only the old eighteenth-century analogy of America as the New Hesperia to which the classical values of Troy and Rome have been transmitted.

The Poseys, in contrast, while also a respectable family, come from the border state of Maryland (and now from the border town of

Georgetown), and their values are appropriately alienated and modern. "George Posey was a man without people or place; he had strong relationships, and he was capable of passionate feeling, but it was all personal; even his affection for his mother was personal and disordered. . . ." (179) George in his violent uprootedness is incapable of appreciating the traditional Southern values. "'And by God they'll all starve to death, that's what they'll do. They do nothing but die and marry and think about the honor of Virginia'" (107). At the same time, he seeks an attachment to the Virgilian *pietas* and *ordo* of an established family like the Buchans in an effort toward self-awareness and self-restraint.

> In a world in which all men were like him, George would not have suffered—and he did suffer—the shock of communion with a world that he could not recover; while that world existed, its piety, its order, its elaborate rigamarole—his own forfeited heritage—teased him like a nightmare. . . . All violent people secretly desire to be curbed by something that they respect, so that they may become known to themselves.
>
> (180)

It is this fateful confrontation of types, the Old South and the modern world, that determines the outcome of the Civil War, and its implications for the traditional way of life, even before the first shot is fired. This is how Lacy Buchan, the sole surviving member of his family, justifies the narrative that he undertakes many years later.

> Is it not something to tell, when a score of people whom I knew and loved, people beyond whose lives I could imagine no other life, either out of violence in themselves or the times, or out of some misery or shame, scattered into the new life of the modern age where they cannot even find themselves? Why cannot life change without tangling the lives of innocent persons?
>
> (5)

The collapse of the Buchan family begins a year before the war—symbolically enough, with the funeral of Mrs. Buchan, the last occasion at which the whole family is assembled. Thereafter, in a series of scenes the inevitable denouement takes place: George Posey marries Susan Buchan, who quickly goes mad; George finds himself in a situation that causes him, impulsively, to kill Lacy's brother, Semmes. Shortly after the outbreak of hostilities Major Buchan, though himself opposed to secession, commits suicide rather than hand his home at Pleasant Hill over to the Union troops. George, who is basically in sympathy with the industrial North, initially goes with the South and becomes a smuggler of military supplies for opportunistic reasons. When his actions make it impossible for him to serve the South any longer, he disappears into the turmoil of the war, while Lacy joins the Confederate forces, survives the war, fulfills a career as a physician, and then sits down many years later to write the account of his family.

The only explicit allusion to the Virgilian analogy is indirect: The molding in the Buchan's house has a "Wall of Troy design" (32) reminiscent of the bronze on George Washington's mantelpiece. However, in light of Tate's earlier "Aeneas" poems that analogy provides the clue to the entire work and enables us to understand the various associations. There are few parallels of plot: E.g., Major Buchan's suicide in his own house has been compared to the death of Priam.[79] The wily George Posey, who sets out on his wanderings following the symbolic fall of Troy at Pleasant Hills, bears a more than accidental resemblance to Odysseus. Above all, the analogy enables us to understand how the *Aeneid* was appropriated after the Civil War by the South, which now saw its own defeat at the hands of the Union as a parallel to the defeat of the older and nobler Trojan civilization by the upstart Greeks with their modern ways. By the time Lacy Buchan writes his account he has matured from Trojan "timelessness" to a Virgilian awareness of history. It is characteristically Virgilian *pietas* that motivates Lacy to set out half a century later in his narrative to recapture the order and beauty of that lost paradise of the Trojan South and to preserve the memory of "the Fathers." Like many critics of recent decades, Lacy has come to regard Aeneas as "a civilized man fallen into a barbaric age."[80]

Given the prevalence of the analogy, it is hardly surprising to find a late echo of the Southern Aeneas in the work of a third Kentuckian, Robert Penn Warren's *A Place to Come To* (1977). Like *The Fathers*, Warren's *bildungsroman* is another retrospective account—this time by a poor Southern boy who grows up to become a scholar of medieval literature and, at age sixty, looks back at his life. Jed Tewksbury comes from rural Alabama, where he is encouraged by a high school teacher to learn Latin, and then attends a small Alabama college on a football scholarship. At college Jed is prompted by his classics professor to apply to the University of Chicago for graduate study with the great German scholar, Dr. Stahlmann. Although his application is rejected, Jed makes his way to Chicago and talks his way into graduate school where, following service in World War II, he completes his degree with Stahlmann. He then gets a job in Nashville, where he has an affair with a woman he knew in high school. Following this episode, the central affair in his life and in the narrative, Jed returns to Chicago, where he marries, has a son to whom he is passionately devoted, gets divorced, and fulfills a distinguished career. The story is rounded off with an account of Jed's visit to his mother's grave back home in Alabama. "When your parent dies—the last to survive, I mean, for I can speak only for myself and the death of my father occurred before I had reached the age of speculation—you begin to count deaths, even those on the obituary page of the *New York Times*" (382). It is this experience of death that, in turn, justifies the act of Virgilian *pietas* that the novel constitutes.

The allusions to the *Aeneid,* while rather more overt than in Tate's novel, are strictly personal and have none of the national breadth that they imply in *The Fathers.* It is his knowledge of Latin that provides the basis for Jed's academic career, a knowledge that begins in rural Alabama.

> By the time I got out of high school I had read a lot more than the parts of the *Gallic Wars,* the *Aeneid,* and Cicero's *Orations* that were laid out in Dugton High but never got finished. My reading was due to old Miss McClatty. By Christmas of my first year she got me in Caesar; then on past the *Aeneid* to more Virgil, then lots of Horace, Catullus, Tacitus, and Sallust, not to mention lots of Cicero.
>
> (26)

It is also the topic of Latin that first brings up and introduces Rozelle Hardcastle, the girl from his hometown with whom he subsequently becomes involved in Nashville. Rozelle is at first the "star" of the freshman Latin class until Jed is promoted out of the class to a higher level. Because this early acquaintance and the ensuing affair are mediated by Latin, it is appropriate that their second encounter years later in Nashville is announced in Virgilian tones.

> When Aeneas came to Carthage, he moved, in a protecting cloud provided by Venus, toward Dido the Queen, whom he was to love, and then, in the fulfillment of his mission, leave her to the fate of the flames. Well, when I came to Nashville, my cloud was a ramshackle bar car, and if my progress was presided over by the Goddess of Love, she was embodied in the poor, drunken, courageous female with the clanging charm bracelet and the bum gam. But even if Nashville was scarcely Carthage—only a thriving middle-size commercial city of the Buttermilk Belt—I was to find a queen there.[81]

The key has been transposed from major to minor and from the group to the individual, but the explicit allusions to Virgil, the explicit analogy to the Dido episode, the equation of Carthage with Nashville, and the *pietas* to the dead that motivates the narrative, all leave the reader with the distinct sense that Warren is paying final allegiance to an analogy that played a central role in the thinking and mythmaking of the Agrarians among whom he began his literary career.

In sum, whether as an analogy for the bringing of rule and order to the "chaos" of the frontier in *The Great Meadow*, or for the Troy-like destruction of the Old South and the pious preservation of its memory in *The Fathers*, or for the Carthaginian love affair of a young classicist, the three Kentucky novelists turn with an almost instinctive attraction to Virgil's epic in the assumption that the familiar work will lend a subtext of additional meaning to their fictions.

THE DETRACTORS

The unusual unity and coherence of the Southern view of Virgil and Aeneas are even more striking if we consider, by way of contrast, three non-Southern writers of the period. Wallace Stevens, to be sure, numbers Virgil along with Dante, Shakespeare, and Milton as one of the great representative poets.[82] And his poetry contains a fair number of references to what, in "Notes toward a Supreme Fiction" (1942), he called "his Virgilian cadences, up down, / Up down."[83] Yet the various references—from a journal entry in 1899 to quotations, half a century later, from C. Day Lewis's translation of the *Georgics*[84]—cannot conceal the extreme fragmentation of Virgil's image in Stevens: Virgil does not represent, as he did for the Southerners, a coherent vision of life but rather a model for Virgilian sonorities and disconnected literary allusions.

In two of Stevens's only slightly younger contemporaries, however, we encounter a conspicuously different attitude. Ezra Pound is, along with Robert Graves, the most conspicuous *obtrectator* of the twentieth century. It is not that Pound did not know Virgil: Pound, as his *Homage to Sextus Propertius* and other works make clear, was thoroughly at home in the Latin classics.[85] In his literary essays, Pound found frequent occasion to belittle the poet he considered little more than a Tennysonized Homer. Thus he notoriously (and irrationally) claimed that Gavin Douglas's sixteenth-century translation of the *Aeneid* was "better than the original" because the Scottish poet "had heard the sea."[86] And as early as 1914, he was warning the readers of *Poetry* magazine: "Not Virgil, especially not the Aeneid, where he has no story worth telling, no sense of personality. His hero is a stick who would have contributed to *The New Statesman*. He has a nice verbalism."[87] For all the often gratuitous attacks in Pound's prose, Virgil is conspicuously absent in the elaborate cultural pastiche of the *Cantos*, as Donald Davie has pointed out.[88] For this reason, Davie correctly urges, it is especially striking "when the Virgilian voice *does* irrupt" into the late Pisan Cantos—notably in Canto LXXVIII, which borrows from Gavin Douglas's translation to make the analogy between Aeneas's departure from Troy and Pound's own flight from Rome at the end of World War II:

Slow life of long banners
Roma profugens [*sic!*] Sabinorum in terras
And belt the sitye quahr of noble fame
the lateyn peopil taken has their name
bringing his gods into Latium
saving the bricabrac. . . .[89]

What Davie regards as a poignant moment in literary history—"For a poet so hostile to Virgil to discover that *in extremis* only Virgil had foreseen and foresuffered his predicament, and thereby eased it"—goes well beyond poignancy to irony. Davie believes that Pound's hostility to Virgil stems from his fundamentally American hopefulness, which was repelled by that melancholy that appealed to the Southern writers. Bianca Tarozzi explains the antagonism on more literary grounds, arguing that for Pound Virgil was "a sort of modest Victorian ecclesiastic" who was not at home in the world of seafaring heroes he set out to describe.[90] Either interpretation confirms the difference between Pound's rejection of Virgil and the acceptance by the Southern writers.

Another American expatriate living in Paris during the years immediately following the bimillennial celebrations adopted Virgil as the principal image of his contempt for a world of order and temporality, one that exists on "the plateau of good health where one reads Vergil and Dante and Montaigne and all the others who spoke only of the moment," in contrast to the "peaks of drunkenness" where everything is simple and timeless and whole.[91] In Henry Miller's second book, *Black Spring* (1936), the section entitled "A Saturday Afternoon" bears the motto: "This is better than reading Vergil." The section begins harmlessly enough when Miller poses and answers his own rhetorical question, "What is better than reading Vergil or memorizing Goethe (*alles Vergängliche ist nur ein Gleichnis*, etc.)? Why, eating outdoors under an awning for eight francs at Issy-les-Moulineaux" (46). At this point, when the critical evaluation could still conceivably go in either direction, the reader does not yet realize that the question will assume leitmotivic force in the course of the section. Miller's Saturday afternoon bicycle ride leads him from the pleasant lunch by way of an epiphany on the "eternal moment" to a rhapsody on the *pissoirs* of Paris. Standing blissfully at the urinal, Miller reflects: "For, whenever I think of Vergil, I think automatically—*what time is it?*" (56). This apparently incongruous association leads to a brilliant passage in which Miller recalls his high school Latin teacher in Brooklyn.

Vergil to me is a bald-headed guy with spectacles tilting back on his chair and leaving a grease mark on the blackboard; a bald-headed guy opening wide his mouth in a delirium which he simulated five days a week for four successive years; a big mouth with false teeth producing this strange oracular nonsense: *rari nantes in gurgite vasto.* Vividly I recall the unholy joy with which he pronounced this phrase. A *great* phrase, according to this bald-pated, goggle-eyed son of a bitch. We scanned it and we parsed it, we repeated it after him, we swallowed it like Cod Liver Oil, we chewed it like dyspepsic pellets, we opened wide our mouths as he did and we reproduced the miracle day after day five days in the week, year in and year out, like worn-out records, until Vergil was done for and out of our lives for good and all.

(56)

Although by this time we have begun to grasp Miller's feelings about Virgil, we still do not have the key to the associations that triggered the reminiscence.

But every time this goggle-eyed bastard opened wide his mouth and the glorious phrase rolled out I heard what was most important for me to hear at that moment—*what time is it?* Soon time to go to Math. Soon time for recess. Soon time to wash up. . . . I am one individual who is going to be honest about Vergil and his fucking *rari nantes in gurgite vasto.* I say without blushing or stammering, without the least confusion, regret or remorse that recess in the toilet was worth a thousand Vergils, always was and always will be. At recess we came alive.

(56–57)

Having thus disposed of Virgil, Miller explains his literary preference for writers like Petronius, Apuleius, Boccaccio, and Rabelais: "That salty tang! That odor of the menagerie! The smell of horse piss and living dung, of tiger's breath and elephant's hide. Obscenity, lust, cruelty, boredom, wit" (60–61).

Miller does not indicate whether, in the course of those painful years, he ever got beyond line 118 of the first book of the *Aeneid,* but in an earlier section of *Black Spring* he does allude to the Fourth Eclogue in similarly disparaging terms as the epitome of ethereal irreality. "Either you start with pure melody or you start with listerine. But no Purgatory—and no elixir. It's Fourth Eclogue or 13th Arrondissement" (14). As we survey the nostalgia for Virgilian *ordo* and *pietas* that permeated conservative circles in Europe and the Western hemisphere in the twenties and thirties, it is well to keep in mind, for the sake of perspective, Henry Miller's earthy rejection.

——— ❧ ———————————————————————

Virgil *Redivivus*

In light of the widespread Virgiliophilia between the two world wars and the corresponding vividness achieved by the figure of Virgil in the modern cultural consciousness, it seems inevitable that some admirers should have longed to establish personal contact with the revered poet. The South African scholar T. J. Haarhoff (cited in Ch. 1) reported that Virgil, accompanied by Euripides and speaking German,[1] manifested himself to him on at least one occasion. Jackson Knight (discussed in Ch. 4), who was introduced to psychic matters by Haarhoff in 1946, never became a complete convert to spiritualism, thanks largely to his mother's skepticism. However, he had long been obsessed by ancient views of death and the underworld, as is evident in his first book, *Vergil's Troy* (1932; reissued in 1967 under the title *Vergil: Epic and Anthropology*). His second major work, *Cumaean Gates* (1936), adduced Jung's theory of the collective unconscious to explain the myths and rituals of the megalith builders. Knight's ambivalence regarding spiritualism caused him, following his mother's death when he was working on his translation of the *Aeneid* (1956), to accept Haarhoff's offer to interrogate Virgil on various matters of textual interpretation. Accordingly Haarhoff put Knight's questions to the Roman poet who, responding initially in German through a medium and subsequently every Tuesday evening in Latin through Haarhoff's automatic writing, expressed his interest in Knight's effort, praised his industry, and offered various textual emendations and explications. Given this background even among reputable scholars, it is hardly surprising that other writers sought to come to grips with Virgil through fictional representations.

The most obvious possibility of representation is the historical novel, in which the modern writer portrays characters from the past in their historical context—often with a unique fictional twist. In Ernst Schnabel's *Der sechste Gesang* (1956) Odysseus shows up at the court of the Phaeacians (hence "the sixth book" of the *Odyssey*), where he encounters the poet Homer who, still young and not yet completely blind, persuades the adventurer to fulfill his destiny by forsaking the temptations of the Phaeacians and returning to Ithaca. In Christoph Ransmayr's *The Last World* (*Die letzte Welt,* 1988) the poet Ovid is exiled to the remote Roman colony of Tomi, which is depicted with details borrowed from the dictatorship of modern Rumania. Robert Graves with *I, Claudius* (1934), Marguerite Yourcenar with *Hadrian's Memoirs* (*Mémoires d'Hadrien,* 1951), and Thornton Wilder with his *Ides of March* (1948) have attained worldwide successes with novels based on the lives of historical figures from classical antiquity.

The novel offers another imaginative possibility of depicting figures from the historical past—to introduce them, or their reincarnations, into fictions set in the present.[2] Thus—to take the example of a single figure—both Hermann Hesse in his *Journey to the East* (*Die Morgenlandfahrt,* 1931) and Peter Henisch in *The Tales of Hoffmann: Notes of a Confused German Teacher* (*Hoffmanns Erzählungen: Aufzeichnungen einer verwirrten Germanisten,* 1983) pay their respects to the German Romantic writer E.T.A. Hoffmann by giving the historical character a walk-on role in their fictions, which are set in twentieth-century reality. It is this possibility that we want to consider first as background and context for the major modern novel based on the life of Virgil.

VIRGILIUS REDUX

Perhaps no American writer is more conspicuously indebted to the European cultural heritage, and specifically in its manifestation as Christian humanism, than Thornton Wilder.[3] Following his graduation from Yale in 1920, where he minored in Latin, Wilder's father staked him to a year at the American Academy in Rome, where as a special student (because the twenty-three year old was not academically qualified to be a regular fellow of the Academy) he pursued his interests in archaeology while preparing himself to teach high school Latin.[4] On his return to the United States, while teaching French at the Lawrenceville School and subsequently taking a Master's degree in Romance Languages at Princeton University, Wilder worked on his fictional "Memoirs of a Roman Student," which were published in 1926 under the title *The Cabala.* This first novel, published in the same year as was Hemingway's *The Sun Also Rises,* appears on the surface more Jamesian than Virgilian, depicting as it does the encounter of a young American cultural pilgrim[5] with a group of sophisticated but enervated European aristocrats. Set in Rome immediately after World War I, it portrays in its three major episodes, and through the consciousness of an American student designated only as Samuele, the moral tragedies of four members of a mysterious clique known to the citizens of Rome as the Cabala. In one episode Marcantonio, already sex-crazed and morally corrupt at age sixteen, commits suicide after succumbing to the taunting temptation to incest with his decadent sister. In another, the beautiful Princess Alix d'Espoli falls in love with the Harvard classicist James Blair—Wilder's shrewd anticipation of the contemporary academic hustler—and is humiliated and spiritually shattered when she is rejected by the cold rationalist, who is incapable of appreciating her fine sensibility. The third episode links two stories: The first is about the wealthy Marie-Astrée-Luce de Morfontaine, dedicated quixotically to the return of royalism in France through a revival of Catholicism, whose almost fanatical religious devotion is so profoundly shocked by the rationalism of the famous Cardinal Vaini that she attempts to shoot him; the second story centers on Cardinal Vaini himself, once reputedly the greatest missionary known to the Church since the Middle Ages, who has lost his faith and, seeking to recover it by returning to China to regain touch with the people, dies and is buried anonymously at sea.

Wilder's narrator survives the experiences of these European aristocrats, whose confidant he becomes. Although he appreciates the cultural dimensions they represent, he does not believe that their personal tragedies mark the end of culture. Like his contemporary Allen Tate, he is staunch enough in his own convictions and values to believe that in a grand movement of history the course of cultural empire is moving westward to the America to which he returns at the end of the book. This is where Virgil comes in. Indeed, the book opens with reminiscences of Virgil. In the first paragraph, as a train bears the narrator across the Campagna toward Rome, we are alerted to the interplay between Roman antiquity and modern Italy that dominates the book. "It was Virgil's country and there was a wind that seemed to rise from the fields and descend upon us in a long Virgilian sigh, for the land that has inspired sentiment in the poet ultimately receives its sentiment from him" (23).[6] At many points throughout the account, the poet's memory is invoked in passing. Looking down at the street near the Spanish Steps, he "tried to remember whether Virgil had died in Rome . . . no, buried near Naples" (44). When he meets a famous scholar, a member of the French Academy, and praises his work on Church history, the distinguished man replies:

Why read me at all? . . . There are too many books in the world already. Let us read no more, my son. Let us seek out some congenial friends. Let us sit about a table (well-spread, pardi!) and talk of our church and our king and perhaps of Virgil.

(55)

When Princess Alix asks James Blair to explain his maps to her, "coldly, haughtily, and with long quotations from Livy and Virgil, he harangued my guest" (85). A preposterous Rosicrucian-Swedenborgian *magister hieraticorum* (whose séances Alix attends in her despair, substituting superstition for true religion) relates "how Virgil never died, but was alive still on the Island of Patmos, eating the leaves of a peculiar tree" (106). And there are other less explicit allusions. During his first week in Rome, the narrator meets a dying young poet (based loosely on Keats), who is so dissatisfied with his works that, when he dies, he wants every copy to be destroyed, just as Virgil demanded the destruction of the *Aeneid* (47). And when Samuele leaves Rome, he "set aside several days for the last offices of piety, piety in the Roman sense" (138).

All these passages prepare us for the culminating moment in the last section, which is entitled "The Dusk of the Gods." I do not mean the fantastic ideas of Miss Grier, the wealthy and learned American spinster who fills "the moneyed emptiness of her days" (36) by choreographing the activities of the international set in Rome. When Samuele, shortly before his departure, asks Miss Grier to "throw some light on the Cabala," she develops a mad theory of spiritual transmigration and reincarnation to explain their character and behavior. "The gods of antiquity did not die with the arrival of Christianity," she assures him (140). "When one of them died his godhead was passed on to someone else; no sooner is Saturn dead than some man somewhere feels a new personality descending upon him like a strait jacket" (140–41). Although the narrator is too tactful to demand of her "the application to the Cabala of all these principles" (144), according to this doctrine the actions of all the members of the Cabala can be interpreted as analogies to the gods they reincarnate: Miss Grier herself as Demeter, Cardinal Vaini as Jupiter, Marcantonio as Pan, and Alix and James Blair as Venus and Adonis.[7] As she tells Samuele explicitly, "I sometimes think that you are the new god Mercury" (141), destined to serve as the messenger and secretary of the gods.

The narrator is much too pragmatic and sensible to be taken in by this far-fetched theology, which Wilder seems to have introduced in an effort to lend some unity and continuity to his otherwise episodic narrative. For one thing, he points out ironically, he has had none of the headaches that allegedly symptomize the act of deification. Yet he does not reject out of hand the analogical relationship itself, a relationship already signaled by the repeated references to Virgil and one that provides the novel with a more profound and persuasive sense of unity.

On the night that my steamer left the bay of Naples I lay sleepless in my deck chair until morning. Why was I not more reluctant at leaving Europe? How could I lie there repeating the Aeneid and longing for the shelf of Manhattan? It was Virgil's sea that we were crossing; the very stars were his: Arcturus and the showery Hyades, the two Bears and Orion in his harness of gold.

(144)

Recalling that Mercury is not only the messenger of the gods but also the conductor of the dead, he reflects:

> If in the least part his powers had fallen to me I should be able to invoke spirits. Perhaps Virgil could read my mood for me, and raising my two palms I said in a low voice (not loud enough to reach the open portholes behind me):
>
> > Prince of poets, Virgil, one of your guests and the last of barbarians invokes you.
>
> (144)

Believing that he can make out "the shimmer of a robe and the reflection of the starlight on the shiny side of a laurel leaf," he presses his advantage by appealing with the words of Dante to the *anima cortese mantovana.*

> Now indeed the shade stood in mid-air just above the handrail. The stars were glittering and the water was glittering, and the great shade, picked out in sparks, was glittering furiously.
>
> (145)

In the hope of making the image clearer, he invokes it with the "one title that might avail more with him than those of poet or Roman":

> Oh, greatest spirit of the ancient world and prophet of the new, by that fortunate guess wherin you foretold the coming of Him who will admit you to His mountain, thou first Christian in Europe, speak to me!
>
> (145)

At this point "the gracious spirit became completely visible with pulsations of light, half silver and half gold," urging the "importunate barbarian" to be brief and not to detain him from the company of his peers in eternity, Erasmus, Plato, and Augustine. Asked about Dante, Virgil becomes indignant at the memory of "that soul of vinegar," who judged the souls of the dead more harshly than God did. He goes on to praise Milton's "noble Latin" but notes that Shakespeare is greater, even though in eternity "he sits apart, his hand over his eyes" and does not participate in the community of the spirits.

Finally the "importunate barbarian" asks a personal question. "Master, I have just spent a year in the city that was your whole life. Am I wrong to leave it?" (146). Virgil, who dedicated his own works to the

notion of the *translatio* of gods and men from Troy to Rome, assures
his young American interlocutor that the process continues.

> I spent my whole lifetime under a great delusion—that Rome and
> the house of Augustus were eternal. Nothing is eternal save
> Heaven. Romes existed before Rome and when Rome will be a
> waste there will be Romes after her. Seek out some city that is
> young. The secret is to make a city, not to rest in it. When you
> have found one, drink in the illusion that she too is eternal. Nay,
> I have heard of your city. Its foundations have knocked upon our
> roof and the towers have cast a shadow across the sandals of the
> angels. Rome too was great. Oh, in the pride of your city, and
> when she too begins to produce great men, do not forget mine.
> When shall I erase from my heart this love of her? I cannot enter
> Zion until I have forgotten Rome.
>
> (146–47)

With these words Wilder's Virgil confirms the interpretation of the
Fourth Eclogue as a precursor of Christianity while the narrator implicitly attributes to him the role of Father of European humanism. To this
extent Wilder anticipates and is consistent with the view of Virgil advanced a few years later by such Christian humanists as Theodor
Haecker and T. S. Eliot. But in the extended notion of *translatio imperii* Wilder, returning from his year in Rome to the United States, attributes to his Virgil a view that would have been incomprehensible to
most Europeans and to his own American contemporaries, who in the
1920s were flocking to Paris in search of a cultural experience that they
found missing at home. Wilder's Virgil counsels no elegiac absorption
in the past, whether of Rome or any other culture. He urges the young
American to return to the United States, where New York waits to be
made into a city that will rival Rome in its greatness. The novel can
therefore end with a sublime optimism: Although Virgil's shade may
disappear, the enthusiasm that he brought to the Rome of his own age
is the appropriate spirit for the young writer of the twentieth century
to bring to his own metropolis:

> The shimmering ghost faded before the stars, and the engines
> beneath me pounded eagerly toward the new world and the last
> and greatest of all cities.
>
> (147)

It seems utterly appropriate that, only a few years later, this American
apostle of Virgil's humanism should have returned to North Africa and
Italy as an officer in Air Force Intelligence; there it was his chief responsibility, during World War II, to support the resistance movements

against the dictatorships of Mussolini and Hitler. As in so many cases
that we have already observed, the preoccupation with Virgil turned
out to be an ideological gesture.

It is perhaps inevitable that *Virgilius redux* should bear a different message when speaking to a young American returning to a
young country than when addressing a fellow countryman in an Italy
undermined by the moral decay detected by Wilder in the aristocrats of
The Cabala. One of the oddest literary curios produced by the bimillennial excitement was the eighty-page Latin poem by Anacleto
Trazzi entitled *Vergilius Redux* (1930).[8] This composition—with about
two thousand lines roughly the same length as the *Georgics* and, like
Virgil's poem, divided into four parts—has the astonishing elegance
that we might expect from a Doctor of Theology who went on to win
the international prize in Latin poetic composition of the Royal Neth-
erlandic Academy of Sciences.[9] By no means a cento, although quite a
few properly footnoted lines from Virgil's works are built into the text,
the style is distinctly Virgilian and contains a number of linguistic
allusions: e.g., *Cur igitur tantae in fratres mortalibus irae?* ("Why do
mortals harbor so much wrath against their brothers?" [34]; cf. *Aen.*
1.11); or

> Iam novus Italiae saeclorum nascitur ordo.
> Si qua manent vero sceleris vestigia prisci
> Irrita sincerae Pacis mox pignore fient.
>
> (38; cf. *Ecl.* 4.5 and 13–14)

(Already the new order of centuries is born in Italy. Yet, if there
remain any traces of past crime, let them straightway be made
invalid by the pledge of pure Peace.)

The first part (*De laudibus Vergilii ac de eius monumento novissimo*,
"On the Praise of Vergil and the Newest Monument to Him") finds the
author, on the eve of the poet's two-thousandth birthday, perusing his
works while all Mantua sleeps. Suddenly he is moved by terror as the
image of the poet materializes before his eyes and stands silently before
him. The author overcomes his shock to greet Virgil in effusive terms
and, as his visitor remains silent, to describe for him in considerable
detail the celebrations that attended the unveiling of the famous monument on the Piazza Virgiliana in Mantua on April 21, 1927. At last
Virgil breaks his silence to explain that he has returned from the Shades
neither to hear praise and acclaim nor to see the monument designed
by Luca Beltrami, but impelled by an overpowering love to see his
sweet fatherland:

Visere si placuit, tanto post tempore, dulcem
Italiam, Patriamque meam, civesque nepotes,
Ipsius Patriae vehemens amor impulit unus.

(19)

(To see, if possible after so many years, sweet Italy, and my Country, and its citizen-descendants—a powerful love of Country
impelled me.)

But the next section (*De vitae commoditatum profectu ac de morum de-
fectibus*, "On the Advancement of Life's Amenities and the Deficiencies of Morals"), which begins with the poet's acknowledgment of such
achievements as steamships, airplanes, radios, and other modern accomplishments, soon turns to their evil uses—notably war—that have
been made worse:

Quam graviora modo studio fecistis et arte,
Igne, cruore, fuga, per se nimis horrida bella!

(29)

(How much worse you have made war, frightful enough in itself
with its fire, gore, and flight, through diligence and skill!)

Even worse is the spiritual deterioration of a civilization in which prize-
fighters earn more than scholars do and in which soccer stadiums are
filled while the schools stand empty:

Num deceat pugilem, perparva temporis hora,
Ditari decies centenis millibus aeris,
Cum, vel qui musas doceant artesque, sub ipsum
Elysii limen, longe post tempora vitae
O scelus indignum! turpis divexet egestas?
Num deceat populi turmas complere palaestras,
Calcibus impingunt ubi plenas aëre sphaeras,
Dum docti coetus vacui cernuntur alumnis?

(40)

(Is it fitting that the pugilist, for a brief hour of time, is rewarded
with ten hundred thousand coins when, on the very threshold of
Elysium and following a long lifetime, shameful poverty—o, dis-
graceful state of affairs!—distracts even those who teach the muses
and the arts? Is it fitting that throngs of people fill the stadiums
where they kick spheres full of air while learned assemblies can be
seen empty of the young?)

Part 3 (*De vita urbana et rustica*, "On City and Country Life") addresses
the sad conditions that have caused the rural populace to emigrate or to

move into the city, which like a *nova Circe* (48) teaches innocent girls to wear shameless dress exposing their legs, shoulders, and breasts (*Ut fere nuda tamen spectatu crura relinquat, / Et nudos omnino humeros et pectora nuda,* 50) and corrupts youth with sexual license and drug addiction:

> Ex plantis quippe elicitis blanda illa venena
> Quae · · · · · · · · · · ·
> Naribus hausta modo, tantum vel dente retrita,
> Sic hilarant animos, sic ebrietate suavi
> Sensibus illudunt, ea demum visa stupenda
> Praetendunt menti ut, curas oblitus acerbas,
> Se quisque Elysiis credat iam vivere lucis,
> Sentiat ac prorsus sese omni ex parte beatum.
>
> (53)

(those alluring poisons extracted from plants which, merely inhaled into the nostrils or ground by the teeth, so exhilarate the spirits, so deceive the senses with their suave intoxication and finally hold out to the mind such stupendous visions that, forgetting bitter worries, each victim believes that he is already living in Elysian groves and feels himself wholly blessed from every side.)

The only remedy is *ad rura reverti* (45, "to go back to the land"). Nor have the arts fared any better in modern times, as Virgil continues in Part 4 (*De arte recentiore eiusque vitiis,* "On Modern Art and Its Defects"). Without any patience or discipline, artists ignore Truth for the sake of the beautiful appearance of truth (*pulchrum nitorem veri,* 71) and appeal to the lowest common denominator of taste. Virgil is particularly offended by the fashionable free verse:

> Adspice sed versus; omni prope lege solutos,
> Omnibus et numeris.
>
> (77–78)

(Just look at the poetry: freed virtually of all rule and all meters.)

Warming up to his subject, Virgil is prepared to recommend to his modern descendants the study and practice of the ancient languages (*Romanae Linguae ut studio cultuque vacetis,* 81). But suddenly a loud noise startles the author—the fireworks celebrating the poet's bimillennium.

> Tormenta tonabant
> Bellica, quae festis Ipsius prima Poëtae

Laeto signa dabant strepitu (sed sulphure tantum
Ac nitro) magno circum resonantia Vati.

(81–82)

(Warlike cannons thundered, which with a joyous sound [albeit produced merely by sulphur and nitrate] gave the first signals for the festivals of the Poet Himself, echoing round in honor of the great Bard.)

Realizing that what he has experienced was a dream or vision, the awakening author watches Virgil's image disappear into thin air. The poem concludes with a distinct reminiscence of the last line of the *Aeneid*:

Dixeris at tamen Illum ipsum rediisse sub umbras.

(But you would have said that He himself returned to the shades.)

When we remind ourselves that Trazzi was writing contemporaneously with Montale, Quasimodo, and Ungaretti, it seems evident that the Latin language provided him with a shield behind which he was able to take critical liberties unavailable to poets writing in the vernacular—even in the often impenetrable vernacular of the Hermeticists.

THE CASE OF HERMANN BROCH

In 1944, the *annus mirabilis Virgilianus* that witnessed in England Eliot's "What is a Classic?" Connolly's *The Unquiet Grave*, and Jackson Knight's *Roman Vergil*, an Austrian refugee was sitting on the other side of the Atlantic, making the final revisions of a work that seems to embody Eliot's claims for the exemplary universality of the Roman poet as well as Haecker's view of Virgil as the *anima naturaliter christiana*. Hermann Broch (1886–1951) had chosen Virgil as the central figure of a lyrical novel, *The Death of Virgil* (*Der Tod des Vergil*, 1945), in which he sought to expose the crisis of Western civilization. As Broch described his work-in-progress in a 1939 proposal to the Guggenheim Foundation, "Virgil, standing on the threshold between two ages, exemplified the ethic poet par excellence; he summed up antiquity, as he anticipated Christianity."[10]

Broch was convinced from the start that he was creating a modern classic. "You know I do not overestimate the importance of literature, and today less than ever," he wrote to Willa Muir in 1940; "but within its realm I am quite sure that this *Vergil* is approaching to a new border of human expression, to a new border of the soul or of the world (for all these things mean the same)."[11] Three years later he explained to Thornton Wilder (whose *The Cabala* he gives no indication of knowing although the two writers were in close touch during the years when Broch was working on *The Death of Virgil*) that he did not regard the problem of art as the most urgent one at present. "But as far as art has its right of existence, I know that the Virgil is a forward step in the realm of German poetry and I wouldn't like to have it wasted by the ignorance or inability of the public, or the critics, to understand it."[12] In 1944 he confided to his publisher Daniel Brody that he regarded his novel "perhaps even as the most important literary product of these years."[13] In the half-century since the book's publication, Broch's evaluation has been seconded by many critics. Jean Starr Untermeyer, who accomplished the heroic feat of translating the massive work into English, entitled the chapter of her autobiography in which she described that labor "Midwife to a Masterpiece."[14] The scores of monographs and articles devoted to the appreciation of Broch's *opus magnum* have established it firmly in the canon of twentieth-century classics.[15]

Broch's work, which revolves around the legend according to which the dying poet wanted to burn his *Aeneid*, depicts in four parts the last eighteen hours of Virgil's life (September 21–22 of the year 19 B.C.). Returning from Greece with the Emperor Augustus, Virgil arrives at the harbor of Brundisium one evening. Because he is quite ill, the poet is borne on a litter through the reeking streets of the slums up to the palace of Augustus ("The Arrival"). In the course of a fitful night ("The Descent"), during which he is beset by visions from his past, the poet is tormented by self-recrimination at what he now regards as the waste of a life devoted to poetry. In Virgil's mind his poetry, and especially the *Aeneid*, has become a symbol of his own imperfection. Just as he has carefully filtered all disturbances and ugliness out of his life, so too has he distilled the reality of his poem until nothing is left but an unproblematic beauty. Instead of any profound cognition of life in all its aspects (what Broch calls "cognition of death"), Virgil has devoted himself to the lovely surface of things, praising the historical reality of Caesar's Rome rather than the transtemporal reality of the new era whose arrival he senses. The *Aeneid* is thus a living memorial to his "perjury" of reality, and he feels that he can atone for his guilt only by consigning his work to destruction. As dawn breaks he falls at last into a deep sleep that lasts well into the morning.

He spends his last day ("The Expectation") talking with various friends. Literary gossip with Plotius Tucca and Lucius Varius and medical discussions with the Greek physician Charondas are interspersed with phantasmagoric scenes involving a boy who seems to represent Virgil's own youth, a Syrian slave who utters proto-Christian sentiments, and the apparition of his one-time beloved Plotia, who embodies elements borrowed from Virgil's own figures of Dido, Eurydice, and the Sibyl.

The centerpiece of the work is a great encounter of poet and emperor, which Broch wittingly cast in the form of a Platonic dialogue.[16] Augustus has gotten wind of Virgil's decision to burn the *Aeneid*, his hymn to imperial Rome, and in a brilliant exercise in dialectics covering almost precisely one-fifth of the pages of the work, the representatives of two cultural epochs expound their positions. Augustus is an idealized totalitarian; for him all life revolves around the state, and the individual finds meaning only through service to the state. Virgil, in contrast, is what Broch called a pre-Christian—he has his foot all but on the threshold of a new system of Christian values in which a concern for personal freedom will outweigh the totalitarian concept of imperial Rome. Because neither of these strong-willed men is willing or able to understand the other, the dialogue never becomes true communication but remains a statement of positions in which they talk past each other. It exemplifies what is called in the novel the dilemma of "no longer and not yet," for Augustus represents an age that is virtually past while Virgil speaks with the voice of an era that has not yet come. (Actually, the theme of "no longer and not yet," which occurs elsewhere in Broch's works, has been subtly altered in this novel to "no longer and yet already," because Virgil has vivid premonitions of a future era that will be born only two decades later in Israel.) While Virgil tries to explain his decision to destroy his poem as a sacrificial act, Augustus objects that the poet has fulfilled his ethical responsibility by creating a symbol of the state in all its glory. He is offended when Virgil insists that the existing Roman state, far from being eternal, is nothing but the symbol of a human reality that is in the process of changing into a new and greater kingdom of the spirit.

At this point the story takes the twist that is foreordained by history. The two men have grown increasingly heated in the defense of their positions and, as the argument becomes more and more personal, Augustus angrily accuses Virgil of simple envy of his worldly power. Suddenly Virgil, relenting with no apparent motivation, agrees to relinquish the manuscript. He has perceived—Broch implies this rather than stating it—that it requires an even greater sacrifice to forgo his desire to burn the manuscript in what he perceives to be its imperfection. By destroying his poem, he would merely have gained a passing satisfaction: The act would amount to little more than a gesture of defiance. But by renouncing this wish, he is able to commit an act of human love, thus anticipating in his own way the kingdom of love and spirit which is to come. In return he asks of Augustus simply that his slaves be freed upon his death. Following Augustus's departure with the manuscript, Virgil spends another hour with Plotius and Lucius, adding terms and codicils to his will and testament.

Sitting with his friends that afternoon ("The Homecoming"), Virgil glides gently into death. As his consciousness fades, he slips into what he thinks of as a "first eternity"—that is, a state of exalted consciousness in which, liberated by his act of love, he comprehends first Lucius and Plotius but then Augustus and other friends, both dead and still alive, in their true essence and not through the merely superficial perception of ordinary reality. Gradually transcending all sensory perception, he moves into a "second eternity"—that is, a state of universal timelessness and unity with all being. First experiencing a kind of paradisical state, based on images from the *Eclogues* as well as the Bible, he sinks progressively through earlier stages of being; through the stages of animal, plant, and mineral life; back through the original separation of light and dark to the source of all being. At that point, two pages from the end of the book, concentrated into the purity of a cognitive eye, he turns around and in one dazzling epiphany surveys all life and reality. From this new perspective of reunification with the All, he can now make out the pattern of wholeness in a life from which all the polarities have disappeared. In his final vision, he witnesses the moving scene of a child in his mother's arms and the smile that links them both; but at this point, that image is no longer the recollection of a scene from his own fourth *Eclogue* but an anticipation of the birth of the new era that is on the point of replacing the glory of the Roman empire.

Part of the difficulty in dealing with this work lies in the fact that Broch was consciously striving to create a new genre; to measure it by the standards of ordinary novels is to criticize it unfairly. Alone among Broch's major prose works, it does not bear the designation "novel." In his letters and essays as well as the various statements he wrote in an effort to explain his undertaking to friends, editors, and foundations, Broch regularly referred to it as a lyrical work. He observed that the book is "a poem, though not in the sense of a single lyrical outburst and also not in the sense of a poem cycle on a central theme; yet a poem and, moreover, one that extends in a single breath over more than five hundred pages."[17]

From the very first pages, we are struck by a barrage of contrasts: above and below, within and without, here and beyond, past and present, motion and rest, I and All. Especially in the first section, life is presented as fragmented; nothing is whole. Virgil becomes increasingly aware of the dissonances of life and of the necessity to resolve them in order to attain any semblance of harmony in his own life. Such a resolution is possible only when all aspects of reality can be brought together in an all-encompassing vision: past, present, and future as well as life and death. A resolution of this sort can be accomplished only by means of sentences of a grand scope, and so Broch conceived as the underlying pattern of his book "one thought, one moment, one sentence."[18] His almost monomaniacal consistency produced some of the longest sentences ever written in the German language—sentences beside which even the more adventurous efforts of Thomas Mann pale. "One can probably claim," Broch boasted, "that the sentences in the adagio of the second part belong to the longest in world literature."[19] He justified this stylistic elephantiasis by his assumption that only a poetic form is "capable of producing unity of the disparate and making it plausible, for in a poem the utterance does not fulfill itself in the rational expression, but in the irrational tension between the words, between the lines, in short: in the 'architecture of meaning.'"[20]

Broch buttressed this "architecture of meaning" in various ways. Each of the four sections has a central symbol (water, fire, earth, and air) as well as a basic mood, which Broch conceived in musical terms (*andante, adagio*, [no specific term], *maestoso*).[21] The repetition and development of the various motives is treated consciously as musical variation. Broch's essays on the composition indicate how elaborately even the slightest details of the work have been plotted to intensify the "architecture of meaning."

Within this "symphonic" framework, the book has a distinct rhythm of development. In "The Arrival" Virgil is shocked into an awareness of the disjointedness of life. His feverish state makes him keenly aware of polarities: the leisure on board the ship and the agonies of the slaves groaning over the oars below, the blue sky above and the dark water below, the stench of poverty of the slums and the luxury of Augustus's lofty palace. That night, as these impressions fuse with memory in his feverish vision, he comes to the frightful realization that in his life as well as his work he has excluded an entire half of existence; he has willfully shut out grief and ugliness for the sake of beauty and empire. What the first part presents in visual contrasts and the second part in a lyrical inner vision, the third part recapitulates in dialectical arguments between Virgil and Augustus. In "The Homecoming," finally, all the conflicting elements are resolved in a grand epiphany of unity.

The monumentality of Broch's undertaking can easily obscure the fact that *The Death of Virgil* is not in the last analysis primarily about Virgil at all: It is a profound meditation on the meaning and value of art in the face of human existence and death. In one of his statements about "The Goals" of his novel, Broch stated that it was not merely his intention to describe the poet Virgil and his earthly life, but simultaneously also to reveal in the hero of the narrative those aspirations that are common to every artistic creation. The eternally valid theme with which all great poetry in all ages has concerned itself, namely the problem of approximation to death ("Annäherung an den Tod"), this theme that unavoidably forces itself upon all poetic creation, is likewise the principal concern of the present work.[22]

In many sections of the novel, especially in parts 2 and 4, Virgil is ignored for pages on end. Indeed, the so-called "Elegies of Fate" (*Schicksalselegien*), into which Broch concentrated the philosophical essence of his work, can be taken out of the novel and printed separately (as they have been) among his poems. Many of the meditations on time and mortality, on death and cognition, could just as well occur in novels called *The Death of Novalis* or *The Death of Rilke*—that is to say, novels about other writers obsessed by the same epistemological and eschatological questions that obsessed Broch.

At the same time, Broch had his reasons for putting Virgil at the center of his work. In the first place, a novel revolving around the destruction of a literary work requires for that purpose not just any poem but a work that matters to humanity; otherwise why should we care? Not many works fit that specification. But as Lawrence Lipking has observed, "To burn the *Aeneid* would be to destroy the thousands of poems, the millions of lives, that have been built on it—a holocaust devouring the very basis of civilization."[23] Second, as a member of his generation Broch was aware of the Roman analogy that played a constitutive role in European thought between the two world wars. But in Broch's mind, the political analogy took on pronounced religious tones. As he put it in a statement he prepared in 1939 for Viking Press:

> Following a decades-long bloody strife, which displays many analogies to the happenings of our time, Augustus pacified again the Western sphere of civilization and brought it to a new prosperity. Augustus' goals—the reconstitution of Roman glory, of the Roman spirit, of Roman paternal piety—seem on the whole to have been realized. Yet the after-effects of the profound disruptions could not be eradicated from the souls of men through such a total conservatism. Spiritually something new had to emerge, and it became Christianity.[24]

If this is correct, as he continued in the same statement, he hoped that his work might have a further analogous function and specifically

> that this book—precisely in a time like ours today, in a time searching for its lost religion, in a time of the resolution of all

ethical values and the search for their refoundation—will be able to provide something for many people, namely the beginnings of the ethical support that the world today needs just as in Virgil's time.

In reality, however, the theme of the novel did not emerge nearly so smoothly as Broch later presented it. Broch was hardly unaware of the festivities surrounding the bimillennial of Virgil's birth in 1930. But unlike almost all the writers discussed so far, he had no particular interest in, or knowledge of, Virgil. Indeed, he only gradually realized that the Roman poet fitted the ideological specifications that he had in mind for his work. According to an often quoted letter to Hermann J. Weigand, who wrote the first (and still fundamental) interpretation of *Der Tod des Vergil*,[25] it was not choice but chance that brought him to the Roman poet.[26] As Broch explained the circumstances, he was asked by Radio Vienna in 1935 to introduce the Pentecost program with a reading from his poetic works. Opposed in principle to such readings, Broch proposed to the director of the station a talk on the topic "Literature at the End of a Culture." Because for technical-budgetary reasons such a talk was unacceptable, Broch decided to incorporate his ideas on the decline of culture into a short story, and it did not require much deliberation (given the publicity surrounding the bimillennial, although Broch nowhere mentions it) to think of the parallels between the first pre-Christian century and our own age:

> civil war, dictatorship, and a dying off of old religious forms; yes, there was even a striking parallel to the phenomenon of emigration—that is, in Tomi, the fishing village on the Black Sea. Further, I knew about the legend according to which Vergil had wanted to burn the *Aeneid* and therefore might assume—accepting that legend—that a mind like Vergil's was not driven to such an act of desperation by trivial reasons, but that the entire historical and metaphysical meaning of the epoch played a role.

Even subsequently, when it occurred to him that it was Ovid and not Virgil who had been exiled to Tomi, Broch decided to stay with Virgil for the subject of his story. Yet "chance" is not a wholly satisfactory explanation for the inception of Broch's work. Even "chance" requires a certain background of circumstances in which to occur.

Thanks to various recent publications, we now understand the genesis of *The Death of Virgil* in considerable detail.[27] Scholars have been aware for some time that Broch's memory was playing tricks on him when he wrote to Weigand. There was no such immediate connection between the radio talk and the Virgil story as he implies. The talk entitled "Die Kunst am Ende einer Kultur" was actually written in 1933, not 1935.[28] The first version of the Virgil story, entitled "Die Heimkehr des Vergil" ("Virgil's Homecoming"), was not composed until 1936.[29] But Broch did read the first half of that story on the radio on March 17, 1937. Later that same year Broch returned to his story and, retaining essentially the outline of the original, expanded it fivefold.[30] When he was taken into custody by the Nazis in March 1938, he was reworking his story for the third time—an even more radical expansion whose new title, "Erzählung vom Tode" ("Story of Death"), suggests the new emphasis produced by the imminent threat to his life.[31] By 1939, now in American exile, Broch had undertaken yet another revision and expansion of his text under the working title "Die Heimfahrt des Vergil" ("Virgil's Journey Home"). This manuscript of roughly 160,000 words, completed in February 1940, constituted the basis for the fifth and final version, which Broch kept expanding and revising until the beginning of 1945—virtually until the moment of the book's publication.[32]

Although all five stages share the four-part structure of the original story—Virgil's arrival in Brundisium on a September evening, his restless night of memories and visions, his conversations the following day with friends, and his death some eighteen hours after his arrival—they differ conspicuously in detail and in emphasis. If we are going to talk with any precision about Broch's image of Virgil, we must therefore always specify the stage of composition. For instance, although Virgil's wish to burn the *Aeneid* constitutes the central problem of the novel as we know it today, that motif plays no role at all in the first version of the story, despite Broch's asseverations in the letter to Weigand. Similarly, his reference to parallels between Virgil's Rome and the modern age implies a familiarity with Virgil's life that is belied by his confusion of Ovid and Virgil in the same communication.

This confusion alerts us to a significant difference between Broch and almost all the other writers with whom we have been concerned: Broch had enjoyed no systematic training in Latin or the classics. Although as a boy he wanted to attend a classical gymnasium, his father, a textile manufacturer, insisted that the study of classics was "impractical"; so he sent his son to the Königlich-Kaiserliche Staats-Realschule in Vienna, where the future heir to the family business learned French and English rather than Latin and Greek. It was not until he was almost forty that Broch finally had the need and opportunity to rectify his educational deficiencies. In the 1920s, when he gave up business and returned to the university in the hope of obtaining a doctorate, a command of Latin was still required for the degree. The records show that Broch registered for elementary Latin courses over a period of five semesters, from 1925 through 1927, but he worked at it so indifferently that he did not even bother to take the qualifying examination.[33] Although these courses no doubt provided him with the rudiments of Latin, he acquired neither a thorough command of that language nor a familiarity with the tools of classical philology. Moreover, prior to 1936 there is no allusion in his essays or correspondence to the figure of Virgil. In fact, with the exception of occasional references to ancient philosophers, his writings display no interest in matters classical. We must therefore rely wholly on internal evidence to determine what Broch knew about Virgil when he first turned to his figure in 1936.

If we scrutinize the seventeen-page typescript that Broch called the "Ur-ur-ur-Vergil," we find very little indeed. Apart from a few rudimentary details, there are virtually no biographical facts: Virgil was born a farmer's son in the village of Andes near Mantua; traveling in Greece at age fifty, he encounters Augustus in Athens and is persuaded by the emperor to return with him to Brundisium, where he dies; and he expresses the desire to be buried outside Naples. As we noted earlier, the legend that constitutes the main theme of the final version—Virgil's wish to destroy the manuscript of the *Aeneid* at the time of his death—is missing here. The story revolves around Virgil's perception that Rome is beset by a crisis of faith, and this crisis causes him to entertain grave doubts concerning the validity and usefulness of poetry—a theme consistent with Broch's radio talk three years earlier. But he is pleased at the thought that his works will remain after his death as his bequest to his friends, particularly Maecenas and Augustus, to whom respectively the *Georgics* and the *Aeneid* are dedicated.

Another curious circumstance deserves to be noted. Although his authorship of the *Georgics* and the *Aeneid* is mentioned in passing, in this early version Virgil is essentially the poet of the *Eclogues*. There are only two allusions to the *Aeneid*, and one of those is incorrect: Broch confuses the son with the father, causing Anchises to carry Aeneas through the burning streets of Troy. Otherwise the few direct allusions all refer to the *Eclogues* (1 and 4). This emphasis is of course consistent with the theme of the first version, which focuses on civil war and the crisis of values, as do Virgil's early poems. Because the question of destroying the *Aeneid* has not yet become central, there is no reason to highlight that work.

In sum, the first version of Broch's story does not yield evidence for more than a casual familiarity with Virgil's life and works. Yet the very sketchiness of the evidence enables us to establish his source with a fair degree of probability, for both the biographical details and the interpretation of the life correspond with a high degree of coincidence to the presentation in Theodor Haecker's *Virgil, Father of the West* of 1931. Haecker's book also contains conspicuously few biographical facts, but it utilizes almost exactly those few details that Broch picks up in "Die Heimkehr des Vergil." More importantly, Haecker's interpretation of Virgil parallels Broch's: He stresses the political turmoil of Virgil's age, he insists on the fundamental importance of the *Eclogues* vis-à-vis Virgil's later writing, he emphasizes the power of love in Virgil's works, he accepts the analogy between past and present as a key to the understanding of modern Europe between two world wars, and he does not mention the legendary wish to burn the *Aeneid.*

We know from a letter to Aldous Huxley that Broch read and appreciated Haecker's book—especially Haecker's view of Virgil as a proto-Christian.[34] And in his appendix to the published novel, Broch states that he used Haecker's translation of the *Eclogues* for all passages from those poems that he incorporated into the various stages of his novel. Indeed, in Broch's copy of Haecker's *Hirtengedichte* (Leipzig: Hegner, 1932; now in the Yale University Library), most of the quoted passages are underlined in pencil. So it is plausible to assume that Broch got his information about Virgil's life as well as the translations from Haecker—in fact, that he knew nothing about Virgil that was *not* in Haecker's two works. We can be even more precise. In 1934 Broch mentions Haecker several times as a thinker whose ideas are quite congenial with his own. In April of that year, for instance, he twice wrote to his publisher Daniel Brody of his high esteem for Haecker's philosophical tract *What is Man?* (*Was ist der Mensch?* [1933]) and urged Brody to read Haecker's other works.[35] In the absence of any references to a story about Virgil prior to this date, it seems reasonable to assume that Broch's interest in the Roman poet was kindled specifically by Haecker's book of 1931 and his translations in the edition of 1932, which Broch probably read sometime after 1934.

We can now begin to reconstruct the situation. We know from Broch's radio talk "Art at the End of a Culture" and from letters of the period that by 1933 the author of the impressive novel *The Sleepwalkers* (*Die Schlafwandler,* 1931–32) had gradually become convinced that literature is no longer a viable or even legitimate mode of expression in the present age. His reading of Haecker's book suggested to him that Virgil might well provide a suitable figure through whose consciousness the situation might be explored fictionally—by means of the analogy between past and present that had been widely publicized during the Virgil celebrations in 1930. When he set down the first brief and preliminary version of the story, he was concerned only with the problem of art in an age of crisis—not with the burning of the *Aeneid.* He was an autodidact with no classical background, and his knowledge of Virgil was limited essentially to what he learned from Haecker.

When Broch began to revise and expand his story in 1937, he added very little new biographical detail apart from the figure of Augustus—an addition probably introduced in response to the intense publicity accompanying the bimillennial of the emperor's birth that same year. (In the first version, the conversation in part 3 takes place between Virgil and Maecenas.) But he did make one major change: He introduced the motif of Virgil's wish to destroy the *Aeneid* as a gesture denying the legitimacy of art. Where did Broch get that motif? In 1931 Broch had met, through his publisher Brody, Ernst and Emmy Ferand, who operated a dance school in the Laxenburg Palace in Vienna.[36] During the first half of 1935, Broch occupied a room in the palace, and Emmy Ferand translated one of his stories into Hungarian. Knowing that Frau Ferand enjoyed reading Latin literature in the original, Broch presented her with a nineteenth-century Latin edition of the *Aeneid*, which he had bought in an antiquarian bookshop.[37] Frau Ferand, when she realized that Broch was himself working on a story about Virgil, translated the first few paragraphs of the vita that she found in the front of the volume and gave them to him as a surprise in late 1936 or 1937—in any case after the first version had already been written. It was this translation that Broch subsequently attached as an appendix to the published novel, stating misleadingly (in the first edition) that he had found it in a seventeenth-century German translation of the *Aeneid*. (In subsequent editions Broch acknowledged Emmy Ferand as the translator.) This vita recounts the legend according to which Virgil wanted to burn the *Aeneid*. It seems clear, then, that Emmy Ferand's translation provided, sheerly by chance, the source for the central theme of the novel as it developed.

That shift of emphasis necessitated in turn a major change in the texture of the work, for Virgil could no longer be presented primarily as the poet of the *Eclogues*. He must now appear as the author of the great Roman epic. Accordingly, it became desirable to introduce into the text allusions to and quotations from the *Aeneid*. Where did Broch get those passages? In his appendix to the published novel, Broch states that all passages from Virgil's works, apart from Haecker's translations of the *Eclogues*, represent new translations from the original ("Neuübertragungen aus dem Originaltext"). Readers were long inclined to take Broch at his word. But how "original" are in fact the translations from the *Aeneid* and the *Georgics* that Broch incorporated into his novel? If we simply consider the published text, it looks very much as though Broch did make his own translations, for the passages are stylistically consistent with the lyrical prose that Broch created for the purposes of his work. Moreover, a survey of the roughly half-dozen German translations available at the time, including Schröder and Trendelenburg, reveals no source for the cited passages. But the matter turns out to be less straightforward than it appears.

If we work our way back through the various stages of composition, we note that the translations from Virgil also change from stage to stage. By the time we get back to the second version of 1937, in which for the first time Broch included passages from the *Aeneid*, the quotations stand out conspicuously from Broch's own prose. To make a long story short, the quotations from the *Aeneid* are lifted almost without change from the translation of Virgil's works published by Johann Heinrich Voss in 1799[38] and recently (1926) reprinted in the inexpensive paperback editions of Reclams Universal-Bibliothek. With each successive revision, Broch also revised the incorporated translations until finally they bear only a slight resemblance to their source. For instance, in the conversation with Augustus, Virgil quotes the words from the beginning of the *Georgics* in praise of Caesar. The Latin text goes as follows:

> anne novum tardis sidus te mensibus addas,
> qua locus Erigonen inter Chelasque sequentis
> panditur (ipse tibi iam bracchia contrahit ardens
> Scorpios et caeli iusta plus parte reliquit):
>
> (*Geo.* 1.32–35)

(whether you insert yourself as a new star into the slow months, where between [the constellation] Erigone and the trailing Claws a space spreads wide (even now blazing Scorpio draws back his arms and has left you more than a fair share of the sky).

Voss translates quite literally as follows:

> Ob du, ein neues Gestirn, den langsamen Monden dich an-
>   fügst,
> Dort wo Erigone weit den folgenden Scheeren vorangeht;
> Schau, wie er selbst, dir weichend, die Klaun einzieht, der ent-
>   brannte
> Skorpion, und mehr denn schuldigen Himmel dir räumet.
>
> (Voss translation, 1.124)

Broch's "original" translation, which first appears in the "Heimfahrt" and is carried over with the same wording into the final version, reads as follows:

> Dir, dem neuen Gestirne, von langsamen Monden umfüget,
> dort, wo Erigones Bahn den Skorpionen heranlockt, dir
> weichet selbst dieser, der feurig Entbrannte, vor dir zieht
> die Klauen er ein und räumt dir den dienenden Himmel.
>
> (*Tod des Vergil*, 358)

Most of the passages cited or alluded to can be traced back in this manner to Voss. For the final version, as Broch acknowledges in his appendix, the verse translations of several longer passages were provided by Erich Kahler (in whose house Broch was living at the time); but up to the point of Kahler's intervention precisely the same progression is still evident. In part 2, for instance, the boy Lysanius quotes an extensive passage from *Aeneid* 8 beginning:

> miratur facilisque oculos fert omnia circum
> Aeneas capiturque locis et singula laetus
> exquiritque auditque virum monumenta priorum.
>
> (*Aen.* 8.310–12)

(Aeneas marvels and, turning his mobile eyes this way and that, is captivated by the scene and happily inquires about each thing and hears the records of the men of old.)

Again Voss's rendition is highly literal:

> Aber Aeneas bewegt die fertigen Augen um alles,
> Angereizt von den Orten, und staunt; und des einzelnen
>   fröhlich
> Forscht er umher, und vernimt die Denkmal' alter Geschlechte.
>
> (Voss 3.101)

Broch picks this up in the untitled version of 1937 with only one change in vocabulary (*munter* for *fertig*) and with minor modernization of spelling and punctuation:

> Aber Äneas bewegte die munteren Augen um alles,
> Angereizt von den Orten und staunt, und des Einzelnen
>   fröhlich
> Forscht er umher und vernimmt die Denkmal' alter Ge-
>   schlechter.
>
> (*Materialien*, 57)

The "Erzählung vom Tode" makes further minor modifications (achieving an unfelicitous rhythm in the first two lines):

> Aber Äneas bewegte die freundlichen Blicke um alles,
> Angeregt von den Orten, staunend und froh jeglichen Dinges

Forscht er umher und vernimmt die Denkmal' alter Ge-
schlechter.

(Materialien, 157)

In "Die Heimfahrt des Vergil" (1940) Broch plays around somewhat
more boldly with the text:

Voll Verwunderung wirft Aeneas die regsamen Augen
Rings auf alles, gereizt von den Gegenden, und mit Vergnügen
Forscht und vernimmt er die Kunde von Heldenmalen der
Vorzeit.

(Materialien, 323)

The version that Erich Kahler provided for the published version, finally, departs in most respects from Voss and manages to make Virgil
sound almost like Broch:

Alles um ihn herum verlockte den Geist und die Blicke,
Schwer von Vergang'nem die Gegend und trächtig von Taten
der Vorzeit
Und so lauschte Äneas den stumm sich eröffnenden Sagen.

(Tod des Vergil, 183)

Scores of briefer passages from the *Aeneid* and *Georgics* alike are taken
without exception from Voss's translation with Broch's own modifications. Some undergo fairly extensive revisions and show up in the published volume looking more like Broch than Voss. Other passages display few signs of stylistic adaptation. In any case, the manuscripts yield
absolutely no evidence to suggest that Broch prepared, as he claimed,
new translations from the original: They are, to put it most accurately,
adaptations of Voss—a procedure consistent with what we have seen to
be Broch's limited command of Latin. He knew enough to collate a
translation with the original and to make adjustments, but he could not
easily translate afresh from the original text.

Even with the texture afforded by the increased incorporation of
Virgilian texts from the second version on, Broch realized that his story,
as it grew longer, was conspicuously thin in vivid biographical detail.
On March 10, 1938, when he was well into the third draft, he wrote to
his friend Joseph Bunzel, asking for information concerning Virgil: "I
now feel obliged after the fact to expand the source study that I have
greatly neglected."[39] Again we must rely largely on internal evidence,
for there is no record of the material that Bunzel or others may have
suggested to Broch. And, as he subsequently wrote to Weigand, the
emphasis in the book on the central experience of death required him
to play down merely "cultural materials" (*Bildungsmaterial*).[40] Begin-

ning with the third draft, however, we find a certain amount of new biographical data, including such details as the names of Virgil's family and friends, the story of his love for Plotia Hieria, as well as his affection for two youths called Cebes and Alexander, and various other facts that lend color and substance to the narrative. Where did Broch get this information?

In the appendix to the published novel, Broch states that he used all available information concerning the life of Virgil. Claiming that he consulted the standard reference works, he maintains that it would be superfluous to provide a bibliography of sources. Instead he includes the three-page translation by Emmy Ferand from a work that he identifies as a representative example of the legends that grew up around the figure of Virgil in the Middle Ages. Broch characterizes the roots of the legend as typically medieval. In a slightly different version of the afterword attached to the working manuscript that he presented to Hannah Arendt Broch goes on to say that he lost his notes, including the bibliographical information, during his flight from the Nazis and that he has not succeeded in identifying the edition in American libraries.[41]

Broch could not have looked very hard. At the time he was expanding the fourth into the final published version, he was living within six blocks of the finest Virgil collection in the Western hemisphere, the Junius S. Morgan Collection in the Princeton University Library. But ten minutes of research in any reasonably comprehensive classics library would have provided him with the needed information. The passage appended to his novel amounts to the first few pages of the so-called "expanded" Life of Virgil by Donatus, the famous vita attached to scores of editions from the fifteenth century down through the nineteenth, including the standard Heyne-Wagner edition that was widely used well into the twentieth century (see Ch. 2).

Broch's failure to recognize the source provided by Emmy Ferand is illuminating for several reasons. It suggests, first of all, that we must not take Broch too seriously when he claims to have consulted all the standard works of Virgilian biography. He could not have used the recent German biography by Walter Wili (1931), the English biography by Tenney Frank (1922), the standard German and English studies of the ancient lives of Virgil by Henry Nettleship (1879) or Ernst Diehl (1911), or Comparetti's magisterial study of *Virgil in the Middle Ages* (1872) without learning the name of his source. It suggests, second, that Broch is putting on airs when he characterizes the text as medieval and its language as monastic Latin (*Klosterlatein*), for the quoted passage is taken from that part of Donatus Auctus which is essentially classical. Moreover, the accounts of miraculous prophecies concerning Virgil's birth, which strike Broch as medieval, are in fact characteristically ancient, based as they are on legends that arose during Virgil's own lifetime. Finally, an amusing mistake in Ferand's translation suggests that Broch did not know enough about classical antiquity to question an egregious error and that he did not know enough Latin to check it.

One of the prophecies concerning Virgil's birth states that his mother Maia dreamed while she was pregnant that she had given birth to a laurel branch (*praegnans eum mater Maia somniavit enixam se laureum ramum*[42]) which, as soon as it touched the ground, took root and sprouted up into a large tree with blossoms and fruit—a variation on common prophecies concerning the birth of illustrious men who will live to earn the laurel wreath for their achievements. In Ferand's translation, however, the passage is given a new twist: Maia does not give birth to the laurel branch; she climbs up on it—no small feat for a pregnant woman in her ninth month who is about to deliver her child the following morning! ("Die schwangere Mutter Maja träumte, sie sei auf einen Lorbeerast gestiegen.") What matters here is not that Emmy Ferand slipped while translating but that the same error was carried over from edition to edition and even into the English translation by Jean Starr Untermeyer, which was made with Broch's constant collaboration.[43] Broch did not know enough classical philology to identify the standard life of Virgil; he did not know enough about the Roman context to detect a patent absurdity in his text; and he did not know enough Latin to distinguish medieval Latin from classical Latin or to pick up a howler of a translation error. Nevertheless, he attempts in his appendix to the published volume to give the impression of competence and authority both in Virgilian studies and in Latin—and many students of Broch and his novel have taken him at his word.

However, the main point is this. Almost every biographical detail in the entire novel, in drafts three through five, can be found in the passages from Donatus Auctus that Broch quotes in his appendix—from Virgil's olive complexion and kinky sexual preferences to his schooling in Cremona and his house on the Esquiline hill. The few details that are not included in the portion printed in the novel—e.g., the name Flaccus for Virgil's brother and Proculus for his stepbrother, the mention of the early compositions *Aetna* and *Culex*, as well as the details concerning his will and testament—are contained in later sections of the same vita. Indeed, a few details are to be found only in Donatus Auctus and not in other vitae: e.g., the spelling Maia (rather than Magia) for Virgil's mother, or the fact that Cebes and Alexis achieved a certain fame as poet and grammarian respectively. It seems most likely that Emmy Ferand's translation was originally more extensive than the passage actually quoted in the novel; as we have seen, Broch stated that his notes were lost during his flight from Austria and that he retained only one sheet by accident.[44] It is also possible that Broch asked Ferand about certain details from the untranslated passages of the vita. However, there is absolutely no indication that Broch made any attempt, either in Europe or later in the United States, to go beyond the biographical information available in Donatus Auctus.

What Broch did add to the later stages of the novel was material of two kinds. Throughout he inserted—this is evident in the final manuscript—a number of leitmotifs from Virgil's works: the gates of ivory and horn (*Aen.* 6.893–96), the frozen snake (*Ecl.* 8.71), the Golden Bough (*Aen.* 6.136–48), the Age of Saturn (*Ecl.* 4.6), and others. Even in the final draft, Broch noted in the margins the specific source (with book and line number) of all the allusions to Virgil's works.[45] In keeping with his original emphasis on Virgil as the author of the *Eclogues*, we find references to all ten of those poems, with particular emphasis on the fourth. The *Georgics* are mentioned only a few times and, apart from the tale of Orpheus and Eurydice, play no constitutive role in the novel. Most books of the *Aeneid* are alluded to at least once, but Broch was clearly more familiar with the first half, and specifically with Book 6, which is frequently cited. In general, Broch takes the quotations out of their Virgilian context and reintroduces them "intertextually" into his own work for the new meanings that they assume there.[46]

In addition, into the conversation between Virgil and his friends Plotius and Lucius, Broch injects as casual literary gossip a certain amount of handbook knowledge concerning contemporary Roman literature and literary figures—lore that could easily have been obtained from any history of literature. In fact, the manuscript of the second draft (Yale University Library) has numerous notes written into the margin to indicate additions to be included in the third draft: e.g., the name Marcus Terentius Varro along with the titles of his principal works; the notation that Tibullus died in the same year as Virgil; the fact that the booksellers Sosii had bought Horace's *Carmen saeculare* (an anachronism because Horace's great poem was written two years after Virgil's death). But to repeat: Nothing suggests that he went beyond Donatus Auctus for information concerning the life of Virgil. Indeed, in the summer of 1939 he complained to René Spitz that Virgil was "at the moment intimately familiar to me but no less boring for that reason."[47] Small wonder that he did not trouble to stroll over to the Princeton University Library to verify his facts or to discover new ones.

It is tempting to point to the conspicuous parallels of biography and thought that might have enabled Broch to salute in Virgil a kindred spirit. Both writers were initially destined by their fathers for practical careers; both turned to literature during their maturity; and both around age fifty toyed with the idea of renouncing poetry in order to devote themselves to philosophy. Both men displayed a pronounced dedication to work: the tag from the *Georgics*—*labor omnia vicit improbus*—would have been an appropriate motto for Broch, who liked to boast to his correspondents that he was working eighteen hours a day. As writers, both men composed their works by a process of constant revision and through the integration of familiar material rather than by the invention of new material. The Virgilian reverence for *ordo*—the harmonious relation of parts to the whole—is evident not only in the literary work of both writers but also in the ethical impulse that constitutes a conspicuous component of their character. Both men shared a cyclical conception of history—the conception that permitted Broch to detect in Virgil an anticipation of his own social concerns. Virgil's obsession with *fatum*, finally, is reflected in the *Schicksalselegien* that enter Broch's novel in the later stages.

But to cite such parallels as the basis for any sympathy that Broch might have felt for Virgil would be contrary to the facts. First, the few passages outside the novel in which Broch talks about Virgil as a historical figure suggest that Broch was unaware of those implications. In the studies on mass psychology that occupied Broch in 1943, he characterizes Virgil briefly in passing as a peasant shattered by the disintegration of his social class, by the horrors of the civil war, and by the metaphysical unrest of his age—a forerunner of Rousseau and Tolstoy appalled by the new Roman urban proletariat and driven, for that reason, into his dreams of a primal paradise.[48] Second, we have Broch's own word for the fact that he was bored by Virgil as a person and that he found his poetic accomplishments less significant than his dubious credentials as a proto-Christian. Third, to overestimate the importance of these parallels would be to attribute to Broch a knowledge of Virgil's life and thought that he did not possess. Finally, the main conclusion of our findings would be obscured: that Broch knew little and cared less about the historical Virgil, using him merely as a figure upon which to impose his own views and concerns. Unlike almost all the other writers we have considered, who were initially enchanted by Virgil's poetry, which they had read in Latin, Broch came to the poetry only after he had been alerted to Virgil's role as the poet of Rome at the end of a cultural epoch.

The purpose here is not to denigrate Broch or to play down the magnificent achievement of his novel but to put matters into a proper perspective. If Broch did not bother to inform himself in great detail about Virgil's life, the reason was that his own image of Virgil had increasingly taken precedence over the historical Virgil. The legend concerning Virgil's wish to destroy the manuscript of the *Aeneid* goes back to classical antiquity and plays a role in the earliest vitae, and classical scholarship has had no reason to doubt the motivation given in the earliest versions of the legend: that Virgil was dissatisfied artistically with his epic, which would have required according to his estimate at least three more years of careful polishing in Greece before it would be suitable for posterity. When we recall that Virgil spent three years composing the roughly eight hundred lines of the *Eclogues* and seven years polishing the two thousand lines of the *Georgics*, it is easy to appreciate that this same poet—who, it is estimated, composed his *Aeneid* at the rate of roughly one line a day for twelve years—would have been reluctant to release a work that he did not regard as perfected. Therefore, when Broch attributes Virgil's decision to burn the *Aeneid* to metaphysical doubts involving the crisis of values and the illegitimacy of art, he is projecting onto an ancient author modern anxieties that have no basis in history or the extant texts. Furthermore, as Broch was working on the third draft of his novel in 1938, the threat of death at the hands of the Nazis loomed ever more imminently, and the constant preoccupation with death gradually shattered the framework established by the figure of the historical Virgil and his oeuvre. "It was no longer the dying of Vergil," Broch wrote in the letter to Weigand, "it become the imagining of my own dying." This shifting emphasis helps us to understand why the working title of the novel kept changing over the nine years between its inception and its publication.

Paradoxical though it may be, in a novel based on the theme that art is irrelevant and even immoral, Broch became increasingly obsessed with the artistry of his own work. It is symptomatic that the essays he wrote about his novel, which served as the basis for the publishers' promotion and for the translator's afterword to the English version, mention only in the first sentence the substantive basis of the book— that it deals with the figure of the historical poet Virgil.[49] Most of the time Broch is intent upon stressing what he regarded as the technical literary achievement of his own work: notably the four-part musical structure of the whole, the lyrical character of the language, and the sentences that he proudly calls the longest ever written in the German language. But this estimate of his accomplishment is consistent with what we have seen to be his attitude toward Virgil. Broch was not essentially concerned with Virgil at all. He imposed upon the Roman poet the problematics of his own consciousness, and for that reason he could not make too much use of historical or biographical evidence, for it might have undermined his motivation of the poet's character. After all, the historical Virgil was not Broch's Virgil—a distinction that he stresses in the letter to Weigand. This means, in turn, that we are dealing essentially with a work of integration rather than one of innovation—a novel that grew from stage to stage by creative integration of materials that Broch found readily at hand. He did not make new translations of Virgil nor exhaust the biographical and scholarly-critical sources. Using Voss's translations and a fragment of the vita by Donatus, he worked and reworked the passages and details that he found there into a brilliant fabric depicting his own twentieth-century consciousness superimposed onto the figure of the historical Virgil.[50] To this extent Broch's achievement resembles nothing more closely than another German novel written during those same years in Princeton that also revolves around the portrayal through memory, dream, and conversations of a great writer's consciousness and, by a curious coincidence, takes place within a few hours of another September 22: Thomas Mann's *The Beloved Returns* (*Lotte in Weimar*, 1939).[51]

OTHER "DEATHS OF VIRGIL"

While *The Death of Virgil*, at least to the extent that it is largely dependent upon Haecker's book and translation of the *Eclogues*, is at least indirectly indebted to the bimillennial celebrations, there is nothing to suggest that Broch was even remotely aware of the extensive literary response among other contemporary writers in Europe and the United States. Indeed, all his utterances imply that he was convinced of the absolute originality of his return to Virgil. At the same time and more than in any other case we have considered, Broch's Virgil is little more than a mold into which the writer poured his own modern problematics. For that reason we must be more than usually cautious when we speak of Broch's image of Virgil or his reading of the *Aeneid*. At the same time, it is only when we put Broch's novel into the context of the times that we appreciate its true originality, which can be seen— to put it drastically—in what is *non*-Virgilian in his book: in the concept of the lyrical novel and in the meditations on aethetics and mortality. The Virgilian matter, in contrast, is wholly derivative and, in fact, less original than, say, the treatments by Gide or Eliot or Tate—a fact overlooked by critics who tend to consider Broch's work in isolation from the rest of contemporary literature and to give him credit simply for placing Virgil at the center of a novel. Indeed, if we look around, we realize that even the initial idea of a story revolving around the Roman poet's death is not unique to Broch.

In 1930, as its own gesture toward the bimillennial celebrations, the *Atlantic Monthly* published a story entitled "Anima Candida" by Anne C. E. Allinson (1871–1932).[52] The author, a Bryn Mawr Ph.D. in classics, had made her reputation in American education as a teacher of Greek and Latin and as Dean of Women first at the University of Wisconsin and then at Pembroke College of Brown University. But it was especially as a columnist for the Providence *Evening Bulletin*, as a reviewer and essayist for wide-circulation magazines, and as the author of popular books on early Christianity and Roman culture that she earned a national readership. As early as 1917, Allinson published in the *Yale Review* an essay on "Virgil and the New Patriotism," which takes the Roman poet as an occasion to discuss the contemporary dilemma of the perceived immoral consequences of patriotism.[53] "We see that while devotion to country entails the final sacrifice of self, it entails also the most unhumane sacrifice of others" (98). Yet the problem is not a new one, Allinson claims. Our ethical uncertainty can be found in Virgil who, though born fifty years before the first Christian church was founded in Rome, "almost anticipated the New Testament" (98). Indeed, Virgil can be seen as "the apostle of imperialism and the prophet of humanity" (99).

The essay continues with a graceful account of Virgil's life and works based on the ancient vitae and interweaving many quotations from the poetry. We hear about the "progressive patriotism" that inspired the *Georgics* (106) and about Virgil's growing concern at the spiritual dangers to which the empire was exposed in its power and wealth. Coming to believe that only a "reverence for the early strength, for the gravity and constancy and dignity of the Roman character" (107) could save the people, he undertook to write an epic about the founding of Rome. But although he never questioned the "ethical precedence" of Aeneas's enterprise, Virgil was not unaware of its cost. Reminding us that Napoleon scorned the warfare of the *Aeneid*, Allinson pays especial attention to the second half of the epic, pointing out that Virgil, unlike Homer, "describes war with horror instead of with joy" and therefore "must appeal to the tortured conscience of our new age" (110–11). For this reason Virgil's patriotism was utterly different from that of the Germans whom the United States had just engaged in war. "No German is more convinced of the 'Ideal, Mission, Destiny' of his own people than Virgil was of Rome's. But quite un-German was his conception of the character of the civilization which must be forced upon other peoples" (117). Rather than the power and efficiency of the empire, its vision of justice and simplicity and tranquillity inspired Virgil's admiration. If Virgil's patriotism made him the exemplary poet of his age, his poetry has survived because it was "haunted by the spiritual presences of absent things" (118). And for that reason, Allinson concludes, Virgil would have been quite comfortable with the new religion that Paul was to bring to Rome only two generations later.

Many of these sentiments, and essentially the same view of Virgil, minus the patriotic fervor of World War I, are evident in Allinson's bimillennial story. Of relevance here is the first of the story's four sections, which introduces Virgil lying on a couch of tortoise shell and ivory at the portico of his sick room. "It was an afternoon of late September, and the sun over Brindisi was still almost as hot as that sun over Megara which, ten days ago, had seemed to drop a burning shaft upon the poet's head" (145).[54] Racked with fever, Virgil is the houseguest of Tullus, an intimate friend of the emperor, where he is attended by Augustus's personal physician and cared for by several slaves skilled in nursing. As he rests near the garden fountain, "his patient, kindly face relaxed from its habitual attentiveness" (146), and his thoughts wander over present concerns and his past life in an extended interior monologue. The physician has told him that he has a chance to live. But "life had rarely seemed to him worth the struggle, and now that he had passed the half century, fulfilled his ten lustrums, why should he struggle longer?" (147). He has no wife or children. His brothers and parents are dead as well as Gallus, the favorite comrade of his youth. His remaining friends—Horace, Varius, Tucca—can get along without him. "As for Maecenas, as for Augustus, these bright stars would shine on in the firmament of Rome, losing no ray of light because a poet died" (147).

The thought of Augustus and Maecenas reminds him by association of his first visit to Brindisi twenty years earlier when he journeyed down with a literary party accompanying Maecenas, who was mediating between Octavian-Augustus and Antony. "Horace had started with him, and Varius, Tucca, and Virgil himself had joined on at Sinuessa. Horace had written it up in his inimitable way. Who else would have thought of informing the public that when Maecenas played ball he and Virgil took a nap!" (148). (Virgil is paraphrasing the *Satire* (1.5.40–48) in which Horace coined the phrase that provides the story's title:

> Plotius et Varius Sinuessae Virgiliusque
> Occurrunt, animae, quales neque candidiores
> Terra tulit · · · · · · · · · · ·
> Lusum it Maecenas, dormitum ego Virgiliusque.)

(Plotinus and Varius and Virgil joined us at Sinuessa, spirits than whom the earth has borne none brighter. . . . Maecenas goes off to play, Virgil and I to sleep.)

These memories lead Virgil back in time through his student days in Rome, his decision not to go to Athens for further study, and his exploration of his beloved Italy, from the snowy Alps to the warm seas of Sicily. As Virgil's thoughts slip back to his boyhood, to his father's farm near Mantua, and to games with his brother, images from the *Eclogues* and *Georgics* color the narrative.

Once he had plunged his hand down among purple hyacinths and touched a snake—even yet he remembered its slimy coldness. Apple trees were safer—the red fruit was so firm and fresh in the hand when you had stood on tiptoe and pulled down a heavy bough. Always there had been something interesting, from the spring ploughing and planting to the autumn vintage. The cattle and even the bees were playmates. On rainy days the farm hands welcomed help in mending the tools or parching the corn or plaiting the baskets, and filled the hours with old country stories and songs.

(149)

He recalls childish dreams of Rome, which his father had described to him. At that time, like Tityrus in the first *Eclogue,*

The only town he knew was Mantua, to which he was taken on market days, and he had merely enlarged it into Rome, because he had seen that puppies looked like dogs and kids looked liked their dams!

(150)

The thought of Rome brings him back to the present. "In her service he had been long enlisted. She was his commander, his goddess, his mistress" (150). The return to present awareness produces an excited flush in his face and a sudden anxiety.

He must accomplish his purpose before it was too late. The *Aeneid* must be destroyed. It was not worthy of Rome. Incomplete, imperfect, it must die with him.

(150)

Too weak to get to his feet, he summons the slave who takes letters and dictates a strict order to Varius that his unfinished works must not be published. In the very act of dictation, his voice subsides and his flushed face becomes pallid. Before midnight Virgil is dead.

The remaining sections can be summarized quickly. We learn that the publisher Sosius, shortly after the poet's death, spends a few days with Varius and Tucca in Virgil's villa at Posilipo, where the friends have just buried Virgil and are now dealing with the house, the slaves, and the literary bequest. Varius is distressed because they have been compelled by Augustus to go against Virgil's testamentary wish by publishing the *Aeneid.* But Tucca reassures him that Virgil had undertaken the epic as an imperial service and that it therefore could not be regarded as a private matter. They review the poet's reasons for his decision: There are incomplete lines and passages, Virgil intended to reshape the twelve books into a more harmonious whole, and an "inner iconoclasm" had destroyed the poet's confidence in his power to serve Rome. For the benefit of Sosius, who is unfamiliar with the manuscript, they characterize its style—especially the similes—and recapitulate the entire plot of the epic (part 3). They whet Sosius's business appetite by telling him that the fourth book, the love story of Dido and Aeneas, would make his fortune if he issued it separately. Following this extended plot summary, Sosius consoles Virgil's chief copyist, Geta, with the request that he should accompany him to Rome "and help me to make your master still live" (163).

The fourth section is cast in the form of a letter from Horace to Maecenas. Writing from his Sabine farm, Horace recalls a visit years earlier when Virgil had walked about his few acres with him, testing the soil. With his gentle shyness, Virgil was in every sense a countryman. Yet he had a powerful vision of a better age that survived from the *Eclogues* to the end of the *Aeneid*. At the same time, his patriotism was not without fear. "Only the one who hopes most for Rome can know the full measure of terror for her short-comings" (165). It was his longing for a purer life among the people that persuaded him to write an epic to glorify Rome by portraying its early history and nobility. As the autumn wind rises and his fire grows cold, Horace expresses his conviction that "our Virgil was the whitest soul among us" (166).

There is no need to make a detailed comparison between this story of twenty pages and Broch's novel of five hundred. Moreover, because it is highly unlikely that Broch was aware of Allinson's story, there is no question here of literary influence. Yet it is striking that most of the major elements of Broch's masterpiece are present at least *in nuce* in Allinson's piece: the interior monologue of the dying poet in Brundisium, the decision to destroy the *Aeneid*, the discussions (albeit after the poet's death) of the pros and cons of that decision, and a review of Virgil's life and works set in the context of imperial Rome. Both works create their texture by the extensive use of quotations and allusions, direct as well as hidden, that are woven into the fabric. As Tityrus remarked to Meliboeus: *sic canibus catulos similis, sic matribus haedos* (*Ecl.* 1.22). Yet we cannot deny a certain generic similarity between the pups and the dogs, between the kids and the goats. Behind "Anima Candida" and *The Death of Virgil*, we recognize the bimillennial celebrations and the literary technique of integration that characterized many works of the period.

Through Broch's influence the image of the dying Virgil persisted as a literary topic for several decades. Only four years following its publication, Leonard Bernstein phoned Broch to announce his plan to make *The Death of Virgil* the basis of a symphony in four movements (water, earth, fire, and air).[55] Bernstein's plan apparently never materialized, but the French composer Jean Barraqué (1928–1973) actually did undertake, and complete several parts of, an immense composition based on the novel—a composition, according to rumor among his friends, planned to be longer than Bach's *Passion of St. Matthew* and Wagner's *Parsifal* combined.[56]

One work indebted to Broch was actually completed, the radio play *Vergil Dying* (1979) by the English novelist and playwright Gabriel Josipovici (born 1940).[57] The play is a monologue in seven continuous scenes set in Brindisi, where Virgil has arrived with Augustus's fleet. Suffering from a severe chill, he lies in his room in the royal palace with the metal casket containing the manuscript of the *Aeneid*. As he mumbles to himself, we understand that Virgil had hoped for a new start in Athens: "No more poetry. No more falsehood. Truth. The peaceful study of Truth" (2). (With a Virgilian fondness for wordplay, Josipovici's "Vergil" plays on an assumed etymological connection between his name and the words for "spring" [*ver*] and "true" [*verus*].) With extensive quotations and allusions to his poetry (in C. Day Lewis's translations of the major works and the Loeb translations of the minor poems), Virgil faces the truth about himself—that he has been at most a spectator of life—and about his own poetry: "You sang to avoid yourself. To conjure away the thoughts of death" (25). These thoughts bring him to the realization that the *Aeneid* must go. "It must be destroyed. Nothing but lies. Pollution. The source of pollution" (28).

The play revolves structurally around the almost wordless section 4, in which Virgil, weakened by fever, struggles off the couch and attempts to open the manuscript coffer. When he is unable to do so, the crisis passes and he crawls back to his bed (29). In the last three scenes, Virgil works his way back up to an acceptance of reality. "Accept it all. Sympathy with all. . . . The *beauty* of this earth!" (41). At this point he is able to die in peace, with the image from the last line of the first *Eclogue* in his mind:

> longer falls the shadow cast by the mountain heights
> That voice . . . You? Or you? Or you?
> falls
>   falls the shadow
>   longer falls
>   longer
>   the shadow
> (Whisper) AT LAST!
>
>   (43)

Josipovici has written a detailed account of the composition of his work.[58] He had no classical training and, until the late 1970s, little interest in Virgil. But when he had the opportunity of writing a radio play for Paul Scofield, "At once, for no reason that I could or can fathom, I thought, simultaneously: 'Virgil in the underworld!' and: 'My play!'"(248). Years earlier he had read Broch's *The Death of Virgil*—with initial excitement but increasing disillusionment. By an associative leap, he connected Virgil's wish to destroy the *Aeneid* with Kafka's injunction to his friend and executor, Max Brod, to burn all his unpublished work. To explore this question Josipovici undertook his play, reading and rereading all of Virgil and studying not only the scholarly works but also Donatus. "What really convinced me that I had a subject which was both close to my heart and out there in Virgil was my growing realisation that so much of Virgil's work, like Kafka's, was about *exile* and *doubt*" (251). Added to this was the intuition that Virgil "in talking about Aeneas and his men . . . was talking about Israel" (253). Finally, the work of American scholars on Virgil's number symbolism provided Josipovici with the idea for the "palindromic pattern" (256) of his own work: three sections descending to the single act that constitutes section 4, followed by three precisely analogous sections moving back up to the final resolution.

Josipovici has gone on to create a work that is independent in form and emphasis from the model that Broch provided. (To be sure, the biographical analogy to Kafka and the textual analogy to the Bible would have been quite congenial to Broch.) Yet his radio play would be inconceivable without *The Death of Virgil*, and especially the interior monologue of the novel's second section. So this work, though written almost fifty years after the bimillennial and suggesting no awareness of it, constitutes a late efflorescence of the Virgilian restoration between the wars.

~

Conclusion

VIRGIL IN A POST-VIRGILIAN AGE

The shade of Virgil, so compellingly evoked by the moderns, did not simply subside quietly after 1945 into the eternities from which it had emerged, like the spirits in Anacleto Trazzi's *Virgilius Redux* or Thornton Wilder's *The Cabala*. We have already observed that the momentum of modernism lasted well past the end of World War II to generate the ironized *Aeneid* of Anthony Burgess's *A Vision of Battlements*, the late reflex of Southern Agrarianism in Robert Penn Warren's *A Place to Come To*, and a postmortem of Broch's *The Death of Virgil* in Gabriel Josipovici's *Vergil Dying*.

The decades since 1945 have also produced works in which Virgil figures. But the very fragmentation of his presence among what Auden called "the ruins of the Post-Vergilian City"[1] enables us to calibrate the degree to which the Roman poet has lost his authenticity for writers of a new generation. There is no better example of this than in Carlo Emilio Gadda's *That Awful Mess on Via Merulana* (*Quer pasticciaccio brutto de via Merulana*, 1957), one of the most influential literary works of postwar Italy. Gadda's novel, which is sometimes compared in its effect and stylistic brilliance to Joyce's *Ulysses*, first appeared serially in 1946–47 in the newspaper *Letteratura* and was published as a book ten years later. In its genre the novel appears to be a Dostoyevskian crime story, set in the Rome of 1927, in which a homicide detective, Dr. Francesco Ingravallo, investigates two related crimes—an armed robbery and a savage murder—that have taken place in the same apartment house on the solidly bourgeois Via Merulana. The details of plot are not relevant because the crimes are never satisfactorily solved (hence the "mess," *pasticciaccio*), although Dr. Ingravallo has a very strong suspicion of the truth.

What does matter is the fact that Gadda's novel is also, and primarily, an indictment of the moral depravity of Italian society at every level—from the debauched upper classes through the corrupt bureaucracy to the petty criminals in the streets—under the Fascists, which Gadda describes with a satirical savagery that betrays Virgilian tones:

> The moralization of the Urbs and of all Italy, the concept of greater civil austerity, was then making its way. . . . Crimes and

suggestive stories had abandoned forever the Ausonian land, like a bad dream dissolving. Robberies, stabbings, whorings, pimpings, burglary, cocaine, vitriol, arsenic bought for poisoning rats, abortions *manu armata*, feats of pimps and cardsharpers, youngsters who make a woman pay for their drinks—why, what are you thinking of?—the Ausonian land didn't even remember the meaning of such things.[2]

(88–89)

The individual principally responsible for this decline from ancient Roman grandeur is "the Ass on high" (109), the "Puppet in Palazzo Chigi, yelling from his balcony like an old-clothes man" (116). In the degradation of Mussolini's state, where even the policeman is prevented from enforcing the law, reminiscences of ancient glory, going back to the founding of the city by Romulus and Remus, are constantly present: E.g, the murdered woman, Signora Liliana, scion of a distinguished old family, had a grandfather named Rutilio, whose name is often confused with "Romilio," and she herself had long been secretly in love with a man named "Remo" (148–49). Gadda, portraying a fragmented world, is no longer able to make use of a sustained postfiguration of the *Aeneid*. But scattered elements make their way into the story. Margherita Sarfatti, Mussolini's one-time mistress, is "now reduced to playing Dido Abandoned" (64). And the hero of Virgil's epic shows up in Gadda's tawdry world in the person of Enea Retalli, a nineteen-year-old petty thief. Enea, the son of Anchise Retalli and his wife Venere née Procacci, has the proper genealogy. He is traced by the police when he passes stolen goods to his fiancée, an illiterate peasant girl named Lavinia, and her potato-faced cousin, the seamstress Camilla. This sordid reduction of Roman glory and its great epic exemplifies more vividly than does any editorializing the sorry state of Fascist Italy only three years before the bimillennial celebrations.

The absence of Virgil is also evident in the early poems that Thomas Bernhard published under the title *Ave Vergil*. Although the volume was not published until 1981, the poems were written in 1959 and 1960 in Oxford and Sicily, where the thirty-year-old Austrian author was turning away from the model of such national poets as Georg Trakl and exposing himself to the influence of international modernism—an influence acknowledged by an epigraph from T. S. Eliot's *The Waste Land*. The poems begin rather like demented *Georgics*, with an apostrophe to the still unnamed Roman poet, who appears like a wraith (*Gespenst*) to the young Austrian in the coldness of the modern world. Bernhard tells him that his words, too, sought sheep, swine, oxen, and cows while his father's plow "disfigured the constellations" in ancient books.[3] The conclusion amounts to a paean to the poet's own land and his relation to it, which he has acquired without the mediation of the ancient poet, obtaining his knowledge of heaven and earth from the potato ditches, the darkness of the pigsty, and the rubble of autumn apples. Indeed, his relation to the rivers of his own land stands between him and the Roman poet.

Virgil's name occurs only twice in the fifty pages of the poems: once in a list of "conquerors of the world": Dante, Virgil, Pascal (55). In a more extended passage (20–21), the young Austrian asserts his independence from the authority of the Roman *vates*, stating that he discovered cities two thousand years after Virgil did and learned from the very stars "the language of foreign peoples, Virgil's letters, the speech of my peasants." Bernhard's "farewell to Virgil," in sum, amounts to a symbolic departure from the traditions that still governed the poets of classic modernism. The volume is most significant, in our context, for its appropriation of Virgil as the canonical figure exemplifying the cultural heritage that the postwar generation rejects.

Bernhard's younger fellow Austrian Peter Handke, in contrast, seeks to restore the continuity that Bernhard's generation shattered as a gesture of independence. As Handke observed in one of his literary aphorisms, "Every fairly extensive mystical adventure—of the sort that writing is—makes me clearer, more precise, more rational, and attracts me, as a reader, more and more away from Kafka's shambling [*Geschlenkere*] to the bright day-work of Virgil."[4] Handke's most Virgilian work is the novel *Across* (*Der Chinese des Schmerzes*, 1983), which is at once a celebration of the landscape around Salzburg and the story of a man who overcomes an existential crisis in his life with the spiritual assistance of the Roman poet. Andreas Loser is a high school classics teacher who, in despair at the meaninglessness of his life, has left his job and his family and lives over a supermarket in the southern outskirts of Salzburg—in a "state of abeyance" ("in der Schwebe"), according to the phrase that recurs leitmotivically throughout the account.[5] So out of touch is he with life, such an outsider in his local world and so pained by that circumstance, that an acquaintance gives him the nickname that provides the German title of the book: "the Chinaman of Grief." Loser claims to have taken leave in order to prepare an archaeological report on a Roman villa newly unearthed near the Salzburg airport. Obsessed with thresholds—both real and symbolic ones—he thinks of himself as a "thresholdologist" (*Schwellenkundler*, 24). His state of abeyance (*on* the threshold, so to speak) continues until he is violently reconnected to life when, one evening on his way to a weekly card game with friends, he sees an unknown man spray-painting swastikas on a wall and in a sudden fit of anger kills him with a stone. This impulsive act initiates a series of events that lead to Loser's reintegration into society, his family, and his job.

Although the action of the book may not seem particularly Virgilian, the Roman poet, especially as the author of the *Georgics,* is a constant presence throughout the text, and not simply as the model for the earthy descriptions of the landscape around Salzburg. Early in the story we learn that Loser, slowly and word for word, reads a few lines from the *Georgics* at the end of every day—a work, he says, that he would like to translate in his retirement. "The verses of the *Georgics* also turn time back for me, or put it into another context. . . . You can learn from the poem a good deal about the laws of nature that does not go out of date" (43). Loser tells us how he was able to use Virgil's teachings to care for the grapevines and laurel tree in his own garden.

> The teaching that matters to me, however, I do not derive from these rules for agriculture, but from the enthusiasm (which never becomes an intoxication)—that is, the poem—about things that are still valid: the sun, the earth, the rivers, the winds, the trees and bushes, the domestic animals, the fruits (with their baskets and jugs), the utensils and tools.
>
> (44)

The Roman poet has affected the very way Loser perceives the world: "As I looked up a car from somewhere was turning onto the canal bridge, which thanks to Virgil's verses now shimmered with a particular blue" (46). Though the *Aeneid* is never mentioned, the *Eclogues* and especially the *Georgics* dominate the narrative. Loser knows from the *Georgics* that a storm is signified if the moon appears with a reddish cast (48); salt, we hear, is always paired in Virgil with the modifiers "scarce" or "hidden" (150–51); he is reminded that in Virgil the acanthus "smiles" (154) and that the epithet for hibiscus is "graceful" (190).

The centrality of Virgil emerges most clearly toward the end of the account when Loser, as a penultimate stage in his spiritual rebirth, takes a flight to Milan and, from there, a train to Mantua, where he seeks out Virgil's birthplace.

> A few kilometers south lies a village named Pietole, which was formerly called Andes and is supposed to be Virgil's birthplace. Past the village behind an embankment flows the Mincio, which Virgil once called "huge," streaming "in slow bends" through the lowlands of Lombardy, its banks "overwoven with delicate reeds." Today, one reads in the Virgil editions, the Mincio is only a narrow stream. But standing before it I saw: that is not true; the river corresponds exactly to the two-thousand-year-old description.
>
> (221)

Loser goes swimming in the clay-brown water and then, back in the village, sits in the "Trattoria Andes," where he observes that Virgil could not have known the corn, the potatoes, the tomatoes, and the "false" acacia that are now cultivated in the region. Following his symbolic rebirth from the waters of the Mincio, which is highlighted that night by a dream of his mother's bed, Loser returns—by way of Sardinia, where his own two children were conceived—to Salzburg. Thanks to Virgil, he has crossed the threshold from his earlier state of abeyance into a life of normal human connections.

The *Georgics* also fulfill their traditional function as a point of stability in a world of disorder in Claude Simon's remarkable novel *Les Géorgiques* (1981). The title is both a literary allusion and a pun, and it is the pun that holds together the three parts of this complex narrative structure. The narrator interweaves three levels of wartime experience: the era of the French Revolution, the Spanish Civil War, and the fall of France in May of 1940 (the period that Simon portrayed in his masterpiece, *The Flanders Road*). It is implied, though never stated, that the narrator of this work is the same "Georges" who narrates *La Route des Flandres* (1960). And in the passages concerning the Spanish Civil War the author makes extensive use of George Orwell's accounts. Though those two sections amount to "Georgics" in a punning sense, the third—and major—level of narrative has a literary aspect consistent with an author who studied Latin intensively as a boy with the priests at the Collège Stanislaus in Paris.

Most of the long novel concerns a minor aristocrat whose life involves him in many of the most important stages of French history during the revolutionary era: as a young officer, as a member of the National Assembly, as a general in charge of artillery in the army of Italy, as an ambassador to Naples under the Directory. From wherever his duties may take him—from Tunisia to Prussia, from Spain to Holland—"he writes long letters to his stewardess ["intendente"] Batti to prescribe to her in detail according to the season the chores to be carried out on the lands of his domain" (26).[6] It is in these letters, and in the occasional face-to-face interviews with Batti, that we sense the real meaning of the title: the general's (we never learn his full name) obsession with his ancestral estate in southwestern France leads him to compose epistles that, although owing little in a literal sense to Virgil's poems, amount in spirit to veritable "georgics" in their knowledge and appreciation of country life and that fulfill essentially the same role as did Virgil's, that is, constantly reminding that the cultivation of the land provides a lasting foundation in the tumultuous social and political upheavals of the times, whether they be the Roman civil wars or the revolutionary wars of France. It is the irony of the work—and a sign of Simon's skepticism at Virgil's ability to provide any meaning for the modern world—that the ancestral home falls into decline in the hands of the general's descendants while his own name is retained only as the brandname for a liqueur.

Similarly fragmented Virgilian associations are evident, finally, in Michel Butor's novel *La Modification* (1957).[7] The action of the novel is simple: Léon Delmont, the forty-five-year-old Paris representative of an Italian typewriter company, travels to Rome one weekend in 1955 to inform his mistress Cécile that he has located a position for her in Paris. This would enable the two of them to live together after he has separated from a wife and family from whom he has become almost wholly estranged. But in the course of the twenty-hour train ride, Delmont decides to return to Paris without having looked up Cécile and to write a book explaining reasons for his sudden "modification." In the train compartment, which provides Delmont with the same kind of "abeyance" as does Loser's leave from his job, his reflections are triggered by various associations: memories of earlier trips between Paris and Rome; the mirrors and pictures decorating the compartment as well as scenes beyond, or reflected in, the windows; the other travelers in the third-class compartment; and cultural associations stimulated by the letters of Julian the Apostate, the works of Virgil, and the art of Michelangelo—the latter two representing respectively the poet and architect of the city of Rome, which in Delmont's mind assumes mythic proportions (198).

Butor, who in a 1957 newspaper piece on Mantua used a phrase with a conspicuously bimillennial flavor when he called Virgil the "poète fondamental de la latinité,"[8] includes a couple of allusions to the *Eclogues* as well as the *Georgics* in his text, e.g., the phrase *hic ver assiduum*[9] from the *laudes Italiae* (*Geo.* 2.149). But the principal references come from the *Aeneid*, whose first six books, as we learn, Delmont has previously read in the Budé edition (218). Delmont's decision to abandon Cécile—sensing that transplanted to Paris she would lose her appeal, which resides for him essentially in her identity with the city of Rome—postfigures Aeneas's desertion of Dido.

Butor is more explicit about the sixth book. As he tosses restlessly in the crowded compartment, Delmont dreams (176–86) that he is descending into a grotto where he encounters, crouching before a fire, the Sibyl, whose appearance resembles that of a beak-nosed old Italian woman who had earlier entered the compartment (158–59). She recognizes that, like Aeneas in the underworld, "you are also going in search of your father so that he can teach you the future of your race" (179). But unlike Virgil's Sibyl, this one refuses to help him obtain the golden bough because, as she tells him (180), Delmont still belongs to those who are "alienated from their own desires" (180). In a visionary meeting with Charon (whose apparition is apparently triggered by the entrance of the ticket collector), Delmost slips as he tries to board the metal boat and almost sinks in the mud. But Charon drags him out and transports him across the river to a place that turns out to be the Rome of his longing. It is in the course of this phantasmagoria, just as in Aeneas's descent to the underworld, that Delmont achieves an understanding about his own future and makes the decision that leads to his rejection of Cécile, his return to Paris, and his decision to write the book that we are reading.

Though Butor's novel employs Virgil's works, and specifically Books 4 and 6 of the *Aeneid*, in a loosely prefigurative manner, its post-Virgilianism is evident in the fact that Virgil, as simply one among several cultural sources, is summoned up here not so much for his values, for his *pietas* and *ordo*, as for the purely aesthetic structure that his work provides.

Virgil has been detected elsewhere in the late twentieth century, as for instance in the mythologizing works of Tolkien.[10] Feminist critics have suggested, but not specifically claimed, that Virgil's Sibyl represents the "authentic female voice" in the otherwise male-dominated world of the *Aeneid* while Creusa's death marks the "canonical replacement of female by male creation"—motifs that are traced in the fiction of Gloria Naylor and the cultural theories of Luce Irigaray.[11] Another critic has detected Virgilian echoes in a film by director Spike Lee.[12] In a cycle of poems entitled "Sibyls," the contemporary English poet Ruth Fainlight includes one called "Aeneas' Meeting with the Sibyl," in which Aeneas finds it difficult, in memory, to reconcile the awesome augur who conducted him safely through the underworld with a sibyl who might have come straight out of *The Waste Land*—"like a skinny / gypsy with a joint dripping ash in the corner of her mouth / quizzing the Tarot cards."[13] Yet despite these examples, the decades since World War II provide nothing to match either the great number of Virgilian works in Europe and America in the years surrounding the bimillennial celebrations or the evidence for Virgil's influence on many of the finest and most representative writers of the period. Recent works are too discrete to constitute any groups or to display patterns other than the negative pattern of fragmentation. We do not live in Virgilian times.

THE MEANING OF VIRGIL'S SURVIVAL

Measured against recent as well as preceding decades, the years from 1914 to 1945 were distinctive. The examples discussed in the chapters above, embracing many major figures of literary modernism, should effectively put to rest the widespread misconception, advanced yet again in a recent anthology of English poets' writings on Virgil and other classical authors, that "the achievement of the twentieth century does not justify a very positive closing note."[14] As we have seen, Virgil remained a powerful sustaining presence in the works of such writers as T. S. Eliot, Hermann Broch, Paul Valéry, Giuseppe Ungaretti, Allen Tate, and many others at least through the first half of the century.

Why should this have been so? The survival (or what in German is called the *Nachleben*) of Virgil resulted, as we have seen, from a unique conjunction of factors. First, it was made possible by the fact that so many of the writers as well as their readers had benefited from the thorough grounding in classics that was still standard in European, English, and American schools up to 1914 (and, in fact, until World War II). They were thus familiar with Virgil in Latin as a cultural possession that dated back to their school days. (Remember the staying power of Virgil's lines even in the memory of a detractor like Henry Miller!) The exceptions we noted—Hermann Broch, Giuseppe Ungaretti, Vita Sackville-West, Jean Giono—seem to confirm the rule because all of them took steps in later life, through the belated study of Latin or at least through the use of translations, to compensate for what they came to regard as a serious deficiency in their educations.

Second, the generations that we have been discussing consisted of people who read poetry and to whom poetry mattered. As Noel Annan observed about his own contemporaries in England, "They were a generation who lived through poetry."[15] For this reason, as we have seen in the specific case of Virgil, they read, translated, and anthologized "poetry that spoke to their heart in a way which . . . it did not seem to speak to their successors"—successors who were attracted not only to the theater and the novel, but also increasingly to radio, television, film, and other forms of artistic expression. Anthony Burgess's *A Vision of Battlements* is symptomatic of the resulting cultural downgrading of Virgil, exemplifying as it does the shift from the high seriousness of epic to the ironic comedy of the modern novel. A similar refocusing is evident in Gabriel Josipovici's reduction of Broch's mammoth *The Death of Virgil* to a radio play.

Third, the sense of crisis produced by the First World War and intensified by the chaotic social and political upheavals of the 1920s and 1930s sent writers and their readers back to the past in search of patterns of order and stability, as well as models of personal behavior. Indeed, it is an underlying theme of Ronald Syme's *The Roman Revolution* (1939) that many Europeans of the times, wearied by social and economic uncertainties, were tempted like the Romans of the Augustan Age to sacrifice a degree of personal liberty for the reassurances of political stability. The Roman analogy and, through it, the conservatism evident in the life and works of Virgil, achieved a relevance that had not been apparent to the Victorians, who appreciated Virgil above all for the sonorous beauty of his poetry. This new trend was evident in the popularizing biographies as well as the bimillennial statements.

Finally, the publicity attendant upon the bimillennial celebrations presented Virgil as a particularly appropriate exemplar because literary references to him and his works would not be lost upon culturally interested readers. Here Hermann Broch, who seized upon Virgil after the fact to incorporate his theory of literature in an age of cultural decline, is the paradigmatic example.

Although these factors appear to be constant from writer to writer and from country to country, we observed conspicuous national preferences—virtually a *rota virgiliana* that revolved from *pascua* by way of *rura* to *duces* as we moved westward from Europe by way of England to the United States. The *Eclogues* spoke with a new urgency to continental nations recovering from the war, laboring under a great depression, and seeking for an appropriate response to the forms of totalitarianism emerging all over Europe. Here the examples of the French bucoliasts as well as the German millennialists are exemplary.

The *Georgics* did not play a significant role on the continent—not, at least, until they were taken up in postwar years by Thomas Bernhard, Peter Handke, and Claude Simon—but they were constitutive, as we have seen, in England and the United States, where Virgil's return to the soil appealed in equal measure to T. S. Eliot as a social theorizer, to the English georgicists, and to the Southern Agrarians.

Evidences of the *Aeneid* show up in Ungaretti, Broch, Eliot, Connolly, as well as in many American writers, but conspicuous differences are also evident in their preferences. Only in the United States was the westering theme and the conquest of new lands an important element: in Allen Tate's poems, in Elizabeth Madox Roberts's epic, in Thornton Wilder's novel. For this reason the *translatio imperii* was evoked almost exclusively by the American writers. In Europe, by way of contrast, it was essentially the first half of the epic that commanded the attention of writers: e.g., the Dido tragedy (in Eliot's early poems or in Ungaretti's *La terra promessa*) and the unhappy fate of Palinurus (in Ungaretti and Connolly's *The Unquiet Grave*).

Although such examples as the English georgicists and the French bucoliasts or the German millennialists and the Southern Agrarians seem persuasive, such national groupings should be considered simply as tendencies, not as absolutes. We observed certain ideological affinities that transcend national lines. The appeal of what some felt to be Virgil's proto-Christian attitudes linked Theodor Haecker and Hermann Broch with T. S. Eliot and Thornton Wilder in a fellowship that might be loosely called Christian humanism. While those who sympathized with the totalitarian movements in France and Italy detected a protofascist strain in Virgil's thought, the French bucoliasts as well as the Italian hermeticists turned to the Roman poet as a refuge in their political escapism. In the United States, Virgil was evoked by Robert Frost as a support for a nonparticipatory individualism and by Allen Tate as a witness for political action. Visions of *Virgil Redivivus* inspired writers from Italy and Austria to the United States. Finally, we must not forget the fraternity of Robert Graves, Ezra Pound, and Henry Miller, who were united by their common Virgiliophobia.

In the final analysis, however, common denominators that transcend national or ideological groupings account for the survival of Virgil in the first half of the twentieth century. These, I believe, can be recapitulated in two related themes: the descent to the underworld and the discovery of history—that is to say, Virgil's view of man and his view of mankind.

By the first, the Tartarean theme, I mean Virgil's insight into the dark side of human affairs that was unknown to, or at least ignored by, the Victorians and earlier generations that admired in Virgil essentially, in Dryden's words, "the best Poet." From Gide's apprehension of Virgil's complex sexuality to Connolly's analysis of Palinurus's conflicting emotions (will to failure coupled with remorse), from Lowell's recognition of Aeneas's streak of inhumanity to Broch's exploration of Virgil's own dualities, the writers of the 1920s and 1930s were fascinated by that ambivalence in Virgil's view of humankind that was subsequently defined by Adam Parry in his well-known essay on Virgil's "two voices."[16]

Virgil's profound sense of order, which enabled him to perceive a pattern and direction in human history while acknowledging the necessity of evil as a factor in that process, captured the attention of readers who had been sensitized to disorder by the events of their own times. Recognizing in Virgil's works a response to the violence of the late Republic from which the *imperium* emerged, they began to appreciate for the first time his relevance for the modern world. It is this shock of recognition that speaks to us from C. S. Lewis's theory of "secondary epic," from Eliot's essays, from Tate's poems, as well as from dozens of celebratory writings in every country.

Generations of writers and thinkers between Freud and Toynbee who witnessed the passing of the seemingly stable pre-1914 world now sought Virgil's guidance in their own descent into the spiritual and historical underworld exposed by the war's ravages. What they learned to value in the course of that ordeal was a *vates* whose poems, long considered so perfect as to be morally irrelevant, provided a golden bough for the journey through the extremes of human behavior—our impulse to nobility combined with our capacity for evil, the desire for order set against the terror of history. They came to understand that the *magnus saeclorum ordo* envisioned by the young artist of the *Eclogues* is always qualified by an awareness of the *lacrimae rerum* keenly felt by the poet of the *Aeneid*. It was this recognition that impelled many writers, despite the skepticism of detractors and in the face of a growing public indifference to the past, to reaffirm the cultural continuity linking classical antiquity and the twentieth century, binding Virgil and the moderns in a conspiracy of understanding. This reaffirmation, attained at the cost of great spiritual engagement by our intellectual predecessors, we neglect today at our peril.

_____ ❧ _____

PREFACE

1. Donald Davie, "Virgil's Presence in Ezra Pound and Others," in *Virgil in a Cultural Tradition*, ed. Richard A. Cardwell and Janet Hamilton, University of Nottingham Monographs in the Humanities 4 (Nottingham, 1986), 135.

CHAPTER ONE

1. "Ein Hinweis auf die Verdrängung"; Letter of July 17, 1899; in Sigmund Freud, *Aus den Anfängen der Psychoanalyse: Briefe an Wilhelm Fliess, Abhandlungen und Notizen aus dem Jahren 1887–1902* (London: Imago, 1950), 305. Freud repeats the quotation a few pages from the end of the 1909 edition with the commentary, "The interpretation of dreams is the Royal Way to an understanding of the unconscious in the life of the soul"; *Die Traumdeutung*, 5th ed. (Leipzig und Wien: Franz Deuticke, 1919), 449. For an overly speculative reading of the meaning of the quotation in Freud's thought see Jean Starobinski, *"Acheronta Movebo,"* *Critical Inquiry* 13 (1987): 394–407. Freud's interpretation of another quotation from the *Aeneid, exoriare aliquis nostris ex ossibus ultor* (4.625), is analyzed by August A. Imholtz, Jr., "The Vergilian Context of Freud's 'Aliquis Analysis,'" *Victorians Institute Journal* 17 (1989): 51–62. Northrop Frye adduces the epigraph to demonstrate what he regards as "the Virgilian inspiration of modern scientific mythology"; see "New Directions from Old," in his *Fables of Identity: Studies in Poetic Mythology* (New York: Harvest/HBJ, 1963), 66.
2. Indeed, the same quotation had already been coopted in a political sense by Ferdinand Lassalle, who used it in 1859 as the epigraph for his book, *Der italienische Krieg und die Aufgabe Preußens*, to suggest the socialist appeal to the lower classes. See Carl E. Schorske, "Politics and Patricide in Freud's *Interpretation of Dreams*," in Schorske's *Fin-de-Siècle Vienna: Politics and Culture* (New York: Knopf, 1980), 181–207; here 200–201. Although Freud was familiar with Lassalle, whom he mentions in the same letter, he had read Virgil since his schooldays and had originally planned, as he wrote to Fliess on December 4, 1896 (*Aus den Anfängen*, 184), to use the same quotation to head a chapter in his unwritten book on the psychology of hysteria.
3. *Album Virgiliano. XVII Settembre MDCCCLXXXII* (Mantova: Mondavi, 1883), iii.
4. Robert Graves, "The Virgil Cult," *The Virginia Quarterly Review* 38 (1962): 13–35; here 13.
5. *Ego contra hoc quoque laboris praemium petam, ut me a conspectu malorum, quae nostra tot per annos vidit aetas, tantisper certe, dum prisca tota illa*

mente repeto, avertam. Quoted from *Titi Livi Ab Urbe Condita Libri I. II. XXI. et XXII*, ed. Charles Anthon (New York: Harper, 1891), 25.

6. Karl Jaspers, *Die geistige Situation der Zeit*, reprint of 5th edition of 1932, Sammlung Göschen 1000 (Berlin: De Gruyter, 1947), 67.

7. Rudolf Pannwitz, *Die Krisis der europäischen Kultur* (rpt. Bayreuth: Emil Mühl, 1947), 41: "Es gibt nichts ungeschichtlicheres als die geschichte" (l.c. [*sic*]).

8. Ernst Robert Curtius, *Der Syndikalismus der Geistesarbeiter in Frankreich* (Bonn: Cohen, 1921).

9. Ernst Troeltsch, *Der Historismus und seine Probleme*, Gesammelte Schriften 3 (Tübingen: Mohr, 1922), 1.

10. On the difference between "historism" and "historicism," see Georg G. Iggers, "Historicism," in *Dictionary of the History of Ideas*, ed. Philip P. Wiener, vol. 2 (New York: Scribner, 1973), 456–64.

11. Karl Heussi, *Die Krisis des Historismus* (Tübingen: Mohr, 1932), 20.

12. Troeltsch, 1–8, makes this general point; but it is also noted by such non-German historians as, for instance, Johan Huizinga, "The Task of Cultural History," in the collection of his essays published under the title *Men and Ideas*, trans. James S. Holmes and Hans van Marle (New York: Meridian, 1959), 17–76; here 40. See also G. P. Gooch's 1952 introduction to the new edition of his *History and Historians in the Nineteenth Century* (1913; rpt. Boston: Beacon Hill, 1959), ix.

13. Ernst Troeltsch, "Die Krise des Historismus," *Die Neue Rundschau* 33 (1922): 572–90; here 584.

14. Karl Heussi, *Die Krisis des Historismus*, esp. 22–38; and C. H. Becker, "Der Wandel im geschichtlichen Bewußtsein," *Die Neue Rundschau* 38 (1927): 113–21.

15. Theodor Lessing, *Geschichte als Sinngebung des Sinnlosen, oder die Geburt der Geschichte aus dem Mythos*, 4th ed. (1927; rpt. Hamburg: Rütten und Loening, 1962).

16. H. G. Wells, "The Story and Aim of the Outline of History" (1939), in *The Outline of History*, rev. Raymond Postgate and G. P. Wells (Garden City, N.Y.: Doubleday, 1971), 1.

17. "Rosa Luxemburg als Marxist," in the study edition of *Geschichte und Klassenbewußtsein* (Neuwied: Luchterhand, 1968), 94.

18. "The Task of Cultural History," in *Men and Ideas*, 39–51.

19. Oswald Spengler, *Der Untergang des Abendlandes: Umrisse einer Morphologie der Weltgeschichte* (München: Beck, 1963), 36–39 ("Einleitung," section 10).

20. Spengler, *Untergang*, 1102.

21. Arnold J. Toynbee, *A Study of History*, vol. 4 (London: Oxford Univ. Press, 1939): viii-ix.

22. *A Study of History*, vol. 6 (1939): 284.

23. *A Study of History*, vol. 6, 318.

24. Friedrich Gundolf, *Caesar: Geschichte seines Ruhms* (Berlin: Georg Bondi, 1924), 7.

25. Volker Losemann, *Nationalsozialismus und Antike: Studien zur Entwick-*

lung des Faches Alte Geschichte 1933–1945 (Hamburg: Hoffmann und Campe, 1977), 19–20.

26. Adolf Hitler, *Mein Kampf,* 14th ed. (München: Franz Eher Nachfolger, 1932), 469–70.

27. Karl Christ, *Römische Geschichte und deutsche Geschichtswissenschaft* (München: Beck, 1982), esp. 164–260.

28. Werner Jaeger, *Humanistische Reden und Vorträge,* 2d ed. (Berlin: De Gruyter, 1960), 169.

29. Ronald Syme, *The Roman Revolution* (Oxford: Clarendon Press, 1939), 4.

30. Walther Rehm, *Der Untergang Roms im abendländischen Denken: Ein Beitrag zur Geschichtsschreibung und zum Dekadenzproblem* (Leipzig: Dieterich, 1930), vii. In 1939 Rehm published a second contribution to this discourse, his study of *Europäische Romdichtung,* 2d ed. (München: Max Hueber, 1960).

31. Rehm, *Untergang,* 6.

32. *Europäische Romdichtung,* 244.

33. I rely for the following information on Ugo Piacentini, "Über die Rolle des Lateinunterrichtes und der römischen Geschichte im faschistischen Italien," *Das Altertum* 10 (1964): 117–26. For a more thorough discussion of Gentile's educational reforms, see Lorenzo Minio-Paluello, *Education in Fascist Italy* (London: Oxford Univ. Press, 1946), 68–75.

34. Edmund G. Gardner, *Virgil in Italian Poetry.* Proceedings of the British Academy 17 (London: Humphrey Milford, 1931), 23.

35. *Latinité* 2 (1930): 478–80.

36. *Master Vergil: An Anthology of Poems in English on Vergil and Vergilian Themes,* ed. Elizabeth Nitchie (Boston: Heath, 1930), 23.

37. "Rudolf Borchardt über Virgil," in Ernst Robert Curtius, *Kritische Essays zur europäischen Literatur,* 2d edition (Bern: Francke, 1954), 29.

38. "Zweitausend Jahre Vergil," *Neue Schweizer Rundschau* 23 (1930): 730–41; rpt. *Wege zu Vergil,* ed. Hans Oppermann (Darmstadt: Wissenschaftliche Buchgesellschaft, 1976), 29–42.

39. In the journal *Atene e Roma,* N.S. 5 (1924): 225.

40. *Enciclopedia Virgiliana,* ed. Umberto Cozzoli (Roma: Instituto della Enciclopedia Italiana, 1984ff.), 2: 469–72 ("fascismo e bimillenario della nascita di Virgilio").

41. Albert R. Bandini, "The Fortune of Vergil," *Catholic World* 132 (1930): 66–74; and V. Ussani, "La celebrazione bimillenaria di Virgilio," *Nuova Antologia* 348 (1930): 263–69.

42. Herbert L. Willett, "Vergil and Mussolini's Italy," *The Christian Century* 47 (1930): 1445–47.

43. V. Ussani, "La celebrazione bimillenaria," 263.

44. "Vergilzitate auf italienischen Briefmarken," *Gnomon* 6 (1930): 670–71. These stamps are reproduced in the *Enciclopedia Virgiliana,* 2:496–97, plate XXXV.

45. Susan Ford Wiltshire, "Introduction. *Novus Ordo Seclorum*: Vergil's Rome and the American Experience," *The Augustan Age,* Occasional Papers Number One, ed. Robert J. Rowland, Jr. (College Park, Md.: The

Vergilian Society of America, 1987), 1–4; and J. Edwin Hendricks, "Charles Thomson and the Creation of 'A New Order of the Ages,'" in *America: The Middle Period*, ed. John B. Boles (Charlottesville: Univ. Press of Virginia, 1973), 1–13. The Great Seal of the United States, which is incorporated on the reverse of the dollar bill, was designed in 1782 by Charles Thomas, secretary to the Continental Congress and a former teacher of Greek and Latin.

46. Ann Pearl MacVay, "In Honor of the Two Thousandth Birthday of Vergil," *The Phi Beta Kappa Key* 7 (1930): 464–71. The quotation is the familiar passage from *Ecl.* 5.43.

47. Edward Kennard Rand, *The Magical Art of Virgil* (Cambridge, Mass.: Harvard Univ. Press, 1931), viii.

48. Oscar M. Voorhees, "Phi Beta Kappa and the Vergilian Bimillennium," *The Phi Beta Kappa Key* 7 (1931): 771–75.

49. *A Pageant Celebrating Virgil's Two Thousand Years* B.C. *70*—A.D. *1931*. Presented by the Germantown Friends School at Wistar Brown Field, Germantown, Philadelphia, Pennsylvania, May 6, 1931. [Philadephia: Engle Press, 1931.]

50. *Vergilian Bimillennium*. Program of the Celebration at the College of William and Mary, October 15, 1930.

51. *The Classical Weekly* 23 (1930): 143.

52. George Edward Woodberry, *Virgil* (1907; rpt. New York: The Authors Club, 1930).

53. George Meason Whicher, *Vergiliana* (Amherst, Mass.: The Bookmart, 1931).

54. Felix Peeters, *A Bibliography of Vergil*, The American Classical League Bulletin 28 (New York, 1933), 76–80.

55. *To Virgil on His Twentieth Centenary*. A.D. *MCMXXX*, a limited edition of two hundred copies printed in San Francisco: Grabhorn Press, 1935.

56. *Laudes Virgilianae*. Auctore Henrico Woods e soc. Jesu in universitate Santae Clarae . . . A Joanne Henrico Nash . . . editae. . . Sancti Francisci MCMXXX.

57. Melville Best Anderson, *The Fate of Virgil as Conceived by Dante*. A Dialogue of the Dead and the Living between Walter Savage Landor and Willard Fiske. San Francisco: John Henry Nash, 1931.

58. Aurelio Espinosa Pólit, S.I., *Virgilio, el poeta y su misión providencial* (Quito: Editorial Ecuadoriana, 1932), ix–xiii.

59. Aurelio Espinosa Pólit, *La Ascensión espiritual de la crítica Virgiliana* (Quito: Editorial Ecuadoriana, 1933).

60. Ussani, "La celebrazione bimillenaria di Virgilio," 267.

61. Jean Rivain, "Le Message de Virgile," *Revue des deux mondes*, 1 April 1930, 696–99.

62. Maurice Bardèche, cited from Marc Chouet, "Brasillach et Virgile," *Cahiers des Amis de Robert Brasillach* 17 (1972): 57–61; here 57.

63. Borchardt, "Vergil," in his *Reden*, ed. Marie Luise Borchardt and Silvio Rizzi (Stuttgart: Klett, 1955), 254–71; Fraenkel, *Gedanken zu einer*

deutschen Vergilfeier (Berlin: Weidmann, 1930); Johannes Stroux, *Vergil* (München: Max Hueber, 1932); the speeches by Schadewaldt and Otto reprinted in *Wege zu Vergil* (above, note 38).

64. Fraenkel, *Gedanken*, 17; Curtius, "Zweitausend Jahre" (above, note 38), 31.

65. "Vergilius zu seinem 2000. Geburtstage," *Deutsche Rundschau* 225 (1930): 12–22; here 12.

66. "Zu Vergils zweitausendstem Geburtstag," in Carl Hosius, *Zwei Rektoratsreden* (Würzburg, 1930), 50.

67. The *Enciclopedia Virgiliana* includes a number of separate entries on Virgil in various countries. See also the essays in *La Fortuna di Virgilio*, ed. Marcello Gigante (Napoli: Società Nazionale di Scienza Lettere e Arti in Napoli, 1986).

68. Bronislaw Bilinski, *La Fortuna di Virgilio in Polonia*, Biblioteca e Centro di Studi a Roma dell'Accademia Polacca delle Scienze Biblioteca, Conferenze 93 (1986); see also *Enciclopedia Virgiliana* 4:191–92.

69. *Enciclopedia Virgiliana* 4:608–17.

70. "Virgil and the New Morality," *South Atlantic Quarterly* 30 (1931): 155–67; here 155.

71. "Vergil, the Modern Poet," *Harper's Monthly Magazine* 161 (1930): 280–86; here 282.

72. *Corona* (May, 1931), 744.

73. *Wege zu Vergil* (above, note 38), 47.

74. "Virgil und die geschichtliche Welt," in Friedrich Klingner, *Römische Geisteswelt* (1943; 5th ed. München: Heinrich Ellermann, 1965), 297–98.

75. *Vergil. Vater des Abendlands* (Leipzig: Hegner, 1931), 40.

76. *Reden* (above, note 63), 271.

CHAPTER TWO

1. Cf. Friedrich Gundolf, *Caesar: Geschichte seines Ruhms* (Berlin: Bondi, 1924); Heinz Kindermann, *Das Goethebild des 20. Jahrhunderts*, 2d ed. (Darmstadt: Wissenschaftliche Buchgesellschaft, 1966); there are many books on the image of Napoleon in Italy, France, Germany, and England.

2. Duane Reed Stuart, "Biographical Criticism of Vergil since the Renaissance," *Studies in Philology* 19 (1922): 1–30.

3. I rely in this section principally on *Vitae Vergilianae antiquae*, ed. Colin Hardie (Oxford: Oxford Univ. Press, 1966); Werner Suerbaum, "Von der Vita Vergiliana über die Accessus Vergiliani zum Zauberer Virgilius: Probleme—Perspektiven—Analysen," in *Aufstieg und Niedergang der römischen Welt*, ed. Hildegard Temporini and Wolfgang Haase, vol. 31/2 (Berlin: De Gruyter, 1981), 1157–1262; and *Vergil-Viten*, ed. Karl Bayer, in Vergil, *Landleben*, ed. Johannes and Maria Götte, 5th ed. (München und Zürich: Artemis, 1987), 212–59 (text) and 407–69 (commentary).

4. W. F. Jackson Knight, *Roman Vergil* (London: Faber, 1944), 34.

5. For a convenient list of the questioned lines, see Bayer, *Vergil-Viten*, 414–15.

6. For purposes of proportion, I refer to the line numbers in Bayer's *Vergil-Viten*, 214–28 (= two hundred lines).

7. See Suerbaum, "Von der Vita Vergiliana. . . ," 1261–62.

8. See also John Webster Spargo, *Virgil the Necromancer: Studies in Virgilian Legends* (Cambridge, Mass.: Harvard Univ. Press, 1934).

9. For a list of these see Bayer, *Vergil-Viten*, 466–68, and Suerbaum, "Von der Vita Vergiliana . . . ," 1165.

10. The text of *Donatus Auctus* is conveniently available in *Die Vitae Vergilianae und ihre antiken Quellen*, ed. Ernst Diehl (Bonn: Marcus und Weber, 1911), 26–37. Most later editions—e.g., Hardie and Bayer—do not include the postclassical material added to the VSD.

11. Charles-Augustin Sainte-Beuve, *Etude sur Virgile suivie d'une étude sur Quintus de Smyrne* (Paris: Calmann Lévy, 1891), 29.

12. See Ruth E. Mulhauser, *Sainte-Beuve and Greco-Roman Antiquity* (Cleveland: Case Western Reserve Univ. Press, 1969), 60–62.

13. Sellar, *Virgil* (Oxford, The Clarendon Press, 1877).

14. André Bellessort, *Virgile. Son oeuvre et son temps*, 10th ed. (Paris: Perrin, 1927).

15. Tenney Frank, *Vergil* (New York: Holt, 1922).

16. J. W. Mackail, *Virgil* (Boston: Marshall Jones, 1922).

17. See *Horizonte der Humanitas*. Festschrift Walter Wili, ed. Georg Luck (Bern-Stuttgart: Haupt, 1960).

18. Walter Wili, *Vergil* (München: Beck [1930]).

19. Cf. Max Rychner's extensive appreciation, "Vergil und die deutsche Literatur," *Neue Schweizer Rundschau* 23 (1930): 721–29; rpt. in Rychner, *Zur europäischen Literatur zwischen zwei Weltkriegen* (Zürich: Atlantis, 1943), 11–20.

20. Tenney Frank, *Virgilio. L'uomo e il poeta* (Lanciano, 1930); André Bellessort, *Virgilio dopo la sua morte* (Piacenza, 1930).

21. Paolo Fabbri, *Virgilio: Poeta sociale e politico* (Milano: Società editrice Dante Alighieri, 1929).

22. I take most of the biographical information from the early chapters of William R. Tucker, *The Fascist Ego: A Political Biography of Robert Brasillach* (Berkeley: Univ. of California Press, 1975).

23. The first four chapters, published in *Revue universelle* 41 (April 15, 1930): 151–75, are preceded by a quotation from the right-wing writer Léon Daudet, linking the bimillennial of Virgil with the centennial of Mistral, the two poets who, along with Dante, constitute the purest mirrors of "l'esprit latin et la civilisation éternelle" (151).

24. Tucker, *The Fascist Ego*, 68–69.

25. Ibid., 114.

26. Maurice Bardèche in a review cited by Marc Chouet, "Brasillach et Virgile," *Cahiers des Amis de Robert Brasillach* 17 (1972): 57–61; here 57.

27. Jean Madiran, *Brasillach* (Rennes: Club du Luxembourg, 1958), 180.

28. Robert Brasillach, *Présence de Virgile* (1931; rpt. Paris: Plon, 1960).

29. P. Plessis and P. Lejay, *Oeuvres de Virgile* . . . avec une introduction biographique et littéraire (Paris: Hachette, 1919).

30. See *Theodor Haecker 1879–1945*, ed. Hinrich Siefken, in *Marbacher Magazin* 49 (1989), an issue devoted to the catalogue of the 1989 exhibition at the Schiller-Nationalmuseum in Marbach.
31. *Der Brenner* 8 (1923):9, cited in Siefken's Haecker catalogue, 5.
32. *P. Vergilius Maro: Bucolica. Hirtengedichte.* Deutsch von Theodor Haecker. Mit zwanzig Holzschnitten von Richard Seewald (Berlin: Euphorion, 1923).
33. *Vergil. Vater des Abendlands* (Leipzig: Hegner, 1931).
34. "Betrachtungen über Vergil. Vater des Abendlandes," *Der Brenner* (November 1932): 433–74.
35. *Enciclopedia Virgiliana* 4:967.
36. Aurelio Espinosa Pólit, *Virgilio. El poeta y su misión providencial* (Quito: Editorial Ecuatoriana, 1932).
37. That Espinosa's views have not been shared by all modern Catholic critics is evident, for instance, from the much less sympathetic discussion of Virgil in Hans Urs von Balthasar, *Herrlichkeit: Eine theologische Ästhetik*: 3, pt. 1 (Einsiedeln: Johannes Verlag, 1965), 226–51. As a German-Swiss, Balthasar shares the German preference for Homer over Virgil (238, 249); as a Catholic theologian, he sees Virgil as limited by the law of ancient religion (251).

CHAPTER THREE

1. *Le message de Virgile* (Paris, 1930), 20–21.
2. See Benedetta Papàsogli, "Francia," in *Enciclopedia Virgiliana* 2: 573–85; esp. 583–85.
3. Cited according to the text in Victor Hugo, *Poésie*, ed. Bernard Leuilliot (Paris: Seuil, 1972) 1:366–415.
4. Benedetta Papàsogli, "Hugo" in *Enciclopedia Virgiliana* 2: 865–67.
5. "'L'Heure du Berger': Mallarmé's Grand Eclogue," in Poggioli, *The Oaten Flute: Essays on Pastoral Poetry and the Pastoral Ideal* (Cambridge, Mass.: Harvard Univ. Press, 1975), 283–311.
6. Paul Fort, *Les Idylles antiques* (Paris: Société du Mercure de France, 1900), esp. 117–58.
7. Francis Jammes, *Oeuvres* (Paris: Mercure de France, 1921), 151–221.
8. The seven books ("chants") of Jammes's *Georgiques chrétiennes*, each consisting of some four hundred lines of alexandrine couplets, are of roughly the same length as Virgil's *Georgics* and deal with such traditional topics as viniculture (2), the cultivation of grain (3), and the care of animals (4). But the cloyingly pious context, beginning with a "harvest of angels" and ending with "the presence of God," is quite remote from Virgil's religiosity and *pietas*.
9. Gide, *Oeuvres complètes* (Paris: Gallimard) 2:450n.1.
10. This passage and the following one cited according to Jean Delay, *The Youth of André Gide*, trans. by June Guicharnaud (Chicago: Univ. of Chicago Press, 1963), 277.
11. Gide, *Oeuvres complètes* 3:2–11.

12. On the exemplary role of Ménalque in Gide's works, see Wallace Fowlie, *André Gide: His Life and Art* (New York: Macmillan, 1965), 44–45. Justin O'Brien, "Gide's *Nourritures Terrestres* and Vergil's *Bucolics*," *Romanic Review* 43 (1952): 117–25, proposes an even closer parallel between the two works.

13. "Postface" in André Gide, *Romans*, ed. Yvonne Davet and Jean-Jacques Thierry (Paris: Gallimard, 1958), 1476–79.

14. I cite the text according to my own translation from the Pléiade edition.

15. Although the noun *palus* and the adjectival form *paludéen* (and other derivatives) occur in standard French, as well as the nominal forms *palun* and *palud* in dialects, no form exists that would generate the plural *paludes*, which is cited in the dictionaries as Gide's formation.

16. See the notes in *Romans*, 1471–75, for quotations from some of the reactions.

17. Annabel Patterson, *Pastoral and Ideology: Virgil to Valéry* (Berkeley: Univ. of California Press, 1987), 303–6, briefly discusses *Paludes* but misses this point because she is under the impression that *Le Prométhée mal enchaîné* was written and published in 1889, before *Paludes*, rather than four years later.

18. Cited according to my translation from the text in *Romans*, 335–41.

19. *Oeuvres de Virgile*, ed. E. Benoist, 3d ed. (Paris: Hachette, 1884), 1:14. It would be interesting to study more closely the influence upon Gide of the edition(s) that he used.

20. See Catharine Savage Brosman, "The Pastoral in Modern France: Forms and Reflections," *French Forum* 9 (1984): 212–24; and A. Bourgery, "*Les Bucoliques* de Virgile dans la poésie moderne," *Revue des Etudes Latines* 23 (1945): 134–50.

21. See Georgia Hooks Shurr, *Marguerite Yourcenar: A Reader's Guide* (Lanham, Md.: University Press of America, 1987), 7–19.

22. "Postface," in Marguerite Yourcenar, *Anna, soror* (Paris: Gallimard, 1981), 131–59.

23. *Alexis*, trans. Walter Kaiser (New York: Farrar, 1984), 105.

24. From the 1963 preface, in Kaiser's translation, xiii.

25. I follow the account provided by Fernand Mazade in his "pages liminaires" that accompany Xavier de Magallon's translation of *Les Bucoliques* (Paris: Librairie de France, 1930; rpt. Paris: Les Bibliophiles Franco-Suisses, 1943), 1–13.

26. *Latinité* 2 (1930): 8–54. Annabel Patterson, *Pastoral and Ideology*, 316–22, discusses the translations by Magallon and Charpentier, but is apparently unaware that the collective effort was in fact published as planned in 1930.

27. Reynaud would have found it awkward to substitute Delille's translation for the second *Eclogue*, rather than the third; the *abbé*, with concessions to contemporary morality, replaced Alexis with Lycoris, thus transmuting the paean to homoerotic love into a purely heterosexual affair. Delille translated all of Virgil (the *Eclogues* in 1806); but he was famous, and

elected into the Académie française, for his translation of the *Georgics* (1769), which was reprinted repeatedly during the eighteenth and nineteenth centuries.

28. *Les Bucoliques*, trans. Henry Charpentier (Paris, 1946).

29. In France the Virgilian bimillennial was often celebrated in conjunction with the centennial of the birth of the Provençal poet, Frédéric Mistral, a fact missed by Annabel Patterson, *Pastoral and Ideology*, 319, who translates this sentence as "these Virgilian celebrations of the Latin fraternity, in a mistral and under a stormy sky."

30. Emile Proveux, trans., *Bucoliques* (Paris, 1929); Fagus (pseudonym for Georges Faillet), trans., *Les Eglogues* (Paris, 1930); M. De Coppet, trans., *Les Bucoliques* (Paris, 1931); and Maurice Rat, trans., Virgile, *Oeuvres* I, Editions Garnier (Paris, 1932). I have not seen these translations, which are listed in Ward W. Brigg, Jr., "A Bibliography of Virgil's 'Eclogues' (1927–1977)," in *Aufstieg und Niedergang der Römischen Welt* 31.2:1270–1399. A further translation by Raymond Billiard—*Les Bucoliques* (Paris, 1934)—is listed in the National Union Catalogue.

31. The translation was first published posthumously in a luxury edition of 245 copies with 44 lithographs by Jacques Villon (Paris: Scripta et Picta, 1953). I cite the text as well as the translator's introduction according to Paul Valéry, *Oeuvres*, ed. Jean Hytier (Paris: Gallimard, 1957), 1:207–81.

32. These details are recapitulated in Roudinesco's introduction, reprinted in *Oeuvres* 1:1691–92.

33. Valéry's variants are printed in *Oeuvres* 1:1693–97.

34. I cite the third edition (Paris: Hachette, 1884).

35. L. A. Bisson, "Valéry and Virgil," *Modern Language Review* 53 (1958): 501–11.

36. Paul Valéry, "Dialogue de l'arbre," in *Discours*, Séance annuelle des Cinq Académies, 25 Oct. 1943 (Paris: Institut de France, 1943), 3.

37. *Les Pages immortelles de Virgile choisies et expliquées par Jean Giono* (Paris: Éditions Corrêa. 1944). The volume contains the *Eclogues* in their entirety and selections from the *Georgics*, both in a translation by Henri Goëlzer; passages from the *Aeneid* are reproduced in the translation by André Bellessort.

38. I refer to the text as printed in vol. 3 of the Pléiade edition of Giono's *Oeuvres romanesques complètes* (Paris: Gallimard, 1974), 1019–68.

39. *Virgile: Bucoliques.* Texte établi et traduit par E. de Saint-Denis (1942), 2d ed. (Paris: Société d'édition "Les Belles Lettres," 1949).

40. See the notes to "Virgile" in the Pléiade edition, 1561–83; here 1569.

41. Ernst Robert Curtius, *Europäische Literatur und Lateinisches Mittelalter*, 2d ed. (Bern: Francke, 1954), 197.

42. For general surveys see Eduard Fraenkel, *Gedanken zu einer deutschen Vergilfeier* (Berlin: Weidmann, 1930), 11–19; and Karl Büchner, *P. Vergilius Maro: Der Dichter der Römer* (Stuttgart: Drukkenmüller, 1957), 459–64.

43. Johann Christoph Gottsched, *Versuch einer critischen Dichtkunst*, 4. vermehrte Auflage (Leipzig, 1751), 474–75 (=I.iv.8)

44. Johann Jacob Breitinger, *Critische Dichtkunst* (Zürich, 1740), I:43.

45. Johann Gottfried Herder, *Ideen zur Philosophie der Geschichte der Menschheit*, ed. Gerhart Schmidt (Darmstadt: Melzer, 1966), 388.

46. Gotthold Ephraim Lessing, *Werke*, ed. Herbert G. Göpfert (München: Hanser, 1974), 6:122.

47. Ernst Grumach, *Goethe und die Antike: Eine Sammlung* (Berlin: De Gruyter, 1949), 1:117–214 (Homer) and 1:353–60 (Virgil).

48. See Johanna Jarislowsky, *Schillers Übertragungen aus Vergil im Rahmen der deutschen Äneis-Übersetzung des 18. Jahrhunderts*, Jenaer Germanistische Forschungen 12 (Jena: Frommann, 1928).

49. See Eberhard Semrau, *Dido in der deutschen Dichtung*, Stoff- und Motivgeschichte der deutschen Literatur 9 (Berlin: De Gruyter, 1930).

50. Written in 1794, the play was not published for some seventy years; see *Dido. Ein Trauerspiel in 5 Aufzügen von Charlotte Albertine Ernestine von Stein-Kochberg*, ed. Heinrich Düntzer (Frankfurt am Main, 1867); also discussed by Semrau, *Dido*, 63–66.

51. Friedrich Schlegel, *Geschichte der alten und neuen Literatur*, ed. Hans Eichner, Kritische Friedrich-Schlegel-Ausgabe 6 (München: Schöningh, 1961), 80.

52. August Wilhelm Schlegel, *Geschichte der klassischen Literatur*, ed. Edgar Lohner, Kritische Schriften und Briefe 3 (Stuttgart: Kohlhammer, 1964), 146–68, esp. 166.

53. Letter of June 12, 1801, to A. W. Schlegel; cited by Fraenkel, *Gedanken*, 18.

54. See Semrau, *Dido*, 62–63; and Jarislowsky, *Schillers Übertragungen*, 22–24.

55. B. G. Niebuhr, *Vorträge über römische Geschichte*, ed. M. Isler (Berlin, 1848), 130.

56. Ulrich von Wilamowitz-Moellendorff, *Hellenistische Dichtung in der Zeit des Kallimachos* (Berlin: Weidmann, 1924), 2:224.

57. Martin Schanz, *Geschichte der Römischen Literatur* II/1 (München: Beck, 1899), 94.

58. Friedrich Klingner, "Virgil: Wiederentdeckung eines Dichters" (1942), in his *Römische Geisteswelt* (München: Ellermann, 1965), 239.

59. E. R. Curtius, "Literarische Unsterblichkeit," *Neue Schweizer Rundschau* 19 (1926): 1065–71. The *Rundschau* was reporting on a recent survey by *The New York Times* (July 25, 1926; viii:4) in which a jury of twelve international men of letters was asked to list twelve immortal writers. According to the survey, Virgil ranked fourth after Shakespeare, Dante, and Homer.

60. Since W. Binder's translation of Virgil's *Idyllen* (1856) and S.C.N. Osiander's translation of the "Idyllen" in Wilhelm Adolf Boguslaw Hertzberg's edition of Virgil's works in German (1856).

61. From the 1927 *Prospectus* as reproduced in Roderick Cave, *The Private Press*, 2d ed. (New York: Bowker, 1983), 146.

62. The National Union Catalogue lists *Probedrucke* from 1910–11, 1912–13, and 1913–14.

63. R. A. Schröder, "Aristide Maillol" (1922), in his *Gesammelte Werke* (Frankfurt am Main: Suhrkamp, 1952), 3:1051–55.

64. *Eclogae* (Weimar: Cranach Presse, 1926). Annabel Patterson, *Pastoral and Ideology*, 311–16, who is concerned exclusively with the woodcuts and not with the text itself, mistakenly attributes this famous German translation to Thomas Achelis and Alfred Koerte, the editors responsible for the Latin text.

65. Rudolf Alexander Schröder, *Gesammelte Werke in fünf Bänden* (Frankfurt am Main: Suhrkamp, 1952), 5:21–58; here 23.

66. "Der Sänger der Äneis," in *Gesammelte Werke* 2:158–69; here 160.

67. See his notes on the fourth *Eclogue* in *Gesammelte Schriften* 5:508–9.

68. "Marginalien eines Vergil-Lesers" (1931), in *Gesammelte Werke* 2:169–78; here 169.

69. Walter Wili, "Grundzüge der Dichtung Vergils," *Neue Schweizer Rundschau* 23 (1930): 742–53.

70. Max Rychner, "Vergil und die deutsche Literatur," *Neue Schweizer Rundschau* 23 (1930): 721–29.

71. Friedrich Fuchs, "Vergiliana," in *Hochland* 28 (Oct. 1931): 75–80.

72. P. Vergilius Maro, *Bucolica. Hirtengedichte* (Berlin: Euphorion, 1923). Haecker's translation was reprinted in 1932 and 1936 (Leipzig: Hegner) and several times after the war: notably in a paperback edition along with *Vergil. Vater des Abendlandes* in the Fischer-Bücherei (1958) and in two bibliophile editions with lithographs by Robert Kirchner (1965 and 1974).

73. "Die vierte Ecloge des Vergil," in *Der Brenner* 6 (August 1920): 401–3.

74. "Wahrheit und Leben," in Theodor Haecker, *Essays* (München: Kosel, 1958), 277–320; here 307–8.

75. *Virgils Ländliche Dichtungen*, verdeutscht und erklärt von Adolf Trendelenburg (Berlin: De Gruyter, 1929).

76. "Rudolf Borchardt on Virgil," in Ernst Robert Curtius, *Essays on European Literature*, trans. Michael Kowal (Princeton, N.J.: Princeton Univ. Press, 1973), 18.

77. E. R. Curtius, "Zweitausend Jahre Vergil," in *Wege zu Vergil*, ed. Hans Oppermann (Darmstadt: Wissenschaftliche Buchgesellschaft, 1976), 35.

78. Wolfgang Schadewaldt, "Sinn und Werden der vergilischen Dichtung," in *Wege zu Vergil*, 53–54.

79. Eduard Fraenkel, *Gedanken zu einer deutschen Vergilfeier*, 38.

80. "Vergiliana," in *Hochland* 28 (April 1931): 78.

81. Bruno Snell, "Arkadien, die Entdeckung einer geistigen Landschaft," in *Wege zu Vergil*, 338–67; here 359.

82. *Die Geburt des Kindes*, 2d ed. (Leipzig: Teubner, 1931).

83. Oswald Spengler, *Der Untergang des Abendlandes* (München: Beck, 1963), 465 (=I.5.xvi).

84. Arthur Moeller van den Bruck, *Das dritte Reich*, 3d ed. (Hamburg: Hanseatische Verlagsanstalt, 1931), 300–322.

85. Julius Petersen, *Die Sehnsucht nach dem Dritten Reich in deutscher Sage und Dichtung* (Stuttgart: Metzler, 1934), 51.

86. Theodore Ziolkowski, *The Novels of Hermann Hesse* (Princeton, N.J.: Princeton Univ. Press, 1965), 34–51.

87. Hanns Heiss, "Virgils Fortleben in den romanischen Literaturen," *Das Erbe der Alten*, 2. Reihe, 20 (1931): 99–117; rpt. *Wege zu Vergil*, 301–19. Heiss focuses on Dante, Camoes, and Victor Hugo.

88. Vladimir Zabughin, *Vergilio nel Rinascimento Italiano da Dante a Torquato Tasso*, 2 vols. (Bologna: Nicola Zanichelli, 1921–23); Edmund G. Gardner, *Virgil in Italian Poetry*, Proceedings of the British Academy, 17 (London: Humphrey Milford, 1931); the *Enciclopedia Virgiliana* has, rather than a national entry for Italy, separate rubrics for periods and individual authors.

89. Gardner, *Virgil in Italian Poetry*, 3, assumes the former reading; Charles S. Singleton, in his commentary on *The Divine Comedy* (Princeton, N.J.: Princeton Univ. Press, 1970), I/1:14, proposes the latter.

90. *Vergilio nel Rinascimento Italiano*, 2:398–99.

91. See the rubrics on all three poets in the appropriate volumes of the *Enciclopedia Virgiliana*.

92. Herbert Frenzel, *Virgil in der modernen Lyrik Italiens*, Schriften und Vorträge des Petrarca-Instituts in Köln, 10 (Krefeld: Scherpe, 1957), 41–42. This is virtually the only essay that comes to grips with Virgil in a modern context broader than the works of an individual writer.

93. See Walter A. Strauss, *Descent and Return: The Orphic Theme in Modern Literature* (Cambridge, Mass.: Harvard Univ. Press, 1971); here 238.

94. *Ossi di Seppia*, *Poesie* I (Milano: Mondadori, 1948), 103–5.

95. Frenzel, 40.

96. Montale, *Poesie I: Ossi di Seppia 1920–27*, 7th ed. ([Milano]: Mondadori, 1960), 103–5.

97. Frenzel, 11–14.

98. I refer to the text as published in Quasimodo, *Poesie e discorsi sulla poesia*, ed. Gilberto Finzi, 3d ed. (Milano: Mondadori, 1974), 529–57.

99. "Traduzioni dai classici" (1945), in *Il poeta e il politico e altri saggi* (Milano: Mondadori, 1967), 109.

100. Cited by Leone Piccioni, "Le origini della 'Terra Promessa,'" in Giuseppe Ungaretti, *Vita d'un uomo. Tutte le poesie*, ed. Leone Piccioni, 7th ed. (Milano: Mondadori, 1974), 429. All quotations from Ungaretti, unless otherwise indicated, are taken from this edition.

101. Mario Petrucciani, "La discesa nella memoria, il pilota innocente. Ungaretti e Virgilio," in *Atti del Convegno Internazionale su Giuseppi Ungaretti*, ed. Carlo Bo et al. (Urbino: Edizioni 4-venti, 1981), 597–637; rpt. in Petrucciani, *Il condizionale di Didone* (Napoli: Edizioni Scientifiche Italiana, 1985), 131–79; here 132.

102. Glauco Cambon, "Giuseppe Ungaretti," in *European Writers of the Twentieth Century*, ed. George Stade, vol. 10 (New York: Scribner, 1990), 1453–73; here 1458–59.

103. Leone Piccioni, *Vita di Ungaretti* (Milano: Rizzoli, 1979), 174.

104. Comments at the 1956 "Recontre Est-Ouest" in Venice; in Giuseppe Ungaretti, *Vita d'un uomo: Saggi e interventi*, ed. Mario Diacono and Luciano Rebay (Milano: Mondadori, 1974), 867–69; here 868.

105. *Vita d'un uomo: Tutte le poesie*, 566.

106. Michael Hanne, "Ungaretti's *La Terra Promessa* and the *Aeneid*," *Italica* 50 (1973): 3–25. This is Hanne's conclusion, in the most detailed textual comparison of the two works. See also Mario Petrucciani, "La discesa nella memoria, il pilota innocente. Ungaretti e Virgilio"; Petrucciani is concerned less with textual similarities than with archetypal analogies between the two works, notably the motifs of shipwreck and descent.

107. Piccioni, "Le origini," 430.

108. *Vita d'un uomo: Tutte le poesie*, 241–51.

109. Frenzel, *Virgil in der modernen Lyrik Italiens*, 33–34.

110. See Piccioni, "Le origini"; and Frederic J. Jones, *Giuseppe Ungaretti: Poet and Critic* (Edinburgh: Edinburgh Univ. Press, 1977), 145–74, esp. 145–58.

111. Hanne, "Ungaretti's *La terra promessa*," 11–17, suggests a closer connection between this poem and the *Aeneid*, but it is based on such broad similarities as the "spiritual journey of Ungaretti's and the experience of Aeneas in his search for the site on which to found Rome" or the "ironic" references to dawn in both works.

112. Piccioni, "Le origini," 430.

113. Hanne, "Ungaretti's *La terra promessa*," 6.

114. *Vita d'un uomo: Tutte le poesie*, 566.

115. Hanne, "Ungaretti's *La terra promessa*," 19–22.

116. The irony is noted by Cambon, "Giuseppe Ungaretti," 1469.

117. *Vita d'un uomo: Tutte le poesie*, 566.

118. Cambon, "Giuseppe Ungaretti," 1469.

119. Frederic J. Jones, *Giuseppe Ungaretti*, 17.

120. *Innocence et mémoire* (Paris: Gallimard, 1969), 12; cited by Frederic J. Jones, *Guiseppe Ungaretti*, 75.

CHAPTER FOUR

1. Robert Graves, "The Virgil Cult," *The Virginia Quarterly Review* 38 (1962): 13–35; here 13. Essentially the same piece, minus the enframing attack on Eliot, was published under the title "The Anti-Poet" in Graves's *Oxford Addresses on Poetry* (London: Cassell, 1962), 29–53, where the enemy is identified simply as "senior literary churchwardens" (44).

2. *The Collected Poems of Wilfred Owen*, ed. C. Day Lewis (London: Chatto and Windus, 1963), 43.

3. This is the implication of E. Porges Watson, "Virgil and T. S. Eliot," in *Virgil in a Cultural Tradition: Essays to Celebrate the Bimillenium* [*sic*], ed. Richard A. Cardwell and Janet Hamilton, University of Nottingham Monographs in the Humanities 4 (Nottingham, 1986), 115–33. Although the author's interpretation of Eliot is quite incisive, her point of departure tends to isolate Eliot in a misleading way from his contemporaries.

4. Ezra Pound, *ABC of Reading* (New Haven: Yale Univ. Press, 1934), 31.

5. Paul Fussell, *The Great War and Modern Memory* (New York: Oxford Univ. Press, 1975), 7–18, 29–35, and passim.

6. "A Classical Education," in C. M. Bowra, *In General and Particular* (London: Weidenfeld and Nicolson, 1964), 45–61; here 45.

7. *The Aeneid*, ed. with introduction and commentary by J. W. Mackail (Oxford: Clarendon, 1930), vii.

8. Noel Annan, *Our Age: English Intellectuals between the World Wars—A Group Portrait* (New York: Random House, 1990), 92.

9. In *Others to Adorn*, with a preface by W. B. Yeats (London: Rich and Cowan, 1938), 10; rpt. *The Collected Poems of Oliver St. John Gogarty* (New York: Devin-Adair, 1954), 13.

10. *Others to Adorn*, 148–50; *Collected Poems*, 74–76.

11. Louis MacNeice, *Collected Poems 1925–1948* (London: Faber, 1949), 19.

12. *The Great War and Modern Memory*, 278.

13. Virginia Woolf, *To the Lighthouse* (New York: Harvest/HBJ, [n.d.]), 189.

14. L. P. Wilkinson, *The Georgics of Virgil: A Critical Survey* (Cambridge: Cambridge Univ. Press, 1969), 311.

15. W. H. Jackson Knight, *Roman Vergil*, 2d ed. (London: Faber, 1944), viii.

16. Victoria Glendinning, *Vita: The Life of V. Sackville-West* (New York: Knopf, 1983), 166.

17. Ibid., 166.

18. Ibid., 119.

19. Ibid., 166.

20. Anthony Low, *The Georgic Revolution* (Princeton, N.J.: Princeton Univ. Press, 1985).

21. *The Works of John Dryden*, ed. Sir Walter Scott, rev. George Saintsbury (Edinburgh, 1889), 14:2.

22. Ibid., 14:12–19; here 19.

23. Dwight L. Durling, *Georgic Tradition in English Poetry* (New York: Columbia Univ. Press, 1935).

24. Wilkinson, *The Georgics of Virgil*, 303.

25. *The Georgics of Virgil*, trans. C. Day Lewis (London: Jonathan Cape, 1940).

26. C. Day Lewis, *The Buried Day* (New York: Harper, 1960), 73.

27. Day Lewis, trans., *The Georgics of Virgil*, 10.

28. *The Buried Day*, 26.

29. Nicholas Blake, *There's Trouble Brewing* (1937; New York: Perennial, 1982), 63.

30. *Virgil: The Georgics*, in English Hexameters by C. W. Brodribb (London: Ernest Benn, 1928), prefatory note.

31. J. Marouzeau, "Le latin langue de paysans," in *Mélanges linguistiques offerts à J. Vendryes*, Collection linguistique 17 (Paris: Champion, 1925), 251–65; and David O. Ross, Jr., *Virgil's Elements: Physics and Poetry in the Georgics* (Princeton, N.J.: Princeton Univ. Press, 1987), 17–18.

32. *The Buried Day*, 209–11.

33. Ibid., 224.

34. Ibid., 97.

35. Ibid., 233.

36. Ibid., 97–98.
37. Already Dryden, in a note referring to the end of the first book, speaks of wars in Asia and central Europe "as if Virgil had prophesied of this age"(*The Works of John Dryden*, 21).
38. Gary B. Miles, *Virgil's Georgics: A New Interpretation* (Berkeley: Univ. of California Press, 1980), 1–63.
39. Ross, *Virgil's Elements*, 109–45. A similarly "dark" reading of the prophecies in the *Aeneid* has recently been proposed by James J. O'Hara, *Death and the Optimistic Prophecies* (Princeton, N.J.: Princeton Univ. Press, 1990).
40. Miles, *Virgil's Georgics*, 85, cites examples to demonstrate the "unequivocally negative connotations" of *improbus* throughout Virgil's works.
41. Miles, *Virgil's Elements*, 76–77 and elsewhere.
42. L.A.S. Jermyn, *The Singing Farmer: A Translation of Vergil's 'Georgics'* (Oxford:Blackwell, 1947).
43. Jermyn, ibid., describes the circumstances in his preface, v–xi.
44. A good deal has been written about Eliot and Virgil: E. J. Stormon, S. J., "Virgil and the Modern Poet," *Meanjin* 6 (1947): 6–15; Hugh Kenner, "The Urban Apocalypse," in *Eliot in His Time: Essays on the Occasion of the Fiftieth Anniversary of The Waste Land*, ed. A. Walton Litz (Princeton, N.J.: Princeton Univ. Press, 1973), 23–49; Alessandro Perutelli, "T. S. Eliot e il concetto di 'Tradition' nella critica anglo-sassone su Virgilio," *Maia: Revista di letterature classiche* 25 (1973): 118–36; William Arrowsmith, "Daedal Harmonies: A Dialogue on Eliot and the Classics," *The Southern Review* 13 (1977): 1–47; E. Porges Watson, "Virgil and T. S. Eliot," in *Virgil in a Cultural Tradition*, ed. Richard A. Cardwell and Janet Hamilton, University of Nottingham Monographs in the Humanities 4 (Nottingham, 1986), 115–33; and, most recently, Gareth Reeves, *T. S. Eliot: A Virgilian Poet* (London: Macmillan, 1989), who provides accurate summaries of earlier interpretations.
45. "What is a Classic?" in Eliot's *On Poetry and Poets* (1957; rpt. London: Faber, 1986), 53–71; here 68.
46. "Virgil and the Christian World," in *On Poetry and Poets*, 121–31; here 127.
47. Frank Kermode, *The Classic: Literary Images of Permanence and Change* (1975; rpt. Cambridge, Mass.: Harvard Univ. Press, 1983), 15. Kermode quotes Eliot's statement from *Transatlantic Review* (Jan. 1924).
48. "What is a Classic?" 62.
49. "Virgil and the Christian World," 123–24.
50. "The Music of Poetry," in *On Poetry and Poets*, 26–38; here 27.
51. "What is a Classic?" 68.
52. *On Poetry and Poets*, 121–31.
53. Eliot probably had the incorrect phrase from Theodor Haecker, who cites it in that form several times in his *Virgil, Father of the West*, a book that influenced Eliot profoundly, as we shall see.
54. I cite Eliot's poems from *The Complete Poems and Plays 1909–1950* (New York: Harcourt, 1958).

55. This interpretation ignores the possibility that the vocable *aversa* can also—and in these contexts perhaps more suitably—be translated as "askance" or "disdainfully."

56. Gareth Reeves, *A Virgilian Poet*, 11–13.

57. Arrowsmith, "Daedal Harmonies"; and Reeves, *A Virgilian Poet*, 23–27.

58. T. S. Eliot, *The Waste Land. A Facsimile and Transcript of the Original Drafts including the Annotations of Ezra Pound*, ed. Valerie Eliot (New York: Harcourt, 1971), 29.

59. "The Urban Apocalypse," 38–39; Reeves, *A Virgilian Poet*, 28–58, accepts and expands on Kenner's remarks. See also Marjorie Donker, "*The Waste Land* and the *Aeneid*," *PMLA* 89 (1974): 164–73.

60. Eliot's essay first appeared in *Dial*; rpt. in *Forms of Modern Fiction*, ed. William Van O'Connor (1948; rpt. Bloomington: Univ. of Indiana-Midland, 1959), 120–24.

61. Stormon, "Virgil and the Modern Poet"; and Reeves, *A Virgilian Poet*, 60–65.

62. Stephen Spender, "Remembering Eliot," in *T. S. Eliot: The Man and His Work*, ed. Allen Tate (New York: Delacorte, 1966), 38–64; here 49.

63. *Criterion* 12 (1933): 244–49.

64. T. S. Eliot, *Selected Essays*. New edition (New York: Harcourt, 1950), 343n.

65. *Selected Essays*, 295.

66. Edmund Wilson, *Axel's Castle: A Study in the Imaginative Literature of 1870–1930* (1931; rpt. New York: Scribner, 1959), 120. Wilson's characterization of the *Georgics* suggests that he had never actually read Virgil's poem.

67. Eliot, "A Commentary," *The Criterion* 11 (October 1931): 65–72.

68. "A Commentary," *The Criterion* 17 (April 1938): 482–83.

69. Wilkinson, *The Georgics of Virgil*, 273–90.

70. Donald Davie, "Anglican Eliot," in *Eliot in His Time: Essays on the Occasion of the Fiftieth Anniversary of The Waste Land*, ed. A. Walton Litz (Princeton, N.J.: Princeton Univ. Press, 1973), 181–96; here 183.

71. Stormon, "Virgil and the Modern Poet," 15n. The wood in which grows the Golden Bough, which is sometimes mentioned in this context, is of course never called "sacred."

72. E. Porges Watson, "Virgil and T. S. Eliot," 125.

73. On Haecker and Eliot see Frank Kermode, *The Classic* (London: Faber, 1975), 26–28, who is singularly uncomprehending and ungenerous in his appreciation of Haecker's work; and Reeves, *A Virgilian Poet*, 96–116.

74. In his German radio talks, *Die Einheit der Europäischen Kultur* (Berlin: Habel, 1946); rpt. in English as the appendix to *Notes towards the Definition of Culture* (London: Faber, 1948), 116.

75. Haecker, *Virgil, Father of the West*, trans. A. W. Wheen (London: Sheed and Ward, 1934), 51.

76. Notably Reeves, *A Virgilian Poet*, 117–57.

77. Reeves, *A Virgilian Poet*, 127.

78. On the founding of the Virgil Society see the account by G. Wilson

Knight in his biography of his brother, *Jackson Knight* (Oxford: Alden, 1975), 267–79.

79. W. F. Jackson Knight, *Roman Vergil*, rev. ed. (Harmondsworth: Penguin, 1966), 9.

80. W. B. Stanford, in the *Irish Times* of March 18, 1944; quoted in *Jackson Knight*, 280.

81. *Roman Vergil*, 2d ed. (London: Faber, 1944), 130.

82. *Jackson Knight*, 262.

83. C. S. Lewis, *A Preface to Paradise Lost* (1942; rpt. New York: Oxford Univ. Press, 1961), 29–30.

84. C. M. Bowra, *From Virgil to Milton* (London: Macmillan, 1945), 28.

85. Cited according to *On Poetry and Poets*, 53–71.

86. Charles-Augustin Sainte-Beuve, *Etude sur Virgile* (1857; rpt. Paris: Calmann Lévy, 1891), 104.

87. *A Virgilian Poet*, 1.

88. Annan, *Our Age* (above, note 8), 212.

89. *The Condemned Playground* (London: Routledge, 1945).

90. Cyril Connolly, *The Evening Colonnade* (New York: Harcourt, 1975), 223.

91. Annan, *Our Age*, 213.

92. *The Unquiet Grave. A Word Cycle by Palinurus* (London: Horizon, 1944). The epigraph is missing in the revised edition, with an introduction by Cyril Connolly, from which all following quotations are taken (New York: Persea, 1981).

93. In *Nones* (New York: Random House, 1950), 40.

94. "Secondary Epic," in Auden's *Collected Shorter Poems 1927–1957* (London: Faber, 1966), 296–97.

95. Anthony Burgess, "Introduction," *A Vision of Battlements* (New York: Norton, 1965), 7–9.

96. Burgess also employed a prefiguring pattern as the shaping basis for his next comic novella, *The Eve of Saint Venus* (written 1950), which is based on the medieval legend of Venus and the Ring; see Theodore Ziolkowski, *Disenchanted Images: A Literary Iconology* (Princeton, N.J.: Princeton Univ. Press, 1977), 71–75.

97. In this connection see A. A. DeVitis, *Anthony Burgess* (New York: Twayne, 1972), 29–39.

98. The ultimate reductio ad absurdum of this British literary Virgilianism surely is attained at the moment when Roger Micheldene, the antihero of Kingsley Amis's satirical novel *One Fat Englishman* (1963), "urgently" recites to himself the opening lines of *Aeneid* 2— simply as a means of self-distraction to postpone the climax of the sexual intercourse in which he is engaged.

CHAPTER FIVE

1. Leo Marx, *The Machine in the Garden: Technology and the Pastoral Ideal in America* (1964; rpt. New York: Oxford Univ. Press/Galaxy, 1967), 3. Although Marx was the first to focus on pastoralism mainly as a literary

mode, he cites several other studies that have emphasized the idealization of rural values in American social thought: notably Richard Hofstadter, *The Age of Reform: From Bryan to F.D.R.* (New York: Knopf, 1955); and Henry Nash Smith, *Virgin Land: The American West as Symbol and Myth* (Cambridge, Mass.: Harvard Univ. Press, 1950).

2. Susan Ford Wiltshire, "Aeneas in America," *Vergilius* 25 (1979): 2–9; here 2.

3. Cited by Wiltshire from *A Voyage to Virginia in 1609*, ed. Louis B. Wright (Charlottesville: Univ. Press of Virginia, 1964), 78.

4. Howard Mumford Jones, *O Strange New World* (1952; rpt. New York: Viking, 1964), 238.

5. Richard M. Gummere, *The American Colonial Mind and the Classical Tradition* (Cambridge, Mass.: Harvard Univ. Press, 1963), 15.

6. Meyer Reinhold, "Vergil in the American Experience from Colonial Times to 1882," in *Vergil at 2000: Commemorative Essays on the Poet and His Influence*, ed. John D. Bernard (New York: AMS, 1986), 185–205; here 197. Reinhold's essay also appears as a chapter in his volume *Classica Americana: The Greek and Roman Heritage in the United States* (Detroit: Wayne State Univ. Press, 1984), 221–49.

7. Meyer Reinhold, "Vergil in the American Experience," 197.

8. Ruth W. Brown, "Classical Echoes in the Poetry of Philip Freneau," *Classical Journal* 45 (1949), 29–34; here 32–33.

9. Meyer Reinhold, "Vergil in the American Experience," 198–99; see also Bianca Tarozzi, "Virgilio nella cultura americana," in *La fortuna di Virgilio*, ed. Marcello Gigante (Napoli: Società Nazionale di Scienze Lettere e Arti in Napoli, 1986), 475–505.

10. *Early American Latin Verse 1625–1825: An Anthology*, ed. Leo M. Kaiser (Chicago: Bolchazy-Carducci, 1984), 236–39.

11. Leo Marx, *The Machine in the Garden*, 209–15; here 212.

12. Meyer Reinhold, "Vergil in the American Experience," 197.

13. See esp. Robert B. Heilman, "Spokesman and Seer: The Agrarian Movement and European Culture," in *A Band of Prophets: The Vanderbilt Agrarians after Fifty Years* (Baton Rouge: Louisiana State Univ. Press, 1982), 93–116; here 100–101. Heilman understands more clearly than do many critics that the Agrarians are less pastoral than georgic in their goals.

14. Erik Ingvar Thurin, *The Humanization of Willa Cather: Classicism in an American Classic*, Lund Studies in English 81 (Lund, Sweden: Lund University Press, 1990), 364. Thurin's thorough study discusses the works that I take up in my discussion, and others as well; but he frequently presses the analogies further than I am willing to do, seeing complex thematic implications in passing references that I regard as no more than loosely allusive.

15. Willa Cather, *Shadows on the Rock* (New York: Knopf, 1931), 122.

16. Cited according to Willa Cather, *My Antonia* (Boston and New York: Houghton Mifflin-Riverside Press, 1954). For other allusions see Mary B.

Ryder, "'Our' Antonia: The Classical Roots of Willa Cather's American Myth," *Classical and Modern Literature* 12 (1992): 111–17.

17. Joseph V. Paterno and Bernard Asbell, *By the Book* (New York: Random House, 1989), esp. 35–46.

18. Marino Barchiesi, "I moderni alla ricerca di Enea," in his *I moderni alla ricerca di Enea* (Roma: Bulzoni, 1981), 11–46; here 33. Essentially the same essay, in somewhat abbreviated form, appeared under the title "Les modernes à la recherche d'Enée," in *Formation et survie des mythes: Travaux et mémoires* (Paris: Société d'Edition "Les Belles Lettres," 1977), 50–65.

19. Rudolf Kettemann, *Bukolik und Georgik: Studien zu ihrer Affinität bei Vergil und später* (Heidelberg: Carl Winter, 1977), 128, uses the term to designate the breakdown of formal boundaries between eclogue and georgic in the "rural lyricism" of the Renaissance.

20. *Master Vergil* (Boston: Heath, 1930), 113–15 and 109–12.

21. From *A Son of Earth* (New York: Viking, 1928), 3–5.

22. First published in *The Phi Beta Kappa Key* 3 (March 1917): 119–22, without the concluding four lines added in December 1917.

23. Louis Mertins, *Robert Frost: Life and Talks-Walking* (Norman: Univ. of Oklahoma Press, 1965), 50.

24. Lawrance Thompson, *Fire and Ice: The Art and Thought of Robert Frost* (1942; rpt. New York: Russell, 1961), 145–46.

25. Both incidents cited by Mertins, *Robert Frost*, 310 and 425.

26. I am interested here, as throughout this study, in the specifically Virgilian analogy, and not in the more general pastoral pattern detected as the "structure of his most representative and important work" by John F. Lynan, *The Pastoral Art of Robert Frost* (New Haven: Yale Univ. Press, 1960).

27. Rpt. in *Critical Essays on Robert Frost*, ed. Philip L. Gerber (Boston: Hall, 1982), 19–21.

28. Cited by Louise Bogan, "Robert Frost," in *Major Writers of America*, ed. Perry Miller (New York: Harcourt, 1962), 2: 643–53; here 647.

29. *The Literary Spotlight*, ed. John Farrar (1924); rpt. in *Critical Essays on Robert Frost*, 57.

30. Elizabeth Shepley Sergeant, *Fire under the Andes* (1927); rpt. in *Critical Essays on Robert Frost*, 85–86.

31. Lawrance Thompson, *Robert Frost: The Early Years, 1874–1915* (New York: Holt, 1966), 433.

32. Robert Frost, *North of Boston: Poems*, ed. Edward Connery Lathem (New York: Dodd, 1977), v.

33. Meyer Reinhold, "Vergil in the American Experience," 197.

34. Bruce Fogelman, "'Pan with Us': The Continuity of the Eclogue in Twentieth-Century Poetry," *Classical and Modern Literature* 6 (1986): 109–25, detects examples of the "pastoral dialogue" in Frost, Yeats, Walter de la Mare, W. H. Auden, Louis MacNeice, Allen Tate, John Crowe Ransom, William Carlos Williams, A. E. Housman, James Agee, and

C. Day Lewis; but he does not assume or suggest any specifically Virgilian influence in any of these cases.

35. W. H. Auden, "Robert Frost," in *The Dyer's Hand and Other Essays* (New York: Random House, 1962), 337–53; here 349–50.

36. See in this connection Stanley Burnshaw, *Robert Frost Himself* (New York: Braziller, 1986), 61–65.

37. *The Poetry of Robert Frost*. The Collected Poems, Complete and Unabridged, ed. Edward Connery Lathem (New York: Holt, 1979), 316–25.

38. See the synopsis of reviews in Burnshaw, *Robert Frost Himself*, 59–60.

39. Allen Tate, *Collected Poems 1919–1976* (Baton Rouge: Louisiana State Univ. Press, 1988), 95.

40. *The Collected Poems of Archibald MacLeish* (Boston: Houghton Mifflin, 1963), 103–5.

41. Tate's poems cited here and subsequently from *Collected Poems 1919–1976* (Baton Rouge: Louisiana State Univ. Press, 1988).

42. Robert S. Dupree, *Allen Tate and the Augustinian Imagination: A Study of the Poetry* (Baton Rouge: Louisiana State Univ. Press, 1983), 146–47, while differing in some details of interpretation, comes to the same conclusion about the meaning of the poem.

43. *Fugitives' Reunion: Conversations at Vanderbilt, May 3–5, 1956*, ed. Rob Roy Purdy (Nashville: Vanderbilt Univ. Press, 1959), 183.

44. *Fugitives' Reunion*, 105.

45. Paul K. Conkin, *The Southern Agrarians* (Knoxville: Univ. of Tennessee Press, 1988), 42.

46. Susan Ford Wiltshire, "Vergil, Allen Tate, and the Analogy of Experience," *Classical and Modern Literature* 5 (1985): 87–98; here 88,

47. "The Bi-Millennium of Vergil," *The New Republic* 64 (October 29, 1930): 296–98.

48. Ford Madox Ford, *Provence: From Minstrels to the Machine* (London: Allen and Unwin, 1938), 291–94.

49. Ford Madox Ford, *The March of Literature from Confucius' Day to Our Own* (New York: Dial, 1938), 223.

50. Allen Tate, "Speculations," *Southern Review* 14 (1978): 226–32; here 226–27.

51. See Susan Ford Wiltshire, "Vergil, Allen Tate, and the Analogy of Experience"; Robert S. Dupree, *Allen Tate and the Augustinian Imagination*, 138–43; and also Lillian Feder, "Allen Tate's Use of Classical Literature," *Centennial Review* 4 (1960):89–114; R. K. Meiners, "The Art of Allen Tate: A Reading of 'The Mediterranean,'" *The University of Kansas City Review* 27 (1960): 155–59; Louise Cowan, "Vergil's Rome and the Cosmos of Southern Literature," *The Augustan Age*, ed. Robert J. Rowland (College Park, Md.: The Vergilian Society of America, 1987), 31–44; Levi Robert Lind, "Aeneas among the Poets," *Rocky Mountain Review of Language and Literature* 34 (1980): 120–32; and M. E. Bradford, "Rumors of Mortality: An Introduction to Allen Tate," in *Generations of the Faithful Heart: On the Literature of the South* (LaSalle, Ill.: Sherwood Sugden, 1983), 91–96.

52. Wiltshire, "Analogy of Experience," 92.

53. E.g., Wiltshire, "Analogy of Experience," 91; Feder, "Allen Tate's Use of Classical Literature," 94; and Lind, "Aeneas among the Poets," 121.

54. Eleanor Winsor Leach, *The Rhetoric of Space: Literary and Artistic Representations of Landscape in Republic and Augustan Rome* (Princeton, N.J.: Princeton Univ. Press, 1988), 30–40, 69–70.

55. Wiltshire, "Analogy of Experience," 90.

56. Lillian Feder, "Allen Tate's Use of Classical Literature," 93.

57. *Collected Poems*, 69, has "struck," which is undoubtedly a misprint; I take the reading "stuck" from *Poems* (New York: Scribner, 1960), 6.

58. "William Faulkner* 1897–1962," *Sewanee Review* 71 (1963): 160–64; here 163.

59. "Vergil's Rome and the Cosmos of Southern Literature," 40.

60. In Davidson's *Still Rebels, Still Yankees and Other Essays* ([n.p.]: Louisiana State Univ. Press, 1957), 159–79.

61. Louise Cowan, "The *Pietas* of Southern Poetry," in *South: Modern Southern Literature in Its Cultural Setting*, ed. Louis D. Rubin, Jr., and Robert D. Jacobs (Garden City, N.Y.: Doubleday-Delphin, 1961), 95–114; here 95–98.

62. Donald Davidson, *Poems 1922–1961* (Minneapolis: Univ. of Minnesota Press, 1966), 15–16.

63. Radcliffe Squires, *Gardens of the World* (Baton Rouge: Louisiana State University Press, 1981), 34–35; see Susan Ford Wiltshire, *Public and Private in Vergil's Aeneid* (Amherst: Univ. of Massachusetts Press, 1989), 34–36.

64. Henrietta Holm Warwick, *A Vergil Concordance* (Minneapolis: Univ. of Minnesota Press, 1975). In this connection see also Wiltshire, *Public and Private in Vergil's Aeneid*, 127.

65. Letters, *The New Republic*, February 8, 1933.

66. Originally in *Virginia Quarterly Review* (1933); rpt. *The Collected Essays of John Peale Bishop*, ed. Edmund Wilson (New York: Scribner, 1948), 3–13; here 12.

67. *The Collected Poems of John Peale Bishop*, ed. with a preface and a personal memoir by Allen Tate (New York: Scribner, 1948).

68. See the interpretations by Louise Cowan, "The *Pietas* of Southern Poetry," 103–4; and Levi Robert Lind, "Aeneas among the Poets," 126–28.

69. "The South and Tradition," 12.

70. See Robert Lowell, "Visiting the Tates," *Sewanee Review* 67 (1959):557–59, for an account of that visit.

71. Cited according to *The Mills of the Kavanaughs* (New York: Harcourt, 1951), 24–27.

72. Richard J. Fein, *Robert Lowell*, 2d ed. (Boston: Twayne, 1979), 54–60; here 54.

73. "Aeneas among the Poets," 128–32.

74. *Eneas Africanus* was reprinted in various illustrated editions during the 1920s and 1930s. I refer here to the edition illustrated by Ernest Townsend (New York: Grosset and Dunlap, 1940).

75. Jo Reinhard Smith, "New Troy in the Bluegrass: Vergilian Metaphor and *The Great Meadow*," *The Mississippi Quarterly*, 22 (1968–69): 39–46.

76. Elizabeth Madox Roberts, *The Great Meadow* (New York: Viking, 1930), 13.

77. In his *res gestae* Augustus spoke of the need for *pietas erga deos patriamque*; v. *Res Gestae divi Augusti*, ed. P. A. Brunt and J. M. Moore (Oxford: Oxford Univ. Press, 1967), 35–36.

78. Allen Tate, *The Fathers* (New York: Putnam, 1938), 210.

79. Wiltshire, "Analogy of Experience," 98.

80. Stephan Medcalf, "Vergil's 'Aeneid,'" in *The Classical World*, ed. David Daiches and Anthony Thorlby (London: Aldus, 1972), 297–321; here 303.

81. Robert Penn Warren, *A Place to Come To* (New York: Random House, 1977), 123.

82. In *The Necessary Angel* (London: Faber, 1951), 16.

83. *The Collected Poems of Wallace Stevens* (1954; rpt. New York: Random House-Vintage, 1982), 407.

84. Eleanor Cook, *Poetry, Word-Play, and Word-War in Wallace Stevens* (Princeton, N.J.: Princeton Univ. Press, 1988), 110–11.

85. John P. Sullivan, "Ezra Pound and the Classics," in *New Approaches to Ezra Pound*, ed. Eva Hesse (Berkeley: Univ. of Calfornia Press, 1969), 215–41.

86. "How to Read" (1928), in *The Literary Essays of Ezra Pound*, ed. T. S. Eliot (London: Faber, 1954), 35.

87. "The Renaissance," in *Literary Essays*, 215.

88. Davie, "Virgil's Presence in Ezra Pound and Others," in *Virgil in a Cultural Tradition*, ed. Richard A. Cardwell and Janet Hamilton, University of Nottingham Monographs in the Humanities 4 (Nottingham, 1986), 143–46.

89. *The Cantos of Ezra Pound* (New York: New Directions, 1948), 56–57.

90. Tarozzi, "Virgilio nella cultura americana," in *La fortuna di Virgilio*, ed. Marcello Gigante (Napoli: Società Nazionale di Scienze Lettere e Arti in Napoli, 1986), 491–92.

91. Henry Miller, *Black Spring* (1936; rpt. Paris: Obelisk Press, 1938), 48. Andrea Mariani, the author of the rubric "Stati Uniti" in *Enciclopedia Virgiliana*, IV: 1015, suggests that the section is meant as a satire against Hemingway and Gertrude Stein. Though possibly valid, such a reading would not vitiate the critique of Virgil, which is consistent with Miller's statements in other places.

Chapter Six

1. See the title piece in T. P. Wiseman, *Talking to Virgil: A Miscellany* (Exeter, England: Univ. of Exeter Press, 1992), 171–209; here 201.

2. See "Figures on Loan: The Boundaries of Literature and Life," in my *Varieties of Literary Thematics* (Princeton, N.J.: Princeton Univ. Press, 1983), 123–51.

3. Ruth Fichtner, *Elemente ausseramerikanischer Kulturkreise in Wilders Werk* (Birkach: Ladewig, 1985), 158–73.

4. For the biographical background on Wilder's year in Rome, see Richard H. Goldstine, *Thornton Wilder: An Intimate Portrait* (New York: Saturday Review Press, 1975); and Gilbert A. Harrison, *The Enthusiast: A Life of Thornton Wilder* (New Haven: Ticknor and Fielding, 1983).

5. I appropriate the term from Rex Burbank, *Thornton Wilder*, 2d edition (Boston: Twayne, 1978), 31.

6. Cited according to the text in *A Thornton Wilder Trio*. Introduction by Malcolm Cowley (New York: Criterion Books, 1956), 21–147.

7. See Burbank, *Thornton Wilder*, 31.

8. Anacleto Trazzi, *Vergilius Redux seu De Vita Recentiore* (Asola: Scalini and Carrara, 1930).

9. Anacleto Trazzi, *Ruris facies vespere. Carmen in certamine poetico Hoeufftiano praemio aureo ornatum* (Amsterdam: Academia Regia disciplinarum nederlandica, 1933).

10. *Materialien zu Hermann Broch 'Der Tod des Vergil'*, ed. Paul Michael Lützeler, suhrkamp taschenbuch 317 (Frankfurt am Main: Suhrkamp, 1976), 204–5; henceforth *Materialien*.

11. Letter of March 17, 1940; *Materialien*, 207.

12. Letter of March 6, 1943; Hermann Broch, *Briefe 2 (1938–1945), Kommentierte Werkausgabe* 13/2, ed. Paul Michael Lützeler (Frankfurt am Main: Suhrkamp, 1981), 310–11.

13. Letter of May 19, 1944; *Briefe 2*, 388.

14. Jean Starr Untermeyer, *Private Collection* (New York: Knopf, 1965), 218–77.

15. The articles, dissertations, and books in many languages devoted to *The Death of Virgil* have become unsurveyable. A research report on the most important ones is provided by Luciano Zagari, "Hermann Broch e l'antimito di Virgilio," in *La Fortuna di Virgilio*, ed. Marcello Gigante for the Società Nazionale di Scienza Lettere e Arti in Napoli (Napoli: Giannini, 1986), 315–90.

16. Letter of October 22, 1945, to Robert Neumann; *Materialien*, 230–31.

17. Most of these essays are reprinted in the edition of *Der Tod des Vergil* in vol. 4 of P. M. Lützeler's *Kommentierte Werkausgabe* (1976); here 490.

18. *Der Tod des Vergil*, 476.

19. Ibid., 492.

20. Ibid., 494.

21. Ibid., 492.

22. Ibid., 472.

23. Lawrence Lipking, *The Life of the Poet: Beginning and Ending of Poetic Careers* (Chicago: Univ. of Chicago Press, 1981), 135.

24. *Der Tod des Vergil*, 457.

25. "Hermann Broch's *Death of Vergil*: Program Notes," *PMLA* 62 (1947): 525–54.

26. Letter of February 12, 1946; *Materialien*, 233–39; also printed in English translation at the end of Weigand's article.

27. See especially Lützeler's *Materialien* and the material appended to his edition of *Der Tod des Vergil*; Theodore Ziolkowski, "Broch's Image of Vergil and Its Context," *Modern Austrian Literature* 13 (1980): 1–30; and Paul Michael Lützeler, *Hermann Broch: Eine Biographie* (Frankfurt am Main: Suhrkamp, 1985), trans. Janice Furness (London: Quartet, 1987).
28. The radio talk has been published in the *Kommentierte Werkausgabe* 10/2 (Frankfurt am Main: Suhrkamp, 1977): 53–58.
29. The story exists in various typescripts. One has been published in *Materialien* 11–22. I refer to a 17-page, double-spaced copy (in my possession) that Broch presented to Hermann J. Weigand at Christmas 1950 with the inscription "Der Ur-ur-ur-Vergil als Santa Klaus für Manos in Liebe und Freundschaft."
30. *Materialien*, 23–87.
31. *Materialien*, 88–169; only the first two sections of this fragment are still extant.
32. This fourth version is available as a microfilm from the Poetry Collection of the Lockwood Memorial Liberary at the State University of New York-Buffalo.
33. Lützeler, *Hermann Broch*, 98.
34. Letter of May 10, 1945; *Materialien*, 226.
35. Letters of April 4 and April 11, 1934; Hermann Broch–Daniel Brody, *Briefwechsel 1930–1951*, ed. Bertold Hack and Marietta Kleiss (Frankfurt am Main: Buchhändler-Vereinigung, 1971), 323.
36. Lützeler, *Hermann Broch*, 190–91.
37. I am indebted for my information to P. M. Lützeler (letter of Sept. 4, 1980), who at my request, while he was interviewing Emmy Ferand in preparation for his biography, asked her specifically about this matter.
38. Johann Heinrich Voss, *Des Publius Virgilius Maro Werke*, 3 vols. (Braunschweig: Vieweg, 1799). Unlike his classic renditions of the *Iliad* and the *Odyssey*, Voss's translation of Virgil has been regarded, from his contemporaries down to the present, as less than inspired.
39. *Materialien*, 200.
40. *Materialien*, 236.
41. Yale University Library; *Der Tod des Vergil*, 496–502.
42. Bayer, *Vergil-Viten*, 214.
43. The mistake was finally corrected in the paperback edition of *Der Tod des Vergil* published by Deutscher Taschenbuch-Verlag (3d printing; München, 1968), where the editor, without explanation or justification, changed the text to read that Maia "einen Lorbeerreis geboren habe" (471). I am grateful to P. M. Lützeler for pointing out this amusing example of editorial tampering.
44. *Der Tod des Vergil*, 499.
45. I have consulted the manuscript in the Yale University Library.
46. This I take to be the principal conclusion of Kathleen L. Komar, "*The Death of Vergil*: Broch's Reading of Vergil's *Aeneid*," *Comparative Literature Studies* 21 (1984): 255–69.
47. *Materialien*, 203.

48. *Massenwahntheorie: Beiträge zu einer Psychologie der Politik*, in Kommentierte Werkausgabe 12 (1979): 144–49.
49. See, for example, "Bemerkungen zum *Tod des Vergil*," in *Der Tod des Vergil*, 473.
50. See Thomas Koebner, "Vergil als Leitfigur? Zu Hermann Brochs *Der Tod des Vergil*," *Würzburger Jahrbücher für die Altertumswissenschaft*, N.F. 8 (1982): 161–70.
51. Theodore Ziolkowski, "Hermann Brochs *Tod des Vergil* und Thomas Manns *Lotte in Weimar*. Zwei Exilromane," in *Hermann Broch: Das dichterische Werk. Neue Interpretationen*, ed. Michael Kessler and P. M. Lützeler (Tübingen: Stauffenburg, 1987), 263–72.
52. The story first appeared in *Atlantic Monthly* 146 (1930): 83–92; it was later reprinted in Allinson's *Selected Essays*, ed. Gertrude Slaughter (New York: Harcourt, 1933), 145–67.
53. *Yale Review* 7 (1917): 140–58; I quote the text as reprinted in *Selected Essays*, 96–120.
54. Cited according to *Selected Essays*.
55. Broch mentions Bernstein's call in a letter to Daniel Brody of November 23, 1949; *Materialien*, 245.
56. "Musical Events," *The New Yorker*, May 17, 1982: 116.
57. Published by Span, the Windsor Arts Centre Press, 1981, from which I quote.
58. "*Vergil Dying*," in *Virgil and His Influence: Bimillennial Studies*, ed. Charles Martindale (Bristol: Bristol Classical Press, 1984), 245–64.

CHAPTER SEVEN

1. W. H. Auden, "Memorial for the City," in *Nones* (New York: Random House, 1950), 40.
2. Carlo Emilio Gadda, *That Awful Mess on Via Merulana*, trans. William Weaver (New York: Braziller, 1965).
3. Thomas Bernhard, *Ave Vergil. Gedicht* (Frankfurt am Main: Suhrkamp, 1981). I have paraphrased the relevant passages because the Estate does not permit excerpts from Bernhard's poems to be reprinted.
4. Peter Handke, *Phantasien der Wiederholung* (Frankfurt am Main: Suhrkamp, 1983), 90–91.
5. Peter Handke, *Der Chinese des Schmerzes*, suhrkamp taschenbuch 1339 (Frankfurt am Main: Suhrkamp, 1986). For an analysis that enumerates textual parallels, albeit with little context, see Barbara Feichtinger, "*Glänz mir auf, harte Hasel. Schweb ein, leichte Linde*. Zur *Georgica*-Rezeption in Peter Handkes *Chinese des Schmerzes*," *Arcadia* 26 (1991):303–21.
6. Claude Simon, *Les Géorgiques* (Paris: Editions de Minuit, 1981).
7. For the most detailed analysis as well as a summary of the other studies, see Wolfgang Hübner, "Vergils Aeneis in Michel Butors Roman 'La Modification,'" in *Würzburger Jahrbücher für die Altertumswissenschaft*, NF 8 (1982): 171–82. See also Werner Suerbaum, "Vergil nineteen eighty-

four—Anstöße der *Aeneis*-Interpretation," in *Lateinische Literatur, heute wirkend,* ed. Hans-Joachim Glücklich (Göttingen: Vandenhoeck & Ruprecht, 1987), 1: 81–109.

8. "Mantoue," *France-Observateur,* December 5, 1957: 24; cited by Hübner, "Vergils Aeneis," 181.

9. Michel Butor, *La Modification* (Paris: Editions de Minuit, 1957), 48.

10. David Paul Pace, "The Influence of Vergil's Aeneid on The Lord of the Rings," *Mythlore* 6 (1979): 37–38.

11. Margaret Homans, "The Woman in the Cave: Recent Feminist Fiction and the Classical Underworld," *Contemporary Literature* 29 (1988): 369–402.

12. Dana L. Burgess, "Vergilian Modes in Spike Lee's *Do The Right Thing,*" *Classical and Modern Literature* 11 (1991):313–16.

13. Ruth Fainlight, *Sibyls and Others* (London: Hutchinson, 1980), 14–15.

14. Stuart Gillespie, *The Poets on the Classics* (London: Routledge, 1988), 219.

15. Noel Annan, *Our Age: English Intellectuals between the World Wars—A Group Portrait* (New York: Random House, 1990), 449.

16. Adam Parry, "The Two Voices of Virgil's *Aeneid,*" *Arion* 2 (1963): 266–80. The "dark" side of Virgil's poetry, in the *Eclogues* as well as the *Georgics,* has subsequently been explored by many scholars. See, for instance, Gary B. Miles, *Virgil's Georgics: A New Interpretation* (Berkeley: Univ. of California Press, 1980); A. J. Boyle's introduction to his translation of *The Eclogues of Virgil* (Melbourne: Hawthorn, 1976); Charles Segal, *Poetry and Myth in Ancient Pastoral: Essays on Theocritus and Virgil* (Princeton, N.J.: Princeton Univ. Press, 1981); and M. Owen Lee, *Death and Rebirth in Virgil's Arcadia* (Albany: State Univ. of New York Press, 1989).